Tokens and Social Life in Roman Imperial Italy

Tokens are under-utilised artefacts from the ancient world, but as everyday objects they were key in mediating human interactions. This book provides an accessible introduction to tokens from Roman Imperial Italy. It explores their role in the creation of imperial imagery, as well as what they can reveal about the numerous identities that existed in different communities within Rome and Ostia. It is clear that tokens carried imagery that was connected to the emotions and experiences of different festivals, and that they were designed to act upon their users to provoke particular reactions. Tokens bear many similarities to ancient Roman currency, but also possess important differences. The tokens of Roman Italy were objects used by a wide variety of groups for particular events or moments in time; their designs reveal experiences and individuals otherwise lost to history. This title is also available as Open Access on Cambridge Core.

CLARE ROWAN is Associate Professor in the Department of Classics and Ancient History at the University of Warwick. Her previous books, *Under Divine Auspices: Divine Ideology and the Visualisation of Imperial Power* (Cambridge University Press, 2013) and *From Caesar to Augustus: Using Coins as Sources* (Cambridge University Press, 2018), have demonstrated the enormous potential of coin evidence for understanding the Roman world. She held a European Research Starting Grant, entitled *Token Communities in the Ancient Mediterranean*, from 2016 to 2021, and this volume represents the findings of this work. She is currently the ancient editor for the *Numismatic Chronicle*.

Tokens and Social Life in Roman Imperial Italy

CLARE ROWAN
University of Warwick

CAMBRIDGE
UNIVERSITY PRESS

Shaftesbury Road, Cambridge CB2 8EA, United Kingdom

One Liberty Plaza, 20th Floor, New York, NY 10006, USA

477 Williamstown Road, Port Melbourne, VIC 3207, Australia

314–321, 3rd Floor, Plot 3, Splendor Forum, Jasola District Centre, New Delhi – 110025, India

103 Penang Road, #05–06/07, Visioncrest Commercial, Singapore 238467

Cambridge University Press is part of Cambridge University Press & Assessment, a department of the University of Cambridge.

We share the University's mission to contribute to society through the pursuit of education, learning and research at the highest international levels of excellence.

www.cambridge.org
Information on this title: www.cambridge.org/9781316516539

DOI: 10.1017/9781009030434

© Clare Rowan 2023

This work is in copyright. It is subject to statutory exceptions and to the provisions of relevant licensing agreements; with the exception of the Creative Commons version the link for which is provided below, no reproduction of any part of this work may take place without the written permission of Cambridge University Press.

An online version of this work is published at doi.org/10.1017/9781009030434 under a Creative Commons Open Access license CC-BY-NC-ND 4.0 which permits re-use, distribution and reproduction in any medium for non-commercial purposes providing appropriate credit to the original work is given. You may not distribute derivative works without permission. To view a copy of this license, visit https://creativecommons.org/licenses/by-nc-nd/4.0

All versions of this work may contain content reproduced under license from third parties.

Permission to reproduce this third-party content must be obtained from these third-parties directly.

When citing this work, please include a reference to the DOI 10.1017/9781009030434

First published 2023

A catalogue record for this publication is available from the British Library

A Cataloging-in-Publication data record for this book is available from the Library of Congress

ISBN 978-1-316-51653-9 Hardback
ISBN 978-1-009-01574-5 Paperback

Cambridge University Press & Assessment has no responsibility for the persistence or accuracy of URLs for external or third-party internet websites referred to in this publication and does not guarantee that any content on such websites is, or will remain, accurate or appropriate.

For Richard

Contents

List of Figures   [*page* viii]
Acknowledgements   [xvi]
List of Abbreviations   [xviii]

1 Introduction   [1]

2 Tokens and the Imperial Family   [37]

3 Creating Identities in Rome, Ostia and Italy   [78]

4 Cult, Euergetism and the Imagery of Festivals   [127]

5 Tokens, Finds and Small-Scale Economies   [170]

6 Conclusion: Tokens and the History of Roman Imperial Italy   [213]

References   [217]
Index   [243]

Figures

All images of coins and tokens are reproduced at 2:1.

1.1 Bone gaming piece with a portrait of Nero. Reproduced courtesy of the BnF, FRBNF45877682, Froehner no. 171. [*page* 5]

1.2 AE token with portrait of Augustus, 22 mm. Reproduced courtesy of the Heberden Coin Room, Ashmolean Museum. Rowan, 2020b: no. 1.   [6]

1.3 AE token (*spintria*) with a sexual scene, 22 mm. The Hunterian, University of Glasgow. Bateson, 1991: H, 3. Photograph by author.   [6]

1.4 AE token of Gaius Mitreius, 19 mm. Münzkabinett Winterthur R 6047.   [14]

1.5 AE token of Gaius Mitreius, 20 mm. Heberden Coin Room, Ashmolean Museum. Rowan, 2020b: no. 10.   [15]

1.6 Palombino marble mould half, 108 × 76 × 29 mm. Reproduced courtesy of Harvard Art Museums, inv. no. 2008.118.   [19]

1.7 Palombino marble mould half, 93 × 108 × 28 mm, 561 g. *TURS* 3578 (Pl. XII, 6). © ANTIKENSAMMLUNG, STAATLICHE MUSEEN ZU BERLIN – PREUSSISCHER KULTURBESTIZ, photographer Johannes Kramer, TC 8217, 183.   [24]

1.8 Pb token with the legend M VALERI | M F | ETRVSC. *TURS* 1327. Reproduced courtesy of the Münzkabinett, Staatliche Museen zu Berlin, 18268125.   [24]

1.9 Pb token decorated with Victory standing right / Wreath. *TURS* 1913. Harvard Art Museums 2008.116.32.   [25]

1.10 Countermarked AE token. Cohen vol. VIII, 271 no. 47. Reproduced courtesy of the BnF, inv. no. 17062.   [26]

2.1 Pb token showing Claudius and Messalina. From London Ancient Coins, Auction 60 (14 February 2017) lot 362.   [40]

2.2 Pb token showing Nero and Mars (or a soldier). *TURS* 13. The Hunterian, University of Glasgow, RLT 42. Photograph by author.   [41]

List of Figures   ix

2.3   Pb token with the legend MARCI·MANI· around. *TURS* (Supplement) 3601 (previously unpublished). Reproduced courtesy of the Münzkabinett, Staatliche Museen zu Berlin, 18256008.   [42]

2.4   Pb token showing Nero and Claudia Augusta (?). *TURS* 34, Rostovtzeff and Prou, 1900: no. 32. Reproduced courtesy of the BnF, source gallica.bnf.fr.   [44]

2.5   Pb token bearing an image of an oyster. From a private collection. Dalzell, 2021: 88 no. 2.   [46]

2.6   Orichalcum token with the legend IO IO TRIVMP. Reproduced courtesy of the Heberden Coin Room, Ashmolean Museum. Rowan, 2020b: no. 19.   [48]

2.7   Pb token, 17 mm, showing a palm tree on a platform with two wheels. *TURS* 34. Reproduced courtesy of the Münzkabinett, Staatliche Museen zu Berlin, 18256020.   [50]

2.8   Pb token, 19 mm, showing a palm tree on a platform with two wheels. *TURS* 34, *BMCRLT* 942. © The Trustees of the British Museum.   [50]

2.9   Pb token, 14 mm, with the legend IVDE. *TURS* 39, Rostovtzeff and Prou, 1900: no. 33b. Reproduced courtesy of the BnF, source gallica.bnf.fr.   [52]

2.10 Pb token, 19 mm, showing nude figure before palm tree. *TURS* 3194, *BMCRLT* 1224. © The Trustees of the British Museum.   [53]

2.11 Pb token, 19 mm, showing Vespasian, Domitian and Titus. *TURS* 40. The Hunterian, University of Glasgow, RLT 24. Photograph by author.   [55]

2.12 AR denarius showing Vespasian, Domitian and Titus. *RIC* II.1^2 16. American Numismatic Society 1944.100.39897.   [55]

2.13 Pb token, 23 mm, showing a two-horned rhinoceros. *TURS* 645, Rowan, 2020b: no. 49. Reproduced courtesy of the Heberden Coin Room, Ashmolean Museum.   [59]

2.14 Pierced bone gaming piece (?) showing the Colosseum on one side and VI incised on the other. Froehner 282. Reproduced courtesy of the BnF, source gallica.bnf.fr.   [60]

2.15 Pb token, 19 mm, naming Titus and Domitian. *TURS* 44, Rostovtzeff and Prou, 1900: no. 33e. Reproduced courtesy of the BnF, source gallica.bnf.fr.   [62]

2.16 AE token, 18 mm, with the legend A·P·P·F. Rowan, 2020b: no. 21. Reproduced courtesy of the Heberden Coin Room, Ashmolean Museum. [63]
2.17 Pb token, 18 mm, with the legend HAD | AVG / PPF. *TURS* 66. Reproduced courtesy of the Münzkabinett, Staatliche Museen zu Berlin, 18256023. [65]
2.18 Pb token, 20 mm, showing Antinous. *TURS* 1552, Rostovtzeff and Prou, 1900: no. 525a. Reproduced courtesy of the BnF, source gallica.bnf.fr. [68]
2.19 Pb token, 12 mm, with a triumphal arch. *TURS* 107, *BMCRLT* 2268. © The Trustees of the British Museum. [70]
2.20 Pb token from Egypt, 20.5 mm, showing Venus and a triumphal arch. Dattari-Savio Pl. 323, 11706 (this token). From Naville Numismatics Ltd., Auction 32, lot 340. [72]
2.21 Pb token, 27 mm, showing two male busts. *TURS* 71, Reproduced courtesy of the Münzkabinett, Staatliche Museen zu Berlin, 18256024. [73]
2.22 AE sestertius, 40 mm, with a *congiarium* scene. *RIC* I^2 Nero 160, reproduced courtesy of the American Numismatic Society, 1954.203.156. [76]
3.1 Pb token, 14 mm, with the legend GPR FELICITER. *TURS* 1573, Rostovtzeff and Prou, 1900: no. 361b. Reproduced courtesy of the BnF, source gallica.bnf.fr. [81]
3.2 Pb token, 19.5 mm, with Roma and the legend G P R F. *TURS* 1576, *BMCRLT* 371. © The Trustees of the British Museum. [85]
3.3 Pb token, 13.5 × 12 mm, showing the she-wolf suckling twins and the *Ficus Ruminalis*. *TURS* 1667, *BMCRLT* 1778. © The Trustees of the British Museum. [85]
3.4 Pb token, 20 mm, showing a river deity holding a long reed and cornucopia. *TURS* 1682, Rostovtzeff and Prou, 1900: no. 420a. Reproduced courtesy of the BnF, source gallica.bnf.fr. [87]
3.5 Pb token, 19 mm, showing a river god reclining on an urn from which water flows. *TURS* 526, *BMCRLT* 768. © The Trustees of the British Museum. [88]
3.6 AE sestertius showing a view of the harbour at Ostia. *RIC* I^2 178. American Numismatic Society 1967.153.118. [89]
3.7 Pb token, 13 mm, showing a Genius accompanied by the legend VICI. *TURS* 1613, *BMCRLT* 124. © The Trustees of the British Museum. [91]

List of Figures   xi

3.8 Pb token, 15 mm, showing three *Fortunae*. *TURS* 501, Rostovtzeff and Prou, 1900: no. 335a. Reproduced courtesy of the BnF. Photograph by author. [93]

3.9 Pb token, 14 × 12 mm, showing a lit lighthouse of three tiers. *TURS* 59, Rostovtzeff and Prou, 1900: no. 98. Reproduced courtesy of the BnF, source gallica.bnf.fr. [95]

3.10 Pb token, 24 mm, showing a lit lighthouse of four tiers. *TURS* 61, Museo Archeologico Nazionale di Palestrina bag no. 97.36, no. 1445 in Rowan's unpublished catalogue. Photograph by author. [95]

3.11 Pb token of Oxyrhynchus, 23 mm, decorated with a bust of Athena and Nike. See Milne 5291, Museo Archeologico Nazionale di Palestrina, bag no. 97.39, no. 1446 (= Pensabene, 2001–3: no. 38). Photograph by author. [98]

3.12 Pb token, 24 mm, with the legend TRA and two people in a *cymba*. Private collection, ex Classical Numismatic Group 55 (13 September 2000), lot 1201 (part of) (www.cngcoins.com). [99]

3.13 Pb token, 20 mm, with the legend M ANTONIVS GLAVCVS. *TURS* 1127, Rowan, 2020b: no. 55. Reproduced courtesy of the Heberden Coin Room, Ashmolean Museum. [101]

3.14 Pb token, 22 mm, showing a female portrait. *TURS* 1546, Rostovtzeff and Prou, 1900: no. 439a. Reproduced courtesy of the BnF, source gallica.bnf.fr. [103]

3.15 Pb token, 18 mm, displaying male busts and the legend VERRES and PROCVLVS. *TURS* 1332, Rostovtzeff and Prou, 1900: no. 427b. Reproduced courtesy of the BnF, source gallica.bnf.fr. [104]

3.16 Pb token, 22 mm, with the legend P·TETTIVS | RVFVS. *TURS* 517, Reproduced courtesy of the Münzkabinett, Staatliche Museen zu Berlin. [106]

3.17 AR denarius of L. Livineius Regulus. *RRC* 494/27. American Numismatic Society 1937.158.312. [106]

3.18 Pb token, 19 mm, with the legend P GLITI GALLI. *TURS* 1238, Rowan, 2020b: no. 57. Reproduced courtesy of the Heberden Coin Room, Ashmolean Museum. [108]

3.19 Pb token, 18 mm, showing an elephant emerging from a shell. *TURS* 1903, *BMCRLT* 810. © The Trustees of the British Museum. [111]

3.20 Pb token, 19 mm, with a *gryllus* design. *TURS* 2897, *BMCRLT* 343. © The Trustees of the British Museum. [112]

3.21 Pb token, 19 mm, with the legend CWC|IOY. *TURS* 1319, Rostovtzeff and Prou, 1900: no. 432. Reproduced courtesy of the BnF, source gallica.bnf.fr. [113]

3.22 Pb token, 18 mm, decorated with the figure of a *saccarius*. *TURS* 1033, Rostovtzeff and Prou, 1900: no. 418b. Reproduced courtesy of the BnF, source gallica.bnf.fr. [115]

3.23 Orichalcum token, 20 mm, showing Augustus on one side and a *saccarius* on the other. Cohen vol. VIII, 254 no. 101, BnF 16979. Reproduced courtesy of the BnF, source gallica.bnf.fr. [116]

3.24 Marble relief showing *saccarii* offloading *amphorae* from a ship. DAI Rom Negative 33.1329. [117]

3.25 Pb token, 21 mm, decorated with a wheel with eight spokes. *TURS* 832. Museo Archeologico Nazionale di Palestrina, bag no. 121.5, no. 669 in Rowan's unpublished catalogue. Photograph by author. [119]

3.26 AR denarius, decorated with the triple cult statue of Diana Nemorensis. *RRC* 486/1, American Numismatic Society 1937.158.302. [123]

3.27 Pb token, 19 mm, decorated with three women standing frontally with arms raised. *TURS* 1345, Rostovtzeff and Prou, 1900: no. 430f1. Reproduced courtesy of the BnF, source gallica.bnf.fr. [124]

4.1 Pb token, Athens, 18 mm, Hellenistic period, showing the 'cart of Dionysus'. Gkikaki, 2020: cat. no. 21. Photo courtesy of the Archaeological Institute of Göttingen University. Photograph by Stephan Eckardt. [128]

4.2 AE token, 19 mm, with the legend VOTA PVBLICA. Ramskold 2016: no. 33, pl. 1. Reproduced courtesy of the Münzkabinett, Staatliche Museen zu Berlin, 18236298. [129]

4.3 Pb token, 18 mm, decorated with Isis standing left on a ship. *TURS* 3184. Museo Archeologico Nazionale di Palestrina bag no. 97.56, no. 1486 in Rowan's unpublished catalogue. Photograph by author. [131]

4.4 Pb token, 19 mm, showing Anubis and Isis, or their priests. *TURS* 3190, *BMCRLT* 16. © The Trustees of the British Museum. [132]

4.5 Pb token, 18 mm, decorated with the mask of Anubis. *TURS* 3206, Pl. X, 13. [134]

4.6 Pb token, 18 mm, decorated with a cat (?) and left hand. *TURS* 3185, Rostovtzeff and Prou, 1900: no. 446b. Reproduced courtesy of the BnF, source gallica.bnf.fr. [135]

4.7 Pb token, 17 mm, decorated with the head of Sarapis and a river deity. *TURS* (Supplement) 3731, Rostovtzeff and Prou, 1900: no. 646. Reproduced courtesy of the BnF, source gallica.bnf.fr. [136]

4.8 Pb token, 17 mm, showing Isis or a worshipper of Isis. *TURS* 3179, *BMCRLT* 1286. © The Trustees of the British Museum. [136]

4.9 Pb token, 17 mm, with the legend IO SAT IO. *TURS* 507, Rostovtzeff and Prou, 1900: no. 103. Reproduced courtesy of the BnF, source gallica.bnf.fr. [139]

4.10 Pb token, 12 mm, decorated with Victory and the legend SAT. *TURS* 508. Reproduced courtesy of the Münzkabinett, Staatliche Museen zu Berlin. [141]

4.11 AR denarius, c. 19 mm, decorated with four wreaths. *RRC* 426/4a. Reproduced courtesy of the American Numismatic Society, 1937.158.206. [142]

4.12 Orichalcum token, 19 mm, showing a scene of triumph on a camel. Buttrey, 1973: B25 XIX. The Hunterian Museum *Tessera* 19. Photograph by author. [143]

4.13 AE token, 25 mm, with four knucklebones. Cohen vol. VIII, 266 no. 5. Reproduced courtesy of the BnF (AF 17092), source gallica.bnf.fr. [145]

4.14 Orichalcum token, 21 mm, showing two boys or men playing a game. Reproduced courtesy of the BnF (AF 17088), source gallica.bnf.fr. [146]

4.15 Three-handled jug from the Rhône valley, and an enlarged image of the decorative medallion. Metropolitan Museum of Art, 17.194.1980, public domain. [148]

4.16 Pb token, 17 mm, showing two spectators applauding. *TURS* 537 variant (no fly). Reproduced courtesy of the Münzkabinett, Staatliche Museen zu Berlin. [152]

4.17 Pb token, 15 mm, showing a woman standing left holding a cloth over her head in an arch. *TURS* 2149. Reproduced courtesy of the Münzkabinett, Staatliche Museen zu Berlin. [153]

4.18 Pb token, 16 mm, with the legend DIES VENAT. *TURS* 578, Bertolami Fine Arts E-Auction 73, lot 1947. [154]

4.19 Pb token, 16 mm, decorated with the image of a charioteer. *TURS* 749, *BMCRLT* 1086. © The Trustees of the British Museum. [157]

4.20 Pb token, 22 mm, showing Victory inscribing a shield. *TURS* (Supplement) 3603. Reproduced courtesy of the Münzkabinett, Staatliche Museen zu Berlin. [158]

4.21 Pb token, 21.5 mm, decorated with an image of Victory crowning a boxer (?). *TURS* 550, *BMCRLT* 770. © The Trustees of the British Museum. [161]

4.22 Pb token, 15 mm, decorated with the image of an amphora with two palm branches. *TURS* 434, *BMCRLT* 1982. © The Trustees of the British Museum. [162]

4.23 Pb token, 23 mm, showing a loaf of bread seen from above. *TURS* 1021, Rostovtzeff and Prou, 1900: no. 609. Reproduced courtesy of the BnF, source gallica.bnf.fr. [165]

4.24 Pb token, 18 mm, decorated with the image of a *modius*. *TURS* 372, Rostovtzeff and Prou, 1900: no. 79. Reproduced courtesy of the BnF, source gallica.bnf.fr. [166]

5.1 Pb token, 17 mm, with the legend HS ∞. *TURS* 1460. Reproduced courtesy of the Münzkabinett, Staatliche Museen zu Berlin, 18262461. [171]

5.2 Pb token, 14 mm, decorated with the image of a *lituus*. *TURS* 1072. Reproduced courtesy of the Münzkabinett, Staatliche Museen zu Berlin. [174]

5.3 Copper *quadrans*, 18.5 mm, decorated with a garlanded altar. *RIC* I^2 Augustus 425. Reproduced courtesy of the American Numismatic Society, 1944.100.38382. [174]

5.4 Pb token, 18 mm, with the legend BALI|NEVM / GER|MANI. *TURS* 886, Rostovtzeff and Prou, 1900: no. 415b. Reproduced courtesy of the BnF, source gallica.bnf.fr. [182]

5.5 AE token, 13 mm, showing a male bather (?). Unpublished, BNF inv. FRBNF45877423. Reproduced courtesy of the BnF, source gallica.bnf.fr. [185]

5.6 AE token, 22 mm, showing two standing figures. Cohen vol. VIII, 266 no. 9. Reproduced courtesy of the BnF, source gallica.bnf.fr. [186]

5.7 Pb token, 17 mm, showing a nude male bending at the knees with both arms outstretched before him. *TURS* 901, Pl. X, 21. [187]

List of Figures xv

5.8   Pb token, 19 mm, showing jug and strigil. *TURS* 899, Rostovtzeff and Prou, 1900: no. 105bis. Reproduced courtesy of the BnF, source gallica.bnf.fr.   [188]

5.9   Pb token, 22 mm, showing a dolphin accompanied by the legend BAL. Museo Archeologico Nazionale di Palestrina bag no. 124.5, no. 608 in Rowan's unpublished catalogue. Photograph by author. See Overbeck, 2001: no. 50.   [188]

5.10 Pb token, 14.7 mm, showing a ring with two strigils hanging down on either side of a container of oil (*aryballos*). *TURS* 563. Reproduced courtesy of Harvard Art Museums 2008.116.6.   [189]

5.11 Pb token, 19 mm, showing an eagle, a peacock and an owl. *TURS* 869, Rostovtzeff and Prou, 1900: no. 247c. Reproduced courtesy of the BnF. Photograph by author.   [194]

5.12 Pb token, 22 mm, with the legend ROM|VLA. *TURS* 1478. Reproduced courtesy of the American Numismatic Society, 1967.160.7.   [197]

5.13 AE token, 12 mm, with the head of Mercury right. BM 1940, 0401.60. © The Trustees of the British Museum.   [202]

5.14 AE token, 17 × 15 mm, showing a nude female figure beneath a domed canopy. BnF inv. F 7917. Reproduced courtesy of the BnF, source gallica.bnf.fr.   [203]

5.15 Orichalcum token, 19 mm, with *modius* and cantharus. BnF inv. 17070. Reproduced courtesy of the BnF, source gallica.bnf.fr.   [205]

5.16 Orichalcum token, 16 mm, with *modius* and cantharus. The Hunterian Museum Glasgow, *Tessera* no. 25. Photograph by author.   [205]

5.17 AE token, 19 mm, with *modius* and cantharus and the legend Θ E. Ex BCD collection, Numismatik Naumann Auction 69 (2 September 2018), lot 342.   [205]

5.18 Pb token, 14 mm, decorated with the image of a phallus. *TURS* 919. Reproduced courtesy of the American Numismatic Society, 2000.26.1.   [207]

5.19 Pb token, 18 mm, decorated with an image of Fortuna. *TURS* 1502, Rostovtzeff and Prou, 1900: no. 430a. Reproduced courtesy of the BnF, source gallica.bnf.fr.   [209]

5.20 Pb token, 15 mm, with the legend C PE|DANI. *TURS* 1299, Rostovtzeff and Prou, 1900: no. 426a. Reproduced courtesy of the BnF, source gallica.bnf.fr.   [209]

Acknowledgements

This book is the product of the wonderful support given by the European Research Council and has been written as part of the project *Token Communities in the Ancient Mediterranean*, which received funding under the European Union's Horizon 2020 research and innovation programme under grant agreement no. 678042. My sincere thanks are due to the wonderful intellectual environment provided by my fellow researchers on the project, Denise Wilding, Mairi Gkikaki and Antonino Crisà, as well as the fruitful discussions with Cristian Mondello as he conducted work on the tokens of late antiquity. I am particularly grateful for the collaboration we have formed, and the generosity of spirit in which everyone has shared data and photographs from various research campaigns.

Thanks are also due to all those who participated in the numerous conferences and workshops on tokens that have been held over the last few years: the multi-disciplinary Tokens: Culture, Connections, Communities at the University of Warwick in 2017, the Tokens, Value and Identity workshop at the British School at Rome in 2018, as well as the Tokens: The Athenian Legacy to the Modern World event at the British School at Athens in 2019. This book also owes a debt to all who gave feedback on various papers delivered on this topic over the years, as well as those who presented their own work on tokens in smaller settings (individual papers, smaller workshops, exchanges over coffees and drinks). Particular thanks are due to Yoav Farhi and our ongoing discussions over tokens found in Israel; Bill Dalzell, who found tokens as a topic well before I did; as well as Bernhard Woytek, Christina Kuhn and Jack Kroll for their sustained support and intellectual exchanges. I must also thank all those who participated in discussions and identification debates over Twitter. I also wish to thank the two readers of the manuscript, who have improved the final product. Any mistakes, of course, remain my own.

The book, and our knowledge of tokens, would not have been possible were it not for the support of various museums and their curators: thanks are due to the Münzkabinett in Berlin (particularly Bernhard Weisser and Karsten Dahmen) and the staff at the Altes Museum; the British Museum,

Department of Coins and Medals (the entire staff, but especially Amelia Dowler, Richard Abdy, Vesta Sarkhosh Curtis, Henry Flynn, Eleanor Ghey, Helen Wang), and the Department of Greek and Roman Antiquities; the Ashmolean Museum (particularly Chris Howgego, Volker Heuchert, Jerome Mairat and also Denise Wilding for doing the photography); the Fitzwilliam Museum (Adrian Popescu for sending photographs of the tokens of the collection during lockdown); the Hunterian Museum (Jesper Ericsson for his hospitality and time); the Capitoline Museum (Maria Cristina Molinari); the Museo Archeologico Nazionale di Palestrina (Roberto Fatiganti and Roberto Darelli); the staff at archives and deposits at Ostia; Museo Nazionale Romano (Gabriella Angeli Bufalini); the BnF (especially Julien Olivier); the ANS (thanks to all staff and to Denise Wilding who spent a summer there); as well as the staff at Harvard University Art Museums (and especially Carmen Arnold Biucchi for her hospitality). The arrival of Covid-19 prevented exploration of further collections, but the campaign to that time had already furnished more material than I thought possible.

I must also thank the wonderful administrative staff at Warwick (Kymberley O'Hagan, Susan Doughty, Donna Davis, Gabrielle Grant, Colette Kelly, Perminder Dhesi) and at the British School at Rome, who helped me in more ways than I can list in terms of organising travel, expenses and access, and negotiating the challenges involved in running a large grant. My colleagues at the Department of Classics and Ancient History at Warwick are wonderful, and kept me afloat while I negotiated what was, at the time, a largely unknown field of research.

Finally, all my thanks to Richard Hassell, who shared a Covid-19 lockdown space with me during the writing period, and who ensured a ready supply of coffee, cake and fresh air was to hand.

Abbreviations

Unless otherwise stated, all translations are those of the Loeb Classical Library. Abbreviations of classical texts follow those of the *Oxford Classical Dictionary*, journals are abbreviated according to *L'Année Philologique*. Additional abbreviations used frequently throughout are as follows:

AE	*L'Année Épigraphique* (1888–)
AJN	*American Journal of Numismatics*
ANS	The American Numismatic Society
BM	The British Museum
BMCRLT	Thornton, M. K. (unpublished). 'Roman Lead Tesserae in the British Museum' (unpublished manuscript in the Department of Coins and Medals, the British Museum)
BnF	Bibliothèque nationale de France
CIL	*Corpus Inscriptionum Latinarum* (1863–)
Cohen	Cohen, H. (1880–92). *Description historique des monnaies frappées sous l'Empire romain communément appelées, médailles impériales* (8 vols). Paris.
FMRD	*Die Fündmünzen der römischen Zeit in Deutschland* (1970–)
GdS	*Giornale degli Scavi di Ostia*
HN *Italy*	Rutter, N. K. (2001). *Historia Numorum: Italy*. London.
NC	*The Numismatic Chronicle*
NSc.	*Notizie degli scavi di antichità*
RIB	Collingwood, R. G. and Wright, R. P. (1965–). *The Roman Inscriptions of Britain*. Oxford.
RIC	*The Roman Imperial Coinage* (1923–). London. (A digital version of the catalogue is available at http://numismatics.org/ocre/).
RPC	*Roman Provincial Coinage* (1992–). London. (Select volumes available digitally at http://rpc.ashmus.ox.ac.uk/)
RRC	Crawford, M. H. (1974). *Roman Republican Coinage* (2 vols). Cambridge. (A digital version of the catalogue is available at http://numismatics.org/crro/).

TURS	Rostovtzeff, M. (1903). *Tesserarum urbis Romae et suburbi plumbearum sylloge*. St Petersburg, with the supplement Rostovtzeff, M. (1905). *Tesserarum urbis romae et suburbi plumbearum sylloge. Supplementum I*. St Petersburg.
TURS (Supplement)	Refers to token types not known to Rostovtzeff and which have been published online at https://coins.warwick.ac.uk/token-types/.

1 | Introduction

Tokens remain one of the most enigmatic and under-utilised bodies of evidence from antiquity. Monetiform objects of varying materials have been known from Rome since the eighteenth century and yet our understanding of these objects has made precious little progress in the years that have followed.[1] Many tokens remain unpublished, and the few individuals that have attempted the study of these objects have despaired at their elusive nature. Rostovtzeff, whose catalogue and doctoral dissertation on Roman lead tokens still remains the most detailed work on the topic to date, observed that the volume of the material, the wear on most of the pieces, as well as the seeming unending array of inscriptions and representations on these pieces are enough to warn anyone off studying them, especially when, as he noted, the study does not appear to have any scientific promise.[2] Rostovtzeff's frustration with the subject matter manifested into a hope that future studies might better elucidate the pieces he could not understand, noting that a better understanding of tokens in the East, particularly Athens, would likely result in a better understanding of these objects in Rome.

More than one hundred years later, and with the tokens of Athens now much better understood, this work resumes Rostovtzeff's study of tokens in Roman imperial Italy.[3] It is now clear that monetiform objects were manufactured and used in multiple regions in the Roman Empire, although the tokens from Rome and Ostia remain one of the largest corpora currently known. The sheer variety of designs on these tokens can indeed be bewildering at times and many of the legends remain enigmatic. The majority of tokens from Roman Italy are made of lead, which certainly does not last as well as other metals. But these same characteristics also reveal to us how these particular artefacts functioned: a profusion of designs reflects an abundance of makers and contexts, the enigmatic legends must have contributed to a sense of belonging to a particular group (who could understand the meaning), while the popularity of lead

---

[1] Ficoroni, 1740. [2] Rostovtzeff, 1905b: 9.
[3] The excavations of the Athenian Agora have contributed enormously to our understanding of how tokens worked in the city; see Lang and Crosby, 1964.

for these objects suggests that, in the main, tokens were created cheaply for use over a relatively short period of time. The challenges presented by this material are thus a gateway to better understanding their function.

It is hoped that this volume will demonstrate that the challenges of studying tokens are more than repaid by the insights gained. It is rare that a category of evidence from the Roman world has remained neglected for so long. An examination of the tokens of Roman Italy thus offers the opportunity to uncover new insights into Roman history and society. Tokens reveal acts of euergetism and different social groupings (cultic groups, *collegia*, Roman families and their networks). They shed light on particular Roman festivals, imagery and ideologies. They provide evidence for the imperial image and its reception, for particular identities and for the lived everyday experience of the ancient city. In sum, the potential of tokens as a source are manifold, and undoubtedly other ways in which tokens can be informative will come to light as the artefacts are once more integrated into mainstream scholarly discourse.

When the present author was studying these materials first hand, it became evident to her that Rostovtzeff's catalogue of this material (*Tesserarum urbis romae et suburbi plumbearum sylloge* = *TURS*) contained numerous errors and omissions. The work still remains a feat of scholarship, especially given the early date at which it was compiled.[4] Nonetheless, as part of research into the area, a new and updated catalogue has been made available in English online, and readers wishing to find further detail on particular types are encouraged to make use of the resource.[5] A database of images, specimens and finds has also been compiled, and photographs of numerous tokens (which for obvious reasons could not all be illustrated in this volume) are available online.[6]

Defining Roman Tokens

Rostovtzeff identified some of the lead pieces presented in his dissertation as the *tesserae* of ancient texts, picking up on the terminology used in the

---

[4] Rostovtzeff, 1903b, with a supplement published as Rostovtzeff, 1905c.
[5] https://coins.warwick.ac.uk/token-types/. Additional types not included in Rostovtzeff's original catalogue are given *TURS* (Supplement) numbers in this database.
[6] https://coins.warwick.ac.uk/token-specimens/. It should be noted that the tokens from Roman Italy in the BnF in Paris are now also online with images in Gallica (https://antiquitebnf.hypotheses.org/11049), and all the tokens of the British Museum are also photographed and available online through their online catalogue. For example, for the Roman lead tokens in the British Museum see www.britishmuseum.org/collection/search?keyword=bmcrlt.

nineteenth century.⁷ *Tessera*, derived from the ancient Greek word *tessares* or 'four', refers to an object that has four sides. As Rostovtzeff noted, *tesserae* encompassed different things (e.g. cubic pawns, dice, tablets), meaning the word was often qualified – as *tesserae nummariae*, for example, or *tesserae frumentariae*.⁸ Since then various scholars have sought alternative identifications for these objects. Van Berchem, for example, argued that many of the monetiform lead pieces from Rome were *calculi* or reckoning pieces.⁹ Thornton suggested they might have acted as emergency small change, a sort of 'peasant's money'.¹⁰ More recently, scholarship has become more sceptical of a 'one size fits all' interpretation. Turcan, for example, observed that these objects likely served multiple uses, with the purpose of the vast majority of these pieces remaining unknown to us.¹¹ Virlouvet's exhaustive study, *Tessera Frumentaria*, noted that the word *tessera* possessed multiple meanings; she concluded that the monetiform lead objects we possess are not the *tesserae frumentariae* of our texts and that we should see these objects as private, rather than official, products.¹²

That we encounter issues in attempting to definitively define a 'token' is unsurprising. The enormous quantity and variety of work performed by tokens in societies across time is often overlooked, no doubt due to their unassuming nature.¹³ Tokens are objects that represent something else: this might be people, objects, values, relationships, emotions, prestige, hierarchy or a particular entitlement. In ancient Greek a token was known as a *symbolon*.¹⁴ In addition to *tesserae*, tokens might be described in Latin with the words *missilia* or *nomismata*. The former, which refers to things that might be thrown, is similar in sense to the French word for token, *jeton*, which derives from *jeter* (to throw, or to add up accounts). The words for token in Greek and Latin, as in modern languages today, embodied a large variety of objects and functions, some of which probably referenced the bronze and lead pieces that form the focus of this volume. But there can be no simple equation between a particular term mentioned in a classical text and these artefacts – tokens, after all, might also be

---

[7] Ruggiero, 1878: 149 ('tessere di piombo'); Dancoisne, 1891 ('tessères romaines de plomb'); de Belfort, 1892; Scholz, 1894 ('Römische Bleitesserae'); Rostovtzeff, 1905b: 4.

[8] Rostovtzeff, 1905b: 10; Crisà, Gkikaki and Rowan 2019a: 2. The term *tesserae nummariae* comes from Suetonius (*Aug.* 41) and is thought to refer to something akin to 'money tickets' or a medium to enable the distribution of certain sums. It is to be distinguished from *tesserae nummulariae*, rectangular labels thought to be attached to bags by financial officials to act as a guarantee of the contents within. On the latter see Herzog, 1919.

[9] van Berchem, 1936. [10] Thornton, 1980. [11] Turcan, 1987: 51.

[12] Virlouvet, 1995: 321, 362. [13] Crisà, Gkikaki and Rowan, 2019a.

[14] Crisà, Gkikaki and Rowan 2019a: 2.

metaphorical or imagined, spoken or written (e.g. *tessera* might also refer to a watchword written on a tablet). As a word that refers to the embodiment of something else, a definitive description of the term and its material manifestations in classical antiquity remains impossible and, realistically, undesirable. Indeed, tokens probably performed even more functions than our surviving texts indicate, since everyday objects and processes rarely formed the focus of classical literature.

This volume is focused on the bronze, brass and lead pieces from Roman imperial Italy, which are mainly, though not always, monetiform in nature. This material definition forms the parameters of the volume. These particular artefacts are different from other objects that have attracted the label *tesserae*, and we might better define Roman tokens by exploring what they are not. Our tokens are different from *tesserae hospitales*, for example. The latter were objects that recorded agreements of mutual assistance between individuals; they exist in bronze, ivory and, occasionally, silver, and come in a wide array of shapes.[15] *Tesserae nummulariae*, small ivory or bone rectangular objects that might be inscribed and which carry a hole in order to be attached to something, have been interpreted as artefacts that were attached to bags of money to indicate that the contents had been inspected and found to be sound.[16] Again, this is a very different category of object to the coin-like material presented here.

Similar in shape to the *tesserae nummulariae* (and indeed, at times often grouped with them) are the so-called *tesserae lusoriae* – rectangular bone or ivory pieces with a circular 'handle' at one end. These pieces are inscribed with playful words and numbers (the latter at times accompanied by an A or Λ).[17] The words mainly describe a person and can be positive or negative (e.g. *fortunate, amator, pernix, victor*); although found in 'sets' it seems there was no standard design for these pieces. *Tesserae lusoriae* are believed to have been used in a game or games of some kind and appear to be a phenomenon of the Roman Republic.[18] A further series of gaming pieces often labelled as *tesserae* (and at times conflated with the monetiform pieces that form the focus of this volume) are the circular bone and ivory pieces that carry a variety of designs in relief on one side (including imperial portraits and Egyptian imagery), with a legend identifying the image and a number (often in both Latin and Greek) incised on a flat surface on the other. Figure 1.1 is one example of this type of artefact: the bust of Nero is presented on one side,

---

[15] Sánchez-Moreno, 2001; Luschi, 2008.
[16] The objects often carry reference to a slave – *s(ervus)* – and carry the word *spectavit* (looked at or inspected). See Herzog, 1919; Andreau, 1999: 80–9; Kay, 2014: 125–6.
[17] Banducci, 2015: 203.   [18] Rodríguez Martín, 2016: 207.

Figure 1.1 Bone gaming piece, 31 mm. Bare bust of Nero left / V | NEPWN | Ɛ.

while the other side names the image in Greek, with the number five given in both Latin and Greek. The discovery of a 'set' of these pieces in a child's tomb in Kerch in Crimea overthrew the traditional interpretation of these artefacts as theatre tickets and today they are accepted as gaming pieces, used in an unknown game.[19] Bone gaming pieces may also carry no imagery, or come in a variety of shapes without legends.[20]

Many of the bronze and brass monetiform pieces referred to as 'tokens' in this volume have traditionally been identified as gaming pieces. The presence of numbers on tokens of the Julio-Claudian period (some accompanied by an A) has been central to this argument. Figure 1.2 is one example of this series (further examples can be seen in Figures 4.12 and 4.14), which is characterised by numbers within a wreath on the reverse.[21] The obverses of this series carry a variety of designs, most famously Julio-Claudian imperial portraiture and sexual imagery. The latter series is frequently dubbed *spintriae* in modern scholarship, although these objects were not known as such in antiquity; an example of a *spintria* is reproduced here as Figure 1.3.[22] The discovery of a *spintria* (likely a contemporary imitation) covered in gold leaf in a tomb in

---

[19] Rostovtzeff, 1905a on the Kerch discovery, since then see the studies of Alföldi-Rosenbaum, 1971; Alföldi-Rosenbaum, 1976; Alföldi-Rosenbaum, 1980; Alföldi-Rosenbaum, 1984; Bianchi, 2015.

[20] Bianchi, 2015: 62 for circular pieces without imagery and simply numbers inscribed on the flattened side; Mlasowsky, 1991: nos. 113–210 provides a good illustration of the variety of this type of material.

[21] Some have identified the wreath as the *corona triumphalis*, see Martini, 1999: 13; Campana, 2009: 55.

[22] Campana, 2009: 43–4 on the term and 62–5 on the sexual scene shown in Figure 1.3.

Figure 1.2 AE token, 22 mm, 4.52 g, 4 h, 27 BC–AD 57. Laureate head of Augustus right, FEL beneath, all within linear border and wreath / XIII within dotted border and wreath. Buttrey 1973, B5/XIII.

Figure 1.3 AE token (*spintria*), 22 mm, 4.92 g, 6 h, 27 BC–AD 57. Sexual scene. A man wearing a cape kneels on a *kline* and enters his partner from behind, who rests on her elbows. Drapery above, beneath the *kline* crouching figure on the left and jug on right / III within dotted border and wreath. Buttrey 1973, A9/III = Simonetta and Riva 1984 Scene 4.

Mutina dated to AD 22–57 provides a *terminus ante quem* for this series.[23] In a seminal work on these pieces in 1973, Buttrey suggested one possible use for these objects was as counters in gaming: this theory has since been developed by Campana.[24] In spite of the presence of numbers on these pieces and gaming counters, the current state of material evidence suggests that we should not interpret the so-called *spintriae* as gaming pieces. After all, these artefacts form a small subset of a broader collection of bronze, brass and lead monetiform pieces, of which only a few carry numbers. Moreover, objects

---

[23] Benassi, Giordani and Poggi 2003.
[24] Buttrey, 1973: 54; Campana, 2009: 55. The idea is also discussed by Küter, 2016: 87; Le Guennec, 2017: 425; Martínez Chico, 2019: 109.

used as gaming pieces – the bone *tesserae* with numbers in Greek and Latin, the rectangular *tesserae lusoriae*, other circular bone and terracotta pieces – have been found as 'sets', gathered together ready for play.[25] We have no such find for the *spintriae* or the other monetiform objects discussed in this volume. Although an argument from silence, it does suggest that we should *not* interpret these pieces as counters used for gaming on a board; use in lotteries, however, cannot be ruled out.

It is evident from this brief overview that the word *tessera* not only had a variety of meanings in antiquity but has also been used as a 'catch all' term for numerous objects in modern scholarship. In many cases the application of the word *tesserae* to these objects in publications and museum collections does not reflect ancient usage. Indeed, since the word encompasses a bewildering array of objects (to say nothing of mosaic *tesserae*), the term can be downright unhelpful in the age of keyword searches in electronic catalogues. While *tesserae* might have occasionally been used to refer to tokens of brass, bronze and lead by ancient authors (specific instances will be discussed throughout the volume), there can be no simple equation of the term with these objects. A more fruitful approach is to define Roman tokens on a more material basis: identifying the common characteristics of these objects and the differences between tokens and other categories of artefact.

Since tokens look like coins, another obvious category of material to consider as a point of comparison to tokens is Roman coinage. Several scholars have interpreted the lead pieces found in Rome and Ostia as emergency small change.[26] How do we separate 'tokens' from imitation coinage, lead coinages or test pieces, pseudo-currencies or coin forgeries? While the tokens discussed in this volume may reference the materiality of coinage in terms of imagery, shape and (for some pieces) metal, it is also very clear that the creators of tokens took pains to ensure these artefacts could not easily be mistaken for official Roman currency. The widespread use of lead was an important factor here, as was the design of these pieces. Although tokens might reference particular Roman coin types, no token directly copies a full coin design – these are no imitations or forgeries. As will become clear throughout this volume, the majority of these pieces carry designs that clearly indicate they are products of individuals and groups outside the imperial government. By contrast, lead

---

[25] In addition to the 'set' published by Rostovtzeff, 1905a from Kerch, further 'sets' of circular bone gaming pieces with numbers are known from ancient Rudiae (*NSc.* 1886, 240) and Le Marche (Mercando, 1974: 103). A set of seventeen *tesserae lusoriae* was found in a second century BC tomb in Puglia, and another set of sixteen is known from a Hellenistic tomb from Perugia, see Banducci, 2015: 204. For an overview of the materiality of gaming see Dasen, 2019.

[26] Rostovtzeff, 1905b: 108; Dressel, 1922: 182; Thornton, 1980: 338.

test pieces and lead currencies in antiquity are struck from official dies or carry designs that clearly indicate a governmental authority.[27] Lead currencies might possess 'token' characteristics, in that they represent a value higher than their metal content, and may have been intended as a temporary issue, but they are materially different from the objects that form the focus of this volume.

Indeed, the efforts of token makers to distinguish their creations from official currency appear to have worked: tokens in Roman Italy are not found intentionally hoarded or stored alongside coinage. They were clearly seen as a different type of artefact by their users and treated accordingly. In this way tokens differ substantially from the 'pseudo-coinages' known to exist in Italy, particularly in Pompeii – these pieces have been found in purse hoards alongside official Roman currency, for example, and were clearly used as small change.[28] Another noticeable difference between imitations, pseudo-currencies and tokens is that of scale. While the former were produced in large quantities (as befitting a medium intended to be used to fill a lack of specie in the economy), the production of tokens was, by contrast, far more modest. They were simply not produced in sufficient quantity to have functioned as a replacement medium of small change in the bustling economies of imperial Rome and Ostia.

In terms of bronze and brass pieces, a definitive listing of all known token types has not yet been produced. For bronze tokens carrying numerals, Buttrey identified thirty-nine different scenes, although a few more designs are now known than presented there.[29] Bronze and brass tokens not carrying numbers are not as common but still known; in Cohen's nineteenth century catalogue under *Médailles sans le S.C.* we find some eighteen types that have not since been classified as official coinage (in earlier scholarship anonymous *quadrantes* and sometimes also provincial coinage were misidentified as *tesserae*).[30] Some additional bronze types are now known, but the number of these is not large.[31] Given that Cohen published some eight volumes of material, we might see here the relatively small amount of bronze and brass

---

[27] See de Callataÿ, 2010 for an overview of the different types of lead monetiform artefacts that exist from the classical world, including lead coinages and test strikes in lead.

[28] For example Stannard, 2019; the topic is discussed in more detail in Chapter 5.

[29] Buttrey, 1973: 60–2; Küter, 2019 includes more types (e.g. the MORA board game type, the Mitreius series).

[30] Cohen: vol. VIII, 271–3.

[31] For example, the so-called shipping *tesserae* published in Stannard, 2015b, another issue connected to Gaius Mitreius (published in the auction catalogue *The Thomas Ollive Mabbott Collection Part 2: Coins of the Roman World* no. 5264), a type showing a satyr (published in Arzone and Marinello, 2019: no. 353), and another a *venator* and bull (published in Martínez Chico, 2019: no. 44).

tokens produced in comparison to official coinage. This is also evident in terms of archaeological finds – bronze or brass tokens are not found frequently in excavation, and where they are found it is in small numbers. This suggests a small production in comparison with official coinage. Campana's preliminary catalogue of *spintriae* gathered together 322 examples, which he estimated was some two thirds of what exists today; the study identified thirty-one obverse dies for the tokens carrying sexual scenes.[32] Similar studies for other bronze or brass tokens remain to be performed. But the data suggests a relatively modest production.

By contrast, there are more than 3,750 known types for lead tokens created in Rome and Ostia. This number is very probably going to increase in future as excavations and the exploration of museum collections continue. As outlined below in this chapter, lead tokens in Rome and Ostia were produced from moulds that might carry several designs – a single casting may thus produce multiple different designs at once. It is thus difficult to know how to interpret the overall number of types known, but in comparison with other settlements in Italy (which have a much smaller number of known locally produced types, often just in the tens), Rome and its harbour stand out as a centre of token production. Although the study of tokens across the Roman world is still ongoing, we might identify already some other settlements with relatively large token production as a point of comparison. One of these is Lugdunum (Lyon): c. 2,700 tokens from the region were catalogued within the collection Récamier, with additional specimens published by Turcan.[33] In Palmyra more than 1,500 banqueting *tesserae* are known, while in Athens the excavations at the Agora have resulted in the publication of 900 identifiable lead tokens; further tokens have been found in excavations since and have also been found elsewhere in the city.[34]

How many lead tokens did this quantity of types actually produce in Rome and Ostia? Many types are only known from a single example. More rarely, we read reports of a particular token design being discovered in quantities of hundreds, as with Figure 5.2, discussed in Chapter 5. As this volume will go on to explore, it is likely that lead tokens were meant to be used in a singular context, and then melted down for reuse; the tokens that survive to be excavated are those that did not undergo this life cycle. Unlike coins, it seems that lead tokens did not circulate to be used again and again. When they do turn up in

---

[32] Campana, 2009: 56; de Callataÿ, 2021: 185 points out that most of the surviving *spintriae* seem to have been known before 1800.
[33] Dissard, 1905; Turcan, 1987; with discussion in Wilding, 2020: 166.
[34] Lang and Crosby, 1964: 76 (Athens); Raja, 2015: 165 (Palmyra). A detailed study of the tokens of Athens is in progress by Gkikaki, with a dedicated edited volume imminent: Gkikaki, in press.

archaeological excavation, it is predominately in contexts of fill or abandonment. We thus cannot know whether production in the hundreds was a regular occurrence for lead tokens or a rare one, or to what extent the volume of lead token production varied between issuers and issues.

Another category of material to consider in relation to tokens of the imperial period are contorniates. Contorniates are largely a phenomenon of late antiquity (mid-fourth to fifth century AD) and are monetiform objects that have been given their name due to their raised edges (*contorni*). So-called protocontorniates are known from the imperial period until the fourth century AD, created by people hammering the edges of coins or medallions to create a small raised ridge around the edge. It has been suggested these early pieces may have been converted in this way to serve as gaming pieces (the raised border would protect the design).[35] The contorniates proper of late antiquity, however, are made of bronze and carry designs that differ from the official coinage of the period; long-deceased emperors are portrayed and much of the imagery is related to the games and the circus.[36] Often luck-bringing signs are engraved onto contorniates, recalling the imagery of good luck on earlier tokens discussed in this volume.[37] One contorniate shows the consul of AD 433 and 443, Petronius Maximus, seated frontally holding a *mappa* as a sponsor of the games; Valentinian III is shown on the other side.[38] A unique representation for contorniates, the portrayal of game giver and emperor on a single object is very similar to earlier lead tokens that name the *curator* of the games on one side and portray the emperor on the other.[39]

The precise purpose of contorniates remains the subject of debate. Similar to tokens of the earlier imperial period, contorniates have been viewed as objects produced by private individuals, with some specimens perhaps issued in a more official, governmental capacity. Mittag has proposed that contorniates were multi-functional, used as gifts for a variety of recipients in a variety of contexts.[40] Those carrying representations of the emperor may have functioned as gifts during new year's festivities, while the group labelled

---

[35] Mittag, 1999: 19–25.
[36] Mittag, 1999; Mondello, 2019: 145. Mittag's catalogue collects contorniates that show Alexander the Great, Roma, theatre masks, authors (e.g. Euripides, Homer, Apuleius), emperors (e.g. Augustus, Caligula, Nero, Galba, Vespasian, Trajan, Hadrian, Antoninus Pius, Caracalla, Philip the Arab and rulers of late antiquity), empresses (Agrippina, Faustina I, Faustina II, Lucilla), Antinous, chariot racers, scenes of *venatio* and scenes from the Circus Maximus. Scenes from myth (e.g. Hercules) are also shown.
[37] Mittag, 1999: 193–4.   [38] Mittag, 1999: 184–6, no. 204.
[39] See the example of Oinogenus, discussed in this chapter in the section 'Authority'.
[40] Mittag, 1999: 182–214.

as the 'Reparatio-Muneris-Serie' by Mittag are probably to be connected with the *munera* of AD 400.[41] Holden further suggested some contorniate gifting must have been connected to games and spectacles.[42] Indeed, one contorniate design appears to show the distribution of these objects to recipients before an event; the image has close similarities to a Palmyrene relief that has traditionally been interpreted as three men playing a board game but may actually represent three individuals distributing banqueting tokens.[43] It thus seems that late antique contorniates played similar roles to some of the imperial tokens explored here, in that they were material objects connected to ephemeral events and may have served as mementoes.

Recent scholarly work on tokens has begun to identify the characteristics of this category of artefact. Tokens represent something or someone and, as mentioned above, they might also exist within a text or a speech, or represent emotions, relationships or intentions, concepts beyond the purely material.[44] In this way they function as a form of information storage. When tokens are studied across time and space, one notices that they frequently have a cryptic nature: the heterogeneity of designs on tokens from the classical world forms a part of this, no doubt intended to prevent fraud in many cases. Tokens also frequently function as credentials: they might identify a particular individual or demonstrate that an individual belonged to a particular group, and/or was entitled to a particular privilege. Various examples of this function are presented in the following pages: the characteristic is also seen elsewhere in the classical world. Clay tokens from Athens carrying the names of military commanders were used to identify specific individuals (or their representatives) and as already mentioned, clay tokens from Roman Palmyra entitled the bearer to access a particular religious banquet.[45] Many tokens are utilised over a short period of time and in one-off exchange: in other words they are characterised by singularity. Tokens may represent a single object, may only be used once, or only amongst a small group of individuals. This singularity can create or reinforce social hierarchies.[46]

---

[41] Mittag, 1999: 213–14.   [42] Holden, 2008: 123; Mondello, 2020b: 299.
[43] Albertson, 2014. An image of the relief can be found at https://collections.mfa.org/objects/151400 and the contorniate design at https://ikmk.smb.museum/object?id=18200483.
[44] Crisà, Gkikaki and Rowan 2019a: 2–3.   [45] Kroll and Mitchel, 1980; Raja, 2015.
[46] Crisà, Gkikaki and Rowan 2019a: 6.

Material

This volume is focused on the bronze, brass and lead tokens from Roman Italy, since these survive in greatest number. But we need to acknowledge that tokens might also have been created in clay, bone, stone or wood. A terracotta token now housed in the library at Columbia University carries the image of a facing head of Jupiter Ammon on one side and on the other is inscribed TIBI ME | XXIII (?).[47] Terracotta tokens are known from other regions in classical antiquity (discussed in more detail below), but seem to be rare within Roman imperial Italy. The situation may be coloured by the fact that tokens have traditionally been published alongside other lead objects (e.g. seals), and museum storage practices often mean that terracotta objects are stored alongside other antiquities of the same material, while metal monetiform objects are placed within coins and medals departments.[48] But a search of existing literature does suggest that very few terracotta tokens from Roman imperial Italy have been uncovered.

Bone items are also normally stored and published in different places to lead or bronze objects, and while a bone token is known from Republican Italy (from Fregellae, discussed below), such artefacts also seem rare amongst the surviving material culture from the imperial period. The David Eugene Smith collection, now housed at Columbia University library, provides some intriguing artefacts in this regard. A circular bone piece with a hole in the centre is inscribed 'L. Lucius cons. II' on one side, with the number II incised on the other (flat) side. Further bone pieces are inscribed with references to legions on one side and a corresponding number on the other (LEG III and III, LEG VI and VI, LEG VIII and VIII, LEG XL and XL). Another shows a representation of the Circus Maximus on one side with the number III incised on the other; a piece that recalls the bone artefact showing the Colosseum reproduced here as Figure 2.14.[49] The functions of such pieces remain a mystery; they might

---

[47] Columbia University Library, David Eugene Smith Professional Papers, 1860–1944, Box D6, inv. no. 214. The accompanying ticket says 'Tessera found at Rome'. My deepest thanks to Evan Jewell for bringing this specimen and other Roman objects in this collection to my attention, and for supplying me with photographs and data.

[48] On lead tokens published as one of many lead items see, by way of example, Ficoroni, 1740; Turcan, 1987.

[49] Columbia University Library, David Eugene Smith Professional Papers, 1860–1944, Box D6, inv. nos. 260-4, 268, 271, 275. The piece showing the Circus Maximus (no. 261) is accompanied by a ticket that records 'Tessera found in the via Torrina, near the American Church, Rome'. See Murray, 2012: 70 for a photograph of all the *tesserae* in the collection.

have served similar purposes to the tokens that form the focus of this volume, but there are simply not enough examples known for a detailed discussion. After all, bone pieces would each need to be individually carved, a process that would have taken considerable time and skill. It is thus logical to conclude that the state of the evidence reflects the reality: these pieces were likely rarer in antiquity than, for example, the lead pieces presented below, which could be produced cheaply in large numbers.

A passage of Cassius Dio discussing the opening of the Colosseum suggests tokens might be made of wood. Dio describes wooden balls, each inscribed with a word referring to a different object, being thrown amongst the crowd by Titus – those who managed to obtain a ball could later exchange it for the article inscribed upon it.[50] This author knows of no surviving wooden tokens from the Roman world, however, even from regions where the natural climate and environment preserves this type of material. Tokens of stone are known from Aquileia.[51]

Although tokens existed in a variety of materials in the Roman world, the vast majority surviving from Italy are made of bronze, orichalcum (brass) or lead. To date, most scholarship on these pieces has focused either on those issued in bronze/orichalcum, or on those of lead.[52] But this division of material obscures the many similarities these tokens possess. Similar to the so-called *spintriae*, lead tokens exist that carry sexual imagery on one side and a number on the other, for example.[53] Further iconographic similarities are explored throughout this volume. Both lead and bronze tokens also carry similar legends (e.g. variations on *feliciter*).[54] The similarities go beyond imagery: a close study of tokens related to Roman youth organisations reveal that these groups issued tokens in differing materials – they are thus best studied together.

When Buttrey published his study of *spintriae* he noted that the pieces carrying sexual imagery and those bearing portraits of the Julio-Claudian imperial family were tightly die connected. The dies used to strike the reverses were used both for tokens carrying the imperial portraits and the tokens with sexual imagery. Buttrey interpreted this as evidence that the two

---

[50] Dio 66.25.5. Discussion in Virlouvet, 1995: 321.
[51] Scholz, 1894: 14; Mainardis, 2002: 572 (= *CIL* V, 8211).
[52] Sample of studies focused on (a subset) of bronze/brass tokens: de Belfort, 1892; Buttrey, 1973; Jacobelli, 1997; Martini, 1997; Campana, 2009; Küter, 2019. Focused only on lead: Rostovtzeff, 1897; Rostovtzeff, 1905b; Thornton, 1980; Spagnoli, 2017a.
[53] *TURS* 912 (II within wreath on side b), 913 (AI on side b, which recalls the series of *aes* tokens that carry a sexual scene on the obverse and the letter A before a number on the reverse, Simonetta and Riva, 1981: Groups A and B).
[54] Rowan, 2020b: 99.

series were produced at the same time and perhaps intended to be used together; he suggested the overall effect was a material manifestation of gossip surrounding the imperial family after Tiberius' retreat to Capri.[55] Since Buttrey's work, several more die links have been found, although an exhaustive study of the group is still needed. The reverse dies, carrying numbers or the legend AVG (referring to the emperor) within a wreath, were also used to create brass tokens that bear the image of two boys or men playing a board game on the obverse.[56] The dies were also used to create a series struck for a *magister iuventutis* named Gaius Mitreius.[57] Otherwise unknown, this magistrate produced a series of tokens carrying a Julio-Claudian period portrait on one side (which I suggest is Mitreius himself) and numbers within a wreath on the other (Figure 1.4).[58] He is also the authority behind another series that carried the same obverse with a reverse showing what is likely a basilica, with different numbers incised into the exergue (Figure 1.5).

Both sets of Mitreius' tokens carry numbers, but in different ways; one might see here two series. For one series an existing set of dies within the workshop were used (the numbers within wreath), while for the other series a different reverse design was desired, the basilica. Since this necessitated the creation of a new reverse die, the series was produced from one die

Figure 1.4 AE token, 19 mm, 3.61 g, 6 h, 27 BC – AD 57. Bare male head right, cornucopia (?) below, C. MITREIVS L. F. MAG. IVVENT around (NT ligate). Dotted border (same die as Figure 1.5) / I within dotted border within wreath.

---

[55] Buttrey, 1973: 56–8.
[56] Martínez Chico, 2018: 546; Rowan, 2020b: 107–8. The obverse type is Cohen: vol. VIII, 266 no. 6.
[57] Rowan, 2020b: 108.
[58] Rowan, 2020b: 101–5. Since the publication of that article a further specimen has come onto the market, with VI inscribed below the basilica in the exergue (CNG Electronic Auction 490, 21 April 2021, lot 245). Cristian Mondello has also kindly alerted me to a further token of this series with X within a wreath on the other side, now in Bologna.

Figure 1.5 AE token, 20 mm, 3.58 g, 6 h. Bare male head right, cornucopia (?) below, C. MITREIVS L. F. MAG. IVVENT around (NT ligate). Dotted border (same die as Figure 1.4) / A two-storey building with five columns on each floor (basilica?) and a curved roof. On the building, between each floor, L. SEXTILI· S.P. In the exergue, X incised. Rowan, 2020b: no. 10.

and then engraved with numbers after production – for what seems to have been an exceptionally small volume (less than c. ten specimens are known to the author), this was far cheaper and easier than producing a die for each number required.

Lead tokens also carry the names of magistrates associated with Roman youth organisations, some also carrying what is likely a portrait of the magistrate accompanied by a legend naming him. *TURS* 834, for example, carries a male portrait on one side accompanied by the legend P PETR SABI with the legend MAG | VIIII | IVV on the other – the token refers to a P. Petronius Sabinus, *magister iuvenum*, and carries the number nine.[59] One of the stone tokens from Aquileia (in 'giallo antico') also references a magistrate of the youth; one side is inscribed M | IVVEN | MAG. VI | I.[60] Tokens of differing materials were thus used by youth groups in Roman Italy; the example demonstrates the gains to be had by studying tokens of differing materials alongside each other.[61] Further parallels in the iconographic themes between tokens of differing materials are presented throughout this volume.

Manufacture

The reverse die connections between the Julio-Claudian bronze and brass tokens also suggest something about the method of production. These

---

[59] *TURS* Pl. V, 70 for an image, discussion in Rowan, 2020b: 104.
[60] *CIL* V, 8211; Mainardis, 2002: 572.
[61] A fact also acknowledged by Rostovtzeff, 1905b: 59–60.

particular tokens must have been produced in the same workshop, which reused dies for different series. Given that the die connections are for the reverse (the side carrying numbers or the legend AVG), one might posit that for each customer requesting tokens, the workshop may have created a new obverse design, but then simply reused the numerical reverse dies. This would have been a cost and time saving measure in a production process that likely only ever resulted in a relatively small number of pieces (since larger productions would have required multiple reverse dies). Indeed, if differing numbers were integral to the use of these pieces, as seems to be the case, then the reuse of reverse dies was both economical and suited to the final function of these pieces. That a workshop reused reverse dies for different customers over time might also explain the fact that numbered brass and bronze tokens are known showing both the living and the deified Augustus.[62]

The high quality of these early imperial orichalcum tokens suggests that the workshop may have been in the Roman mint. At the very least the workshop appears to have employed highly skilled individuals. Martini suggested these tokens were an 'official' mint product, noting that orichalcum was used for the production of official small change in this period.[63] Küter, observing the similar iconographic emphasis of the imperial portrait tokens and the official coinage issue of AD 23 (which focused on the imperial dynasty under Tiberius), wondered whether the mint created these tokens as gaming pieces to be given away as gifts.[64] Without further information it is difficult to be definitive, but the presence of Mitreius on the tokens of this workshop suggests that (at least some of) these pieces were unlikely to be 'official' products. Figure 1.1 carries the legend FEL beneath the laureate head of Augustus; it is more likely that the good wishes (*feliciter*) of this token issue are directed towards the emperor, rather than from the emperor to the populace. This further suggests an authority other than the ruler.[65] Indeed, perhaps attempting to categorise these objects as official or not is not the best approach; like many monuments referencing the ruling authority (e.g. triumphal arches), these artefacts may have honoured the imperial family and contributed to their public image without having been 'officially' authored by the ruling power.[66]

Some of the lead tokens of Rome and Ostia also possess a high quality of design, and were obviously created by skilled artisans. Other lead tokens,

---

[62] Buttrey, 1973: cat. nos. 1–3 (Augustus laureate or bare headed), 4–6 (Augustus with radiate crown); see Rowan, 2020b: 109.
[63] Martini, 1999: 13.   [64] Küter, 2019: 91–2.   [65] Burnett, 2016: 77.
[66] On this phenomenon see most recently Russell and Hellström, 2020b.

however, carry imagery that is little more than stick figures, or, in the case of animals, might only be described as a quadruped.[67] The large variety in the quality of imagery on lead tokens must reflect the fact that manufacture of these objects was dispersed across the region, an observation also supported by the scattered finds of token manufacturing materials, discussed further below. Different workshops, and indeed different individuals and groups, must have contributed to the creation of token moulds. The diversity in manufacturing locations has resulted in a category of artefact that has far greater diversity in terms of image quality than other portable objects from Rome whose production was based in workshops of one kind or another (e.g. coins, lamps). The works of ancient authors describing, for example, portraits of the emperor that look nothing like their subjects, hints at the fact that this variety in image quality was characteristic of daily life in the Roman world.[68]

Tokens continued to be produced into late antiquity. In addition to the contorniates discussed above, other token objects of different materials and styles were produced, for different groups and contexts.[69] After the early Julio-Claudian period, imperial portraiture on tokens of bronze or orichalcum disappears, and the use of numbers becomes much less frequent. Information remains scarce, but one imagines these pieces continued to be produced in one or more workshops, which may or may not have been attached to the mint. One also imagines that the shift away from imperial representations and numbers may reflect the development of tokens as a medium, or their use in widening or changing contexts. We cannot know. But tokens do move away from their early Julio-Claudian precedents, and discussions of their purpose need to consider the broader picture: numbers, sexual imagery and imperial portraiture are only found on a portion of a much wider corpus.

Tokens in lead also appear to carry more Julio-Claudian imperial portraits than later emperors.[70] Lead tokens also carry numbers, although as with their bronze and orichalcum counterparts, many do not. Perhaps the

---

[67] For example, Rostovtzeff and Prou, 1900: no. 552 and 554, with images online at https://coins warwick.ac.uk/token-specimens/id/bnf.rost.prou.552 and https://coins.warwick.ac.uk/token-specimens/id/bnf.rost.prou.584.

[68] For example, Arrian, *Periplus Ponti Euxini* 1.2–3 (statue of Hadrian); Fronto, *Ep.ad M. Caes.* 4.12.4 (portraits of Marcus Aurelius), with discussion in Rowan, 2020a: 247.

[69] Woytek, 2020a: 134 dates a bronze token referencing the Roman mint to the third or fourth centuries AD. The *vota publica* tokens of late antiquity are discussed in Alföldi, 1937; a new and revised catalogue is currently being prepared by Laurent Bricault and Cristian Mondello: see Bricault and Mondello, in press. Further publications of late antique token material can be found in Kulikowski, 2017; Mondello, 2020b; Mondello, 2021.

[70] Rowan, in press a.

closest parallel to the numbers found on the brass tokens discussed above are a lead series, all now housed in the Vatican Museums. This series all share the same design on one side – Concordia seated right holding a cornucopia and patera, flanked by two smaller figures identified as Cupids. On the other side are the legends CFP | I, CFP | II, CFP | VIIII, CFP | X, CFP | XI, or CFP | XII.[71] The meaning of CFP is unknown: C might refer to Concordia, or to a proper name (Gaius), but ultimately the abbreviation remains a mystery. Numbers, then, were clearly necessary for some functions of tokens, but their precise role cannot be known given current evidence. They might have been deployed on token series that had to fulfil multiple or differing roles, or which had to represent different objects or values, but this is speculative.

Some lead tokens from Rome and Ostia appear to have been struck or impressed with a die or stamp carrying a negative design. The vast majority, however, were cast from moulds.[72] The method of manufacture for lead tokens means it is not appropriate to use the standard numismatic terminology 'obverse' and 'reverse', since these terms connect to the use of dies and an anvil for production ('obverse' refers to the side of the coin produced by an obverse die, 'reverse' to the side produced by the reverse die). As an alternative, this volume uses the terms 'side a' and 'side b' to describe the designs on each side of a cast token.

Several of the moulds used to cast tokens survive to the present day; they are largely made of palombino marble (a material that allows finely detailed carving) and have been found throughout Rome and Ostia (Figure 1.6).[73] As mentioned above, the dispersed nature of the finds demonstrate that tokens were not artefacts produced in a single government workshop, but cast in multiple locations by different groups of people. The finds of casting waste from these moulds in different spots in Ostia further supports this idea.[74] The use of lead for many tokens is also likely the result of this dispersed manufacture – lead has a relatively low melting point (327.5 degrees Celsius), meaning that melting the required material, was, relatively speaking, much easier than melting

---

[71] *TURS* 1734–9, Pl. VI no. 64; Rowan, 2020b.

[72] For examples (not exhaustive) of struck issues see *TURS* 927 (Pl. X no. 29), 1542 (Pl. XI no. 54), 1701 (Pl. VIII no. 67; Rowan, 2020b: no. 69), 3170 (Rostovtzeff and Prou, 1900: no. 648).

[73] Rowan, 2019 provides an overview of known findspots.

[74] For example, lead casting waste from these moulds has been uncovered during the excavations of the Baths of the Swimmer from a room identified as a *popina* or wine bar (Carandini and Panella, 1977: 271; Rowan, 2019: 100–1).

Manufacture 19

Figure 1.6 Palombino marble mould half, 108 × 76 × 29 mm, 389.2 g. The mould would have cast seven circular tokens decorated with the image of Fortuna standing left.

copper (1085 degrees) or silver (961.8 degrees). Lead was also much cheaper to obtain than other metals.[75]

Using marble moulds to manufacture lead tokens appears to be characteristic of the imperial capital and its port.[76] The overwhelming majority of token moulds have been found there, although there are scattered token moulds elsewhere in Italy. A token mould half now in the Museo Archeologico Nazionale di Firenze was reportedly found in Corneto (Tarquinia); two lead tokens (of different designs) were also reportedly found in the region.[77] A further token mould half was reported in Telesia, although Rostotovtzeff had doubts as to its authenticity.[78] Nineteenth century excavations in Como in Northern Italy also uncovered what was interpreted at the time as a soapstone mould half for round *tesserae* bearing the numbers IV, V, VII, VIII, VIIII, IX, X, XII and XIII; no associated tokens are known.[79] More mould halves might come to light as this material becomes better recognised. Most of these moulds have only been found as a single half, missing its counterpart, although some have been found fully intact.[80]

The moulds that survive to the present day reveal that at least one half was carved with channels for the lead to pour through, branching off into individual depressions into which the design of the token was carved. Figure 1.6 provides an example, with holes in the top right and lower left corners still containing the remains of the nails that would have tightly fastened the mould half to its partner. The use of nails (possibly consolidated with the use of wire wrapped around the mould once joined together) would ensure that the mould halves stayed together as the metal was poured; the use of fixed nail points would also ensure that each mould half was correctly aligned.[81]

---

[75] Boulakia, 1972: 139, 143.
[76] Other tokens from the Roman world were cast, but moulds similar to those presented here have not been found – the material and method was thus likely different. Many of the clay tokens from Palmyra, for example, were produced from moulds, but these moulds do not seem to have been found in the city or are not well published (Ingholt, Seyrig et al., 1955: iv; Raja, 2016: 346. Milne, 1945: 134–5 mentions that token moulds were found in Palmyra and that one entered the Ashmolean Museum collection, but the mould he mentions could not be located by the author).
[77] On the mould (inv. no. 79209), which produced tokens showing Mars and Hercules, see Mondello, 2020a. On the two tokens, both of the same design (L·AP / seated figure with patera) see *CIL* XI, 6722 no. 19; Rostovtzeff, 1903c: 217 no. 15.
[78] *TURS* 3599.
[79] Nogara, 1917. Thanks are due to Susann Lusnia for bringing this article to my attention.
[80] For example, Vatican Museums inv. nos. 64247.2.1–2, reproduced in Rowan, 2019: 96. Another mould with both halves is now housed in Ostia (inv. nos. 5920 a–b); see Spagnoli, 2001; Rowan, 2019: no. 51.
[81] Pardini et al., 2016: 652; Rowan, 2019: 95–6.

The top left corner of Figure 1.6 carries two finely etched concentric circles; the inner circle is c. 14 mm, the same size as the finished token cavities. The outer circle may be an error, or it may reveal the method by which the tokens were 'mapped out' on the mould before carving – this particular sketch was never finalised. Many moulds, including Figure 1.6, contain a deep central hole at the centre of each token design. These may have been used to plot the designs and ensure that each side of the mould aligned correctly (a similar process has been suggested for moulds that created coin flans). Alternatively, this deep impression may have been created by the tool used to carve each image.[82] The result is that lead tokens often carry a central protuberance (e.g. see Figure 1.8, which bears a central 'dot' in the centre of the token on the side carrying the text); although this is frequently included as an intentional part of the design in token catalogues we should see these marks as the result of the manufacturing process. A similar phenomenon can be seen on official coinage, where sometimes a central 'dot' can be seen on reverses where the design doesn't cover the centre of the coin (often on coins that contain only text).[83]

The manufacturing process required the intended design to be engraved into the mould as a mirror image. This was not always successful, resulting in several retrograde ('back to front') legends or letters amongst the corpus from Roman Italy.[84] For example Figure 2.3 carries a legend running around the outer edge of the token; the letters are neatly and correctly carved, with the exception of the 'S'. Despite the mechanisms designed to help align the mould halves, it is clear that not all token castings were successful – numerous specimens have one or both sides 'off-cast' – that is, off centre (see, for example, Figure 3.14, which is cast slightly off centre on both sides).[85] Indeed, the true number of rough castings may be hidden by the fact that most lead tokens today survive in major European museum collections; curators likely selected only the 'best' specimens to include.[86]

---

[82] Rostovtzeff, 1905b: 6; Kroll, unpublished: no. LT57; Rowan, 2019: 96–7. See Pilon, 2016: 56 for moulds used for flan casting, which display similar deep central cavities (with thanks to Bernhard Woytek for bringing this last to my attention).

[83] For example, some specimens of *RIC* II Trajan 149 (= Woytek, 2010: no. 225), for example the specimen in Paris https://gallica.bnf.fr/ark:/12148/btv1b104487671.

[84] Examples of tokens that carry retrograde legends are too numerous to list here but include *TURS* 1313, 1124, 2431, 3081, 3329, 3357.

[85] Other representative examples are *BMCRLT* nos. 638, 2080–1.

[86] See, for example, the collection of tokens published from archaeological excavation in Spagnoli, 2017b. The collection currently housed at the Museo Archeologico Nazionale di Palestrina, which has not been subjected to any 'selection' but was seized as the proceeds of illegal excavation activity, also contains far more 'rough' castings than other major museum collections.

The number of tokens moulds that survive is nowhere near the number of surviving token types, but nonetheless they provide a critical insight into lead token series. Although Rostovtzeff organised his catalogue of lead tokens into 'themes' (imperial portraits, types associated with spectacles, types associated with the *iuvenes, collegia,* gods, etc.), the surviving lead token moulds suggest that more than one design (indeed, more than one shape) might be cast from a single mould.[87] While some token moulds carry just one design (e.g. Figures 1.6–1.7), others produced tokens in a variety of sizes and shapes, and with varying designs. The complete mould now in the Vatican Museums, for example, would have originally produced eleven circular tokens with differing diameters, ranging from 9 to 12 mm. One half of the mould had cavities all decorated with the same image: standing Fortuna. Thus each token made from this mould would have carried the image of this goddess on one side. The other mould half carried two differing designs. Three cavities at the top of the mould (which were of larger diameter) were engraved with two figures standing facing each other, perhaps Mars and Venus. The remaining eight cavities were engraved with the image of an ant seen from above. A mould half found at 'Monte della Giustizia' (modern day Termini station in Rome) in the nineteenth century also demonstrates the variety that might exist in a single token series. The mould half carried designs for three circular tokens showing a standing ram and four triangular tokens carrying the letters PR.[88] Although the majority of lead tokens in Roman Italy are circular, other shapes also existed: quadrangles, triangles, diamonds and hexagons. Tokens in the shape of a *tabula ansata* or double-headed axe (*bipennis*) are also known.[89]

Because each token cavity was hand engraved, there is also the possibility for small differences to exist even between tokens carrying the same design cast from the same mould – the engraver may forget a small detail on one cavity, or add a small change or flourish on another. The Saturnalia tokens, discussed in Chapter 4, may form one such example of this, although small differences in design are not evident on surviving token moulds – the examples we have show a remarkable uniformity in design between each individual token cavity. Nonetheless there are tokens that are similar in design except for one small detail, and one is left to wonder whether they were cast from a mould that had a slight difference in one or more of the token cavities. The type *TURS* 2581, for example, carries the head of Janus

---

[87] Rowan, 2019 for an overview of moulds (although only those with known findspots).
[88] Ruggiero, 1878: no. 4; Rowan, 2019: no. 9, with further discussion on p. 98.
[89] *TURS* 1996; Giglioli, 1913.

on one side and the legend CCM on the other; one is tempted to see a variant in which the legend reads MCC as an error in engraving, although without a surviving mould it is impossible to know for certain.[90] A mould now in Milan also demonstrates that parts of a mould may be re-carved: on this piece one circular token cavity has a deeper hexagonal token cavity carved within it. While the other token cavities on the mould are decorated with a standing figure, the re-carved cavity is engraved with a phallus. Overbeck suggested the engraver was correcting an error here, although there is nothing to dismiss the suggestion that the mould might have been re-carved at a later stage to produce tokens of a different design.[91]

The ideal method to study lead tokens in Rome and Ostia would be to study them as issues cast by the same mould, but so few moulds survive that this task remains impossible. Indeed, even connecting individual tokens to the moulds that survive remains extremely difficult. Some token moulds, such as the two mould halves that once belonged to Wilhelm Fröhner and are now housed in the Bibliothèque nationale de France (BnF), carry designs that have been found on no lead token to date. One mould half would have created triangular tokens with the legend R|VB, the other circular tokens of differing diameters and designs (blank, dolphin, a standing figure with the legend QA PIN ITIRO around).[92] No triangular tokens carrying the legend R|VB or circular tokens with a legend QA PIN ITIRO are currently known; the meaning of these legends remain a mystery. Similarly, the mould half found on the Esquiline Hill in Rome, intended to make tokens carrying the legend ANTONI (with ligate lettering) has no corresponding tokens.[93] Moreover, several mould halves carry the same designs (e.g. standing Fortuna, the Three Graces); this makes it difficult to connect tokens with relatively common imagery to particular moulds.[94] Although differing diameters may help to distinguish between the products of different moulds, the fact the majority of moulds do not survive means that assigning any commonly used imagery, like the Three Graces, to a particular mould half remains fraught.

That said, in some rare instances it is possible to connect tokens carrying a particularly unusual image or unique legend to a particular mould.

---

[90] Rowan, 2020b: 97 and no. 70. [91] Overbeck, 2001: 66 no. 626.
[92] BnF Froehner IV.127 = *CIL* XV.2 p. 996, recorded as found in Rome in 1883; BnF Froehner V.201.
[93] Cesano, 1904a: 209 no. 2.
[94] A mould now in the Museo Nazionale in Rome would have produced seven circular tokens of 17 mm carrying the image of the Three Graces (Cesano, 1904b: no. 1). A mould half now housed in the Casa Buonarroti in Florence was also designed to cast seven circular tokens carrying the image of the Three Graces, but the diameters of these tokens range between 14 and 15 mm (Mondello, 2020a).

Figure 1.7 Palombino mould half, 93 × 108 × 28 mm, 561 g. The mould would have created 5 circular tokens of c. 25 mm in diameter. *TURS* 3578 (Pl. XII, 6).

Figure 1.8 Pb token, 24 mm, 12 h, 5.04 g. M VALERI | M F | ETRVSC / Togate figure standing left holding a purse (?) in outstretched right hand. *TURS* 1327.

Figures 1.7 and 1.8 are one such example. The identification of token and mould was possible due to the unusual nature of the design: this is the only currently known token representation of a togate male figure holding what

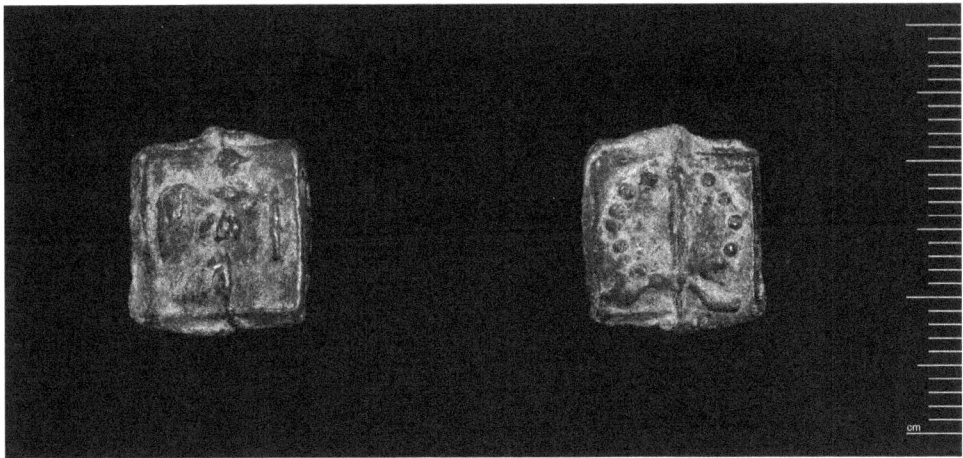

Figure 1.9 Pb token, 15 × 14 mm, 12 h, 4.61 g. Victory standing right / Wreath. *TURS* 1913.

appears to be a purse. The other mould half does not survive, one presumes this was the half that contained the channels for the lead to flow through to the cavities, since these do not exist on the piece we possess. That tokens survive and not their moulds, or vice versa, is a reflection of the partial survival of material from antiquity, particularly in the case of cheaply manufactured everyday goods. But the low survival rates may also reflect the use context of these tokens. As will be explored throughout this volume, lead tokens appear to have been manufactured for use in a particular moment in time, for a specific event or benefaction. One presumes that the lead tokens would normally have been melted down after use; those that survive seem to have escaped their normal life course through accidental loss or curation. It is also perhaps no accident that normally only a single mould half is found: moulds may have been reused, or disposed of in such a way to prevent forgery.

One can also identify tokens from the same mould when there are cracks or errors. Two quadrangular tokens now in Harvard Art Museums, decorated with Victory on one side and a wreath on the other, both have an extra casting ridge running through the centre of the token in precisely the same place on the wreath side; they were clearly cast from the same mould cavity (Figure 1.9).[95] Other tokens of the same design do not carry this fault and were perhaps cast from elsewhere in the mould.[96] This type of error, however, is surprisingly rare on surviving tokens.

[95] Harvard Art Museums 2008.116.31–2.
[96] Harvard Art Museums 2008.116.33; Rostovtzeff and Prou, 1900: nos. 227–9.

Figure 1.10 AE token, 18 mm, 6 h, 3.63 g. *Vexillum*, dotted border, two rectangular countermarks reading NO / Victory advancing right holding wreath in outstretched right hand and palm branch in left; dotted border. Cohen vol. VIII, 271 no. 47.

Countermarking

Tokens in Roman Italy were occasionally countermarked, although there are few studies of this phenomenon.[97] In terms of tokens in bronze and orichalcum, only two types appear to have been countermarked. The first belongs to a series characterised by the common use of a *vexillum*; this type is variously paired with Victory, Minerva or Mars.[98] On many of the tokens with Victory on the reverse, and, remarkably, seemingly *only* on these tokens, a rectangular countermark with the legend ON (or NO) appears twice, struck on either side of the standard (Figure 1.10). Mowat suggested the legend be read as NO and proposed that the countermark may be an abbreviation of *no(vo)* or *no(vata)*, indicating that the token had been 'renewed' for a further use. If so, then the process must have occurred twice or required two countermarks, since the NO stamp is never found in the singular. Mowat further suggested an alternative reading might be *no(tata)*, recording that the token had undergone some sort of control or validation (*nota*).[99]

That the countermarking only occurs on tokens carrying the Victory type may provide clues to the method of manufacture. It may be that, similar to the model proposed above for the brass/bronze tokens with numbers, these tokens are the creation of a single workshop that reused one die (in this case the *vexillum*) as a cost saving measure to create a series of different tokens for different customers over time. For whatever reason, the issue of the '*vexillum* / Victory' tokens underwent countermarking. Although the double countermark is frequently found on tokens of this type, it is not present on all known specimens. This suggests that the

[97] Mowat, 1898.   [98] Cohen: vol. VIII, 271–2 nos. 46–9.   [99] Mowat, 1898: 24.

counfermarking took place after the tokens had been issued, perhaps to renew those 'collected' for use in a new context, or to indicate the token had been validated.[100] It may be that the tokens with Victory indicated a type of object or experience that was different to the tokens carrying Minerva or Mars (hence requiring countermarking in a way the other tokens did not).

The other known instance of countermarking on bronze tokens is found on a series characterised by the use of different letters as types (D, T, ligate TR, as well as a type showing a galley).[101] On some specimens of the type 'ligate TR / D', a rectangular countermark containing a ligate THR appears above the ligate TR.[102] Again the countermark only appears on a single subset of the series (the 'ligate TR / D' combination), but it is not found on *all* specimens of this type.[103] The context of the countermark then is likely to be similar, if not the same, as the '*vexillum* / Victory' type discussed above.

Countermarks on lead tokens from Rome and Ostia are similarly only found on a very small number of types. The countermarks might take the form of legends or images.[104] As with bronze tokens, on the rare occasions when countermarks occur they are not found on all the tokens of a series, although in several instances there is only one (countermarked) specimen of a type known.[105] For these examples, we cannot know if the entire series was originally countermarked or not. The textual countermarks may refer to names or numbers, while the figurative countermarks draw from an array of everyday imagery (e.g. Amor and Psyche, dolphin, elephant, crescent). Once again the impression is of a practice applied after the token series had been manufactured and distributed, perhaps to repurpose the token for a secondary context, or to indicate the token had been used. Overall, token countermarking remains relatively rare in comparison to other regions, particularly Roman Athens. In Athens tokens have been found together in assemblages with countermarks, and the same countermark has been found on tokens of different designs, which Crosby believed

---

[100] Rowan, 2020b: no. 11, for example, is not countermarked.
[101] Cohen: vol. VIII, 272–3 nos. 56–7, 60. Bronze tokens combining a ligate VL with various letters (e.g. Cohen: vol. VIII, 273 nos. 61–2) may be connected to this series, or may form a separate series. The bronze tokens with letters are currently the subject of a study by Bernhard Woytek.
[102] BnF inv. 1933,133; BM 1867,0101.2360; Berlin Münzkabinett 18203172 and Rowan, 2020b: no. 18 also appear to carry the countermark as well, but it is a fainter impression. See also Mowat, 1898: 24–5.
[103] For example, BnF inv. nos. 17074–5 are without the countermark.
[104] Rostovtzeff, 1903b: 423 provides a list of countermarks and graffiti found on tokens included in *TURS*.
[105] For example, *TURS* 450, 567, 775, 1842, 2414 are only known through a single specimen, which is countermarked.

was an indication they had been issued by the same authority.[106] No such similar assemblage, or use of a single countermark across multiple token types, has been found in Rome or Ostia. One imagines that when countermarking occurred, it was an unusual event, the precise circumstances of which remain elusive to us.

Authority

We are reliant on the tokens themselves to reveal who was responsible for their issue. Sometimes tokens carry detailed information in this regard, while other examples bear only an image or letter on each side, which makes it impossible for us to know the authority. Yet this is in itself revealing: it is evident that tokens were issued to small groups within particular contexts – unlike coinage or other media (e.g. triumphal arches), tokens did *not need to communicate their authority to a wide audience*. Rather, one imagines that tokens were given to people who already knew the issuer and the particular context in which the token was to be used. In such contexts, and given the dispersed nature of manufacture, intricate and detailed legends seem to have given way to pure imagery (which must have been chosen to enhance a particular occasion or communicate a particular identity), or abbreviations intended to spark recognition in the mind of a user who already knew the name of the issuer. There appears to be a widespread use of abbreviations, for example, which referred to particular *tria nomina*. Canting types, punning imagery referring to a particular Roman *gens*, also occur and are explored in Chapter 3.

Ancient texts reveal that the emperor produced tokens – for example, the wooden balls created on behalf of Titus mentioned by Cassius Dio. Bronze and lead tokens also carry portraits of the emperor, although we cannot presume that the emperor was the authority in every case. As explored in Chapter 2, it is evident that the imperial image might be chosen to decorate the tokens of a particular magistrate. An example is the token issue of one Oinogenus, *curator*, which carried the portrait of Tiberius on one side.[107] Given the varying quality of tokens carrying the imperial image without reference to another authority, we must also entertain the idea that the imperial image may have been chosen for the decoration of tokens

---

[106] Lang and Crosby, 1964: 83, 116; Gkikaki, 2019.
[107] *TURS* 514b; Franke, 1984; Harris, 2000.

issued by other sectors of Roman society, who may not have deemed it necessary to name themselves on their issues.

Tokens carrying reference to the imperial family, however, are a minority within the broader array of tokens from Roman Italy. The tokens themselves suggest they were issued by a wide variety of different groups and individuals, including women. As mentioned above, tokens can carry the names of magistrates associated with Roman youth groups, as well as *curatores*, generally thought to be curators of Roman games and spectacles.[108] Tokens also carry the names of male and female Roman individuals, as well as *collegia* and other organisations or establishments, for example individual bathhouses. The range of groups issuing tokens is also reflected in the distributed nature of token finds. The full variety of token issuers will be explored in more detail throughout this volume; the material forms an important glimpse into the experiences of multiple groups in Roman Italy, particularly in Rome and Ostia. It is worth drawing attention to the fact that such variety in terms of authority is not universally found elsewhere in the Roman Empire. In Roman Egypt, for example, tokens were anepigraphic or carried the name of particular settlements (e.g. Oxyrhynchus, Memphis).[109] In Palmyra, tokens seem to have largely been the preserve of priests in the city.[110] In Gaul (with the exception of Lugdunum) tokens carried the names of settlements or tribes.[111] Who issued tokens, then, was just as localised as the approach to manufacturing these items.

Date

Rostovtzeff believed that the Romans adopted tokens in the late Republic after having seen the medium in practice at Athens.[112] Tokens of varying sorts, however, existed in Italy from an early period; inspiration need not have come from Athens. In the city of Rhegion spherical terracotta tokens have been found carrying names and demes in Ionic or Chalcidean-Ionic script; they are believed to be connected to the functioning of the democracy in the city and are dated to the fifth century BC; similar spherical objects have been found in Sicily and are thought to have been used in sortition processes (e.g. distribution of land).[113] These pieces form an

---

[108] Rowan, in press b on the tokens issued in connection with imperial games by *curatores*.
[109] Milne, 1930; Milne, 1971; Wilding, 2020.   [110] Raja, 2015: 178.
[111] Weiller, 2000; Wilding, 2020.   [112] Rostovtzeff, 1900: 103; Rostovtzeff, 1905b: 27.
[113] *I.Rhegion* 26A–D. The pieces are now on display in the Museo Archeologico Nazionale di Reggio Calabria. For a good overview of the material in Sicily see Walthall and Souza, 2021.

interesting contrast to the far better known *symbola* associated with classical Athenian democracy. It may be that several Greek democracies made use of tokens, but the form tokens took in each city was unique.[114]

Monetiform objects carrying civic numismatic types made in lead and clay are also known in Magna Graecia.[115] The possible purpose of these artefacts remains unknown. Clive Stannard's work on the 'Italo-Baetican' assemblage demonstrates the use of lead tokens among business communities in central Italy in the late second and first centuries BC.[116] The name was given to this assemblage because of the similarities in design between the lead pieces from central Italy and those from Baetica in Spain; it is believed these pieces were used by Italians involved in mining or agriculture in Roman Hispania.

Fregellae, destroyed by the Romans in 125 BC, has also furnished tokens that date to the second century BC. During excavations of the site in 1987 a circular bone token was found, inscribed on one side with the word BALN (or BALIN, the LN is ligate) and on the other with the name L. Atin(ius) Mem(mianus) (L·ATIN | MEM, with IN ligate).[117] On the basis of palaeography and archaeological context the token has been dated to c. 150–125 BC. Five cast lead tokens were later found in the bathhouse at Fregellae, all decorated with the same design: the head of Mercury facing right with three pellets before him on one side, and on the other side a dolphin swimming right.[118] The tokens were found together in a small drain near the south entrance of the baths along with other finds that suggest the context was one of haphazard accumulation and later spoliation. The tokens are thought to date to around the middle of the second century BC. The use of Mercury and pellets recalls Roman Republican coinage from this period: the head of Mercury appeared on Roman bronze coinage in the third century BC, frequently with a prow design on the reverse. The design appeared on the *sextans* denomination (indicated by two pellets on the coin) and in the late third century on the *quadrans* (indicated by three pellets).[119] The three pellets on the lead tokens may thus have been intended to represent a value (perhaps the price of entry to the baths). But in spite of some similarities

---

[114] See also the use of lead strips at Camarina and differing shapes of clay tokens found at Mantinea (Robinson, 2002). The scholarship on tokens and democracy in classical Athens is large, but see by way of example, Lang, 1959; Lang and Crosby, 1964; Bubelis, 2011; Kroll, 2015. A new monograph exploring tokens in Athens is forthcoming by Mairi Gkikaki.
[115] Mannino, 1993; Siciliano, 1993; Siciliano, Natali and Boffi 1995.
[116] Stannard, 1995; Stannard, 2015a; Stannard et al., 2017; Stannard, Sinner and Ferrante 2019; Stannard, 2020.
[117] Sironen, 1990. [118] Pedroni, 1997. [119] For example, *RRC* 97/5c.

with Roman bronze coinage, the use of lead here, and the dolphin reverse, served to clearly distinguish these tokens from official money.

It is thus evident that Italy had a tradition of using tokens and Rome need not necessarily have taken inspiration only from Athens. But there is currently no archaeological evidence for the use of tokens in the city of Rome before the late Republic. Remarkably, many of the earliest tokens we can connect to Roman authorities were issued overseas. Lead tokens found in Athens carrying variations of the legend CEBACTOC (*sebastos*) and the image of a nude youth holding an aplustre and spear were connected to Augustus by Rostovtzeff on the basis of style; Rostovtzeff argued the image is likely a statue of the first *princeps*. A token with the legend CEBAC|TOY and corn-ears, and another with the legend KAI CAP and a laureate male head with a star before (identified as Apollo or the deified Caesar), have also been connected to Augustus' presence in Athens, and a grain distribution.[120] A token bearing the portrait of Marc Antony accompanied by a corn-ear or caduceus has also been found in Athens.[121] A further lead piece, likely from Carnuntum in Austria, displays the portrait of Antony accompanied by the remnants of the legend –NIVS IIIVIR; worn figures decorate the other side.[122] Seventy-eight tokens discovered by metal detecting, all from Fos-sur-Mer in Southern France, have tentatively been connected with Julius Caesar and his Gallic campaigns.[123] A token showing Augustus has also been found in Sardis.[124] Token use by the Romans, then, appears to have developed during the civil wars of the late Republic. It was at this time that Roman politics, patronage and euergetism was played out across the Mediterranean in a way previously not seen before.

Although there is no definitive evidence, some of the tokens from Rome also suggest use from the late Republic. The deified Julius Caesar appears on a token likely issued under Augustus in Italy, and tokens are known from the region bearing Augustus' portrait.[125] A token series bearing the name Sosius in Greek accompanied by a male portrait that looks Republican in style (although on worn tokens style can be difficult to discern) is likely connected to Gaius Sosius, who supported Antony in

---

[120] Postolacca, 1868: no. 174; Rostovtzeff and Prou, 1900: 50; Rostovtzeff, 1903a. Hoff, 1992 suggests the tokens may have been connected to a grain distribution in Athens in 31 BC (which, if correct, is the earliest known evidence for Augustus' public connection to Apollo).
[121] Rostovtzeff, 1903a: 309. [122] Dembski, 1973/4. [123] Sciallano, 1987; Wilding, 2020.
[124] DeRose Evans, 2018: no. 216.5 (the portrait is accompanied by the legend S C).
[125] Julius Caesar: Rostovtzeff and Prou, 1900: 33, the portrait is reportedly accompanied by a star, *lituus* and the legend DIVI IVLI. For Augustus see the orichalcum pieces published in Buttrey, 1973, and for the lead see Overbeck, 2001: nos. 1–4 (no. 1 may be a coin forgery).

the civil wars before changing sides and returning to Rome to build the temple of Apollo Sosianus (see Figure 3.21).[126] In spite of the Greek legend, the fabric of the tokens suggests it was manufactured in Italy. Another token, purchased by Rostovtzeff in Rome, carries on one side a male figure carrying another on their shoulders, while the other side is decorated with an oath scene, in which two soldiers flank a kneeling figure carrying a pig.[127] Both scenes are also found on Republican coinage. The former image is either one of the Catanaean brothers or Aeneas with Anchises.[128] The oath scene occurs on coins of the later third century BC, on issues of 137 BC, as well as on coins struck by the Italians during the Social War.[129] Although the imagery might have been used on the token well after the coins were issued, it is possible this piece was made in the later Republican period.

It is thus evident that tokens were used by Romans from the late Republic. The first archaeological evidence of their use and manufacture in Rome comes from the early imperial period. Two mould halves were excavated from the *Curiae Veteres* on the Palatine from Neronian *strata*, which provides a *terminus ante quem*.[130] As mentioned above, both bronze and lead tokens carry reference to the Julio-Claudian dynasty. A fragment of a token mould from the Baths of the Swimmer in Ostia demonstrates that lead tokens were still being manufactured in the third century AD.[131] A token that carries the name CARINVS in Greek and Latin was connected by Rostovtzeff to the emperor of the same name; if correct this is further evidence for the continued production of lead cast tokens into the second half of the third century. A rough date range for the production of the majority of lead tokens in Rome and Ostia might thus be given as c. AD 1–300. Token use continued into late antiquity, when it seems specimens were largely made out of bronze rather than lead. Woytek dated a bronze token showing a scene of minting and the *tres Monetae* to between AD 290 and 350 on the basis of comparative iconography.[132] The latest excavation context of bronze or brass tokens known to the author is an orichalcum token decorated with a *modius* on one side and cantharus on the other (for

---

[126] Ficoroni believed the portrait was of Antony (Ficoroni, 1740: 89), but Sosius is just as likely, given that the medium is a token, not a coin.
[127] *TURS* 2014a.
[128] *RRC* 458/1 (47–46 BC), 494/3a–b (42 BC), with discussion in Zarrow, 2003.
[129] *RRC* 28/1–2 (225–212 BC), 29/1–2 (225–214 BC), 234/1 (137 BC); *HN Italy* nos. 425, 428.
[130] Pardini et al., 2016: 656.
[131] Found in Stratum I of 'Ambiente XVI', which dates from the middle of the third century AD to the middle of the fourth century; Carandini and Panella, 1977: 271.
[132] Woytek, 2013: 249.

the type see Figure 5.15), found in a hypogeum in Lepcis Magna that ceased to be used around the middle of the second century.[133] But the iconography of several bronze tokens, which carry representations of late antique emperors and in some cases incorporate Christian motifs, suggest token use continued into at least the fifth and sixth centuries AD.[134] This volume focuses on brass and bronze tokens that were (likely) created in the imperial period before c. AD 300.

As already mentioned, the vast majority of tokens in Roman Italy come from Rome and Ostia; finds from other Italian cities are known, but are smaller in number. Not every settlement seems to have produced tokens. The biggest lacunae in this regard are Pompeii and Herculaneum – no lead or bronze tokens have been found among the excavations in these cities, although bone gaming pieces have often been mistakenly published as Pompeian *tesserae* or theatre tickets. Without further data we cannot know the reason behind the absence of tokens in these now infamous settlements – it may be that Pompeii used a media other than tokens in daily life, or tokens made out of a perishable material like wood. Token use may have reached its zenith after Vesuvius' eruption; much of the data from Ostia, for example, seems connected to the flourishing of the town in the second century AD.

Tokens in the Roman Empire

The piecemeal adoption of tokens by settlements in Roman Italy is paralleled by uneven token use across the Roman Empire. Not all cities made or used tokens. Indeed, token use seems particularly scarce (although not unknown) along the northern frontier and in the more northern provinces.[135] But even within a single province there appears to be significant variation: in Syria, for example, hundreds of tokens have been excavated in Palmyra, while at nearby Dura Europos not a single token has been found.

During the Roman imperial period, relatively large bodies of tokens can be connected with Athens, Ephesus, Lugdunum, Palmyra and towns in

---

[133] Di Vita-Evrard et al., 1996: 129. Several tokens of the same type were found in tombs dating to roughly this period, see Chapter 5.
[134] Kulikowski, 2017; Mondello, 2020b; Mondello, 2021.
[135] Britain: *RIB* 2408.2–3 with discussion in Boon, 1986; Mattingly, 1932; Wilding, 2020. Liberchies, Belgium: van Heesch, 2000. Dalheim, Luxembourg: Weiller, 1994; Henrich, 2009. Carnuntum: Dembski, 1973/4. Lavant, Austria: Kainrath, 2005.

Egypt (e.g. Oxyrhynchus).[136] The picture will no doubt change as the material becomes better recognised and hence better published; for example there are many more tokens associated with Caesarea Maritima than have been published to date.[137] Smaller numbers of tokens have been connected to numerous other settlements, too numerous to detail here.[138] Tokens, for example, have been excavated at Sardis and at a variety of different sites in Gaul.[139] The current state of the evidence is still incomplete, but it nonetheless does allow us to situate the tokens of Roman Italy within a broader context of token use across the Empire.

What the evidence from the Roman imperial period reveals is that where tokens were used, the design and manufacture of these pieces occurred in a very localised manner. The designs, materials and manufacturing techniques of tokens varied from region to region, and even from settlement to settlement. The palombino moulds of Rome and Ostia, for example, are not found beyond Italy. While the tokens of Lugdunum are characterised by very small diameters and the use of a three-letter legend, those of Roman Athens are often anepigraphic. The majority of tokens from Palmyra are made of terracotta rather than lead; many of the lead pieces from Ephesus are uniface (single sided). The tokens of a particular region carry imagery that is particularly local, and were manufactured in accordance with local traditions. Rome and Ostia are also local in the design and manufacture of tokens. This grants the historian an archive of material directly related to the local communities, ideologies and events in the imperial capital and its harbour.

Although our knowledge of tokens will undoubtedly change in future years, the relative absence of tokens in Britain and along the northern frontiers is likely to be a reality. This, in addition to the abundance of tokens in cities like Rome, Athens and Ephesus, provides evidence for one of the main contentions of this volume: that tokens were used for euergetism, to aid in community distributions and communal events. Such events occurred with lesser intensity along the northern frontier, and communal

---

[136] Athens: Lang and Crosby, 1964. Ephesus: Gülbay and Kireç, 2008. Lugdunum: Dissard, 1905. Palmyra: Du Mesnil du Buisson, 1944; Ingholt, Seyrig and Starcky 1955. Egypt: Milne, 1971: nos. 5276–447 (5280–319 Oxyrhynchus); Dattari, 1901: nos. 6412–547.

[137] Communication of Dr Yoav Farhi. Only a small number of tokens from Caesarea have been published to date, see Oestreicher, 1962; Hamburger, 1986.

[138] Postolacca, 1868 includes find information for tokens where it is available, including locations in Greece outside Athens; de Callataÿ, 2010 brings together various studies in a general discussion.

[139] Sardis: Buttrey et al., 1981: 223, nos. 1–14; DeRose Evans, 2018: nos. L1, L3–L10, L24, 113.1, 114.1, 216.5. Gaul: Le Brazidec-Berdeaux, 1999; Dubuis and de Muylder, 2014; Weiller, 2000; Hollard, Le Brazidec and Gendre 2015; with discussion and synthesis in Wilding, 2020.

events may have not required the medium of tokens if they took place in the small, closed communities found within a Roman fortress.

Tokens and Social Life in Roman Imperial Italy

The designs and findspots of tokens in Roman Italy, particularly in Rome and Ostia, reveal them to be artefacts of everyday life, created by an assortment of groups to facilitate communal events. As local artefacts, the designs chosen for these objects offer an insight into how the inhabitants of Italy adapted the imagery that surrounded them to shape identities, experience and feelings of belonging. The imagery *not chosen* is just as important to our understanding of the process as that selected – what imagery is appropriated and made one's 'own', and what is ignored?[140] Once created, tokens and their imagery would have served to consolidate feelings of belonging to a particular group. This would be further underscored by the fact that some would possess tokens and others would not. Tokens often seem to have been used during group events; they might bestow wealth or prestige on a person as they were exchanged for a particular good or service. The excavations of Ostia suggest they were spread throughout the settlement, acting to reinforce the particular beliefs of their owners, even unconsciously.

This volume explores four key aspects of tokens in Roman Italy. The use of tokens as expressions of relations between the imperial family and the population of Italy form the focus of Chapter 2. Tokens carrying imperial portraiture, both those likely issued by emperors and those issued by others, are discussed here. The material opens up new understandings of the imperial image and its semantic flexibility.[141] I then move on, in Chapter 3, to consider the identity of token issuers and users, and the role of tokens in fostering feelings of community and connection. In the fourth chapter, the volume considers the tokens that carry chants or imagery related to Roman festivals. Festivals and spectacles were popular motifs on objects of daily life in Roman Italy, and the prevalence of this imagery must have served to shape the anticipation and memory of particular events. The fifth chapter turns to the idea, often put forward in modern scholarship, that at least some of these tokens served as emergency small change. There is simply no evidence that these objects acted in the

---

[140] de Certeau, 1984: 97–101.
[141] On the social dynamics of the imperial image see most recently Russell and Hellström, 2020b.

same way as other alternative currencies from antiquity; nonetheless their existence may have eased the burden on supplies of small change in Rome and its environs. This chapter examines the possible exchange contexts of these artefacts (e.g. to access Roman bathing facilities) and in doing so highlights once again how these unassuming artefacts shaped everyday experience in antiquity.

Although Roman economic historians may be disappointed not to have discovered a previously unstudied cache of circulating small change, the existence and materiality of these tokens does offer an important insight into the impact of Roman currency on its users. While much work on Roman coinage has highlighted the communicative potential of these objects (and indeed the author herself has been active in this regard), evidence of the reception of numismatic imagery remains slim: we are reliant on the mention of coin types in particular texts, for example, or the scattered reuse of coins as stamps or jewellery. The tokens of Roman Italy provide an important new source: the circular shape of the majority of these tokens, the use of portraits with encircling legends, and the adaptation of numismatic imagery (particularly the reproduction of the images of deities that are otherwise known from coinage), all provide concrete confirmation of the role of money in shaping Roman identities and mentalities.

This volume is offered in the context of a resurgence of token studies in modern scholarship; the themes explored here form only a selection of what this material can tell us.[142] As material manifestations of human relationships, as objects that can represent emotions, value, or identities, tokens have played powerful roles throughout human society, whether this be contributing to the invention of writing and abstract number, or facilitating democracy.[143] The role and impact of tokens in the Roman world has only just begun to be understood; despite Rostovtzeff's reservations the artefacts hold enormous promise.

---

[142] See Arzone and Marinello, 2019; Crisà, Gkikaki et al., 2019b; Martínez Chico, 2019; Raja, 2019; Gkikaki, 2020; Mondello, 2020b; Raja, 2020; Rowan, 2020b; Rowan, 2020a; Mondello, 2021 for a selection of the most recent work on tokens from classical antiquity.
[143] Lang and Crosby, 1964; Schmandt-Besserat, 2010.

2 | Tokens and the Imperial Family

Representations of the imperial family appear on a small number of tokens from Roman Italy. Emperors, empresses and their offspring are named and/or shown on these specimens. Some of these tokens may have been issued on behalf of the emperor; others carry reference to the authority of magistrates or groups. Tokens are thus a medium that communicated both official and non-official representations of imperial power. They form an important, and to date overlooked, source for the reception and use of imperial ideology by differing groups. For those outside the imperial government, the use of imperial imagery offered an opportunity to express a particular connection with the ruling power; the imagery also contributed to status and, subsequently, social structure.[1] In this way the imperial image, as well as tokens themselves as artefacts, contributed to the maintenance of social hierarchy and social relationships.

The emperor's image was likely employed on tokens used during imperial celebrations; at least this is what is suggested by some of the messages carried on these pieces. Although it is dangerous to unthinkingly connect a particular image to a particular purpose, several of these tokens make reference to specific ceremonies through their legends (*dies imperii*, triumphs, *liberalitas* distributions). This suggests that at least some of these pieces were used in such contexts. The following chapter explores how tokens might be used to identify how the imperial image, and imperial ideology, were mobilised at specific moments in time. Festive celebrations offered an opportunity for people to actively engage with the imagery of the imperial family. These event-based, momentary but active iterations of imperial ideology provide an important perspective for the study of the formation of the Roman imperial image more broadly.

As discussed in Chapter 1, individuals were named on tokens during the late Republic (e.g. Julius Caesar, Marc Antony). With the arrival of the principate, emperors were named and portrayed on these objects. The appearance of the imperial family on tokens appears to reach a peak in the Julio-Claudian period, before declining in the second half of

---
[1] Russell and Hellström, 2020a: 11.

the second century AD. This chapter outlines this phenomenon and discusses some potential reasons for it. The Flavians form a particular focus in this chapter, since this period has not seen as much recent scholarship as other dynasties, despite the rich evidence available.

The Julio-Claudians

Augustus and the Julio-Claudians are the best-represented dynasty on tokens of lead and bronze alloy; the surviving material from Italy carries more representations of the imperial family from this period than any other. The possible reasons for this (changing attitudes towards imperial *liberalitas*, changing visual culture connected to festivals and tokens) are discussed at the end of this chapter.

The representation of a wide range of Julio-Claudian imperial family members on tokens has been repeatedly observed in scholarship.[2] The best-known tokens bearing portraits of the Julio-Claudians are the orichalcum series connected to the so-called *spintriae*, briefly discussed in the introduction (see Figure 1.2). As mentioned there, these tokens have die connections with other token series, including tokens carrying sexual imagery and a series issued by a *magister* of the youth, Gaius Mitreius (Figure 1.3 and 1.4). The use of the same reverse dies for multiple series suggests these tokens were produced by a single workshop, perhaps issuing tokens over many years for different individuals.

In terms of imperial portraits, the series carries representations of Augustus (both living and deified), Augustus and Livia, Livia alone, and another female portrait most recently identified as Livilla, wife of Drusus the Younger.[3] Tiberius is also portrayed (bare headed or laureate with *lituus*), and a young male portrait that is likely Drusus (shown cuirassed). Two young boys wearing tunics and with stars above their heads have been identified as the twin sons of Drusus the Younger, Tiberius Gemellus and Germanicus Julius Caesar.[4] Drusus the Younger and his deceased twin sons are also portrayed on a lead token series.[5] Another series, of a different style and produced from different dies, shows the emperor Claudius, while a further orichalcum token now in the British Museum shows a young, bare headed Julio-Claudian prince on the obverse and an eagle holding

---

[2] Küter, 2016; Küter, 2019; Rowan, 2020a; Rowan, 2020b.   [3] Küter, 2019: 80–2.
[4] Küter, 2019: 82–3.
[5] Dressel, 1922: Pl VI no. 7 and the Münzkabinett Berlin 18237641, https://ikmk.smb.museum/object?id=18237641.

a sceptre standing on a globe on the reverse.[6] The different style of these last tokens further strengthens the model proposed in Chapter 1: these artefacts seem to have been produced over a period of time.

These tokens displayed an array of imperial family members, both alive and deceased. Lead tokens also carry representations of the imperial family, discussed further below. Unfortunately we cannot know the use context of these Julio-Claudian pieces, but the fact that the dies were used to create other designs suggest that the 'imperial portrait' types were just one category of token. Other obverse designs included a facing head of Medusa, a Capricorn, a *quadriga*, a *biga*, two individuals playing a game (Figure 4.14) and female musicians.[7] Since these pieces are not found together as 'sets', one imagines that a person likely received only a single token. If this was a token with an imperial portrait it was perhaps distributed during an event connected with the imperial family. Importantly, the use of an imperial portrait for a token design constituted a choice – other imagery was available, used for other occasions and by other groups.

The dynastic presentations on Julio-Claudian tokens in orichalcum and bronze can also be found on issues in lead. Tokens in all these metals were perhaps created for use during occasions that emphasised the reigning dynasty and its heirs; the medium does seem to place an emphasis on imperial children. For example, Augustus' successors Gaius and Lucius Caesar appear seated on curule chairs on a lead token found in the Tiber. The other side of the token carries the image of two shields and two spears: these were voted to Gaius and Lucius by the equestrian order.[8] The token likely celebrates the promotion of both Gaius and Lucius to the role of *principes iuventutis* ('leaders of the youth'): this title, as well as the shields and spears, also appears on coins struck in significant quantity towards the end of Augustus' life.[9] Indeed, the token is likely to have drawn inspiration from the numismatic imagery, adapting it to suit the different medium and context.[10]

---

[6] Claudius: Göbl, 1978: pl. 9 no. 94 (V within wreath); BM R.4459 (XVIIII within wreath), Classical Numismatic Group Mail Bid Sale 57, lot 1051 (II within wreath). The same style of wreath is found on a series that carries Cupid in different poses on the obverse (see Münzkabinett Berlin inv. no. 18203166, Campana, 2009: 53 Group II); both series are likely from the same workshop. Campana suggested the Cupid series may have been a later (post-antique) creation, but seems to have been unaware of the similarity to the Claudius specimens. Julio-Claudian prince and eagle: BM R.4432.

[7] Küter, 2019 for an overview.   [8] *TURS* 3; *Res Gestae Divi Augusti* 14.1; Cooley, 2009: 166–7.

[9] *RIC* I^2 Augustus 205–7, 209–12; *Res Gestae Divi Augusti* 14.1, with discussion in Wolters, 2002; Cooley, 2009: 166–7; Rowan, in press a. *RIC* I^2 Augustus 208 is likely a restoration issue of Hadrian, see Woytek and Blet-Lemarquand, 2017.

[10] The coin design is also imitated on a gem, now in Florence. See Vollenweider, 1963-1967.

Germanicus' sons Nero and Drusus also appear on a lead token that was probably found in Rome. One side of the token shows the busts of Nero and Drusus facing each other, while the other side shows the two young men galloping to the right on horses.[11] This last image again recalls Roman coinage, which shows both Nero and Drusus on horseback as *Caesares*.[12] Suetonius records that Tiberius gave a *congiarium* to the populace upon the formal introduction of Nero and Drusus to the Senate and one imagines that this token was used within a similar context: to mediate a distribution or other activity during an occasion focused on the imperial heirs.[13]

Claudius' rule also saw the representation of numerous family members on tokens, with Messalina (Figure 2.1), Britannicus, Antonia the Younger and the future emperor Nero all making an appearance.[14] As Figure 2.1 illustrates, these tokens have obvious reference to the official coinage produced at the mint of Rome in terms of size, shape, the use of imperial portraiture and the placement of the legend. But tokens also carry otherwise unknown combinations of imagery, and designs not associated with the emperor on coinage. Messalina, for example, does not appear on the imperial coinage produced at the Roman mint.[15] A further example of this phenomenon is found in Figure 2.2. The token carries a portrait of Nero accompanied by a legend naming him;

Figure 2.1 Pb token, 19 mm, 2.16 g. Bare head of Claudius left, TI CLAVDIVS CAESAR / Bust of Messalina right, MESSALINA.

---

[11] *TURS* 8, Pl. I no. 11; Héron de Villefosse, 1893: 353–5.   [12] *RIC* I² Caligula 34, 42, 49.
[13] Suet. *Tib.* 54.
[14] A token of the same type as Figure 2.1 showing Claudius and Messalina was found in the sanctuary of Hercules at Alba Fucens, see Ceccaroni and Molinari, 2017. Britannicus: *TURS* 11. Antonia: *TURS* 910 and Mitchiner, 1984: no. 2.
[15] She does appear on a didrachm struck at Caesarea in Cappadocia, but the reverse carries the imagery of Octavia, Britannicus and Antonia, not Claudius. *RIC* I² Claudius 124.

Figure 2.2 Pb token, 18 mm, 12 h, 2.48 g. Bare bust of Nero right, NERO CAESAR around / Mars (or soldier) standing left holding spear in left hand and resting right on shield, CLAVDIOR around. *TURS* 13.

the overall effect is very similar to the design of a coin. But the other side of the token shows Mars and bears the legend CLAVDIOR. This particular representation of Mars would only appear on Roman coinage during the civil wars of AD 68–9 and only regularly occurs on coinage from the reign of Trajan.[16] Here the token representation predates that on official coinage. Moreover, the legend *Claudior(um)*, 'of the *Claudii*', is never found on coinage. If the adjective refers to Nero (as seems likely), the piece specifically links the emperor to the Claudian *gens*. Nero is normally represented as the (adopted) son of Claudius (*Claudi f.*), rather than a member of the *Claudii* more broadly.[17]

Nero's portrait on Figure 2.2 is certainly not as finely detailed as on other tokens, suggesting an authority other than the imperial government may have created this issue. Indeed, tokens offer an insight into how the imperial portrait was utilised by differing groups. Similar to provincial coinage (where imperial portraiture is used on issues struck under the authority of local magistrates) or other monuments in the capital (e.g. arches erected by the Senate and People of Rome), tokens (and their associated events) formed a medium through which particular sectors of Roman society might contribute to imperial ideology. Tokens were not long-lasting objects: they reflect the conscious use of imperial portraiture by differing groups for specific moments in time. This in turn may reflect methods of interaction

---

[16] *RIC* I² Civil Wars 20, 23, where the god is identified as Mars Ultor; *RIC* II Trajan 161–3. It may be for this reason that Rostovtzeff identified the figure as 'Mars or a soldier'. The figure may be a soldier, but it so closely resembles later depictions of Mars it is likely the deity who is represented, perhaps the cult statue in Augustus' temple of Mars Ultor. Nero reportedly had a statue in the temple of Mars Ultor the same size as the statue of Mars, see Tac. *Ann.* 13.8.

[17] Nero was officially known as Nero Claudius Caesar Augustus Germanicus, but the name Claudius is often omitted on coinage (which frequently bears the legend NERO CAESAR AVGVSTVS); see Hekster, 2015: 52 for a discussion.

with Roman imperial portraiture more broadly across Roman society: a statue or portrait of an emperor, for example, may sit 'in the background' of daily life for a period of time before being mobilised or re-activated for a particular ceremony or occasion, as Tran explores for the imperial *imagines* in the club houses of *corpora* in Ostia.[18] The same might be said for the imperial portrait on coinage: the faces of the imperial family might form a 'background' to monetary exchange until a particular set of circumstances 'mobilises' the image (e.g. the decision to erase the portraiture of emperors who had been subjected to *damnatio*).[19] Time, then, is an important dimension in understanding the roles played by the imperial image in Roman society, although not every particular context can be uncovered in the modern day.

Figure 2.3 is a clear example of a token issued by an authority other than the emperor. On one side we find a Julio-Claudian portrait (Augustus?) accompanied by the legend CAESAR, and on the other side the *praenomina* of the individuals responsible for the token, Marcus and Manius. The S in CAESAR is retrograde (back to front), reflecting an error in the workshop that created the mould. Unfortunately the token itself offers no further information about who Marcus and Manius were, or the context in which the token was manufactured.

Other tokens carrying imperial portraits, however, are issued by individuals whose magistracy is specified; this is often a *curator* or *magister*.[20] The occurrence of *curator* (frequently abbreviated to CVR on tokens) was

Figure 2.3 Pb token, 19 mm, 12 h, 1.7 g. Bare male head (Augustus?) right, CAESAR around / MARCI·MANI· around. *TURS* (Supplement) 3601 (previously unpublished).

---

[18] Tran, 2020: 231.   [19] Calomino, 2016.
[20] For example *TURS* 514b, a token issued by the *curator* Q. Caecilius Q.f. Oinogenus f., with a portrait of Tiberius on the other side. See Rostovtzeff, 1905b: 48; Franke, 1984; Harris, 2000; Rowan, in press a. The second 'f.' in the name should be read as *filius* – that is, 'the younger', see Harris, 2000: 263.

believed by Rostovtzeff to mostly refer to the position of *curator ludorum*, a magistrate in charge of games. The magistracies named on tokens might refer to civic positions or positions within smaller organisations, for example Roman youth groups.[21] The example of Gaius Mitreius has already been discussed. A further example is the *cur(ator) iuv(enum)* responsible for a token issue that bore a female portrait accompanied by the legend CLAVDIA AVG, a reference to Nero's daughter Claudia Augusta who died at four months in AD 63.[22] The female bust shows a young woman with her hair tied in a bun at her neck; Rostovtzeff suggested it was perhaps Claudia's mother Poppaea shown here rather than the deceased infant. Poppaea is shown on provincial coinage with her hair plaited and tied at the base of her neck (she is not shown on coinage struck at Rome).[23] The token may then indeed represent her. However, given the legend, it is equally likely that the portrait was intended to represent Claudia Augusta: she was the first imperial child to undergo *consecratio* at Rome and thus there was no established representational precedent.[24] Evidence for portraits of the deified infant Claudia exist and it has been suggested that a prototype bust of Claudia Augusta was created immediately after her death showing her as a young child, which served as a model for her representation across the Empire.[25] A surviving marble bust proposed to be Claudia does not look like the representation on the token (it shows a young child without a plait), but it may be that, in the absence of a known portrait type, the token issuer here may have simply represented Claudia in a manner akin to her mother – the quality of token designs, as we have already noted, could vary significantly. The representation may have been intended to show Claudia as the young adult she may have become, had she lived.

The legends CLAVDIA AVG and CLAVD AVGVSTA also appear on other lead tokens accompanied by a very similar female portrait. On one specimen, found in the Tiber, the portrait is paired with the legend M L D T arranged in a cross on the other side; we do not know what the

---

[21] Patterson, 1992: 235; Bruun, 2007: 131; Lott, 2013: 176; Laes and Strubbe, 2014: 132 on the position of *curator* in various contexts.

[22] *TURS* 874, pl. V no. 68.   [23] For example, *RPC* I 1352A, 2924, 3564.

[24] McIntyre, 2013: 225.

[25] Cipriani, 2018: 179. The bust discussed in this article shows a young child without a plait, a portrait previously identified as a young Nero. An adult figure also seems to represent the deified Claudia on provincial coinage, see *RPC* I 4846 (also identified as Poppaea) and McIntyre, 2013: 227–8. By contrast, Domitian's son, who must have been around seven or eight when he died, was represented as a baby on coinage marking his deification (*RIC* I^2 Domitian 152).

Figure 2.4 Pb token, 18 mm, 12 h, 2.92 g. Bare head of Nero right, NERO CAESAR around / Head of Claudia Augusta (?) right, CLAVD AVGVSTA. *TURS* 34, Rostovtzeff and Prou, 1900: no. 32.

legend refers to.[26] Another type carries the portrait and legend CLAVD AVGVSTA, with the portrait of Nero and the legend NERO CAESAR on the other side (Figure 2.4). For this type Rostovtozeff did not hedge his bets by describing the portrait as 'Claudia or Poppaea' but rather described the portrait simply as Claudia. An example of this token type was found in the Garigliano river, eighty miles south of Rome and thirty-five miles north of Naples.[27] Nero gave his deceased baby daughter the title Augusta and deified her; a *pulvinar*, a temple, and a priest were granted to her by the Senate.[28] It is entirely possible that Claudia, shown as a young female very similar in appearance to her mother, was incorporated into the imagery of tokens, which may have been used during celebrations in her honour, for example during her consecration.[29] Given the absence of the title DIVA, we cannot rule out the idea that some of these tokens may also have been used during the celebrations of Claudia's birth or some other event in her short life. Ultimately, we cannot be certain as to the identification of the female figure, but the recurring reference to Claudia (and not Poppaea) suggests it is the young daughter of Nero intended here. The context in which these tokens were produced can also only be speculative.

As well as heirs, imperial ancestry might also be celebrated. One token, carrying a representation of the emperor Claudius' mother Antonia the Younger wearing a wreath of corn-ears, specifically records that the piece was used within a ceremony of imperial *liberalitas* (EX | LIBERAL|ITATE TI CLAVDI | CAE AVG).[30] The token was likely used to facilitate the distribution; it might have been given to individuals during the ceremony and exchanged later for money, grain or other goods. Alternatively, the

---

[26] *TURS* 875; Tomassetti, 1887: no. 4d.   [27] Mitchiner, 1984: no. 4.   [28] Tac. *Ann.* XV.23.
[29] Epigraphic evidence attests to activity in honour of the infant: *CIL* VI, 2043–4 (Arval brothers), *CIL* XI, 6955 (dedication in Luni). See discussion in Cipriani, 2018: 174–8.
[30] *TURS* 10; Scholz, 1894: no. 8; Kloft, 1970: 96.

token might have granted access to the distribution. Textual accounts record the distribution of gifts by different emperors, mentioning *tesserae*, *sparsiones* and *missilia* – the latter two words indicate the method by which these tokens were distributed ('scattered' or 'thrown').[31] These words may not necessarily indicate the use of tokens on each occasion. They may equally describe the scattering of smaller prizes, for example meats and sweets.[32] But Cassius Dio's mention of Agrippa, as *aedile*, using *symbola* to distribute prizes in the theatre suggests that, at least on some occasions, imperial and magisterial gifting was mediated by lead tokens.[33] The associated tokens were then designed with particular imagery to further enhance the message of the gesture and its political context.

Suetonius records that while on Capri, Augustus watched the exercises of the ephebes, and then gave them a banquet during which he distributed *missilia* to be exchanged for food and other goods.[34] The particular context, interaction with Italian youth, is of particular note given the assortment of tokens surviving that mention *iuvenes*.[35] Cassius Dio records that during a gymnastic contest Caligula scattered *symbola* and then distributed gifts to those who managed to get hold of one, an act that 'delighted the rabble' but 'grieved the sensible'.[36] Nero is also associated with the distribution of *missilia* that represented multiple types of goods: grain, clothing, gold, silver, precious stones, pearls, paintings, slaves, beasts of burden, trained wild animals, ships, *insulae* and farms.[37]

Although Fortuna is a popular motif on the surviving lead tokens in Rome and Ostia (perhaps a reference to the role of luck in managing to obtain a token thrown from above), the representation of specific goods, as described by our textual sources, remains rare. They do exist, however, and Figure 2.5 is one such example. It depicts an oyster on one side, and gives the Latin for oyster (OSTREVM) within a wreath on the other (perhaps to clarify the image). This may be an example of a token used in a distribution ceremony, imperial or non-imperial; alternatively, it might be connected to some other patronage or business in Rome or Ostia.[38] There might be several reasons why tokens like this are scarce. Most tokens may have not needed to carry such obvious imagery (goods may have been represented in other ways). Alternatively, lead tokens used in these contexts were likely, by and large, to have been redeemed, and

---

[31] Rostovtzeff, 1905b: 4; Nibley, 1945; Simon, 2008. [32] Simon, 2008: 768–9.
[33] Dio 49.43.4–5. [34] Suet. *Aug.* 98.3. [35] For example, *TURS* 833–52; Rowan, 2020b.
[36] Dio 59.9.6–7. See also Suet. *Calig.* 16.4–5. [37] Suet. *Ner.* 11.2.
[38] Dalzell, 2021: 79 observes that oysters were considered a food of the elite and thus were unlikely to be involved in official food distributions.

Figure 2.5 Pb token, 21 mm, 3.18 g. Oyster on an oyster shell / OSTREVM in two lines within wreath. From a private collection, Dalzell, 2021: 88 no. 2.

thus do not survive to the present day. Upon presentation and exchange, one imagines the tokens were then melted down to allow the lead to be reused.

Numerous individuals thus likely made use of tokens to facilitate the distribution of goods or benefactions within Rome. Although lead tokens may not always have been the medium of choice on such occasions, those that survive provide insight into the array of imagery used within specific contexts and moments in time. Some of these tokens bore imperial portraits, underscoring how the imperial image might be mobilised and become 'visible' at particular moments in time. I now turn to a more detailed case study, which has seen far less discussion in scholarship: the use of lead tokens under the Flavian dynasty.

Triumph over Judaea under the Flavians

Two contemporary accounts of Roman ceremony and spectacle are preserved from the Flavian dynasty. Josephus' account of the triumph over the Jewish people in AD 71 in Book 7 of his *Jewish War* is the fullest account of a triumph we have from the Roman Empire.[39] It was also in this period that Martial composed the *Liber Spectaculorum*, a collection of epigrams celebrating various spectacles put on by Domitian and/or Titus, unique among surviving classical literature in its focus on ephemeral displays.[40] Indeed, gift giving and festivals also form a focus of Martial's work elsewhere; several of his books were published for the

---

[39] Joseph. *BJ* 7.5.3–7; Beard, 2003; Millar, 2005: 101.
[40] Coleman, 2006: lxxiv; Lovatt, 2016: 365–6.

Saturnalia.[41] It is perhaps unsurprising that there is such a focus on this theme in authors from this period: the triumph celebrated over the Jews, the public conversion of Nero's Golden House into areas dedicated to public consumption (embodied by the completion of the Colosseum) and the visible connection of military triumph with other building programmes around Rome were key in creating legitimacy for the new dynasty. We also possess a series of tokens that are likely Flavian in date that reference the festivals and spectacles held by these emperors, as well as broader dynastic ideology. The Flavians, then, form an ideal case study for an examination of how tokens operated within contexts connected to the emperor.

The return of Titus to Rome in AD 71 after successfully quashing the uprisings in Judaea was followed by a military triumph in the city. The occasion enabled Vespasian to advertise the new imperial dynasty.[42] In spite of Josephus' detailed account no mention is made of imperial distributions or the use of tokens during the event; one gets the impression that Josephus preferred to focus on other matters, like the route taken through the city. The imagery of several tokens from Rome, however, suggests that these objects may have been used during the triumph of AD 71. Alternatively, imagery connected with the Jewish triumph may have been adopted for later use.[43] While there have been numerous studies of Roman triumphs,[44] the possible connection of tokens to this ceremony has, by contrast, had very little attention.[45]

Scholars have frequently commented that the wreath shown on many bronze and orichalcum tokens is the *corona triumphalis*.[46] This need not suggest these tokens were used in triumphal ceremonies; the imagery of triumph was often adapted for use on objects within broader daily life.[47] But one particular token series carries an even closer reference to the Roman triumph (Figure 2.6). The obverse of the series carries a laurel branch, a symbol of military triumph, accompanied by the cry *io, io triumphe*! Surviving literature informs us that *io triumphe* or *io, io triumphe* was shouted during the triumphal

---

[41] For example, his poems mentioning *sportula* and the Saturnalia, discussed in Harrison, 2001. On the occasion of the books of the *Epigrams* see Coleman, 2005, who suggests Book 6 may have been offered on the occasion of the Matronalia.
[42] Beard, 2003; Tuck, 2016: 111.
[43] Millar, 2005 discusses the evidence for the latter on various other media.
[44] For example, Beard, 2009; Östenberg, 2009; Popkin, 2016.
[45] Rostovtzeff, 1905b: 32; Overbeck and Overbeck, 1996; Woytek, 2015: 480–4.
[46] Martini, 1999; Campana, 2009; Le Guennec, 2017: 421.
[47] For example, on Gallo-Roman vessels, see Desbat, 2011: 21, 24.

Figure 2.6 Orichalcum token, 19 mm, 3.74 g, 12 h, AD 75–125. Laurel branch, IO on left, IO on right, TRI VMP around. Dotted border / Two *armillae* and a torque. Dotted border. Rowan, 2020b: no. 19.

ceremony.[48] Varro provides the best discussion of this phrase, noting that soldiers shouted *io triumphe* as they returned with the general and proceeded through the city of Rome.[49] The reverse of the token series shows articles of the *dona militaria*: a torque and two *armillae* (armbands). These items were awarded to soldiers who had performed well in battle: the tombstone of M. Caelius for example, a soldier who died during the Varian disaster in AD 9, shows the deceased with his *armillae* and torques.[50] It is likely that *armillae* are also represented on lead tokens, although this has previously not been recognised.[51]

The obverse of the token clearly references a triumphal ceremony, although it is by no means certain it was used in this specific context. One specimen of this series was uncovered in Rome and forms part of the 'monete della commissione archeologica' of the Capitoline Museums.[52] We cannot know the precise context or use of the token series, but the choice of imagery is significant. The token issuer(s) did not decorate their series with an image of the emperor in a triumphal chariot, for example, or with images of spoils or captives. Rather, the designs captured the experience of the soldiers themselves: the chant they cried and the objects some of them would have received. Tokens used in other events (e.g. religious festivals) were also designed to appeal directly to the experience of a participant,

---

[48] Hor. *Epod.* 9.21–3, *Carm.* 4.2.49–50; Ov. *Am*.1.2.34, *Tr.* 4.2.51–2; Tib. 2.5.118; Livy 24.10.10; Woytek, 2015: 481; Burnett, 2016: 75.

[49] Varro *Ling.* 6.68.

[50] Linderski, 2001: 3–15; Östenberg, 2009: 108–11. *CIL* XIII, 8648 = LVR-Landesmuseum, Bonn, U82.

[51] *TURS* 1060, 1725; Rostovtzeff and Prou, 1900: nos. 343, 613. Rostovtzeff had identified the image as a horseshoe.

[52] The piece is on display in the museum amongst other numismatic objects.

discussed more fully in Chapter 4. The choice of motifs here forms part of a broader phenomenon in token design.

The IO IO TRIVMP series was originally assigned to the reign of Domitian on the basis of what is now known to be a spurious die link with a *quadrans*.[53] Nonetheless, Woytek proposes that the issue should be dated to the late first or early second century AD: among the *quadrantes* issued by Domitian are types that have previously been identified as an olive branch but which may in fact be a laurel branch, and which form a close parallel to the representation of the branch on the token series.[54] The overall effect of the token (which survives to the present day in relatively large numbers in comparison to the Julio-Claudian numeral tokens) is extraordinary: the user is gifted a 'laurel branch' and the text serves to make the token speak, evoking the senses of the user.[55] Indeed, the recording of the chant, and the gifting of a 'laurel branch' would have created a sense of participation for the user. Even if not used as part of triumphal festivities, the legend and imagery would have evoked the idea (or memory) of a triumphal ceremony.[56] Tokens in Rome and Ostia carry far more acclamations than coins or medallions, perhaps due to their particular connection to specific events. The effect would have been to further reinforce a sense of belonging to a particular community: the process of chanting together unifies a group.[57] If a user was gifted a token before an event, it might serve to create a sense of anticipation (mediated by previous experience), while examining the piece after an event would recall the occasion in the mind of the viewer.

The imagery on several lead tokens suggests that these too must have contributed to the experience of an event and/or its memorialisation via the use of particular triumphal imagery. A lead token with a provenance of Rome and now in the BnF carries a laureate portrait that is likely Vespasian on one side and Victory with wreath and palm branch on the other.[58] A more unusual image can be found on Figure 2.7. One side displays a portrait of Vespasian, while the other side is decorated with a palm tree on a platform with two wheels. Another example of the same type is reproduced as Figure 2.8; this specimen shows that the palm tree was adorned with further palm branches on the left and right. Faint traces of this decoration can also be seen on the left of the palm tree on

---

[53] Woytek, 2015: 482.   [54] *RIC* II.1² Domitian 240–1, 247; Woytek, 2015: 481.
[55] Woytek, 2015: 481. Woytek notes the similarities to the depiction of a soldier standing behind the triumphal chariot on the Boscoreale cup – the figure wears a torque and carries a laurel branch.
[56] Burnett, 2016: 79.   [57] Kuhn, 2012: 298.
[58] *TURS* 1832; Rostovtzeff and Prou, 1900: no. 38.

Figure 2.7 Pb token, 17 mm, 12 h, 2.95 g. Bare head of Vespasian right / Palm tree on a platform with two wheels; palm branch on left and on right. *TURS* 34.

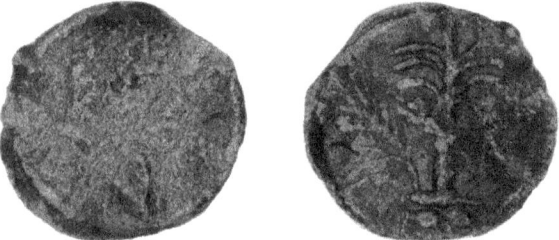

Figure 2.8 Pb token, 19 mm, 3.24 g, 12 h. Bare head of Vespasian right / Palm tree on a platform with two wheels; palm branch on left and on right. *TURS* 34.

Figure 2.7. The palm tree became symbolic of the capture of Judaea; it was shown on coinage, for example, alone or alongside Victory, piles of armour, triumphant members of the imperial family, Jewish captives, or the defeated personification of the region.[59] The palm tree had previously appeared with Victory on coinage of Vitellius in AD 69 (unsurprising given one of Victory's attributes was a palm branch), but under Vespasian it came to symbolise Judaea (and the associated Flavian victory in this region).[60] The representation of this mobile palm tree, however, is unique to tokens.

These tokens might provide evidence that a palm tree was paraded through Rome in the Jewish triumph of AD 71; the representation of Vespasian suggests these pieces were either used in connection with the triumphal ceremony or another context during the emperor's reign. Pliny

---

[59] For example, *RIC* II.1² Vespasian 3–4, 57–9, 159–69, 340–3; Overbeck and Overbeck, 1996: 211; Cody, 2003: 107.

[60] *RIC* II.1² Vitellius 123–4, 142–3, 169. See Plin. *HN* 13.6.26 for the connection between Judaea and the palm tree.

records that a rare balsam tree, reportedly only known from royal gardens in Judaea, was paraded in the triumph of AD 71. In discussing the exhibition of the plant by Vespasian and Titus, Pliny notes 'it is a remarkable fact that ever since the time of Pompey the Great even trees have figured among the captives in our triumphal processions'.[61] Elsewhere Pliny notes that it was an ebony tree exhibited by Pompey, during his triumph over Mithridates.[62] Östenberg suggests that these trees were exhibited alive and upright (as shown on Figure 2.7); they may have been planted after the procession was over.[63] The token imagery here may allude to a painting or image shown as part of the triumphal procession over Judaea, but it most likely represents a physical tree that was paraded through Rome. Given the central role of the palm tree to the representation of Flavian victory in the region, the presence of a physical tree in the triumphal procession is very probable.

The connection between the palm tree and the Flavian victory in Judaea is made more explicit on several other lead tokens. A worn token, now in the British Museum, displays the head of Vespasian on one side and on the other carries the image of a weeping figure (likely the personification of Judaea) beneath a palm tree.[64] The image is very close to that found on official Roman coinage, but is a mirror image, suggesting that perhaps a coin served as inspiration for the design (directly translating a coin image onto a mould would result in a mirror image of the original design on the resulting tokens).[65] Judaea beneath a palm tree is also paired with an image of Jupiter holding a thunderbolt and Victory.[66] The connection between the palm tree and the Judaean victory is also made explicit on Figure 2.9, which pairs the tree with the legend IVDE – Rostovtzeff interpreted this as a reference to *Iudaea*.

Other tokens also carry an image of a palm tree, but are more difficult to connect to Flavian celebrations after the conclusion of the war. One type bears Fortuna on side a, and a palm tree accompanied by the letters T C on side b – Overbeck and Overbeck suggested the legend might refer to T(itus) C(aesar), although the suggestion remains hypothetical.[67] They further argued that *TURS* 1842 (Victory inscribing a shield / the letters T L on

---

[61] Plin. *HN* 12.54.111–12; Totelin, 2012. The plant was a shrub, identified as *Commiphora gileadensis*. The plant on the tokens shows dates beneath the branches, and so should be identified as a palm tree rather than a balsam tree.
[62] Plin. *HN* 12.9.20.
[63] Östenberg, 2009: 184–8; Totelin, 2012: 124 doubts the balsam tree would have been planted, suggesting transplanting trees in this manner would have failed in antiquity.
[64] *TURS* 38; *BMCRLT* 899.   [65] For example, *RIC* II.1² Vespasian 4, 59.
[66] Overbeck, 1995: no. 486.
[67] *TURS* 399 (palm tree misidentified as *modius* and corn-ears) = *TURS* 473; Overbeck, 1995: no. 78; Overbeck and Overbeck, 1996: no. 6.

Figure 2.9 Pb token, 14 mm, 12 h, 1.94 g. IVDE / Palm tree. *TURS* 39, Rostovtzeff and Prou, 1900: no. 33b.

either side of a palm tree) was also a reference to the Jewish wars; various images of Victory inscribing a shield attached to a palm tree appear on Roman coinage under Vespasian.[68] Overbeck and Overbeck noted that the precise function played by these pieces is unknown: they might have been distributed in triumphal ceremonies, as a souvenir, or to be exchanged for other goods.[69] Whatever their context, they served to further consolidate the ideology associated with Flavian legitimacy.

The palm tree also appears on tokens alongside types that cannot be immediately connected to the imperial house. Accompanying designs include two corn-ears, Fortuna, Fides, Mercury, Aequitas, a rhinoceros, a horse, a deer, a flower, the legends CCS, FOR, INS, AMI, CM and a monogram.[70] These tokens need not have necessarily been used during activities sponsored by the emperor, but may have been created by others for local events as part of a broader celebration. We glimpse the existence of such associated events in Josephus' account of the triumph of AD 71: after the arrival of Vespasian at the palace, the 'crowds then betook themselves to festivity' and feasted 'by tribes and families and neighbourhoods'.[71] These very local experiences of a broader imperial celebration may have utilised tokens to control access to banquets or to manage the distribution of goods. The tokens, and the contexts in which they were used, placed imperial ideology within a hyper-local environment.

Not all tokens carrying palm trees, however, are necessarily connected to the Flavians. The palm tree, as with the palm branch, was a general

---

[68] Overbeck and Overbeck, 1996: no. 7; e.g. *RIC* II.1² Vespasian 14, 57, 68–9. The token is overstruck on side a with a rectangular countermark containing the ligate letters MVAL, which Rostovtzeff resolved as M. Val(erius). We do not know what the letters T L might have stood for.
[69] Overbeck and Overbeck, 1996: 215.
[70] *TURS* 425, 471–2, 474–6, 477–9, 480–3, 779, 1691, 2159, 2675, (Supplement) 3749. We do not know what the legends may have stood for.
[71] Joseph. *BJ* 7.1.72–3.

symbol of victory, and supported Victory's shield on official coinage until the early fourth century.[72] The palm tree might also be associated with victories in non-military contexts; for example it is portrayed on a North African Roman lamp next to a victorious racehorse named Regnator.[73] But the portrayal of a palm tree on its own, without accompanying images, does seem, at least in Rome and Ostia (where these tokens are most likely manufactured), to have been connected to Judaea and the Flavian dynasty. Indeed, the palm tree is found on carved marble pieces likely to come from the temple of the *gens Flavia*: entablature pieces from this structure are supported by stylised palm frond capitals and we also possess the remains of male caryatids who are shown with their backs against palm trunk column shafts.[74] These fragments reveal the extent to which the imagery of Jewish conquest, including the palm tree, took on dynastic associations: these were no longer specific references to a particular moment in time, but more enduring images associated with the legitimacy of a dynasty.

Given the association of the palm tree with the Flavian dynasty, Figure 2.10 is of particular interest. A male figure carrying a cornucopia stands before a tree; at the point where the two outer branches of the tree meet the trunk there are two circular shapes suggestive of dates, hinting that this representation is meant to depict a palm tree. The central pellet is the result of the manufacturing technique, detailed in Chapter 1. Rostovtzeff identified the figure as Anubis. Although the figure does have a pointed head that might

Figure 2.10 Pb token, 19 mm, 12 h, 3.06 g. Nude male figure standing left holding cornucopia in left hand and reaching out with right to palm tree before him / LLV. *TURS* 3194.

---

[72] *RIC* VII Lugdunum 28. [73] Getty Museum inv. 83.AQ.377.135.
[74] Koeppel, 1980; Tuck, 2016: 120.

indicate a snout, no ears are visible on this specimen, or on the piece now in the BnF in Paris, which was found in Rome.⁷⁵ The figure then may be a Genius. The embodiment of the people of Rome, or an association within the city, placed before a tree, and represented as the same size as the tree, may have been an instance of localised reuse of Flavian imagery for a particular local context, if the interpretation of the tree as a palm is correct. The LLV on side b of the token might be the initials of a *tria nomina* beginning with Lucius. The use of tokens as a medium that allowed interaction and adaptation of imperial imagery in very localised contexts is discussed further below.

Striking in this context is the apparent absence on tokens of representations of the emperor as *triumphator*. Rostovtzeff records only two occurrences of a *triumphator* on tokens, shown frontally in a *quadriga* holding a globe in his left hand. *TURS* 111 carries, on the other side, the image of a military trophy flanked by the letters F P (the meaning of the legend is not known).⁷⁶ *TURS* 112 carries a radiate lion on the other side. The image of a male figure with a globe in a *quadriga* also fits the god Sol, who appears in a frontal *quadriga* carrying a globe from the third century AD (it is also only from the third century, under Caracalla, that a radiate lion appears on coinage).⁷⁷ Triumphing emperors are normally shown carrying a sceptre and/or branch while in procession; the presence of a globe here does suggest Sol may be the better identification.⁷⁸ The radiate lion, although an uncommon image, seems to be connected with Sol; the god's connection with military victory, particularly in the East, also fits well with the choice of a military trophy as an accompanying image.⁷⁹ The seeming absence of the *triumphator* from tokens is a mystery, one that further research may help to illuminate.

The imperial family do appear in other ways on tokens. As with the Julio-Claudian period discussed above, a dynastic emphasis is found on Roman lead tokens under the Flavians. These tokens may have been manufactured in association with the triumph of AD 71 (the first time the entire dynasty was presented to the Roman people), or at some other point during Vespasian's reign.⁸⁰ Figure 2.11, showing and naming Vespasian on side a, and his two sons on side b, closely recalls coinage issued by the emperor in AD 70 (Figure 2.12).⁸¹ But there are also significant differences between

---

[75] Rostovtzeff and Prou, 1900: no. 478. [76] *TURS* 111, Pl. II no. 30.
[77] *RIC* V Aurelian 77–8; *RIC* IV.1 Caracalla 273A–E.
[78] For example, *RIC* I² Tiberius 221–4, *RIC* II.1² Vespasian 1127. On the development of representations of the emperor as *triumphator* on coinage see Mittag, 2017.
[79] Baldus, 1971: 158; Smith, 2014: 237. [80] Beard, 2003. [81] *RIC* II.1² Vespasian 15–16, 37.

Figure 2.11 Pb token, 19 mm, 12 h, 2.74 g. Laureate head of Vespasian right; IMP AVG VES around / Laureate heads of Titus (on left) and Domitian (on right) facing each other, globe between them; IMP (ligate) above and T DO CAES below. *TURS* 40.

Figure 2.12 AR denarius, 17.5 mm, 6 h, 3.22 g. Laureate head of Vespasian right, IMP CAESAR VESPASIANVS AVG around / Bare head of Titus on left facing bare head of Domitian on right, CAESAR AVG F COS CAESAR AVG F PR around. *RIC* II.1² 16.

the token and the coin. Both Titus and Domitian are shown laureate on the token, with the ties of the wreath flowing down behind their necks.[82] By contrast, both are bare headed on the coin issue. A globe is also placed between the busts on the token, reminiscent of a brass token showing the twin sons of Drusus the Younger, Tiberius Gemellus and Tiberius Germanicus, whose facing busts also had a globe placed between them.[83] The placement of the IMP and CAES on the token is ambiguous: the IMP likely only refers to Titus, but its association with Domitian cannot be ruled out (especially since Domitian is laureate); both Domitian and Titus also bore the name Caesar. In sum, the token takes numismatic imagery to a different level: the temporary nature of the medium, created for a particular (presumably receptive) audience at a particular moment in

---

[82] Although Rostovtzeff originally recorded Domitian was bare headed, Figure 2.11, as well as the specimen in the BnF (Rostovtzeff and Prou, 1900: no. 33b), reveal he is laureate.

[83] Buttrey, 1973: 55 and B19; Küter, 2019: 83.

time, meant that certain ideas and messages might be expressed which did not otherwise feature on other forms of material culture.

We cannot know when in Vespasian's reign Figure 2.11 was produced; the coin imagery may have been adapted years after it was issued. The laureate heads of Titus and Domitian (without the globe) are also found on another token series; the other side of this issue shows a horse rider carrying a spear with the legend IMP AV VES.[84] Bronze coinage under Vespasian carries an image of Titus on horseback spearing a fallen enemy, but the accompanying legend on the token suggests that it is Vespasian who is shown here.[85]

Whatever the specific context of these tokens, their imagery would have contributed to the emotion, experience and memories of certain events. At particular moments in time the image of the imperial family, as well as other imagery closely associated with the emperor and his achievements, were mobilised to underscore the connection of a specific occasion to the imperial house. Imperial imagery would also have communicated status and prestige. We also find this during the spectacles given in conjunction with particular festivals. It is to these we now turn.

Spectacles and the Colosseum under Titus and Domitian

The Flavian triumph in the Jewish War translated into a permanent dynastic ideology through the erection of monuments in Rome, most famously the Colosseum opened by Titus in c. AD 80.[86] In his account of the spectacles staged by Titus in connection with the opening of the amphitheatre Dio records that the emperor 'would throw down into the theatre from aloft little wooden balls variously inscribed, one designating some article of food, another clothing, another a silver vessel or perhaps a gold one, or again horses, pack-animals, cattle or slaves. Those who seized them were to carry them to the dispensers of the bounty, from whom they would receive the article named.'[87] Here we have a detailed account of how tokens (in this case wooden spherical tokens) operated to facilitate distributions during a particular event.

---

[84] *TURS* 41–2, Pl. I no. 38.
[85] *RIC* II.1² 429–30, 474, 497, 564 for Titus. Rostovtzeff suggested the legend on the token be understood as *Imp(erator) Au(gustus) Ves(pasianus)*.
[86] Millar, 2005: 115–18.
[87] Dio 66.25.5: σφαιρία γὰρ ξύλινα μικρὰ ἄνωθεν ἐς τὸ θέατρον ἐρρίπτει, σύμβολον ἔχοντα τὸ μὲν ἐδωδίμου τινὸς τὸ δὲ ἐσθῆτος τὸ δὲ ἀργυροῦ σκεύους, ἄλλο χρυσοῦ ἵππων ὑποζυγίων βοσκημάτων ἀνδραπόδων, ἃ ἁρπάσαντάς τινας ἔδει πρὸς τοὺς δοτῆρας αὐτῶν ἀπενεγκεῖν καὶ λαβεῖν τὸ ἐπιγεγραμμένον.

The opening of the Colosseum and the events that followed also served as inspiration for Martial's *Liber de Spectaculis*.[88] Martial's focus on the consumer culture of Flavian Rome, the playfulness he employs with regards to size (shrinking big to small, transforming small to big), and his project to monumentalise otherwise ephemeral moments means it is little surprise that he mentions tokens on several occasions.[89] The most discussed text of Martial in this regard is 8.78, which was likely written in response to the games of AD 93 held by Lucius Arruntius Stella to celebrate the return of Domitian from the Sarmatian War.

> Each day has its gifts. The wealthy cord takes no holiday and ample plunder falls into the crowd. Now come sportive tokens (*lasciva nomismata*) in sudden showers, now the lavish coupon (*tessera larga*) bestows the animals they have been watching, now birds are happy to fill safe laps and find masters in absence by lot, lest they be torn apart. Martial *Ep.* 8.78.7–12[90]

The phrase *lasciva nomismata* has been the subject of scholarly discussion: the phrase was previously thought to refer to *spintriae* carrying sexual imagery on the basis that *lasciva* meant pornographic, but this view has now been discounted.[91] Buttrey argued that *lasciva* might have been intended to characterise the way the tokens fell from the sky, but, as explored in this volume, metal tokens can also carry playful or satiric imagery that might justify the use of the adjective. *Nomismata* refers to coinage or a coin-like object, like a token. In this passage then it seems that Martial is referencing the use of monetiform tokens to aid in the distribution of gifts during games celebrating Domitian's military success. Indeed, the word *tessera* in the text also suggests the use of tokens to distribute the meat of animals slaughtered in the arena.[92]

Elsewhere Martial uses *nomismata* in the sense of a token to be exchanged for something else. Two separate epigrams focus on one Sextilianus, who, by taking the *nomismata* of his neighbours at a show, managed to drink enough for five rows; although *equites* were only given ten *nomismata* each, Sextilianus managed to procure twenty drinks.[93] *Nomismata* are also given out at the Saturnalia (the connection of lead

---

[88] Coleman, 2006: xiv–lxxiv; Rimell, 2009: 5.   [89] Coleman, 2006: lxxiv; Rimell, 2009: 6, 96.
[90] omnis habet sua dona dies; nec linea dives cessat et in populum multa rapina cadit: nunc veniunt subitis lasciva nomismata nimbis, nunc dat spectatas tessera larga feras, nunc implere sinus securos gaudet et absens sortitur dominos, ne laceretur, avis.
[91] Buttrey, 1973: 56; Virlouvet, 1995: 348; Harrison, 2001; Schmieder, 2008.
[92] Harrison, 2001: 306.
[93] Mart. *Ep.* 1.11 (Cum data sint equiti bis quina nomismata, quare bis decies solus, Sextiliane, bibis?), 1.26 (Sextiliane, bibis quantum subsellia quinque solus: aqua totiens ebrius esse potes; nec consessorum vicina nomismata tantum, aera sed a cuneis ulteriora petis).

tokens with this festival is discussed in Chapter 4).[94] The term may not indicate tokens in each occurrence: Martial also reports *nomismata* found in a goose and these may be coins or tokens.[95] Given Martial's frequent reference to money and the consumerism of Rome we should not be surprised that the poet also uses references to lead tokens in order to communicate his themes. Indeed, although his use of *plumbeos* to characterise his earnings as a poet has been translated as 'coppers' or small denomination coins, one wonders whether Martial in fact was referring to lead tokens. Being paid in lead tokens that could only be exchanged for goods from an individual's holdings paints the poet as a client subject to his patron even more so than someone who was paid in low denomination coinage (which would at least offer the freedom to purchase whatever one might desire within one's means).[96]

Lead tokens, as small objects that referenced much larger benefactions, may also have appealed to Martial as objects: in his work he also used small poems to reference larger events, and, like tokens, he captures a fleeting moment.[97] One can see this particularly in his epigrams focusing on the games, the *Liber Spectaculorum*. In two epigrams Martial presents the two-horned rhinoceros Domitian famously exhibited at Rome, which also appears on *quadrantes* struck under the emperor. Buttrey uses the dates of the coins to date the spectacle to AD 83–5.[98] Rhinoceroses were rarely displayed in the capital, and the capture and presentation of a specimen with two horns must have caused a sensation. Like Martial's poems, the coins would have served as a long lasting reminder to the citizens of Rome of Domitian's spectacular games. One poem celebrates the rhinoceros defeating a bear, while in the other the animal defeats a bull. The latter poem is strikingly similar to a lead token that shows a two-horned rhinoceros on one side and a bull on the other (Figure 2.13). Martial also details a fight between an elephant and a bull, a pairing that is also shown on lead tokens.[99]

---

[94] Mart. *Ep.* 12.62.11 (quam non parca manus largaeque nomismata mensae, quae, Saturne, tibi pernumerentur opes?), see also Stat. *Silv.* 1.6.66.

[95] Mart. *Ep.* 9.31.7 (octo vides patulo pendere nomismata rostro alitis?).

[96] Mart. *Ep.* 10.74.4 (quam diu salutator anteambulones et togatulos inter centum merebor plumbeos die toto, cum Scorpus una quindecim graves hora ferventis auri victor auferat saccos?). On Martial's (relative) poverty see Tennant and Tennant, 2000.

[97] Coleman, 2006: lxxviii; Rimell, 2009: 94.

[98] Mart. *Spect.* 11(9), 26(22); *RIC* II.1² Domitian 248–54; Buttrey, 2007: 110.

[99] Mart. *Spect.* 22(19); *TURS* 623 (Pl. IV, 69), 624 (with the legend FAV above the elephant, we do not know the significance of the legend); Rostovtzeff and Prou, 1900: no.122.

Figure 2.13 Pb token, 23 mm, 6 h, 5.6 g. Rhinoceros with two horns standing right; crescent above / Bull walking right. *TURS* 645.

This token series, and other tokens carrying the image of a two-horned rhinoceros, may have been used during the games held by Domitian in which the rhinoceros appeared, or the imagery may have been appropriated for occasions after the event. On gems and intaglios the rhinoceros was a symbol that communicated victory.[100] In addition to the bull, the rhinoceros with two horns is paired with a bison and a rooster (carrying a wreath in its beak) on tokens.[101] Four specimens of the rhinoceros / rooster type were found in the Tiber river in Rome; the rooster may reference Mercury.[102] On another type the legend AVR is placed above the rhinoceros and a palm branch is depicted on the other side.[103] One type carries the image of a rhinoceros with a single horn, but has a palm tree on the other side, suggesting a possible connection with the Flavian victory in Judaea.[104]

Whether these tokens were used during games in Domitian's honour or some other event, they would have served to heighten anticipation (if distributed before the animal fights) or consolidate one's memory of an occasion (if distributed after the fight). It is difficult, if not impossible, however, to connect particular tokens to particular games. The same problem applies to Martial's *Liber Spectaculorum*: one imagines, with the exception of the rhinoceros, that similar contests were held on multiple occasions; this is what makes dating the work to the reigns of either Domitian or Titus so tricky. Regardless of these difficulties, however,

---

[100] Vendries, 2016: 311.   [101] *TURS* 643–4, 647.
[102] Two specimens recorded by Rostovtzeff as nos. 2–3 under the type in *TURS*, for the other two see Rostovtzeff and Vaglieri, 1900: 2621 nos. 58–9.
[103] *TURS* 651. We do not know the significance of the legend.   [104] *TURS* 477.

both sources provide important insights into the emotions, activities and experience of spectacle in the Flavian age.

Overbeck suggested that a bone token, carved with an image of the Colosseum accompanied by the legend COS on the left and XII on the right, might have been connected with celebrations associated with the opening of the Flavian amphitheatre under Titus.[105] The other side of the token carries the legend FLA COS VES XII around in a circle, with each word clearly delineated from the others via a series of lines. The overall decoration suggests that the legend should be read from left to right and then up and down: FLA VES COS XII. Overbeck noted the piece might also be a gaming token. A bone piece now in the BnF offers a parallel: one side bears a representation of the Colosseum and the other side a number (VI); this particular piece has been pierced, perhaps for later conversion into a necklace pendant (Figure 2.14).

Bone gaming pieces often carry a number on one side, as on Figure 2.14. The mention of a twelfth consulship, and the absence of a number, would make the piece published by Overbeck unusual if it were a gaming piece. A similar bone piece, with no image and only a legend, is in the David Eugene Smith collection in Columbia University. One side carries the engraved legend L·LVCIVS·CONS·II and the number II is engraved on

Figure 2.14 Pierced bone gaming piece (?) showing the Colosseum on one side and VI incised on the other. Froehner 282.

[105] Overbeck, 2001/2002: 53.

the other side – perhaps a number used in a game, but more likely a second reference to the number of consulships held by Lucius.[106] For the Colosseum piece published by Overbeck, the number of consulships may hold the clue to the date: Titus never held twelve consulships (nor did Vespasian), so it is unlikely the piece was created for the opening of the Colosseum. It was Domitian who obtained a twelfth consulship in AD 86, and this piece may then be connected to events held in that year; the representation of the Colosseum, accompanied by the reference FLA VES, served to reinforce the dynastic connections of Domitian. The purpose of these rare bone pieces mentioning magistracies still needs further research. The material and labour involved suggests they might have served a different (more long term?) purpose than their lead counterparts.

After the death of Vespasian, tokens continued to reference Titus and Domitian. One issue shows the busts of the brothers facing each other, with Fortuna on the other side accompanied by the legend SEM.[107] This type may equally have been produced during the reign of Vespasian. During the rule of Domitian and Titus, there seems to be a shift in the design of tokens bearing reference to the emperor: portraits disappear, and the emperors are referred to only via a legend (Figure 2.15).[108] This practice seems to continue into the reign of Domitian: two token series carry nothing but legends, naming Domitian as *imperator* and connecting him to the deified Vespasian.[109] The abbreviation of the emperors' names here (T and DOM) echoes their representation on coin legends under Vespasian.[110] Why there should be a shift in representing the imperial family on tokens at this time is difficult to explain; it may be part of a broader process by which reference to the emperor on these objects slowly disappears.[111]

Overall, reference to the Flavian emperors on tokens emphasises dynastic connections, and the foundational moment of the dynasty, the Jewish War.

---

[106] David Eugene Smith Collection, Columbia University, Roman II (no. 260). With thanks to Evan Jewell for bringing these pieces to my attention, and for so kindly photographing them for me.

[107] *TURS* 47. The meaning of the legend is unknown, perhaps the initials of a name?

[108] *TURS* 43: IMPER|ATORIB | PTF / DOMI|TIANO | CF. Rostovtzeff read the legend on side a as IMPER|ATORIB | TTF and thought it might be resolved as *Imperatorib(us) T(itis duobus) f(eliciter)*, but the specimen in the BnF (Rostovtzeff and Prou, 1900: no. 33d) seems to read PTF rather than TTF. What the P might stand for here is unknown, but it would also be very unusual for Titus' name to be given twice (although TT was resolved as *Tito* by Burnett, 2016: 95). Rostovtzeff resolved the legend on side b as *Domitiano C(aesari) f(eliciter)*. See also *TURS* 45: IMP | TCA / DO | CAE (*Imp(erator) T(itus) Ca(esar) / Do(mitianus) Cae(sar)*) and *TURS* 46 (IMP | TCA / DOM | CAE).

[109] *TURS* 49 (IMP / DOM), 1206 (DOM / DI | VE).

[110] For example, *RIC* II.1² Vespasian 13 (T ET DOM C).   [111] Rowan, in press a.

Figure 2.15 Pb token, 19 mm, 12 h, 1.77 g. IMP | T·CAES (AE ligate) / DOM | CAES. *TURS* 44.

Other themes, for example the very public connection between Domitian and Minerva communicated by coinage, appear to be absent.[112] Tokens bearing representations of Minerva may indeed have been used during the reign of Domitian, but the image of the goddess was not directly placed alongside the emperor, meaning we have no way of deducing the date of tokens carrying the goddess' image. The ideology used during particular occasions, during festivals and their associated feasts and distributions, differed from the imagery that was placed on coinage for repeated daily use over time. A person's experience of the imperial image was thus very much dependant on one's location and the events one attended. Ephemeral events had an important role in shaping the ideology and culture of a dynasty, epitomised in Martial's poetry.

Tokens that Speak: Imperial Acclamations

As the triumphal token discussed earlier illustrates (Figure 2.6), tokens might carry acclamations. As Kuhn observes, chants served to create an ad hoc emotional community, a 'we-feeling' generated by common expression.[113] The presence of these cries on tokens is a further insight into the role of these artefacts in building different types of communities. Several tokens carry imperial acclamations, most commonly expressions of good fortune (*feliciter*) for the emperor (non-imperial acclamations are examined in more detail in Chapters 3 and 4).[114] The earliest numismatic acclamation we possess occurs

---

[112] Carradice, 1998: 112.   [113] Kuhn, 2012: 300.
[114] Burnett, 2016: 77 notes that *feliciter* was often used in imperial acclamations, see also *CIL* VI, 632 and VI, 2086, 16–19.

Figure 2.16 AE token, 18 mm, 2.72 g, 7 h. A·P·P·F within wreath. Dotted border / Bust-topped sceptre left. Dotted border. Rowan, 2020b: no. 21.

on a token carrying a portrait of Augustus with the legend FEL beneath (Figure 1.2).[115]

Often *feliciter* is abbreviated to F, as seen on a bronze token dated to the second half of the first century AD (Figure 2.16). The sceptre shown on this token is topped with what is likely an imperial bust; Woytek consequently connects this piece with the *praeses ludorum*, the overseer of games in Rome that drove in the procession to the circus (*pompa circensis*) in a *biga* carrying a sceptre.[116] The obverse carries a wreath that has been identified as the *corona Etrusca*, the golden wreath held over the head of a *triumphator* by a slave, and which also became associated with magistrates who offered games.[117] The token, then, carries images associated with the *pompa circensis*. Woytek suggests the legend might be understood as *A(ugusto) P(atri) P(atriae) F(eliciter)* – 'good fortune for Augustus, father of his country'. This phrase is also found in Petronius as a toast, and an abbreviated form, *Augusto feliciter*, occurs as a graffito in the House of Maius Castricius in Pompeii.[118] Unlike earlier suggestions for the abbreviation – such as *A(pollinares/-aria) P(ecunia) P(ublica) F(iunt)* or *F(acti/facta)* – Woytek's solution fits well with what we know of tokens more broadly. As demonstrated throughout this volume, *feliciter* (or an abbreviation thereof) appeared on tokens with relative frequency; Figure 2.17, for

---

[115] Mowat, 1913: 46; Buttrey, 1973: B5.XIII.

[116] Woytek, 2015: 488. A third century sarcophagus shows the *praeses* in a chariot holding a sceptre topped with a human bust, see Latham, 2016: 154, fig. 42.

[117] Woytek, 2015: 485–7, noting that the wreath is connected to magistrates providing games in Juv. *Sat.* 10.36–42, and that both the bust-topped sceptre and wreath are found on funerary reliefs of praetors, representing their role in presiding over games at the Circus. See Latham, 2016: 153 fig. 41 for a drawing of the so-called Maffei relief, which shows the *praeses ludorum* with a slave standing behind him holding a wreath over his head.

[118] Petron. *Sat.* 60.6; Benefiel, 2010: 78; Woytek, 2015: 489.

example, also carries the abbreviation PPF, here in reference to Hadrian. For the abbreviations to have been understandable one imagines they must have been employed with relative frequency within Rome.

The reference to the *praeses ludorum* highlights that many of the acclamation tokens were likely created as part of a wider festival or event. The placement of an imperial bust on a sceptre to be held by the presiding magistrate during a public procession, alongside the parade of imperial cult images that occurred within the *pompa circensis* (or the *pompa theatralis*, theatrical processions) form a very real example of how the imperial image might be 'mobilised' at a particular moment in time (the imperial busts that were placed atop sceptres, for example, were likely stored in temples when not in use, including temple porches and porticoes).[119]

The carriages that bore the statues or *exuviae* (attributes) of the imperial family in the procession to the circus are also represented on tokens, for the deified Augustus, for Livia and for Trajan. These tokens may have been used during particular events that had a *pompa circensis*. However one cannot exclude the idea that the tokens took their imagery from Roman imperial coinage, which also showed representations of the *carpenta* (carriages used for women), *tensae* (wagons that carried cult images) and elephant chariots that bore imperial statues and paraphernalia in these processions. The token series carrying the representation of four elephants with riders pulling a statue of Augustus, for example, is very similar to a scene found on Tiberian coinage.[120] Another token series carries a portrait of Livia on one side and a *carpentum* (a wagon drawn by two mules) on the other. The type is also reminiscent of coinage, but on at least one specimen the *curator* of the games adds his name: L SEI.[121] Since game giving and the associated processions to the venue was one of the few remaining avenues in which the Roman elite might visibly increase their prestige during the imperial period, it is not surprising that tokens (likely used at some point during the event, if not in the procession) should represent the *pompa*; such representations are also known from other non-imperial monuments celebrating the achievements of Roman citizens.[122]

---

[119] Elkins, 2014: 81.

[120] Overbeck, 2001: no. 4 = *TURS* (Supplement) 3735; *RIC* I² Tiberius 56, 62, 68; Latham, 2016: 116.

[121] *TURS* 1, 1a, (Supplement) 3736 = Overbeck, 2001: no. 5 (with L SEI CVR). It is tempting to see a reference to Sejanus here, but there is no evidence to confirm this one way or another. One specimen of the 'Livia / *carpentum*' token series (*TURS* 1) was found in Rome, along the Tiber, see Rostovtzeff and Vaglieri, 1900: 258 no. 2.

[122] For example, see the material discussed in Latham, 2016: 161–80.

Tokens connect a *tensa* with the emperor Trajan; no other evidence exists that Trajan was awarded this honour. This token issue, then, created a combination of imagery not found on official coinage, likely to specifically communicate the presence of Trajan's cultic imagery in a procession.[123] Two other token types carry *tensae*: the first is drawn by four lions with a palm branch shown on the other side, and the second drawn by two elephants with Mercury shown on the other side.[124] An elephant *biga* was awarded to Titus' daughter Julia by Domitian, as well as to the deified Nerva and Faustina I, but without further information we cannot know what deities (imperial or otherwise) were connected with these particular carriage representations.[125]

Festive occasions that utilised tokens may have also included the *dies imperii*, the anniversary of the day an emperor came to power. An antiquarian report on the collection of Capranesi found in Rome records the existence of a token that bore the legend DIEI | IMPE|RI on one side and HADR | AVG | FEL on the other – a wish of good fortune (*fel(iciter)*) for Hadrian Augustus on his *dies imperii*.[126] Other token types also communicate good wishes for Hadrian and Sabina. Figure 2.17, for example, expresses good fortune (F) for Hadrian Augustus (HAD AVG), father of his country (PP). Another token issue carries the legend FEL | SABI on one side and the legend AVG | HADR | SAL on the other.[127] Here the FEL likely

Figure 2.17 Pb token, 18 mm, 12 h, 3.04 g. HAD | AVG / PPF. *TURS* 66.

---

[123] *TURS* 55, Pl. I, 41. Rostovtzeff identified the wagon as a *carpentum*. The token is not well preserved, but the image does seem closer to a *tensa* than a *carpentum*, a suggestion that seems to be confirmed by the four horses – *carpenta* are always shown drawn by two mules. Latham, 2016: 125 notes there is no evidence that suggests Trajan or Hadrian were commemorated in the *pompa circensis*, although he does not consider the token evidence.
[124] *TURS* 713–14.   [125] Latham, 2016: 123–8.   [126] *TURS* 65; *CIL* XV.2, p. 995 no. 2.
[127] *TURS* 69. Rostovtzeff suggested the legend be understood as *Fel(ix) Sabi(na) Aug(usta) Hadr(iano) sal(vo)*.

refers to Sabina as *felix* (happy or lucky), as long as Hadrian is safe and healthy (*Aug(usto) Hadr(iano) salvo*). The use of the word *salvus* in connection with the emperor is also known from acclamatory inscriptions, as well as tokens of urban prefects in late antiquity.[128]

The few imperial acclamations that appear on coins and medallions also suggest festive contexts. Coins and medallions issued under Hadrian and Antoninus Pius wish the emperor a happy and auspicious new year on behalf of the Senate and People of Rome.[129] Suetonius records that Claudius was greeted with *feliciter* while presiding over the games, as were Domitian and his wife in the Colosseum.[130] Acclamations formed an important interaction between the emperor and the populace. One wonders whether tokens, distributed in advance of or during an event, may have served to help provoke these 'spontaneous' exclamations. Alternatively, if distributed after an occasion, these tokens reveal that 'spontaneous' acclamations were, in fact, perhaps expected at particular occasions as part of the experience (hence the pre-manufacturing of tokens carrying such cries). It is evident that emperors might encourage or indeed orchestrate acclamations in the theatre or amphitheatre: Suetonius records that Nero organised and planted young men to cheer and applaud him when performing.[131] Tokens may also have formed a device of encouragement.

The legend FELI AVG is also found on two tokens that carry a reference to the golden age (SAEC AVRE).[132] Rostovtzeff interpreted the legend to mean *Saec(ulum) aure(um) feli(x) Aug(ustus)*; the fact that abbreviations of *feliciter* tend to occur at the end of token legends suggests *felix* is probably the correct choice here. Rostovtzeff recorded that on one token issue the legend SAEC AVRE was accompanied by an image of Victory, but close examination of a specimen now in the British Museum suggests that the standing figure is carrying a crook in their right hand and a circular object (shield?) in their left.[133] The identification of this figure thus remains uncertain. The SAEC AVRE and figure design is combined with a laurel tree on one type, and the figure of Fortuna on a second type. Both of these issues carry the legend FELI AVG on side b. Hadrian was the first to proclaim a golden age on official Roman coinage, but the concept is found

---

[128] *CIL* VI, 632, VI, 2086, 16–19; Kulikowski, 2017: 6. For another possible token containing an acclamation (*feliciter*) for Hadrian see *TURS* 68.

[129] For example, *RIC* II.3² 2868–70, *RIC* III Antoninus Pius 527A; Burnett, 2016: 75, 91–3.

[130] Suet. *Claud.* 7, *Dom.* 13; Clarke, 2007: 270–1.   [131] Suet. *Ner.* 20.3; Roueché, 1984: 184.

[132] *TURS* 1815–16.

[133] *BMCRLT* 1093, *TURS* Pl. VII no. 8. No specimens of *TURS* 1816 (Victory standing left) are currently available for inspection to confirm Rostovtzeff's identification of this type.

throughout the imperial period.[134] The tokens might be connected to a saecular festival of some kind; Hadrian's proclamation of a golden age in AD 121 indicates that this proclamation need not align with the celebration of the official saecular games.[135] That the *felicitas* or the luck of the emperor was connected to a golden age is not surprising: the benevolence of the gods towards Rome's ruler naturally meant prosperity for the broader empire.[136] The emotion captured by the use of *felix* on tokens in connection with the imperial family is very similar to that of *feliciter*, and reflects the atmosphere that must have prevailed upon festive occasions.

Tokens, Imperial Ideology and Roman Triumphal Arches

In addition to the giving of games, other acts of euergetism offered an opportunity for the Roman elite to enhance their prestige. Tokens offered a medium to regulate these acts of generosity while reinforcing the status of the patron. It is thus unsurprising that imperial ideology was adapted by a range of individuals for the decoration of tokens to be used in different contexts: the use of imperial imagery would have served to enhance the prestige of the giver. This practice, discussed in detail throughout this section, reveals how the population engaged with particular ideologies and adapted them for their own contexts. Rather than a clear-cut direct message, tokens and other everyday media reveal that the prevailing imagery of the day might have gained multiple associations over time.

Tokens issued by those outside the government creatively referenced the imagery and materiality of Roman coinage (size, shape, placement of legends and portraiture). This practice included the adaptation of specific imperial imagery. For example, a lead token found in the Tiber carried the image of crossed *cornucopiae*, each topped with a small head, with the legend LAS on the other side (perhaps the initials of a *tria nomina*). The image of heads atop crossed *cornucopiae* is otherwise known from the coinage of Tiberius, where the heads are believed to represent Tiberius Gemellus and Germanicus Julius Caesar; the type is also used on the coinage of Antoninus Pius and is believed to reference the twin children

---

[134] *RIC* II.3² 296–7; Boatwright, 1987: 122.
[135] See Overbeck, 2001/2002: 53 for a bone ring token with the legend PRIM CAL NOV SECVL DIANA / XVIII, which also might be connected to a saecular festival of some kind.
[136] Wistrand, 1987: esp. 56 where he notes the *felicitas* of the emperor was particularly pertinent on his *dies natalis* and *dies imperii*.

born to Marcus Aurelius and Faustina the Younger.[137] The image may have been selected for a token series that was to be used within a particular event honouring the imperial family; alternatively the image may have been selected to communicate fecundity, prestige or some other message. The token itself demonstrates that imperial coinage *was viewed*, and that people *actively* interacted with numismatic imagery.

Some tokens connect to imperial ideology not shown on the official coinage of Rome. A series of tokens, for example, show Hadrian's deceased lover Antinous wearing an Egyptian hem-hem crown with the numeral VIII placed on the other side (Figure 2.18).[138] Each of the four known specimens has been subject to a circular punch, which on Figure 2.18 has resulted in a hole in the token to the right of Antinous' bust. One wonders whether this was a mark to indicate that the token had been redeemed. These tokens possess a chunky fabric unlike the majority of tokens found in Rome and Ostia; they may have been manufactured elsewhere in Italy.

The cult of Antinous spread throughout the Roman world after his death, and he is frequently represented on tokens in Egypt with the hem-hem crown.[139] In Italy the cult is perhaps best known through the *cultores Dianae et Antinoi* in Lanuvium, a *collegium* focused on the cult of Diana and Antinous.[140] Among the preserved laws of the association is the stipulation that a feast would be held on the birthday of Antinous (*natalis*

Figure 2.18 Pb token, 20 mm, 12 h, 9.42 g. Bust of Antinous right wearing hem-hem crown. Dotted border / VIII. *TURS* 1552.

---

[137] *RIC* I² Tiberius 42, *RIC* III Antoninus Pius 185A–B, 857, 859, 961 with discussion on p. 10. For a fuller discussion see Rowan, 2020a: 255–6.
[138] Rostovtzeff and Prou, 1900: 525–25a; *BMCRLT* 1004–5. The type was misidentified by Rostovtzeff as the bust of a woman.
[139] Milne, 1971: nos. 5420, 5432–4, 5446; Wilding, 2019.
[140] *CIL* XIV, 2112; Bollmann, 1998: 38; Perry, 2011: 506–7.

Antinoi); one wonders whether the tokens carrying images of Antinous were used in similar feasting or distribution contexts by other groups whose existence has not been preserved in the epigraphic evidence. A further lead token type carries the legend ANTINOI on one side and the image of Fortuna on the other: the use of Antinous in the genitive here may refer to his birthday, or else an association in his honour.[141] Although relatively neglected in the discussion of Antinous' cult, these tokens contribute to our understanding of how the newly created god was celebrated within Italy.

Overall, however, identifying instances in which specifically 'imperial' ideology was adapted on tokens in Rome and Ostia remains difficult. Many of the images that graced the coinage of the emperors (deities, *modii*, clasped hands, eagles, etc) also appear on tokens but were not specifically 'imperial' per se – they formed part of the broader iconography of Roman everyday life. The impression formed by the surviving token corpus from Roman Italy suggests that direct engagement with imagery that specifically references the imperial family (e.g. representations of the emperor performing various activities) is rare on tokens. Direct references to the imperial family may not have been the most appropriate imagery within many of the contexts in which tokens were used (events or distributions sponsored by individuals or associations).

Coinage influenced the design of at least some tokens, but what of other monuments? Representations of structures from Rome on tokens are rare, but several tokens carry representations of triumphal arches. Here it might be significant that these arches were traditionally decreed *from* the Senate and People of Rome *to* the emperor: their authorship, in a sense, was not directly imperial.[142] One token type carries a triumphal arch on one side with what may be the head of an emperor on the other.[143] Other tokens, however, carry legends that suggest the initiative of other individuals (and we cannot rule out that the token carrying the possible image of an emperor was created by someone outside the imperial government). A triumphal arch is found on tokens variously accompanied by the legends DC, SEX CL and RṄR (Figure 2.19), which suggest the initiative of individuals or groups.[144]

---

[141] *TURS* 1379, for an image see https://coins.warwick.ac.uk/token-specimens/id/hunterian.RL T18. *TURS* 1380 carries the legend ANTI, which Rostovtzeff suggested might also reference Antinous in some way; the other side carries the representation of a pair of scales.

[142] Millar, 2005: 120. [143] *TURS* 88, Pl. II no. 14.

[144] *TURS* 107 (Rostovtzeff recorded that one specimen of this type was reportedly incised VICT), 109, 110. *TURS* 108 carried a triumphal arch on one side and a palm branch on the other. We do not know what the legends may stand for, but they may possibly be abbreviations of Roman names (especially in the case of SEX CL).

Figure 2.19 Pb token, 12 mm, 12 h, 0.89 g. Triumphal arch (surmounted by the statue of a horseman right?) / RŃR, palm branch on left. *TURS* 107.

On some issues there is an effort to indicate a specific arch through the inclusion of the statuary group atop the structure. On Figure 2.19 this took the form of a horseman or *quadriga* (the precise details on the known specimens are worn). By contrast, on the issue of SEX CL an elephant standing right was placed atop the structure.

It has long been recognised that the representation of monuments on coins is not a photographic or realistic representation, but rather reflects an engraver's conceptualisation of a structure and what made it distinctive.[145] On several of the tokens showing arches, the statues shown atop the structure are relatively large; this is reminiscent of architectural numismatic representations in the early Empire (from the late first century AD the representations of such architectural features become smaller).[146] This development may provide a possible date range for these particular tokens of the early first century AD.[147] Indeed, it was only under Augustus (after 29 BC) that arches are represented on coins, and a *quadriga*, a horseman and elephants appear as sculptural decoration on arches on coinage in the Julio-Claudian period.[148] Given the rather schematic representations, however, it is not possible to connect a particular image on tokens to a specific monument.

Why would these arches be selected for representation on tokens? The individuals or groups involved might have been involved in their construction; a potential parallel are the monuments shown on the tomb of the *Haterii*, which probably reflect the work of a public building contractor.

[145] Burnett, 1999; Elkins, 2015: 1–2. [146] For example, Rostovtzeff and Prou, 1900: no. 40b.
[147] Zanker, 1997: 181–2.
[148] *RIC* I² Augustus 131–7 (decorated with the emperor in a *quadriga*), 140–3 (a representation of an arch on what is probably a viaduct, with the emperor shown in a *biga* of elephants crowned by Victory), Claudius 3–4 (equestrian statue).

Alternatively, the arches may have been important in forming a sense of location or identity; the role of the physical landscape of Rome and Ostia in formulating identities is explored more fully in Chapter 3. The arches may have communicated triumph and been used during imperial triumphal ceremonies or on other occasions that invited imagery of victory. Or the tokens might have been used during ceremonies connected with the structure's dedication.

Indeed, the possible context of these pieces may be even broader, as suggested by a so-called 'cake or pancake mould' found in Poetovio in Pannonia. Although we cannot definitively know what product these moulds produced, it is generally agreed they were used to create edible or wax items, perhaps a form of *missilia* (gifts that were thrown to crowds); the designs suggest a connection with festivals.[149] The mould found in Poetovio shows an intricately decorated triumphal arch surrounded by statues and surmounted by a statue group showing the emperor in a *quadriga* being crowned by a Victory on either side and flanked by military trophies. An inscription is placed on the arch: VOTIS X ET XX FEL.[150] The text references the vows taken every five years by the emperor for successful rule. This particular ruler had reached ten years of rule (his *decennalia*) and had made vows for his second decade in power.[151] The FEL recalls the good wishes (*feliciter, felix*) of the tokens discussed earlier in this chapter. Here the triumphal arch was utilised to commemorate imperial vows, with the monument perhaps expressing the idea of military victory and skill. The arch, then, might be employed in multiple contexts; the meaning of a particular monument might change according to time and context. The representation of arches on coins of Augustus commemorating building works, for example, likely communicated the idea that road construction was a triumph over nature.[152] The representation of arches on tokens may also have been performed within a ceremonial occasion such as imperial *vota*, or been used to communicate the idea of victory more broadly.

A triumphal arch also appears on a lead token from Egypt (Figure 2.20). The Roman imperial government controlled the mint at Alexandria – unusually for a province – with the result that local coin imagery closely reflected that at Rome, including the representation of triumphal arches

---

[149] Alföldi, 1938–41: 313–14; Floriani Squarciapino, 1954; Boon, 1958; Salomonson, 1972: 101–9; Simon, 2008: 768.
[150] Alföldi, 1938–41: 335–6 and pl. LII.
[151] The formula is also found on coins, see *RIC* III Commodus 229, with the legend VOTIS XX COS VI in the tenth year of his rule and *RIC* V Gallienus 94–5, 599, which bear the legend VOT X ET XX.
[152] Elkins, 2015: 66–7.

Figure 2.20 Pb token from Egypt, 20.5 mm, 5.10 g. Venus standing raising her hands to her hair, snake on right and cupid (?) on left / Triumphal arch surmounted by frontal *quadriga*. Dattari-Savio Pl. 323, 11706 (this token).

erected in the capital.[153] Whether the image of arches on Alexandrian coinage represented actual structures or was a 'stock type' is debated, but representations included the image of a triple span arch surmounted by a *quadriga*, as found on the token. A coin may have thus inspired the design of Figure 2.20, although the imagery has been paired with Venus instead of the imperial portrait. It is unlikely the Egyptian token was used within the context of a triumphal ceremony; the semantic flexibility of the arch is again revealed. Although at first sight the imagery on the token seems quite Roman, the presence of the snake on the right of Venus recalls the famous *agathos daimon* of Alexandria. The embodiment of good luck and health, the *agathos daimon* here probably communicates the same sentiment that *feliciter* or *felix* does on tokens from Rome and Ostia.

Imperial Tokens after Hadrian and Changing Attitudes to Imperial Euergetism

From the surviving evidence, it appears that representations of the imperial family on tokens in Italy became less frequent from the second half of the second century AD. This may be due to a change in the mode of representation that makes imperial portraiture harder to identify. Several tokens, for example, carry portraiture whose style is of the second century AD, but have no legends: a uniface token from the Garigliano, for example, carries a portrait of Marcus Aurelius.[154]

---

[153] For example, *RPC* III 4337.1–2, 4455, 4456.1–5, 4547.1–4, with an overview of scholarly discussion provided by Elkins, 2015: 147–8.

[154] Mitchiner, 1984: no. 6.

Figure 2.21 Pb token, 27 mm, 6 h, 11.08 g. Bearded bare male bust (of an emperor?) left / Bare young male bust (Galerius Antoninus?) right. *TURS* 71.

Another, now damaged, token carries two male busts (one on each side): Rostovtzeff identified these as second century in date, and suggested one was likely an emperor of the Antonine age, with the other perhaps Galerius Antoninus, the son of Antoninus Pius who died before his father ascended to the throne (Figure 2.21). Galerius also appears on select provincial coins, but given the preservation of the token and the lack of an identifying legend it is difficult to make a concrete identification.[155] A clear portrait of Antoninus Pius (without an identifying legend) can be found on a token now in the BnF; on the other side of the token is the worn legend VNISATIS around in a circle. The meaning of the legend is not clear.[156]

Similar uncertainty attaches itself to further tokens that may reference emperors of the second and third centuries. One example, found in the Tiber, carries the legend IMP within a dotted border on one side and the legend MAC on the other.[157] Rostovtzeff suggested the legend might be resolved as *Imp(erator) M. A(urelius) C(ommodus)*, but he remained uncertain. Indeed, MAC might equally reference the *tria nomina* of a particular magistrate or individual creating the token. On a further series Rostovtzeff was not sure whether the bearded bust on the token was Hercules or Caracalla: the two specimens that survive suggest Hercules is the correct identification, but the example demonstrates the issue of identifying

---

[155] *RPC* IV.3 3006, 3131, 5730, 8345–6.
[156] *TURS* 72; Rostovtzeff and Prou, 1900: no. 33i. Rostovtzeff suggested the legend might be a name.
[157] *TURS* 73; Rostovtzeff and Vaglieri, 1900: 259 no. 7.

imperial portraits on media that are of varying quality and without legends.¹⁵⁸ There may then be more imperial portraiture on tokens than scholarship to date has managed to identify.

The Severan dynasty seems to be completely absent on Italian tokens, although they do appear on tokens issued in other regions. Julia Domna is perhaps shown on tokens at Ephesus and Caracalla on what is likely to be a token from Lyon, although these issues do not have a legend and possess the same identification problems as those above.¹⁵⁹ Indeed, after the Antonines the next appearance of an emperor in Rostovtzeff's catalogue is a single token type for Carinus, who is named on a lead token carrying the number IIII.¹⁶⁰ Emperors then reappear in number on bronze tokens in late antiquity, particularly in connection with the festival of Isis.¹⁶¹

How can this shift in imperial representation on tokens from Roman Italy be explained? It might be an accident of preservation, but many of the tokens with known findspots in Ostia come from second century AD contexts (discussed more fully in Chapter 5); the absence of imperial portraiture on tokens in this region during this period appears to be real. It is perhaps significant that there was a slow transformation of elite attitudes towards imperial euergetism over the first and second centuries AD. At the beginning of the principate imperial acts of *liberalitas* only underscored the inequality between the emperor and the elite, undermining the idea of the 'first man among equals'; it is thus no surprise that Augustus avoided the phrase in his *Res Gestae*. But the slow acceptance of imperial *liberalitas* by the elite from the reign of Trajan meant that this virtue could be communicated more widely to the population of the empire. By the second century, *liberalitas* was publicly associated with the emperor, appearing on inscriptions naming Trajan (as well as Pliny's *Panegyric*) and on coinage under Hadrian.¹⁶² As a result of this shift, reference to imperial munificence may have moved from tokens to more durable, far reaching media. Imperial generosity and euergetism could now, without issue, be widely advertised and celebrated across the empire.¹⁶³

The first specific use of *liberalitas* in conjunction with an emperor occurs under Claudius, on a token likely used during an event associated

---

¹⁵⁸ *TURS* 2085; Rostovtzeff and Prou, 1900: no. 377.
¹⁵⁹ Turcan, 1987: no. 120; Gülbay and Kireç, 2008: no. 183.   ¹⁶⁰ *TURS* 74.
¹⁶¹ Alföldi, 1937; Ramskold, 2016; Mondello, 2020b.
¹⁶² *RIC* II.3² Hadrian 959–62; Metcalf, 1993: 338–9.
¹⁶³ Manning, 1985: 73–80; Noreña, 2011: 82–91; Rowan, in press a.

with his deified mother Antonia.[164] There is a significant gap between this occurrence and the mention of the virtue in Pliny's *Panegyric*, although the depiction of *congiaria* distributions on coinage from the reign of Nero onwards represented one particular aspect of imperial benefaction.[165] We should note that the appearance of the phrase on the token and the representation of *congiaria* on coinage are both representations of *specific acts of euergetism* for specific groups of people. The token would have been used within a specific context for a specific group within Rome, who were presumably accepting of the inequality between giver (emperor) and receiver.

Similarly the representation of *congiaria* in Rome on coins under Nero and Trajan communicates that this is a specific occasion for a particular group of people.[166] Numismatic imagery shows different moments from a specific event; on Figure 2.22 for example, the emperor is seated on a platform with a recipient receiving their allotment of coinage below.[167] Architectural details are also occasionally added to locate the scene within a specific space, and the distributions are even numbered: CONG I, II, etc. It is also perhaps no coincidence that these scenes occur on bronze coins, whose circulation was confined to the west. *Congiaria* consisted of distributions of money to the Roman plebs; within this very specific occasion the *liberalitas* of the emperor and the inequality between giver and receiver was clear and unlikely to cause consternation among the Roman elite. The ceremony was thus acceptable for commemoration on bronze coinage (*sestertii*).[168]

Shifting elite attitudes towards imperial *liberalitas* meant that from the early second century the virtue might be celebrated in a more abstract manner. It is under Hadrian that *Liberalitas* appears as a personification standing alone on coinage: this abstract representation might evoke different occasions of imperial generosity in the mind of the user. The imperial government decided to communicate imperial munificence and benefaction on media that circulated throughout the empire. This may have come at the expense of specific representations on tokens, whose audience can only have ever been small. This might explain the gradual disappearance of the imperial portrait from tokens during the

---

[164] *TURS* 10; Kloft, 1970: 96; Rowan, in press a.
[165] For example *RIC* I² Nero 100–3; Kloft, 1970: 91.   [166] Beckmann, 2015: 189.
[167] For *congiaria* types of Trajan see, by way of example, *RIC* III Trajan 381 and Woytek, 2010: nos. 64, 160, 312. On the rectangular object traditionally identified as a *tessera* but which is likely a board used to distribute coins see Beckmann, 2015.
[168] Metcalf, 1993: 339; Noreña, 2011: 85.

76 Tokens and the Imperial Family

Figure 2.22 AE sestertius, 40 mm, 6 h, 26.16 g. Laureate head of Nero right with aegis on his neck, NERO CLAVDIVS CAESAR AVG GER P M TR P IMP P P around / Nero, bare-headed and togate, seated left on platform; *praefectus annonae* standing behind; in front, attendant standing left, giving distribution of coins to citizen right; statue of Minerva facing left behind holding owl and spear; tetrastyle building to left, CONG II DAT POP S C. *RIC* I² Nero 160.

later second and third centuries, if the disappearance is in fact genuine. That said, any specific connection of tokens carrying imperial portraiture with imperial distributions is tiny, with concrete evidence linked only to the single specimen of Claudius discussed above. Without further evidence, we can only speculate.

The disappearance of imperial portraiture can also be traced on bronze and orichalcum tokens: after the Julio-Claudians, no imperial portraits appear on tokens made from these metals either. Whatever the reason, there was clearly a shift in the design culture of tokens. One imagines that distributions and give-aways must still have taken place in the late second and third centuries. It may be that over time tokens as a medium moved away from referencing the coins they so closely resembled in the Julio-Claudian period. This chapter has already noted the shift from the portraiture and legends of Julio-Claudian tokens to the practice of representing the emperor via a legend from the later first century. The development of types may have continued to move further away from coinage, resulting in a decrease in the use of imperial portraiture in favour of other representations (deities, everyday items, animals, chants, etc). In this way tokens might reflect the development of festival iconography, selected and cultivated to enhance the emotional response of the user and their experience of a particular event. Without further evidence it is difficult to be conclusive, but the disappearance of imperial portraiture from tokens is a trend that may tantalisingly reflect a broader shift in the materiality associated with euergetism and festivals in Rome.

3 | Creating Identities in Rome, Ostia and Italy

Tokens form one of the many media of everyday life through which overlapping identities were created, consolidated and performed. An individual possessed multiple identities throughout their life course; someone might have identified with a particular group or been classified into a particular category by others. A person in the Roman world might possess overlapping identities related to class, geographic region, work, gender, family, the military, cult, communal associations, or another type of community. One or more of these identities might come to the fore at different moments in a person's life – a sense of belonging to a particular group, after all, is actively constructed and contested over time.[1]

Rather than seeing 'identity' as a static concept to analyse, sociologists have suggested that instead we might examine the processes through which identities are (or are not) enacted. This focus on process offers a fruitful path to best capture the lived experience of particular individuals. Brubaker advocated an approach he termed 'Groupness', the study of moments of intense solidarity and cohesion amongst a particular group of people. These events might fail in enacting identity, but even if successful remain only a passing moment in time: the solidarity or cohesion felt during a particular occasion may not endure once the event is over.[2] A focus on the *processes* of group-making uncovers the mechanisms by which, and events in which, identities might become salient – that is, the situation in which a particular identity is invoked or performed.[3]

If we are correct in seeing tokens as objects used for particular moments in time, then they form an ideal source to begin reconstructing 'Groupness' – the way in which feelings of cohesion and community might manifest during a particular occasion. Throughout an event different identities might be activated (i.e. become salient). Indeed, many tokens seem to have been designed in a way to call forth particular identities in the user, through the use of imagery and language designed to speak to participants (e.g. representations of worshippers of different types, the presence of chants). Such

[1] Howgego, 2005; Highmore, 2011: 36–7. [2] Brubaker, 2004: 12; Rebillard, 2015: 428.
[3] Brenner, Serpe and Stryker, 2014: 232; Rebillard, 2015: 429.

strategies may reflect an implicit understanding on behalf of token makers that 'Groupness' might fail – material culture was thus employed to actively facilitate feelings of community and cohesion.

Events and their associated material culture played an important role in the creation and performance of different identities.[4] The connection of artefacts to identity in the Roman world has already received significant attention within scholarship; many of the coins of the Roman provinces, for example, are now understood as elite expressions of civic identity particular to a local region.[5] But among the voluminous outputs on the topic of ancient identities, the role of tokens in this process, and the types of identities these artefacts reveal, has not featured at all. This chapter begins to address this lacuna by exploring what tokens can reveal about the differing identities of individuals in Italy, and the processes by which these identities might be activated at particular moments in time.

The designs of tokens from across the Roman Empire reveal that they could form a vehicle for the expression of different types of identity: civic, tribal, cultic or individual identity, for example. A series of Gallo-Roman lead tokens carry direct reference to settlements or tribes, including the settlement of Ricciaco (modern day Dalheim-Pëtzel), the *Alisienses*, *Ambiani* and *Lingones*.[6] Tokens in Egypt might also carry city names accompanied by imagery of local significance: tokens of Memphis, for example, carry imagery connected to the main cult in the region, the Apis bull, and those from Oxyrhynchus represent the local cult of Athena-Thoeris.[7] A lead token found in Tunisia carries the legend GENIO TVSDRITANORV, a reference to the Genius or embodiment of the people of Thysdrus.[8] Tokens from Roman Athens carry imagery intended to enhance the prestige of the issuers, with imagery perhaps consciously chosen to underline the divine ancestry or familial standing of the individuals concerned.[9] Among the imagery found on lead tokens from Ephesus are a bee, a stag and the famous cult statue of Artemis of Ephesus, images that were also found on the provincial coinage of the city and were emblems

---

[4] Pitts, 2007.
[5] The scholarship on identity in the Roman world is vast and cannot be listed in detail here. For provincial coins see by way of example the contributions in Howgego, Heuchert and Burnett, 2005.
[6] Le Brazidec-Berdeaux, 1999; Weiller, 2000.
[7] Milne, 1930; Milne, 1971: nos. 5278–9, 5312–16 (by way of example); Wilding, 2020.
[8] Reported in the *Bulletin de la Sociéte national des antiquaires de France*, 1882, 272; https://coins.warwick.ac.uk/token-specimens/id/heron.1882.p.272.
[9] Gkikaki, 2019.

of civic identity.¹⁰ The use of tokens to activate and/or consolidate different identities in Italy explored here is thus part of a broader phenomenon.

Tokens form an important corpus of material from which to uncover everyday expressions of identities within Rome and Italy.¹¹ Importantly, their decentralised production means that they offer glimpses into the experiences of individuals who are not necessarily well represented in our surviving textual evidence: women or *collegia* for example. The imagery and legends selected for tokens used in hyperlocal contexts reveal the ways in which everyday material culture was marshalled for 'Groupness', those moments in which particular identities might be made salient. This chapter begins with a consideration of what tokens can reveal about civic identities in both Rome and Ostia, before moving on to consider the display of other identities (those formed through work, family, or office-holding, for example). As Rebillard notes, an individual might experience multiple identities, which might be activated simultaneously or successively.¹² The multiplicity of different types of identities expressed on tokens offers the historian an insight into the plural nature of identity for individuals in Roman antiquity.

The City of Rome

Several lead tokens reference the *Genius populi Romani*, the divine personification of the people of Rome. This figure had previously appeared on coinage of the Republic to emphasise the sovereignty and agency of the Roman people; the Genius is variously shown as a youthful male portrait accompanied by a sceptre, holding a cornucopia and crowning Roma with a wreath, or holding a cornucopia and sceptre and being crowned by Victory.¹³ The figure of the youthful male carrying a cornucopia continued into the imperial period. The Genius was an important focal point of identity, both for Rome's inhabitants and for provincial representations of Roman power.¹⁴ In addition to the youthful male Genius, the embodiment of the Roman people was also communicated via the medium of text. Remarkably, several Roman tokens carry nothing but text, referring to the

---

¹⁰ Gülbay and Kireç, 2008: nos. 108–11a, 161–78a, 179–81b. The legends EPHECION and APTEMICION accompany the image of Diana Ephesia on some specimens.
¹¹ On provincial coinage and identity see, by way of example, Howgego, Heuchert and Burnett, 2005.
¹² Rebillard, 2015: 429.   ¹³ *RRC* 329, 393, 397/1, 428/3; Yarrow, 2021: 82, 96.
¹⁴ On the development of the *Genius Populi Romani* and its Hellenistic context see Fears, 1978.

Figure 3.1 Pb token, 14 mm, 12 h, 2.57 g. GPR / FELICITER around. *TURS* 1573, Rostovtzeff and Prou, 1900: no. 361b.

Genius populi Romani via an abbreviated Latin legend: G P, G P R or G P R F, with the last F acting as an abbreviation of the phrase *feliciter* (well wishes).[15] Figure 3.1 bears the abbreviation GPR on one side with the word *feliciter* spelt out in full on the other. The use of *feliciter* recalls the tokens discussed in Chapter 2, which express good wishes for the emperor. Similar to those pieces, these tokens are likely artefacts created as part of a larger event or festival.

The legend G·P·R had earlier accompanied a representation of the Genius of the Roman people on the coinage of the Republic.[16] The letters G P R F also appear as a stamp on Roman lamps, and appear on marble inscriptions in Rome and Ostia – this particular combination of letters was evidently well used and recognised.[17] The ways in which this abbreviated phrase might form part of daily life can be found in a painted inscription (*titulus pictus*) in the *insula Vitaliana* on the Esquiline hill in Rome.[18] The inscription, the only evidence for the name of this particular *insula*, is placed within a *tabula ansata* in a room that is decorated with black and white mosaic pavement and which dates to the second century AD. The inscription is a dedication by the *officinator* of the *insula* P. Tullius Febus, with G P R F placed on the dovetails of the *tabula ansata* (G P on left, R F on right). Beneath the inscription a large coiled snake (perhaps a representation of the *genius loci*) was painted facing right; the inscription and snake sit within a broader painted decorative scheme in the room that involves floral and fruit garlands, and a rooster.[19] Without further information it is difficult to know the precise use of this room, but it contains an

---

[15] For example, *TURS* 1573–605. [16] *RRC* 393.
[17] Lamps: *CIL* XII, 5682 no. 125 (from Avignon, a lamp decorated with Victory carrying a palm branch and wreath), *CIL* XVI, 6195a–c (all from Rome). Marble inscriptions: *CIL* VI, 329 = *CIL* VI, 30738 (an altar from Rome), *CIL* XIV, 4284 (found during the excavation of the piazzale della Vittoria in Ostia, *NSc.* 1910, 31).
[18] *CIL* VI, 33893 = *AE* 2004, 155.
[19] *NSc.* 1895, 80. On snakes as the 'spirits of place' see Flower, 2017: 63–7.

expression of civic identity in a very local context, perhaps juxtaposed against the Genius of the locality in the form of a snake. As well as the image of the youthful male Genius, one can argue that the identity of the Roman people was also shaped by three or four letters: the G P R or G P R F repeated in numerous contexts throughout the city. Glancing at these letters in an *insula*, on a lamp or on a token would have reinforced to the viewer their location within the broader community of Rome. Such everyday encounters (which Billig called 'banal nationalism'), reminding individuals of their place within a particular group, was an important process in maintaining identity.[20]

At times the textual representation of the Genius of the Roman people on tokens is playfully combined with a figurative form. On one token type the Genius is shown holding a patera and cornucopia. On the other side of the token this representation is clarified as *P(opuli) R(omani)*; the token might then be read in its entirety as *Genius* (represented as a figure) *P(opuli) R(omani)*.[21] On other tokens both the figurative and textual reference to the Genius of the Roman People are present; these combinations may have served to further underline the meaning of the letters G P R.[22] The embodiment of the Roman people was thus expressed through figurative or textual form. Other identities might also be expressed via abbreviated text, as explored throughout the rest of this chapter: through the use of abbreviated *tria nomina*, for example, or through abbreviated references to particular legions (e.g. LEG I, LEG II or L. II).[23]

Among the types that appear on tokens in connection with the Genius of the Roman People are: Roma, Victory, Fortuna, Venus, Pietas sacrificing over an altar, a *modius*, a palm branch, numbers (IIII, XVI) and legends (e.g. PSO).[24] The representations of Venus and Fortuna are of particular interest given what we know of the cult to the *Genius populi Romani* in Rome. Cassius Dio mentions that a temple to the *Genius populi Romani* stood in the Roman forum.[25] The *fasti fratrum Arvalium* and the *fasti Amiternini* record that on 9 October sacrifices were made to the *Genius publicus, Fausta Felicitas*, and Venus Victrix on the Capitoline Hill.[26] Coarelli has suggested that three temples to these precise deities stood on the location of the so-called 'Tabularium', a complex planned by Sulla and

---

[20] Billig, 1995; Brubaker, 2004: 2. [21] *TURS* 1598, Pl. VI, 16. [22] *TURS* 1599–600, 1602.
[23] On the abbreviated reference to legionary divisions on tokens see Boon, 1986; Turcan, 1987: 58 and Wilding, 2020.
[24] *TURS* 1576–601. The meaning of PSO is unknown, although it may be an abbreviated *tria nomina*.
[25] Dio 47.2.3, 50.8.2. [26] *CIL* I² pp. 214, 245, 248, 331; Coarelli, 2010: 125–6.

completed by Q. Lutatius Catulus.[27] Coarelli further suggested that the well-known 'Venus Pompeiana' painting (showing Venus in an elephant *quadriga* with the Genius of Pompeii on her left and Fortuna with rudder and cornucopia on her right) might also reflect this Roman triad – the figure carrying a cornucopia and rudder, currently identified as Fortuna, may in fact be Felicitas according to this theory.

Although any conclusions must remain hypothetical given the state of the evidence, one token type might provide evidence to support Coarelli's suggestion. One side carries the legend G P R F around in a circle, while the other shows a female figure standing holding a cornucopia and rudder accompanied by the legend FEL.[28] Rostovtzeff noted the abbreviated legend might refer to *Fel(icitas)* or *Fel(ix)*. FEL might have been placed on the token to indicate that the figure shown is not Fortuna but *Fausta Felicitas*, who shared a day of celebration with the Genius of the Roman People. Another token shows a female figure holding a cornucopia and rudder standing left, accompanied by the legend FELICIT, which may communicate *feliciter* or name the figure as Felicitas.[29] These specimens lend further weight to Coarelli's suggestion that the image of *Fausta Felicitas* was that of a female deity carrying a rudder and cornucopia.

Venus also appears on tokens in conjunction with the *Genius populi Romani*, but the form taken is that of Venus emerging from the bath with her hands raised to her hair. Venus Victrix, by contrast, normally appears accompanied by a helmet and shield, at least on numismatic representations.[30] The appearance of the goddess on these particular tokens, then, is unlikely to have been a representation of Venus Victrix. The representation of Venus Victrix with a helmet and spear does occur on a token. The other side of this token issue bears a goddess holding a cornucopia and a rudder; whether this is Fortuna or *Fausta Felicitas* is difficult to say.[31]

Tokens thus formed a medium that carried representations of the embodiment of the Roman people (Genius), and which actively expressed well wishes for the inhabitants of the city. The cry of *feliciter* may also have served to evoke a response from the user, similar to the chants discussed in Chapter 2. One imagines these tokens were used during localised celebrations on 9 October or similar occasions: that the expression G P R F is found elsewhere in Rome reveals it was deployed in multiple contexts. The

---

[27] Coarelli, 2010. [28] *TURS* 1582, Pl. VI, 11. [29] *TURS* 1783.
[30] *TURS* 1900–1, for example *RIC* II.3² Hadrian 2492 (Venus Victrix holding spear and helmet, shield at feet), *RIC* III Marcus Aurelius 736 (Venus with victoriola and shield).
[31] *TURS* 153.

representation of the *Genius populi Romani* accompanied by legends consisting of three letters, likely to be abbreviated *tria nomina* or other abbreviated forms of names, suggests the creation of tokens of this kind by different individuals for different occasions.[32] The expression of the Genius of the Roman People on tokens, whether in figurative or textual form, would have contributed to an overall sense of community at a particular event. The sense of 'belonging' to the populace of Rome could be evoked and consolidated through particular moments that created a strong sense of cohesion (e.g. communal sacrifice), while the everyday materiality of Rome would have served to remind individuals of their identity on a daily basis.

Tokens conferred benefaction and privilege to particular individuals. Those with a token and access to what it represented formed an 'in' group, set in contrast to the 'out' group who possessed no token; the overall effect would have contributed to a sense of community within the 'in' group. The imagery placed on a token was likely inspected by users – this would have included those who held the privilege the token conferred, and the individual accepting the token in exchange for the benefaction it represented. The message on a token would thus have enhanced the experience of a particular event, its materiality acting upon users to enhance feelings of solidarity and belonging.

Tokens also show the goddess Roma and foundation myths associated with the city of Rome. Figure 3.2 shows Roma seated on one side, with the expression G P R F on the other, an indication of how expressions of good cheer for the Genius of the Roman People might encompass additional expressions of the city's identity. A token of this type was amongst those found in the Tiber in Rome.[33] On *TURS* 1082 the Genius of the Roman People stands alongside Roma; the other side of the token bears the legend IAN|VAR, likely a reference to the month of January or *Ianuarius*. The she wolf and twins also occurs as a type paired with various other images, including the *Ficus Ruminalis*, the fig tree that reportedly stood at the Lupercal on the spot Romulus and Remus came ashore from the Tiber (Figure 3.3).[34] Aeneas, accompanied by Ascanius and Anchises, is represented on several tokens, as

---

[32] *TURS* 1623 (AVL?), 1624 (CFF), 1625 (CAE), 1626 (L·A·G), 1627 (LPP), 1628 (M·A·F).

[33] Rostovtzeff and Vaglieri, 1900: 260 no. 43. For additional types that combine Roma with the Genius of the Roman People see *TURS* 1575, 1577, 1631–2.

[34] See also *TURS* 184 (with rider on a horse on the other side), 702 (*camelarius* with camel), 1661 (Roma), 1668 (ROMA | [A]MICA), Supplement 3726 (Roma), for further appearances of the wolf with twins. For the she-wolf without the twins see *TURS* 186 (with Mars), 254 (AGR|EVO|AVG, which Rostovtzeff suggested might be understood as *Agr* . . . . *evo(catus) Aug(usti)*), 267 (accompanied by the legend XV ROMA with an eagle on a thunderbolt on the other side).

Figure 3.2 Pb token, 19.5 mm, 12 h, 2.48 g. Roma seated right holding Victory in left hand and spear in right / G P R F around. *TURS* 1576, *BMCRLT* 371.

Figure 3.3 Pb token, 13.5 × 12 mm, 12 h, 2.55 g. She-wolf suckling twins / *Ficus Ruminalis*. *TURS* 1667, *BMCRLT* 1778.

is the myth of Mars descending to Rhea Silvia.[35] Tokens thus formed a medium for the expression of foundation myths and other imagery associated with civic identity. In this way they possess similarities to provincial coinage and the official coinage of the Roman mint.[36] But unlike coins, these pieces were small in number and likely viewed by a limited audience. Unlike coinage, which contributes to a sense of community through repeated circulation over time, tokens served to enhance the experience and feeling of community associated with a particular moment in time.

The Tiber, which snaked through the city of Rome and formed an important channel for the movement of goods and people, also appears on tokens. As with the major rivers of other cities, the Tiber formed a central component in the formation of identity in Rome; the personified deity of the river, Tiberinus, famously spoke to Aeneas in Virgil's *Aeneid*, for example.[37] The river god also appears on Roman coinage, reclining and wearing a crown of reeds, variously accompanied by

---

[35] Aeneas: *TURS* 117–20. Mars and Rhea Silvia: *TURS* 326.

[36] On myths on provincial coinage see Price, 2005. The appearance of foundation myths on the coinage of Rome, particularly under Hadrian and Antoninus Pius, has had extensive discussion in scholarship. See, by way of example, Weigel, 1984; Barenghi, 1992; Rowan, 2014.

[37] Verg. *Aen.* 8.31–78; Meyers, 2009.

a prow, an urn from which water flows, and reeds.[38] The presence of the Tiber indicates a specific location on the saecular games coinage of Domitian and Septimius Severus (sacrifices took place during these games by the Tiber river).[39] The connection of the river to identity in Rome is perhaps best expressed on a coin series struck under Vespasian. The reverse of these coins shows Roma seated right on Rome's seven hills, with Romulus and Remus suckling from the wolf below and the Tiber river reclining on lower right of the coin holding a long reed.[40] The colossal statue of the Tiber now in the Louvre shows the river reclining holding a rudder and cornucopia accompanied by the wolf and twins, underlying the connection between the river and Rome's foundation.[41]

The small number of tokens from Rome and Ostia showing river deities suggest the Tiber was conceptualised in multiple ways. One type shows a reclining river deity accompanied by the legend TIB, presumably a reference to the river Tiber or his personified form Tiberinus. The other side of the token shows the deities Fortuna and Mercury, perhaps an expression of the wealth and commerce the river brought to Rome.[42] The same legend (TIB) occurs on a token that carries on the other side what Rostovtzeff described as a Genius seated holding a patera and an urn from which water flows.[43] The combination of image and legend here suggests that what is represented is the Genius of the Tiber, or perhaps one of its outlets (an aqueduct or fountain). The urn with water flowing from it is an attribute of rivers and springs, but the addition of a patera and the lack of reeds here suggest it is a Genius who is shown rather than Tiberinus.[44] This same Genius, holding a patera and an urn that spills water, is also found on a token with a branch or tree on the other side; on this specimen the Genius appears to also have a *modius* on his head.[45] In yet another representation,

---

[38] *RIC* II anonymous 17–18 (crown of reeds), *RIC* III Antoninus Pius 642A–43b (reed, prow, rock from which water flows), *RIC* III Marcus Aurelius 1142–5 (prow, reed, urn from which water flows). *RIC* II Trajan 556 has traditionally been interpreted as showing the Tiber, but Woytek suggests instead the river god (shown with a long reed) is the Danube; Woytek, 2010: 166, no. 199.

[39] *RIC* II.1² Domitian 621, 627, *RIC* IV.1 Septimius Severus 293, 816A–B, 826B; Sobocinski, 2006. Sacrifices were held to the *Moerae*, the *Ilithyiae*, and Terra Mater by the Tiber river, where remnants of the *acta* of the games have also been found; Taylor, 1934: 103.

[40] *RIC* II.1² Vespasian 108, 193.   [41] Meyers, 2009: 234.

[42] *TURS* 1679. Rostovtzeff reports that the river god is carrying a reed, but the only known specimen (*BMCRLT* 1282) is now too worn to certify if this is correct. See also *TURS* 1686–7, which shows a river god reclining left but without a legend.

[43] *TURS* 1680, Pl. VI, 46.   [44] Boyce, 1958: 69 on the representation of rivers with urns.

[45] *TURS* 1681 = *BMCRLT* 753.

the Genius is shown holding two corn-ears (or perhaps it is a V) and the urn, with the legend M | DM on the other side.[46] This representation of the Genius of the Tiber (or one of its offshoots) appears to be unique to tokens among surviving material culture. The *modius* and corn-ears may reference the role of the Tiber in facilitating the supply of grain to Rome.

Iconographic innovation can be found on another token type, which shows a male figure draped from the waist down, holding a cornucopia and reed, with his left foot on a rock (Figure 3.4). One imagines that this also is a representation of the Tiber or one of its outlets, but unusually the figure is shown standing rather than reclining. As noted above, Tiberinus might be portrayed with a variety of attributes, but these occurrences all show the deity reclining. The standing representation of the river might have referenced a now lost statue; the Nile is frequently portrayed standing on coins of Alexandria and one imagines this variation must have existed for the Tiber as well.[47] This particular image may have been more resonant than a reclining Tiberinus for the community using the tokens; it might have referenced a very particular statue and/or location within Rome as opposed to the Tiber more generally. Just as particular attributes served to make Graeco-Roman deities 'local' (e.g. the addition of the *labrys* to Athena on tokens at Oxyrhynchus in Egypt), so too might the alterations to the

Figure 3.4 Pb token, 20 mm, 9 h, 3.9 g. River deity, draped from the waist down, standing right with left foot on rock holding a long reed in his right hand and cornucopia in left; CGA on left and FT on right / VES between two palms or branches. *TURS* 1682, Rostovtzeff and Prou, 1900: no. 420a.

---

[46] *TURS* 1685. The meaning of the legend is unknown.
[47] For example *RPC* III 4316, 4689, 4744.1–4, 4745.1–2. Nilus is also shown holding a reed and cornucopia, and so one cannot rule out that Figure 3.4 shows the Nile. However, representations of the Nile in Rome are normally accompanied by attributes that clearly reference Egypt (e.g. a sphinx, crocodile, and/or hippopotamus, see *RIC* II.3² Hadrian 1436–7).

representation of the Tiber we find on material culture in Rome represent hyperlocal iterations of the river in the city.[48] The meaning of the legend on this token issue remains a mystery.

A river god, most likely the Tiber, appears in yet another iconographic iteration on Figure 3.5.[49] Here the deity reclines on an urn, with a reed curving up and around him, and a dolphin swims beneath. A more worn token that seems to belong to the same series shows the river god with a reed curving up around him on either side (no legend), and Victory accompanied by the legend V A.[50] This variation in design can be explained by the fact these tokens were made from moulds; this allowed for deviation within a particular series, as explained in Chapter 1. The addition of the dolphin to the scene is significant here, since the feature is not normally associated with rivers or the Tiber.

This is evident from the series of coins struck under Nero showing the harbour at Ostia with a reclining deity placed at the bottom of the scene (Figure 3.6). This figure is identified in the *RIC* as the river Tiber holding a rudder and reclining on a dolphin. But the dolphin is more often used to reference the ocean. As a result, the reclining figure on Nero's coinage has convincingly been re-identified as a personified representation of the

Figure 3.5 Pb token, 19 mm, 12 h, 2.43 g. River god reclining left, left arm leaning on urn from which water flows; reed on right curving above the god's head, dolphin swimming right below. ARA around on left / Victory, standing left with wreath in extended right hand and palm branch in left. C on left, ligate VR on right. *TURS* 526, *BMCRLT* 768.

---

[48] For the *labrys* (double-headed axe) and Athena in Oxyrhynchus, especially on tokens, see Wilding, 2020.
[49] Rostovtzeff read the legend above the river as ARR and suggested the token was issued by Arruntius Stella while *curator*, see Rostovtzeff, 1905b: 49–50 and Ruciński, 2012.
[50] *TURS* 527; *BMCRLT* 779.

Figure 3.6 AE sestertius, c. 35 mm, 6 h, 27.69 g. Laureate head of Nero right, with aegis on neck, NERO CLAVD CAESAR AVG GER P M TR P IMP P P around / View of the harbour at Ostia, AVGVSTI above, POR OST beneath flanked by S C. *RIC* I² Nero 178.

harbour at Ostia.[51] Indeed, the representation of a similar figure on coinage of Pompeiopolis (Cilicia), reclining on a dolphin and holding a rudder as part of a harbour scene seems to confirm the identification. The relative rarity of the image and the fact that it appears in reference to these two

---

[51] Boyce, 1958: 70–2; Weiss, 2013: 77; Cuyler, 2014: 125–6.

distinct harbours suggests, as Boyce argued, that this is a particular deity associated with a place where rivers flowed into the ocean.[52] Indeed, if the dolphin had a specific association with seafaring in Ostia, then its use on tokens that show sailing vessels on the other side may have been intended as a specific reference to the fact that these were ocean-going vessels.[53]

To return to the token shown in Figure 3.5, the presence of the urn and reeds indicate that it is a river god shown here. But the presence of the dolphin alludes to the fact that the river, which we might interpret as the Tiber, is connected to the ocean, evoking Rome's harbour in the mind of the user. The token, issued by a *curator* (CVR), again utilised an inventive (and an otherwise unknown) combination of imagery to evoke a particular vision of the Tiber that emphasised the connection of Rome to her harbour and the ocean that ensured her supplies. The multiple representations of the Tiber on tokens likely reflects the fact that these tokens were created by a variety of individuals, representing particular groups who each may have possessed a slightly different vision of the river so central to their city. In this sense the Tiber can be viewed as a 'shared image', the meaning of which was extended by different users. When different groups widened the semantic meaning and associations of the Tiber, the image of the river became a powerful community-building tool that was able to engage a variety of people, all of whom connected with the image, even if each held different associations.[54] The multiplicity and malleability of representations of the Tiber show how images can be deployed to engage a broader variety of individuals than a single static, carefully controlled image.

We also find much more localised expressions of identity. At least three tokens appear to carry direct references to the regions of Rome: *regio* III, VI and XIII.[55] Augustus had divided the city into fourteen regions (*regiones*) and numerous neighbourhoods (*vici*) also existed; each region and *vicus* received annually elected magistrates.[56] In spite of the regional divisions being imposed from the 'top down', so to speak, the repeated reference to particular regions in inscriptions, including tokens, suggest that Romans nonetheless identified with their region, and might act communally within this grouping, at times in conjunction with other *regiones* in the city.[57] Individuals also formed social

---

[52] RPC IV.3 3581; ANS 1944.100.54319 with discussion in Boyce, 1958: 71.
[53] For example, *TURS* 969–70.
[54] Buck-Morss, 2010 on the concept of the 'shared image'; Rowan, 2020a on its applicability to the Roman world.
[55] *TURS* 490–3. [56] Suet. *Aug.* 30.2; Dio 55.8.6; Lott, 2013: 170. [57] Goodman, 2020.

bonds within their neighbourhood or *vicus*, and we find expressions of identity at this level on tokens. One token carries the legend VICI accompanied by the figure of a Genius. The type must, as Rostovtzeff surmised, represent the Genius of the neighbourhood (Figure 3.7). The *vici* served as focal points for communal activity within Rome, particularly among the lower classes and during the *Compitalia* held in honour of the *lares* placed at the crossroads, as well as in connection with the worship of the imperial family.[58] The material expression of these communities can be found in the shrines (*compita*) and altars erected in these locations, as well as on other items of everyday life, like the tokens presented here.[59] The presence of snakes on several token series also hints at representations of local shrines and locations, since snakes might represent the Genius of a place and are represented in association with the altars of *lares* on other media (for example the fresco of the Lararium at VII.6.3 in Pompeii).[60]

Tokens also express more informal formulations of local areas. The regionary catalogues of late antiquity name each region of Rome in relation to a specific feature of the area, for example *Regio XI Circus Maximus*. Since no earlier sources survive for such naming conventions it is unclear whether this practice was created during the compilation of these texts, or whether the catalogues recorded existing, unofficial, terminology.[61] The third region of Rome was labelled *Isis et Serapis* in the catalogues, after the temple (and street) in the region. In this context a lead token carrying the legend AB | ISE ET | SERAP is of interest – it likely refers to the street leading away from the

Figure 3.7 Pb token, 13 mm, 12 h, 1.36 g. Genius standing left holding cornucopia in left hand and patera in right, VICI around on right / Hercules standing left holding club in right hand and lion skin over left. *TURS* 1613, *BMCRLT* 124.

---

[58] Lott, 2013: 176.   [59] Lott, 2013; Flower, 2017: 160–74; Russell, 2020: 27–8.
[60] *TURS* 1558–70. *TURS* 1558 displays two snakes next to an altar, 1566 two snakes on one side and a decorated altar on the other, 1567 a single snake on one side and a lit cylindrical altar on the other. On the association of the snake with *lares* and as the representation of the Genius of a place see Flower, 2017: 63–7.
[61] Lott, 2013: 173.

temple of Isis and Sarapis that gave the third region its name.[62] The other side of the token shows the god Harpocrates with his hand raised to his mouth; the combination reveals an expression of very local identity shaped by the topography of the city. Indications of location are found on other epigraphic monuments in Rome; for example a *cippus* from region VII records the location *ad tres silanos*, presumably referencing three fountains within the area.[63] Suetonius records that Domitian was born at the street called the Pomegranate in the sixth region.[64] Rome was full of such local names, and associated local communities.

These local expressions of identity can be found on several other tokens. Several express a location in relation to Mars: one carries the legend REG MAR (*regio Martis*?), another carries the legend AD MART and another A MART. These tokens all carry imagery of the god Mars as well; the phrase *ad Martis* refers to the area surrounding the temple to Mars in Rome on the via Appia between the first and second milestones from the Porta Capena.[65] One wonders whether the representation of Mars on the tokens, leaning on a spear with one hand and resting his other hand on a shield at his feet, represents the cult statue within this temple.[66] A token also records the location *ad nucem*. Here the meaning of the legend is further elaborated by the representation of a nut next to the legend and a nut tree on the other side.[67] *Pallacina* also appears on tokens, although whether the legend PALLACIN refers to the *vicus* or the bathing establishment in that district is open to debate.[68] A particular location and associated identity might also be represented via imagery alone. Figure 3.8, with a recorded findspot of Rome, shows three statues of Fortuna standing side by side, a likely reference to the location *ad tres Fortunas*.

The temple of the three *Fortunae* was located on the Quirinal, close to the Porta Collina, and Vitruvius records that the area was named *ad tres*

---

[62] *TURS* 494; Platner and Ashby, 1929: 286; Palmer, 1975: 654; Richardson, 1992: 213. The location is also mentioned in *CIL* VI, 2234 (*fanatico ab Isis Serapis* (sic) *ab aedem* (sic) *Bellone Rufiliae*) and *CIL* VI, 32462 (*ab Isis et Serapis*). A similar name for a region seems to have existed in Aquileia, named on a token made from 'giallo antico', *CIL* V, 8211. The token was created by a magistrate of the youth, see Mainardis, 2002: 572.

[63] *CIL* XIV, 2496; Goodman, 2020: 8. [64] Suet. *Dom.* 1.1; Goodman, 2020: 12.

[65] *TURS* 495–7; Platner and Ashby, 1929: 327–8; Richardson, 1992: 244–5; Suet. *Terent.* 5; Cic. *QFr* 25(3.5).8.

[66] Livy 22.1.12 mentions a statue that stood in the temple alongside that of the she-wolf but provides no further detail.

[67] *TURS* 498; Platner and Ashby, 1929: 363; Richardson, 1992: 269. The phrase also occurs on a funerary inscription as referring to a burial location outside the *pomerium*, *CIL* VI, 28644.

[68] *TURS* 500; Platner and Ashby, 1929: 3812.

Figure 3.8 Pb token, 15 mm, 6 h, 1.92 g. Three *Fortunae* standing left, each holding a cornucopia in their left hand and a rudder in their right / A left hand with thumb and index finger touching; SAT on left, A or uncertain object (prow?) on right. *TURS* 501, Rostovtzeff and Prou, 1900: no. 335a.

Fortunas after the temple.[69] The hand shown on the other side of the token is reminiscent of cameos and gems that show a hand pinching an ear as an embodiment of memory.[70] But here there is no ear, and so a more likely explanation is that the hand represents the number ten. The so-called 'finger calculus' is known from antiquity and the middle ages. A series of bone and ivory gaming pieces reveal that the Romans counted on their fingers in a manner that was preserved into the middle ages, but which was different from the method used in contemporary Western society.[71] These gaming pieces carry the finger sign on one side and the corresponding number inscribed in Latin on the other; the number ten is represented by a left hand with the thumb and index finger touching with the remaining three fingers extended, as on Figure 3.8. The token thus uses imagery alone to communicate two phrases: *ad tres Fortunas* and X.

The legend to the left of the hand reveals a possible context for the token: the Saturnalia. The chant associated with this festival, *io Saturnalia io*, was abbreviated to IO SAT IO on tokens, and is discussed more fully in Chapter 4. One possible context for the objects discussed in this section is revealed: these tokens may have been used during very local events held in the context of broader festivals across the city. These events were occasions that sought to activate the identity of particular neighbourhoods and regions, and the iconography chosen for tokens played a role in this process. Alongside a broader sense of 'belonging to Rome', inhabitants of the city also belonged to communities arranged by smaller neighbourhoods or streets. Overlapping identities connected to different types of community within the city meant that,

---

[69] Vitr. *De arch.* 3.2.2; Platner and Ashby, 1929: 216–17; Richardson, 1992: 158.
[70] For example, BM 1814,0704.1630.
[71] Frœhner, 1881; Alföldi-Rosenbaum, 1971: pl. I, no. 10 for the representation of the number ten.

depending on the occasion, an individual might emphasise their membership in one community over another at a particular moment in time.

Maritime Identity in Ostia and Portus

The tokens found at Ostia also reveal overlapping identities. The nature of civic and local identity in Ostia has, surprisingly, not seen the same level of analysis as other regions of the Roman Empire. As Bruun observes, this may be because Ostia lacks an obvious corpus of sources for such a study. Ostia's close relationship with Rome has also led to the port town being treated as a suburb of the capital.[72] Rome was important in the construction of Ostian identity: Ostia was the first *colonia* of Rome, reportedly founded by Rome's fourth king Ancus Marcius.[73] But Ostia's role as a key port also shaped civic identity, a sense of 'Ostianness'. Bruun has observed the 'maritime mentality' of Ostia's inhabitants, witnessed in epigraphic evidence and material culture: Bruun notes here the imagery of boats, lighthouses, anchors, tridents, dolphins and other aquatic divinities and animals in mosaics, sarcophagi, graffiti, lamps and tokens across the town.[74] In fact, the evidence for a sense of 'Ostianness' is rich when one begins to examine the remains of the town more closely. The tokens found in Ostia and referencing the settlement have had only a minor role in discussions of Ostia's civic identity, but they are a powerful corpus of evidence from which to uncover the different communities and identities in the town.

References to Ostia in material culture frequently depict the harbour's lighthouse, and it is unsurprising to find this represented on tokens as well. The lighthouse appears in several mosaics in Ostia, as well as in marble reliefs, graffiti, a wall painting and on imperial coinage referring to the grain supply.[75] On tokens the lighthouse is paired with a variety of legends and imagery that name the port and allude to the maritime nature of the settlement. Figure 3.9, for example, shows a lit lighthouse of three tiers with the letters P T; Rostovtzeff convincingly suggested this should be understood as *P(ortus) T(raianus)* (although we might resolve the legend as *Portus Traiani*). The other side of the token shows Neptune in a hippocamp *biga*, a reference to the ocean. The lighthouse and the legend suggest

---

[72] Bruun, 2007: 125; Bruun, 2014: 348–51.   [73] Livy 1.33.9.   [74] Bruun, 2015.
[75] An excellent collection of the relevant material, along with images, can be found at www.ostia-antica.org/portus/c001.htm.

Maritime Identity in Ostia and Portus 95

Figure 3.9 Pb token, 14 × 12 mm, 3 h, 3.07 g. Lit lighthouse of three tiers, P on left, T on right / Neptune, holding trident in right hand, riding right in a *biga* of hippocamps; star above. *TURS* 59, Rostovtzeff and Prou, 1900: no. 98.

Figure 3.10 Pb token, 24 mm, 12 h, 5.69 g. Lit lighthouse of four tiers, TI on left, S on right / Fortuna seated left holding cornucopia in left hand and rudder in right. *TURS* 61.

that Ostian civic identity must have incorporated the harbour, initially built under Claudius and then enlarged under Trajan, when it became known as the *Portus Traiani*.[76]

A lighthouse of three tiers also appears on a token with the other side carrying the retrograde legend TR|AI.[77] The lighthouse, at times accompanied by the legend TI S, is paired with a seated Fortuna in one series (Figure 3.10; the meaning of the legend is unknown).[78] The image of the lighthouse is also accompanied by the legend ANT, which Rostovtzeff suggested might refer to *portus Antoniniani*.[79] One token displays the lighthouse on one side and a ship sailing on the other.[80] A specimen now

---

[76] On Portus see Keay, Millett et al., 2005.
[77] *TURS* 60; Rostovtzeff, 1902: no. 1, pl. VI 27. Rostovtzeff suggested the legend should be understood as *Trai(anus)*.
[78] *TURS* 61–2. [79] *TURS* 64. [80] *TURS* 961.

preserved in the Museo Archeologico Nazionale di Palestrina pairs the lighthouse with a semi-circular object with a handle (?) on the other side.[81] Another type, found in the Terme sulla Semita dei Cippi in Ostia, shows a three-tiered lighthouse on one side and a nude figure standing frontally on the other.[82] The representation of the lighthouse at Portus on material culture at Ostia varies in terms of the number of storeys and other features (e.g. in the Piazzale delle Corporazioni it is variously shown with three, four, five or six storeys, or only the top of the lighthouse is represented). On tokens, however, the representation seems quite standardised: of the known representations to date, each has three or four (Figure 3.10) storeys.

Tokens showing the lighthouse and Fortuna have reported findspots in several locations in Ostia. An example of the variant with the legend TI S (Figure 3.10) was found during the excavations of a *taberna* in the Baths of Neptune, with another specimen found in the Terme di Serapide, and a third in the Terme bizantine.[83] Another of the same type possibly came from the excavation fill outside the ruins of the city, and yet a further possible example, too worn for precise identification, was found in the Basilica Portuense at Portus in a late antique context.[84] Three of these finds come from bath contexts, as does the find from the Terme sulla Semita dei Cippi mentioned above. The bath contexts may simply reflect the fact that money (and tokens) are frequently lost down drains in these buildings. Significantly, however, the finds reveal that the same type of token was carried by individuals into different bathing establishments across Ostia. If these tokens were to be redeemed for participation in an event or for a particular good, they were distributed in advance of the occasion.

---

[81] Museo Archeologico Nazionale di Palestrina bag no. 97.59, no. 1502 in Rowan's currently unpublished catalogue. This catalogue is a listing of individual tokens in the collection, specimens that the author intends to publish online in the future. See also bag 124.5 no. 612 for another possible representation of the lighthouse, on a diamond-shaped token with a figure holding a cornucopia on the other side.

[82] *NSc.* 1950, 99. It was found below a mosaic pavement, together with a 'sbarretta' of gold and a billon coin (perhaps of Gallienus) showing Sol on the reverse holding a globe in his left hand and with his right hand raised.

[83] Baths of Neptune: *GdS* vol. 3, 1910 p. 227 = Ostia Antiquarium inv. 3575. Terme di Serapide: Pensabene, 2001–3: 497, inv. 4741, Mag. Vet. V, 4. Terme bizantine: Pensabene, 2001–3: 497, inv. 33110, Coll. Magazzino.

[84] Stray find: Pensabene, 2001–3: no. 36, although the token forms part of the much larger collection now preserved at the Museo Archeologico Nazionale in Palestrina, which was seized as the proceeds of illegal excavation activity and which has no reported findspots. Basilica Portuense: Spagnoli, 2011. The token was found in a stratum dating to Period 3c (AD 550–600), associated with the construction of the central nave (US2020). Also found was a radiate *consecratio* issue of Claudius II and numismatic material dating to the fourth and fifth centuries AD.

Alternatively, these tokens may have been used within the economy of the bathhouse itself. As discussed in further detail in Chapter 5, there is good evidence to suggest that tokens were used within bathhouses in Rome and Ostia, likely as an internal accounting mechanism to be exchanged for food, drink or services. The existence of the same token type in multiple establishments may reflect the fact that tokens from one bathhouse may have been reused in another to cut down on manufacturing costs, or that a particular workshop may have manufactured the same type for multiple groups. Alternatively, the tokens with the lighthouse might have represented a civic level of benefaction – the granting of admission to bathing establishments across the town, although the precise findspots of these pieces suggest they were used and lost within the bathhouse rather than acting as an entry ticket. In any of these scenarios, the civic nature of the imagery chosen – a lighthouse and the goddess Fortuna – must have facilitated the acceptance of this particular token type. The imagery would be easily recognisable to the inhabitants of Ostia, and each user would find meaning in the type in a way not possible with a token naming a specific bathing establishment, for example, or a particular local organisation. Tokens in Roman Egypt also display this dual approach to imagery: the image of Nilus, for example, is found on tokens that travelled across the province, while other types possessed very specific imagery and are only found in one location (e.g. the representation of Athena-Theoris with *labrys* is only found on tokens at Oxyrhynchus).[85] The representation of the lighthouse within daily life (whatever the specific context) must have reinforced a particular maritime sense of 'Ostianness', also seen in the mosaics of the Piazzale delle Corporazioni and the other representations across the town.

Three tokens carrying an image of the lighthouse at Ostia were reported to Rostovtzeff by Gauckler as having been found in Hadrumetum in North Africa; two were specimens carrying the design of the 'lighthouse / Fortuna seated', and one was of the 'lighthouse / ANT' type.[86] The colony of Hadrumetum was an important source of grain for Rome and movement between the two port towns must have been regular, which would explain how the tokens ended up so far from their place of manufacture. The tokens might have been converted into a type of emergency small change, or else might have been carried by merchants as mementoes or items they intended to redeem at a later date. In this context it is worth noting that among the tokens

---

[85] Wilding, 2020.   [86] *TURS* 61.3, 62.2, 64.4.

Figure 3.11 Pb token of Oxyrhynchus, 23 mm, 11 h, 13.70 g. Bust of Athena right wearing Corinthian helmet; linear border / Nike standing right on globe holding wreath in extended left hand and palm branch in right; linear border. cf. Milne 5291 for a token of the same type, found at Oxyrhynchus.

preserved in the Museo Archeologico Nazionale di Palestrina there are five tokens from Egypt (Figure 3.11).[87] Since the collection was seized as the proceeds of illegal excavation activity, we cannot know the precise findspots of these items, but it is very likely these pieces were found in Italy. Indeed, the existence of migrants and merchants in Portus and Ostia is well established: the Isiac association of Portus, for example, seems to have been founded and dominated by individuals from Alexandria in Egypt.[88] Tokens rarely travelled between settlements, although there are several cases where tokens travelled (in small number) from one port to another, a reflection of the much broader exchange of people and goods that took place in these towns.[89] Stannard's analysis of a series of quadrangular bronze tokens found at both Ostia and Minturnae has also demonstrated that tokens moved between ports within Italy; Stannard suggested these particular pieces were connected to the workings of the ports and connected river systems.[90]

---

[87] Museo Archeologico Nazionale di Palestrina bag no. 97.14 no 1423 (= Pensabene, 2001–3: no. 14), 97.39 no. 1446 (= Pensabene, 2001–3: no. 38) shown in Figure 3.11, 97.63 no. 1640, 107.8 no. 946, 111.15 no. 1310.

[88] Steuernagel, 2007: 142.

[89] Egyptian tokens were also found in a shipwreck off the coast of Israel, see Meshorer, 2010: 132. A series of orichalcum tokens appear to have been sent to Lepcis Magna as part of a shipment of small change, see Munzi, 1997 and Rowan, 2020b.

[90] Stannard, 2015b. To the corpus compiled by Stannard another token might be added, possibly of Stannard Type 2. A bronze token with a horse running right and blank on the other side was found among the ruins to the NW of the eastern gate of Ostia; *GdS* 1918 p. 39 no.11, Ostia Antiquarium inv. 12801. Unfortunately the author was unable to examine the piece.

A civic identity closely tied to the maritime activity of Ostia is also indicated by other tokens that carry nautical imagery and variations on the legend *Traianus*. The legend may refer to the emperor Trajan, but the juxtaposition of the legend and maritime imagery suggests a reference to the *Portus Traiani* is more likely. Indeed, epigraphic evidence attests to the fact that the inhabitants of a quarter around Trajan's port were known as *Traianenses*, 'those of Trajan'.[91] The legend TRAIANI ('of Trajan') is also found on tokens accompanying imagery of Apollo and Fortuna.[92] The Latin might refer to the fact that the token was issued on behalf of Trajan, but it might equally refer to a group who identified with a particular area of Portus, or it might reference *portus Traiani* more broadly. The legend TRAIANVS was reported on a token now lost, which carried a tuna fish on one side and Neptune holding a dolphin and trident on the other, a likely reference to the port of the emperor.[93] A new type found amongst the collection now in the Museo Archeologico Nazionale di Palestrina shows what appears to be an elephant on one side and the legend TRAIANAS on the other.[94] *TURS* 947, decorated with a ship (*cydarum*) on one side and the legend PT on the other may equally refer to *Portus Traiani*, as on Figure 3.9. Without recorded findspots for these token types we cannot know for certain whether they referred to particular groups within Ostia and Portus, but the evidence suggests that this is probable.

Tokens showing two or three people in a boat on one side and the legend TRA on the other are also known (Figure 3.12). The legend again might

Figure 3.12 Pb token, 24 mm, 6.12 g. Two people in a boat (*cymba*), fish beneath/ TRA.

---

[91] *CIL* XIV, 4; van Haeperen, 2019. [92] *TURS* 53–4. [93] *TURS* 55–6.
[94] Museo Archeologico Nazionale di Palestrina bag. 120.8 no. 100.

refer to some form of the word *Traianus*, but we cannot rule out an abbreviation of *traiectus*, a place where one could cross the river at Ostia via ferry; various groups provided this service. Without further find information it is difficult to say more; one token with the legend TRA on one side and three palm branches on the other was found in the Tiber in Rome.[95]

Only one token type specifically names Ostia. Side a of this token shows a bare male head right, accompanied by the legend GAL AVG (a reference to Galba Augustus), while the other side shows Ceres seated holding a sceptre and corn-ears, accompanied by the legend OSTIAE.[96] The use of the genitive might indicate that this was a token of Ostia, but equally the token may be referencing grain that came from the port. The combination of Galba and Ceres, along with the reference to Ostia, brings to mind the massive *Horrea Galbae*, a large warehouse complex in Rome that served as a depot for grain and other goods, including the *annona publica*. The complex was probably first known as the *Horrea Sulpicia*, but was renamed after Galba (who was of the Sulpician *gens*) during his reign, when the complex came under imperial control.[97] Both Trajan and Galba oversaw activity that directly influenced the experience of Ostia's mercantile inhabitants and which consequently shaped their everyday experience and identity. Whether this token series, and the TRA tokens discussed above, were issued by inhabitants of Ostia or on behalf of the emperor, their existence, and the activities that led to their creation, would have served to further a particular 'Ostian' sense of community.

Status and Self-Portrayal in Rome and Ostia

Many tokens from Rome and Ostia bear the name of individuals, both men and women, as well as references to particular *gentes*.[98] Figure 3.13, for example, bears the name M(arcus) Antonius Glaucus. Tokens of this kind not only expressed emotions and ideologies associated with a particular moment, but also reinforced the prestige of the individual responsible for the token and the benefaction it represented. In addition to carrying the names of individuals, tokens could carry portraits, or representations of paraphernalia associated with a person's office or occupation. Several tokens carry types that are otherwise only found on gems, suggesting that

---

[95] *TURS* 3353; Tomassetti, 1887: 235 no. 4e.   [96] *TURS* 36, Pl. XI 63.
[97] Richardson, 1992: 193.   [98] Rostovtzeff, 1905b: 104–8 for a discussion.

Figure 3.13 Pb token, 20 mm, 6 h, 4.26 g. M in the centre of the token, ANTONIVS GLAVCVS around / Vulcan standing left holding sceptre in left hand and mallet in right. *TURS* 1127, Rowan, 2020b: no. 55.

the imagery of a person's seal (or glass paste) might be used to reference a particular individual. In general, with a few exceptions, the individuals named on tokens are not otherwise known.[99] This is unsurprising: tokens generally appear to have been issued by lower magistracies in charge of games and distributions, as well as individuals involved in communal associations, bathhouses or other commercial establishments. The corpus of material thus provides an invaluable insight into individuals from the Roman world who are otherwise absent from the remaining historical record.

In fact, the full mass of individuals named on lead tokens may not have been fully recognised. Many tokens from Rome and Ostia carry legends of two or three letters; these may very well be abbreviated *tria nomina* (with two letters perhaps referring to women, for whom the praenomen was abandoned relatively early in Roman history).[100] Graffiti, amphora labels and personal stamps from the Roman world reveal that in circles where an individual was well known, initials might be used to represent a particular person. In Pompeii, for example, graffiti referred to individuals by their initials (e.g. LVP), as did campaign posters: one example of the latter on the Via dell'Abbondanza highlights the candidacy of one CIP.[101] This same practice is found in Ostia, where graffiti reveals that one LCF 'was here'.[102] The combinations of two and three letter legends found on many tokens may

---

[99] For example, the Q. Terentius Culleo named on *TURS* 1323 is likely to be the suffect consul of AD 40; Rostovtzeff, 1905b: 105; Dressel, 1922: 181; Gallivan, 1979: 67; Rowan, in press a.

[100] Salway, 1994: 125–6; Benefiel, 2010: 73.

[101] *CIL* IV, 7872; Benefiel, 2010: 73–4. For the practice on amphora labels on the Iberian Peninsula, and the possible connection to tokens in that region see Mora Serrano, 2005.

[102] G0267 at http://www.ostia-antica.org/graffiti/regio3/caseggiato-degli-aurighi-apartment/caseggiato-degli-aurighi-apartment.htm.

thus have acted as a reference to the name of an individual; these tokens were likely used within a small community and a specific context, where the identity of the issuer would have been recognised. Indeed, two token types carry the legend LCF, the first accompanied by a camel on the other side and the second the legend LAM.[103] This is not to suggest that the LCF of the tokens and the graffito in Ostia are one and the same; rather the example demonstrates the practice of naming conventions within daily life. The surviving corpus of tokens may reference far more individuals than has previously been realised.

Tokens also carry the names and portraits of women. A series of tokens was issued by a woman called Hortensia Sperata: two tokens of 19–20 mm in diameter carry the legend HORTENSIA SPERATA or HORTE·SPER· around in a circle on one side. The other side of the tokens are decorated with a palm branch within a wreath. Smaller tokens (13–15 mm) have an abbreviated legend: HOR in a line on one side and SPE or SP on the other.[104] Hortensia may have required two different sizes of token (19–20 mm and 13–15 mm), with each size equating to a different good or value. The differing diameters of the tokens were further underscored by the use of different designs for each size. A token mould half found on the Esquiline Hill in Rome reveals that tokens of different sizes might be cast at the same time. This mould half had two sets of channels, for two sets of tokens: a 17 mm piece with the legend LVE and a 9 mm piece with the same legend ligate.[105] A Hortensia Sperata is known from a funerary inscription in Antium that she erected to Lucius Hortensius Asclepiades, but there is no reason to identify this woman with the token issuer.[106] The palm branch and wreath, also found on other tokens, evoke a festive feeling.

A Domitia Flora is also named on a token issue, as is an Aelia Septimi, Iulia Iust(a) and a Livia Meliti(ne), amongst others.[107] One token issue names Iunia, with the other side carrying the representation of a sistrum, perhaps referencing a context connected to Isis.[108] Other women may also be named, but in several cases it is impossible to distinguish between the name of a *gens* and that of a woman. A token with the legend APRO|NIA, for example, may refer to an individual woman or the *gens* of the same name; the representation of Fortuna on the other side of the token offers no clues as to which interpretation is correct.[109] Similarly the IVL|IA that appears on a token with the representation of a palm branch and corn-ear on the

---

[103] *TURS* 705, 3489.   [104] *TURS* 1240–3.   [105] Cesano, 1904a: no. 4.
[106] Solin, 2015–16; Chioffi, 2017: 54 no. 30; *AE* 2018, 476.   [107] *TURS* 1107, 1207, 1263, 1272.
[108] *TURS* 1270.   [109] *TURS* 1131.

other side may reference an individual or a broader family.¹¹⁰ Two token issues have the legend OP|PIA; the first carries an image of Fortuna on the other side, the second a female portrait. This may indeed be a representation of a woman named Oppia.¹¹¹ Given that women were generally known by the feminine form of their familial names, one imagines this slippage between a woman and her family was something experienced more broadly in the Roman world. Several tokens also bear female portraits without accompanying legends; one imagines these are representations of particular individuals. Figure 3.14, for example, shows a female portrait likely to be of the second century AD, since the hair is plaited and coiled on top of her head in the fashion of this era.¹¹² The absence of an identifying legend accompanying the portrait also echoes the trend of imperial tokens from the second century, in which emperors are shown but not named (discussed in more detail in Chapter 2). Women are also occasionally named on provincial coinage, either because they held eponymous offices, or in their capacity as priestesses; one imagines that both the coinage-issuing priestesses and the token-issuing women of Roman Italy were the sponsors of particular benefactions of varying value.¹¹³

Hemelrijk's study of female patronage demonstrated that, like their male counterparts, women had reduced opportunity for the very prominent

Figure 3.14 Pb token, 22 mm, 12 h, 8.09 g. Female bust right / B|VVPP. *TURS* 1546, Rostovtzeff and Prou, 1900: no. 439a.

---

¹¹⁰ *TURS* 1248.   ¹¹¹ *TURS* 1295–6.
¹¹² D'Ambra, 2014: 158–9. The abbreviation V.P. normally refers to a *vir perfectissimus* and the occurrence of VVPP here might refer to two such individuals, but it is hard to reconcile this hypothesis with the female portrait on the other side of this piece.
¹¹³ Women might also be named alongside their husbands on provincial coinage, and the phenomenon of female signatories appears to be concentrated in the first and second centuries AD. See Burnett, in press.

display of public benefaction in Rome because of the extensive influence and control of the imperial family; it was rather prosperous and densely populated towns outside of Rome that offered greater opportunity for visible participation in civic life and public commemoration.[114] Also like their male counterparts, women did partake of the civic life available to them in Rome, even if they were restricted in the types of public benefaction and commemoration available. Within this new landscape, both men and women performing an act of euergetism may have decided to underscore their munificence and prestige through the issuing of tokens, a small artefact that marked the occasion in a cityscape otherwise dominated by the imperial family.

Male portraits also appeared on tokens, and partnership between individuals was expressed. A token from the Tiber river, for example, carried a female portrait on one side accompanied by the legend CVRTIA FLACCI, with a male portrait accompanied by the legend FLACCVS on the other; one imagines a familial pairing is represented here.[115] Two individual men might also be named alongside each other, perhaps indicating a shared act of euergetism. This might take the form of both individuals being named on one side of the token (e.g. *TURS* 1495, with the legend SEVERI | ET | CRISPI), or a name given on each side of the token (e.g. *TURS* 1417, with the legend FLAC|CVS within a wreath on one side and GAL|LVS within a wreath on the other). Alternatively, both individuals may be named and provided with a portrait, as found on Figure 3.15.

Male portraits might also appear without an identifying legend. Pairs of individual portraits (male-male or male-female) also appear on the same side of a token facing each other.[116] These tokens formed statements of

Figure 3.15 Pb token, 18 mm, 12 h, 3.16 g. Male bust right, VERRES around / Male bust right, PROCVLVS around. *TURS* 1332, Rostovtzeff and Prou, 1900: no. 427b.

---

[114] Hemelrijk, 2015: 339–42. [115] *TURS* 1195; Tomassetti, 1887: 237, h. [116] *TURS* 1512–56.

connection between individuals. The representation of a portrait and legend naming an individual on a monetiform object closely resembles representations of the emperor on coinage; the phenomenon is also present on orichalcum tokens as shown and discussed in Figure 1.4.[117] In the same way that lower classes might use glass pastes to emulate the otherwise elite practice of gem wearing, so too tokens may have afforded the opportunity for individual Romans to present themselves in a manner similar to the emperor. The particular framework of representation, on an object that looked very similar to a coin, might have served to heighten the sense of prestige associated with the token and the benefaction it represented. Incidentally, the clear imitation of certain aspects of coinage clearly demonstrates the role this medium had in influencing the identities and mentalities of those who lived in the Roman Empire.

Full body representations of individuals are also found. Figure 1.8, for example, was issued by one Marcus Valerius Etruscus, son of Marcus. Rostovtzeff identified the figure on the token as Mercury, but he does not carry a caduceus and is wearing a toga; the representation may then be of Etruscus himself carrying a purse, a visual manifestation of the munificence the token represents. The entire image recalls a togate statue, and this elite medium may have been an intentional reference adopted here to communicate status.

Several token types specifically reference the office of the token issuer, a practice that served to emphasise the status of the individual. One example is that issued by Publius Tettius Rufus, whose token series displayed a curule chair flanked by fasces (Figure 3.16).[118] Rostovtzeff identified this individual with the Tettius Rufus who was praetor in the first century AD; he further compared the token with a coin series struck by Livineus Regulus in the late Republic (Figure 3.17).[119] Crawford believed that this coin type, and others struck by Regulus showing a beast fight and *modius* with corn-ears, referred to the curule office of two of Regulus' ancestors and the activities they performed as aediles.[120] The parallel with Republican coinage is instructive, particularly on a token that likely dates to the first century AD. Moneyers in the Roman Republic utilised coinage as vehicles to communicate familial history and prestige; towards the end of the Republic coinage was also frequently utilised to communicate contemporary ideologies.[121] Under Augustus individual references to moneyers and their familial history gradually disappeared from Roman coinage, part of the broader movement

---

[117] Rowan, 2020b. [118] *TURS* 517.
[119] *Prosop. Imp. Rom.*, III, 309, n. 104; Rostovtzeff, 1905b: 45; *RRC* 494/1–34.
[120] Crawford, 1974: vol. 1, 511. [121] Chantraine, 1983; Meadows and Williams, 2001.

Figure 3.16 Pb token, 22 mm, 12 h, 2.78 g. P·TETTIVS | RVFVS / Curule chair with three fasces on either side. *TURS* 517.

Figure 3.17 AR denarius, 4 h, 4.02 g, 42 BC. Bare head of Regulus right, REGVLVS PR. Border of dots / Curule chair with three fasces on either side, L·LIVINEIVS above, REGVLVS below. *RRC* 494/27.

towards the control of public monuments by the emperor.[122] But although references to moneyers disappear from Roman coinage, we still find references to office holding elites on tokens. During the imperial period these artefacts were able to operate in a communicative manner similar to the coinage of the Republic, albeit on a much reduced scale.

A variety of offices, both civic and religious, are referenced on lead tokens. Another representation of a curule chair flanked by three fasces appears on the token of one Herenn(ius) Ruf(us) who names himself as *curator*.[123] The curule chair also appears on a token with a male portrait on the other side, presumably the office holder and token issuer.[124] A *lituus*,

---

[122] Wallace-Hadrill, 1986: 79.   [123] *TURS* 516, Pl. IV, 34.
[124] *TURS* 518; see also *TURS* 519, which has the head of Medusa on one side and a curule chair on the other.

the emblem of an augur, appears on a token of M CAV|C·LF, which Rostovtzeff noted likely referred to a Marcus Caucidius or Caucilius, son of Lucius.[125] The *lituus* also appears on a token with the legend PCI, and another with SA, perhaps the initials of individuals, as well as on other types.[126] That an individual might reference their religious office while issuing a token is demonstrated by one T. Cornelius Paetus, whose tokens name him as both *pontifex* and *curator* (the other side carries the portrait of Tiberius and the legend TI AVGVSTVS).[127] Priestly offices are also referenced by the *apex*, worn by *pontifices, flamines* and *salii*.[128] One token carries an *apex* on one side and the legend PPS on the other, the three letters perhaps an abbreviated *tria nomina*.[129] An *apex* also appears on a token with what Rostovtzeff reported was perhaps a priestly attendant on the other side; another appears next to a palm branch on a token that bears Victory inscribing a shield on a column on the other side.[130] A token of this last type was recovered from the Tiber in Rome in the nineteenth century, while a mould half for making tokens decorated with a *lituus* has been found at Ostia.[131]

But while some tokens referenced particular offices, many more tokens naming individuals carried imagery connected to prosperity. Fortuna, Mercury and Victory, for example, are found on numerous specimens.[132] These same expressions of luck are found on Roman wall paintings; a shop in Pompeii on the street of Mercury, for example, had painted in the doorway an image of Mercury and Fortuna facing each other, a double statement of luck.[133] The choice of deities that evoked prosperity on tokens may be connected to their use context (e.g. festivals or feasting), or these may be the tokens of individuals who had not managed to hold an office.

The moneyers of the Roman Republic had also used visual puns to communicate their names, images called 'canting types' in numismatics. The moneyer Lucius Aquillius Florus, for example, placed a flower on some of the coins issued under his authority, while the moneyer Quintus Pomponeius Musa placed images of the muses on his coinage.[134] This

---

[125] *TURS* 1154.
[126] *TURS* 1077-8, 6 (with Germanicus), 260 (shrine), 778 (horse and legend CD), 1071 (lit altar), 1072 (altar), 1075 (ivy leaf), 1905 (Victory), 2121 (Diana), 2158 (stag and legend CD), 2192 (Fortuna), 2427 (cornucopia and legend ME), 2676 (Mercury), 3208 (sistrum, F L and D M as legends).
[127] *TURS* 514c; Rostovtzeff, 1905b: 49.
[128] On the wearing of the *apex* by the *pontifices* see Helbig, 1880: 492; Woytek, 2003: 120-1.
[129] *TURS* 1079. [130] *TURS* 1840.
[131] Rostovtzeff and Vaglieri, 1900: 266 no. 141; *TURS* 3596.
[132] See the types listed in *TURS* 1108ff. [133] Pompeii VI.7.9, discussed in Clarke, 2003: 85.
[134] *RIC* I^2 Augustus 308-9; *RRC* 410/2a-10b.

visual expression of a name (and hence a personal identity) is also found on other media in the Roman world: Pliny records that the architects of the *porticus Octaviae*, having been denied the right to be commemorated in an inscription, signed their names on a column with the image of a lizard (*saura* in ancient Greek) and a frog (*batrachos*), visual puns on their names Saura and Batrachus.[135] The remains of a bronze bench from the Forum of the Baths in Pompeii included legs shaped like a calf's legs, accompanied by the inscription M. NIGIDIVS VACCVLA P.S (a *vaccula* in Latin was a young cow, the P.S. is to be understood as *p(ecunia) s(ua)*, 'at his own expense').[136] Tombstones also carried such references: representations of mice were at times placed on the tombstones of individuals with the name *Mus*, and one Tiberius Octavius Diadumenianus was referenced on his tombstone through a representation of Polykleitos' *Diadoumenos* statue ('diadem bearer').[137]

It is thus unsurprising to find canting types on tokens of the imperial period. The token of a Publius Glitius Gallus displays the name and portrait of Gallus on one side and a rooster carrying a wreath and palm branch on the other (*gallus* was Latin for rooster) (Figure 3.18). Rostovtzeff believed this was the Gallus named in the conspiracy of Piso, but another Publius Glitius Gallus is also known from the first century AD; equally this may be a third, otherwise unknown,

Figure 3.18 Pb token, 19 mm, 12 h, 2.66 g. Male head right, P GLITI GALLI around / Rooster standing right holding a wreath and palm branch. *TURS* 1238, Rowan, 2020b: no. 57.

---

[135] Plin. *HN* 36.42. Winckelmann believed he had identified this precise column, see MacCartney, 1919: 59.
[136] *CIL* X, 818.
[137] *Mus*: *CIL* VI, 16771 and VI, 38411; discussion in MacCartney, 1919: 60. The tombstone of Diadumenianus is now in the Vatican Museums, see Anguissola, 2014 for a discussion.

individual.[138] A token with the legend AQ|VIL on one side and an eagle (in Latin *aquila*) on the other is also a further probable canting type.[139] One P. Asellius Fortunatus issued a token with a representation of Fortuna on one side and a star and crescent on the other.[140] A calf was also depicted on a token accompanied by the legend VITLA, which Rostovtzeff interpreted as the name *Vit(u)la*.[141]

There may be many more instances of visual punning that we can no longer recognise: if a calf or a mouse appears on a token without an accompanying name, we cannot know if the image served as a visual pun on the name of an individual. The (possible) use of visual puns without accompanying legends might have occurred because the meaning would have been self-evident to the user, who knew the name of the token issuer. The use of such puns may have been designed to bring a smile to the face of the user (particularly in the case of the wreath-toting rooster), or to further emphasise the individual responsible for the particular benefaction.

Moneyers in the Roman Republic could select coin types that reflected the prestige and achievements of their *gens*. Tokens presumably offered a similar communicative opportunity. And yet there seem little, if any, token types connected to familial history. There may be several reasons for this divergence. In spite of their similar physical appearance, coins and tokens may have been conceived of very differently in the Roman world: while Republican coinage was linked to Juno Moneta and Roman memory, tokens may have had different associations, and hence attracted a different type of design.[142] There may also have been a shift in self-presentation in the imperial period. In the Republic moneyers, at the beginning of their careers, were limited to representations of ancestral achievement. But under the principate, which focused on the achievements of a living individual, elite self-representation shifted. Augustus and his successors presented themselves as models of patronage to be imitated; instead of civil war or military conflict, elite competition and display focused upon public benefaction. Those who participated in such activity also widened, with an increased number of equestrians and decurions undertaking these activities.[143] The position of token issuers, who may have been participating in an act of euergetism for a particular group, was very different to that

---

[138] Rostovtzeff, 1905b: 104; Tac. *Ann.* 15.56.71; *PIR* II 119, n. 166. For the other Gallus, who held numerous magisterial positions, see *CIL* XI, 3097 and 3098.
[139] *TURS* 1132.   [140] *TURS* 1137.   [141] *TURS* 1508, Pl. XI, 42.
[142] On Republican coinage, memory and Juno Moneta see Cheung, 1998; Meadows and Williams, 2001.
[143] Nicols, 2014: 106–8, 115.

of moneyers in the Republic, and this context may have resulted in a preference to emphasise the individual rather than the historical achievements of a *gens*.

Several token types are very close or identical to the designs found on gems and glass pastes. These objects were often incorporated into signet rings and used as seals, forming a visual representation of a particular person. Worn on the body, the objects (and their imagery) were personal markers of status and identity.[144] Many of the designs on tokens, gems and glass pastes are drawn from a broader repertoire of imagery within the Roman world: from political and elite images, from imagery considered to have protective properties, the imagery of deities, of the circus, and of objects encountered in daily life.[145] In his exploration of the practice of everyday life, de Certeau examined the effect individuals have on their environments. By adopting and manipulating the elite culture around them, he argued that people might make this 'language' their own. What is not chosen in this context is as significant as what is chosen.[146] Viewed from this perspective, the selection of particular elite images for use in a non-elite context (whether on a glass paste, or a token issued by someone outside the elite) are powerful acts that transform imagery, making it significant to the identity of an individual or group.[147] But the frequency with which other, non-elite, imagery is chosen (e.g. allusions to chariot racing, Fortuna, or mice) should also be kept in mind. Although some individuals chose to represent themselves via particular elite imagery, others, it seems, found other representations more meaningful in this context.

Given the parallels in imagery between gems and tokens we cannot rule out the idea that some designs on tokens may have been intended to replicate the issuer's intaglio stamp, which would have been used in other contexts and recognised within a certain circle as representative of a particular individual. Indeed, tokens and seals that carried the signet ring design of a particular individual might be viewed as 'media of the body' in that they acted to extend the presence of a particular person in time and

---

[144] Henig, 1978: 19; Platt, 2006: 247; Yarrow, 2018. Gem impressions are occasionally found on tokens in Italy; whether this was because the token formed a useful soft material in a workshop to test a design, or for some other purpose relating to the exchange and validity of tokens, is not certain. See Arzone and Marinello, 2019: no. 282 (two identical gem impressions on a worn token).

[145] Catalogues of this material include Zwierlein-Diehl, 1969; Brandt et al., 1972; Henig, 1978 and Vitellozzi, 2010 with discussions in Maderna-Lauter, 1988 and Yarrow, 2018.

[146] de Certeau, 1984: 32, 98–9.   [147] Maderna-Lauter, 1988: 446; Yarrow, 2018: 31–49.

space.¹⁴⁸ In Roman Athens, tokens were often countermarked with particular designs (e.g. 'stork and lizard' and 'dolphin') thought to reflect particular issuers.¹⁴⁹ Alternatively, similar to glass pastes, tokens may have formed an accessible medium for those outside the elite to display the types of imagery seen on more expensive media. The image of an ant seen from above (at times carrying a seed), for example, is known on tokens, gems and glass pastes.¹⁵⁰ On tokens the ant is paired with legends that might be names (e.g. LAR on *TURS* 455), imperial imagery (e.g. a Capricorn, *TURS* 488), as well as more obvious references to individual and familial identity (e.g. the legend AVRELIAE on *TURS* 1141). These different iterations of the same image (ant), combined with different imagery and legends, reflect the process of appropriation that took place in the Roman world, as a language of images was manipulated to express particular identities.

Some tokens carried fantastical and humorous imagery, which is also found on gems. The image of an elephant emerging from a shell, for example, is found on both media (Figure 3.19).¹⁵¹ On the image reproduced here the design is paired with Victory; an elephant emerging from a shell is also paired with a phoenix and appears on the lead tokens of Ephesus.¹⁵² A token in Berlin appears to show a rhinoceros emerging from a shell, with the legend SPE on the other side – various

Figure 3.19 Pb token, 18 mm, 12 h, 3.28 g. Victory standing right with wreath in right hand and palm branch in left / Head of an elephant emerging from a shell right. *TURS* 1903, *BMCRLT* 810.

---

[148] Belting, 2011: 63; Marshman, 2017: 144.
[149] Lang and Crosby, 1964: 88, 116; Gkikaki, 2019: 132–4.
[150] For example, *TURS* 447–56; BM 1756,0102.33, 1814,0704.1449, 1987,0212.393, 1987,0212.395, 1987,0212.397, 1900,0517.4.
[151] Brandt et al., 1972: no. 2371 (with palm branch beneath); Henig, 1984.
[152] Phoenix: *TURS* (Supplement) 3692 = Rowan, 2020b: no. 72. Ephesus: Gülbay and Kireç, 2008: no. 40a (misidentified).

Figure 3.20 Pb token, 19 mm, 12 h, 5.73 g. Helmeted bust right of Roma or Minerva right / Fantastic creature with the head of a horse, legs of a rooster, mask of Silenus on the right side, and a ram's head on the left; sceptre behind. *TURS* 2897, *BMCRLT* 343.

animals emerging from shells served as a popular motif for gems.[153] The *gryllus* or caricature is also found on tokens, consisting of a creature with the head of a horse, legs of a rooster and a body made up of a mask of Silenus and a ram's head (Figure 3.20). The same image is also known from gems.[154] These fantastical representations fall into the same category as other comical and absurd imagery, for example mice in chariots. Although the humour of these representations might have appealed to the owners of these pieces, the imagery also had the potential to serve an apotropaic function.[155] The imagery chosen for intaglios and tokens therefore might simultaneously communicate a particular identity and protect the individual concerned. These images may also have expressed a desire for prosperity, similar to the imagery of Fortuna and Mercury mentioned above.[156]

Identity might also be communicated through language. Although the overwhelming majority of tokens from Italy bear legends in Latin, several token series are in Greek. These might carry references to individuals or a *gens*: the ΙΟΥΛ on *TURS* 1250 is likely a reference to a Julius, or the Julian clan. The design of this token is linked to the cult of Asclepius through the representation of the head of the deity and his serpent-entwined staff. Another token bears the legend ΔΙΟ|ΓΕΝ, a probable reference to a Diogenes (Fortuna is shown on the other side).[157] Figure 3.21 shows

---

[153] *TURS* 463; Richter, 1956:110; Henig, 1984: 244.
[154] Zwierlein-Diehl, 1969: no. 550. Two further examples can be found in the Santarelli collection, see Del Bufalo, 2009: 26 no. n.i.25/85a and 32 no. n.i.47/91g.
[155] Henig, 1984: 244. See Plut. *Quaest. conv.* 5.7.3 for the idea that strange images drew away the evil eye, protecting the wearer.
[156] Sagiv, 2018: 51 notes that many composite or fantastical images are comprised of elements relating to wealth and fertility.
[157] *TURS* 1406.

Figure 3.21 Pb token, 19 mm, 12 h, 4.96 g. CWC|IOY / Bare male head right (Gaius Sosius?). *TURS* 1319, Rostovtzeff and Prou, 1900: no. 432.

a bare male head facing right, accompanied by the legend CWC|IOY on the other side. Rostovtzeff identified this as the Gaius Sosius who originally served as a general of Marc Antony before defecting to Octavian and who was responsible for the temple of Apollo Sosianus in Rome.[158] The style of the portrait is appropriate for the time period of Sosius' life; indeed, the image is reminiscent of the upward-gazing portraits of Alexander the Great. The choice of Greek for these tokens was not only a statement of identity on behalf of the issuer, it was also a statement made by the creator of the token for his audience: the users of these pieces presumably also knew Greek (or else would have known enough to have been suitably impressed by the appearance of Greek in this context).

Indeed, the frequent use of (often very abbreviated) legends on tokens is an important source of evidence for levels and types of literacy in antiquity. The use of legends on tokens, particularly on tokens that carry nothing but a legend as in Figure 3.1, suggests that both the creators and users of tokens were able to recognise these brief texts. The closest parallel to the abbreviated and frequently (to modern eyes) cryptic combinations of letters found on tokens are perhaps the painted inscriptions (*tituli picti*) carried on *amphorae*.[159] When examining these inscriptions, Woolf advocated seeing writing as a set of graphic symbols to be interpreted, with different types of writing (commercial, funerary, military inscriptions) employing different conventions to communicate their message to the reader. Woolf focused on the painted messages on Dressel 20 *amphorae*, which required an understanding of the conventions and systems used by all those involved. Similarly, the creators and users of tokens were likely to have understood the conventions of this particular medium: abbreviated *tria nomina*, for

---

[158] Rostovtzeff and Prou, 1900: no. 432; Shipley, 1930. [159] Woolf, 2015.

example, the occasional use of interpuncts to distinguish between words (e.g. between P and Tettius on Figure 3.16), and recognising that the central dot on these artefacts was related to manufacture rather than any specific message (see Chapter 1).

Indeed, given that tokens were manufactured for a specific audience, only a relatively small group of people needed to understand the conventions employed; the varying designs of tokens between regions suggests that, unlike Dressel 20 *amphorae*, the semiotic system was local to a particular region. In the Latin-speaking West, regions might produce semiotic conventions for tokens within the broader framework of everyday Latin, but each development appears to have been unique. For example, the tokens of Lyon utilise two and three letter Latin legends that appear to be *tria nomina*, but the tokens of this region also make greater use of accompanying signs (e.g. palm branches or ivy-leaves) than similar tokens found in Rome and Ostia.[160] The local form and design of tokens, in this sense, must also have contributed to a sense of local community through semiotic conventions.

Identity through Work

A wide variety of material culture attests to the fact that many in the Roman world identified themselves through their work. Funerary monuments might display the deceased at work, or specifically mention their vocation.[161] The tomb of Eurysaces the baker at the Porta Maggiore in Rome epitomises this phenomenon: this large tomb carries cylindrical spaces which are thought to represent the cavities in which dough is kneaded, the activities of the bakery are shown in relief towards the top of the tomb and Eurysaces is named as a baker (*pistor*) and contractor (*redemptor*) in the inscription.[162] Tokens too carry statements of identity that refer to work. In several instances tokens and their imagery also appear to have reinforced feelings of belonging between members of a *collegium*. This is explored here through two case studies: representations of porters (*saccarii*), and the tokens referring to the coachmen (*cisiarii*) who ferried individuals between Ostia and Rome.

Several tokens carry images of *saccarii*, the porters who carried goods from ships to warehouses along the docks in Ostia and Portus.[163] Figure 3.22 is one such example, issued by an individual named Quintus Fabius Speratus (otherwise unknown). A *saccarius* is also

---

[160] On the tokens from Lyon see Dissard, 1905; Turcan, 1987: 62–4; Wilding, 2020.
[161] Joshel, 1992.   [162] Coarelli, 2007: 205.
[163] Martelli, 2013 on the *saccarii* and their representation more broadly.

Identity through Work 115

Figure 3.22 Pb token, 18 mm, 12 h, 3.21 g. *Saccarius* standing left holding a sack or *dolium* on his shoulders and with right arm raised / Q·FAB·SPE around. *TURS* 1033, Rostovtzeff and Prou, 1900: no. 418b.

portrayed on lead tokens accompanied by the legend AGM or OBB on the other side, or the representation of three corn-ears.[164] Although one might be tempted to link these lead tokens with the mechanics surrounding the operations of the port, these specimens are more likely to be connected to acts of communality and euergetism.[165] If we accept that the three letter legends AGM and OBB may be initials (although we cannot be certain), then three out of the four token types carrying representations of *saccarii* appear to carry personal names, likely advertising an act of munificence for a broader group. There is enough evidence to suggest the *saccarii* of Portus had joined together into a larger, more formal community – the Theodosian code mentions an organisation which might well be a *collegium, corpus, sodalicium* or similar association, while epigraphic evidence suggests a funerary organisation for this group of workers.[166] Commensality, for example communal banquets, would have acted as an occasion in which the identity of the group was made salient and internal hierarchies reinforced; if tokens played a role on these occasions their imagery would have served to further this process.[167] The representation of *saccarii* at work in numerous port scenes (e.g. carrying sacks of 'things' (*res*) on the Isis Giminiana fresco found in a tomb from the Porta Laurentina) demonstrates that these workers had a specific iconography, and were seen as integral to the harbour and its operations.

[164] *TURS* 1034-6. [165] Facella, 2004: 53; Martelli, 2013: 18, 105-6.
[166] *Cod. Theod.* 14.22 (*De saccariis Portus Romae*) discussed in Virlouvet, 2015: 675. See Tran, 2008: 298 for discussion of a *cippus* that recorded the sepulchral concession of the *saccarii*; see also Martelli, 2013: 101 for the possibility of group burial at Isola Sacra. The idea that *collegia* were mainly funerary organisations, however, has been discredited, see van Nijf, 2002: 308.
[167] van Nijf, 2002: 325-30 on commensality in *collegia*.

Figure 3.23 Orichalcum token, 20 mm, 5 h, 7.3 g. Laureate head of Augustus left, within wreath / *Saccarius* standing front holding an amphora over his shoulder; XV in field right. Cohen vol. VIII, 254 no. 101, BnF 16979.

An orichalcum token also shows a *saccarius* carrying an amphora over his shoulder (Figure 3.23).[168] The issue is part of a broader series of orichalcum tokens (including the so-called *spintriae*) issued during the Julio-Claudian period, likely by a workshop in Rome that produced pieces for a variety of individuals or groups.[169] The *saccarius* is nude and decidedly more heroic-looking than on the lead token, although amphora-carrying *saccarii* are also shown nude on marble reliefs. Figure 3.24, for example, shows nude *saccarii* each carrying an amphora off a ship. The porters walk towards three officials, one of whom gives the rightmost *saccarius* an object. The object was thought by Rickman to be a token; he suggested this was a method of ensuring the number of *amphorae* leaving the ship was the same as that entering the warehouse.[170] The precise shape of the object is difficult to discern, but it does not appear to be a small circular token; rather it seems a longer, more rectangular object.

High quality orichalcum tokens and marble reliefs might be thought beyond the financial means of harbour porters, but Virlouvet makes a convincing case that the group comprising the *saccarii* may have also included the officials involved in the transport and distribution of goods beyond the port. The monopoly afforded the *saccarii* in the Theodosian Code, as well as the honours and activities recorded for *saccarii* in Italy and elsewhere in the Empire (e.g. reserved seats in the theatre at Smyrna,

---

[168] The figure was misidentified as Hercules with a club by Cohen. Martelli, 2013: 101 argues that in the absence of evidence for other types of worker (e.g. *amphorarii*), we should conclude *saccarii* carried *amphorae* in Rome's port.

[169] Rowan, 2020b.

[170] Rickman, 1971: 321–2; Keay, 2018: 162 and fig. 27. The mosaic outside *statio* 25 of the Piazzale delle Corporazioni shows a clothed *saccarius* carrying an amphora over his shoulder.

Figure 3.24 Marble relief showing *saccarii* offloading *amphorae* from a ship, 43 × 33 cm. Found in Portus, now in the Torlonia collection (inv. no. 428).

a statue at Perinthus) suggests this group was wealthier than scholarship has traditionally thought.[171] The token and the relief, then, might have been created by one of the *saccarii*, or else the physical identity of these workers was utilised by another group to communicate a port scene, or the abundance of supplies their work ensured.

Virlouvet notes that although *saccarii* frequently appear in mosaics, frescoes and reliefs, they rarely have a central role – the tokens are important exceptions to this rule.[172] Their presence in the 'background' of life in Rome's ports was also physically manifest in the small terracotta figures of *saccarii* found throughout Ostia. Martelli's study of the findspots of these pieces led her to suggest that these were representations of the Genius of the college of the *saccarii*; if she is correct we may also have a Genius represented on the lead tokens discussed above (Figure 3.22). In Ostia, these small statues are mainly found in public places: in niches and locations frequented by numerous people. Whoever erected these figures and whatever their motivation, it is clear that the image of a *saccarius* formed an important backdrop to Ostia; we should not be surprised, then, that they figure so frequently in port scenes.[173] The figure of the *saccarius* was not

[171] Virlouvet, 2015.   [172] Virlouvet, 2015: 678.
[173] Martelli, 2013: 115–18; Virlouvet, 2015: 681–3.

only important to the identity of the porters and their associates, but to the maritime identity of Ostia as a port settlement.

The second example I wish to explore is the assemblage of tokens found in the baths of the *cisiarii* in Ostia. The *cisiarii* were drivers who transported passengers between Ostia and Rome, named for their two-wheeled vehicle, the *cisium*.[174] A bathhouse that may have belonged to the *collegium* of these drivers (perhaps of a semi-public character) has been excavated on the north side of the *Decumanus* in Ostia, near the Porta Romana.[175] Although the baths and their finds have not yet been studied in detail, the surviving decoration reveals a scheme that evoked bathing, the sea, diversion and entertainment, as well as the work of the *cisiarii* themselves. In the frigidarium (Room C) a black and white mosaic depicts city walls at the very edge of the room, likely representing Rome, and a second set of city walls are placed in the centre, likely representing Ostia. Between these walls *cisiarii* are depicted with their carriages, with the names of the mules at times included.[176] Mosaics in other rooms carry maritime motifs (room B), representations of athletes (room E) and a scene of an animal fight (room A). Stucco reliefs in room F depict *gorgoneia*, sea monsters, Nereids, Mercury and erotes. The entirety communicates to the user a setting of relaxation and entertainment within a port city at the gate where the *cisiarii* presumably collected and dropped off their customers.

Spagnoli has recently published the assemblage of forty tokens coming from the 1972–3 excavations of the complex, all coming from Room C, the frigidarium with the mosaic showing the *cisiarii*.[177] The frigidarium, as well as the larger complex, was constructed during the reign of Hadrian on the site of an existing structure; the tokens (which are interpreted by Spagnoli as a single assemblage that was dispersed) come from strata that date to after the construction period and before the renovation of the room towards the end of the third century – that is, towards the end of the second century (late Antonine) and beginning of the Severan era.[178] More specifically, eighteen tokens were found in 'C2', a fill layer, along with an *as* of Lucilla.[179] Five tokens were found in 'C5', another fill layer, alongside two coins of Gordian I, two further illegible coins, hairpins and ceramic fragments, and other finds. Two tokens were found in 'C1' alongside an illegible *as*, and a further two in 'C7', which was a cleaning context. Ten tokens were found in 'C4,

---

[174] Malmberg, 2011: 369–71. [175] Meiggs, 1973: 419.
[176] For a description, plan and photographs see www.ostia-antica.org/regio2/2/2-3.htm.
[177] Spagnoli, 2017b. [178] Spagnoli, 2017b: 186. [179] *RIC* III Marcus Aurelius 1780.

settore F', the fill of a cut, alongside illegible coins, lamps, an incised gem, a gold bead, hairpins, glass pastes, an earring and fragments of glass and ceramics. Two were found in 'C3', a fill stratum beneath a restored mosaic. A further token from 'C6' was found with two *quadrantes* and a *semis*, nine further illegible coins and ceramic fragments.[180] As with many other archaeological excavations of tokens in Italy, fill contexts dominate here, a phenomenon discussed in further detail in Chapter 5.

Several of the tokens from these baths specifically reference the work of the *cisiarii*. Three tokens found in the baths were of the same type, carrying a wheel on one side and a whip on the other, a reference to the *cisium* the drivers used, and the whips they carried (indeed, they are pictured carrying whips in the mosaic in the bathhouse).[181] A token of the same design is shown in Figure 3.25; the addition of the palm branch next to the whip expresses the same sense of festivity that other decorative motifs in the baths capture. Two further tokens were found with the legend CI|SI on one side and an amphora on the other; the legend likely refers to the *cisiarii* or the bathing establishment.[182] It seems probable that these particular tokens were connected with the *cisiarii* in some way, an expression of identity through work as also seen on the mosaic in the bathhouse. *Cisiarii* are also represented at work driving their carriages on tombstones elsewhere in the

Figure 3.25 Pb token, 21 mm, 12 h, 4.43 g. Wheel with eight spokes / Whip on left, next to palm branch on right. *TURS* 832.

---

[180] The *quadrantes* were *RIC* I² Nero 317, and an anonymous *quadrans* (*RIC* II 28). The *semis* was *RIC* II Hadrian 625 = *RIC* II.3² Hadrian 624).
[181] Spagnoli, 2017b: nos. 5–7. Nos. 5 and 6 were found in 'C2', no. 7 in 'C5'.
[182] *TURS* Supplement 3607; Spagnoli, 2017b: nos. 21–2.

Roman world.[183] The baths of the *cisiarii* had two bars (H and J). If the tokens were issued directly by an establishment in the bathhouse, the reference to the *cisiarii* would have reinforced the decorative scheme found in the frigidarium, furthering a sense of identity for the establishment itself – a bathhouse whose public image was closely connected to that of the carriage drivers, and perhaps owned by them. We possess other tokens that carry the names of bathhouses (discussed further in Chapter 5), which suggest these objects were issued in connection with specific establishments.

The remaining tokens found in the Terme dei *Cisiarii* were decorated with the following types:

- elephant / Fortuna
- Fortuna (or Felicitas) / AF[.]
- standing figure / LCF
- anchor / palm branch (2 examples)
- anchor / H E followed by an illegible third letter (7 examples)
- phallus / scales (2 examples)
- amphora / *dolium* (2 examples)
- S C V within wreath / blank (2 examples)
- D / C (2 examples)
- retrograde F / retrograde S (4 examples)
- EK / I (2 examples)
- EK / II
- ЄC / I
- head of a calf / illegible
- AC above MV within wreath / illegible image within wreath (2 examples)
- illegible (4 examples)

The images of Fortuna and the phallus and scales evoke prosperity and wealth (as did the image of Mercury in the surviving stucco), while the elephant recalls the animal fight mosaic in Room A. The anchor is a maritime motif that evokes Ostia's role as a port. The tokens and their imagery would have interacted in the context of their environment: within the community of the *cisiarii*, the bathhouse, and the city of Ostia more broadly. Along with the broader decorative scheme of the baths, they would also have evoked a particular emotional response fitting for Roman bathing: a sense of diversion, of prosperity, and the

---

[183] A carriage driver in a *cisium* approaching a milestone is shown on a funerary monument now in the Rheinische Landesmuseum Trier, inv. no. 1931,276. Another funerary relief in the museum shows a carriage driver above a ship, inv. no. 11408.

anticipation of food, oil and/or beverages (e.g. the amphora and *dolium*).[184] The imagery of the tokens and the bathhouse would have served to call forth the identities of the users, while also communicating that identity to others: the finds of hairpins and the earring suggest the bathhouse was also used by women, a group beyond the immediate community of the carriage drivers.[185]

Other tokens also carry reference to specific occupations. *TURS* 1058 carries the image of a sculptor working on a statue (perhaps Victory) placed on a column; Rostovtzeff interpreted this as the representation of an artisan, but the nude figure might equally be a representation of Prometheus sculpting Man (also a popular image for gems).[186] *TURS* 1059 shows a mallet on one side and a pair of tongs on the other, a probable reference to metalworking. Other references are less certain; the image of a foot, for example, might reference a shoemaker, but this cannot be securely established.[187] Further study of tokens will only further elucidate their role, but the case studies discussed here demonstrate the variety of individuals who issued and used tokens, as well as their role in contributing to moments of 'Groupness' and a sense of community among particular professions and the establishments they frequented.

Beyond Rome

Far fewer tokens have been found in Italy outside of Rome and Ostia. Several of those that have been uncovered, however, carry clear expressions of particular identities. Two tokens, both of which carry the portrait and name of the emperor Claudius, appear to name specific settlements. The first example refers to a *colonia Veneria* with the legend COLO VEN, accompanied by the representation of Venus standing with her left hand resting on a Cupid, who holds a rudder.[188] It is unclear which of the multiple settlements that were a *colonia Veneria* this refers to; the two

---

[184] On the role of the 'everyday aesthetic' in evoking a particular emotional response see Highmore, 2011: 9, 17.

[185] See Ward, 1992 on women and Roman bathing.

[186] With thanks to David Meadows @rogueclassicist for this suggestion. The token is shown in *TURS* Pl. X, 65.

[187] *TURS* Supplement 3662. A chained cobbler is shown with a foot form above his head on a fourth century AD mosaic from Kalibia in Tunisia; Ben Abed, 2006: 148–9. Erotes in a painted cobbler scene from Herculaneum also have model feet above their heads (Museo Archeologico Nazionale di Napoli, inv. no. MN 719).

[188] Stannard Liri 29.015; Mitchiner, 1984: no. 4; with discussion in Rowan, in press a.

known specimens of this type came from the Garigliano and Liri rivers respectively.[189] The second token type bears the legend FLORENTIA MART accompanied by a standing female figure holding a patera and flower, with a rudder on a globe (?) placed on her right. This may be a reference to the colony of Florentia (modern day Florence), accompanied by the representation of a tutelary deity, or a deity that acted as a pun on the settlement's name (*florentia* in Latin referred to blooming).[190]

A token found during excavations of an inner fortification wall in Rocca di Monfalcone in northern Italy carries what is likely a Genius on one side and Hercules on the other.[191] Whether this was the Genius of the settlement, or of a particular community within the area, is impossible to know. Also in northern Italy, in Aquileia, a token found near the circus carried the diademed head of a personification of the city, although the authenticity of this piece is doubtful.[192] A bronze token series carries the city goddess of Aquileia enthroned with a mural crown on her head. She holds a cornucopia in her right hand, and is accompanied by the legend AQVILEIA FELIX, with a reference to the warehouses (*horrea*) of the city (HORR AQVIL) within a wreath on the other side. A variant on this type with a *modius* on the reverse has been identified as a forgery, and a thorough re-examination of the series and the finds from Aquileia is needed to establish whether the *horreum* type too belongs to a series of forgeries that seem to date to the eighteenth century.[193]

Reported finds also reveal the use of tokens to consolidate local cultic identity. The token finds from Nemi and its surrounds include three specimens carrying imagery connected to the goddess Diana. One displayed the Ephesian Artemis on one side with the legend DIA on the other, another displayed Diana in a tunic carrying a bow with the legend LRP|C on the other side, and the third represented Diana with

---

[189] Mitchiner, 1984: no. 4 (erroneous reading of the type) reportedly from the Garigliano; the other specimen is from Stannard's unpublished catalogue of lead said to come from the Liri.

[190] London Ancient Coins, Auction 60, 14 February 2017, no. 363; Rowan, in press a. Cristian Mondello is currently preparing a catalogue of the lead tokens housed in the National Archaeological Museum of Florence and reports that no specimen of the FLORENTIA type is among the collection.

[191] Visonà, 1980: 347, no. 1. A second token carrying an image of Trajan was also found, as well as twelve coins ranging from the third century BC to the seventeenth century AD.

[192] Maionica, 1899; Buora, 2008: 110.

[193] Maionica, 1899: 105; Buora, 2008: 112. A piece in Berlin, initially published by de Belfort, is also likely to be of this type; see de Belfort, 1892: 176 and Berlin Münzkabinett 18203250, https://ikmk.smb.museum/object?id=18203250.

a bow and a stag shown on the other side.[194] Nemi was renowned for its sanctuary to Diana Nemorensis, located on the northern shore of the lake.[195] One of the best-known representations of the goddess today is the tripartite statue representing Diana as Luna, Diana and Hecate (i.e. Diana as huntress, as the moon, and of the underworld). An excellent representation of the statue can be found on coinage of the late Republic issued by the moneyer Publius Accoleius Lariscolus.[196] On this coin three statues, representing the three aspects of Diana, stand side by side with their arms raised and with a cypress grove behind them (Figure 3.26). But the token evidence and the other remains from the site reveal that the worship of the goddess at Nemi was complex, encompassing her role as a huntress, and, if the votives are any indication, as a healing deity.[197] The varied representations of Diana on tokens fit well with this diversity.

Four tokens found at Nemi carry the representation of three female figures standing frontally with their arms raised. Two specimens carried the legend COR | THAL on the other side; one reported by Catalli and another found as a stray find near the lake in the nineteenth century.[198] A further two tokens with this imagery bore the legend APOL within a wreath on the other side; both were found during the

Figure 3.26 AR denarius, 1 h, 3.82 g. Bust of Diana Nemorensis right, draped; P·ACCOLEIVS LARISCOLVS around. Border of dots / Triple cult statue of Diana Nemorensis (Diana, Hecate and Luna) facing; behind, cypress grove. Border of dots. *RRC* 486/1.

---

[194] Catalli, 2013: *tessera* 2 (Diana of Ephesus of type *TURS* 2151), *tessera* 3 (with legend LRP | C, a previously unpublished type whose legend is not yet understood) and *tessera* 4 (with stag, of type *TURS* 2116). The tokens are presented among the coins from the excavations of the terrace and nymphaeum (1989–2009 excavations), but no further find information is given.
[195] Green, 2007.   [196] Green, 2007: 134–5; *RRC* 486/1.   [197] Romano, 2007: 73–161.
[198] Type *TURS* 1193 = Overbeck, 2001: no. 189; Catalli, 2013: *tessera* 1; Tomassetti, 1887: 281. Rostovtzeff suggested the legend might be understood as a name, for example Cor(nelius) Thal(lus) or similar.

early twentieth century excavations of the theatre and the regions SSW and NNE of the structure.[199] The image was identified as the Three Graces by Rostovtzeff. However, the three figures have their hands raised. Representations of the Three Graces normally show the three figures resting their arms on each other's shoulders. The three figures on the token look similar to the triple cult statue of Diana Nemorensis as displayed on the Republican coin, but without the attributes held in the hand of each goddess, and (unlike Figure 3.26) without the sacred grove above.

But the image is also unlikely to be a representation of the cult statue of Diana Nemorensis. The same image, of three women standing frontally, each with their hands raised, is also found on a variety of other tokens, many without connection to Nemi (e.g. Figure 3.27). This image is variously labelled as 'Hecate' or the 'Three Graces' in Rostovtzeff's catalogue, although the image is the same. Hecate is also an unsatisfactory interpretation of the image, since Hecate is normally shown via three female figures standing back-to-back as 'Hecate *triformis*', even on coinage and on tokens.[200] Moreover, lead tokens also carry the image of *two* women standing frontally with their arms raised, which Rostovtzeff suggested was a representation of two *aurae* (winds).[201] What is a more likely interpretation of all these representations is that they show women with their hands open and arms

Figure 3.27 Pb token, 19 mm, 12 h, 4,15 g. L VOLV|SI PRIMI (*L. Volusi Primi*) / Three women standing frontally with arms raised. *TURS* 1345, Rostovtzeff and Prou, 1900: no. 430f1.

---

[199] *NSc.* 1931, 281. The type was unknown to Rostovtzeff and is entered into the tokens database as Nemi 1, https://coins.warwick.ac.uk/token-types/id/nemi1.
[200] For example, *RPC* III no. 386, VII.1 no. 482; *TURS* 2469; Rostovtzeff and Prou, 1900: 414.
[201] *TURS* 1599, Pl. VI, 17.

raised in the traditional Roman *orans* stance associated with prayer or adoration. Although the representation of women in the *orans* stance is perhaps more commonly known from Christian art, it was also a well-known position in the Graeco-Roman period. The (admittedly restored) sculpture of Livia from Ocriculum is one such example, thought to have been placed next to a statue of *Divus* Augustus, highlighting Livia's role as priestess of his cult.[202] Livia's statue became a model for other representations of elite women (with two variations, '*orans A*' and '*orans B*').[203] The image of a woman with both arms raised was also the representation of *pietas* found on imperial coinage from the reign of Trajan.[204] Coinage connected to the saecular games of Domitian show women kneeling with their arms raised in prayer, which likely represents the prayers to Juno given by Roman matrons as part of the ceremonies.[205]

It is therefore likely that the representations of women with raised hands, found on tokens at Nemi and elsewhere in Italy, represent female worshippers, or perhaps even female priests. Tokens showing three women standing behind each other facing left, each with one right arm raised, also likely show worshippers in a procession or priestesses.[206] If these tokens were distributed to worshippers, the users may have been encouraged to identify themselves in the image. The tokens might have been connected to worship, or to the theatre or baths connected to the cult complex.[207] We see a similar phenomenon in the votives left by women at Nemi: the votive terracottas found at the site are thought to represent donors, while the anatomical votives and objects of personal adornment offered would also have carried with them the personal identity and prayers of the dedicants.[208] If the image referenced priestesses, then the tokens served to communicate their role in the maintenance of the cult, just as the tokens issued by priests in Palmyra highlighted their role in particular cultic banquets.[209] Unlike the tokens of Palmyra, however, which named individual priests, these female representations remain anonymous,

---

[202] Museo Pio-Clementino, Sala dei busti, inv. no. 637; Collins-Clinton, 2000: 115–16. The *orans* pose is often equated with the mention of the statue of the worshipping (*adorantem*) woman by Euphranor, mentioned by Plin. *HN* 34.78.
[203] Collins-Clinton, 2000: 115.
[204] For example, *RIC* II Trajan 392; Woytek, 2010: nos. 9, 17, 28.
[205] *RIC* I² Domitian 610–11; Scheid, 1998: 24; Sobocinski, 2006: 592.
[206] *TURS* 2465, Pl. VIII no. 28. See also *TURS* 2956 (three women, clothed, proceeding left).
[207] Hänninen, 2000: 47 discusses the idea the baths and theatre were there to serve visitors to the sanctuary.
[208] Hänninen, 2000: 46.   [209] Raja, 2015.

and largely standardised: the frequent use of three women across multiple token series suggests this was a well used and recognised image. Whatever the particular reference, it is clear that tokens formed a part of the materiality of cultic experience, a theme that will be explored in greater detail in Chapter 4.

Only a small amount of the surviving lead tokens could be discussed here; the larger corpus still offers a rich amount of examples for the student of identities in the Roman world. The examples presented here were chosen to demonstrate the potential of this source base for studies of this kind. Tokens offer us an insight into the identities of a broad segment of the populations of Rome, Ostia and Portus, and reveal the moments in which 'Groupness' might become apparent or particular identities made salient. Tokens also reveal how particular imagery and personas interacted within the broader landscape of Rome and its harbour. The events and contexts in which tokens were used served as moments that consolidated feelings of community and belonging. The use of tokens (creating a sense of community between the 'haves' in contrast to the 'have nots') and the imagery placed upon them would have contributed to this process, forming part of the materiality of the everyday that shaped social life.

4 | Cult, Euergetism and the Imagery of Festivals

Some tokens carry specific chants connected to Roman festivals, while others carry imagery that evoke particular spectacles, processions or celebratory events. It is highly likely that some of the Roman tokens that survive were utilised within particular festivals; this chapter explores what these artefacts can reveal about the emotions and experiences of these occasions. Festival motifs may also have been placed on tokens to evoke particular emotions and memories before or after an event. Representations of objects associated with celebrations provide a rare source base for a better understanding of the paraphernalia associated with individual Roman festivities. We need to bear in mind, however, that the 'festive' imagery used to decorate many tokens is also found on everyday objects across the Roman world: on frescoes, mosaics, coinage, lamps and other artefacts. The imagery on these pieces is thus part of a broader cultural practice that used singular events as a basis for an iconography that evoked good fortune, abundance and a *joie de vivre* within daily life. The imagery of singular celebrations regularly transcended its immediate context in the Roman world to become part of the everyday lived experience. Tokens were designed within this broader cultural phenomenon.

Tokens from other regions reveal that the connection of these objects to festivals was not isolated to Italy. Several tokens from Athens seem to portray items carried in festival processions. Figure 4.1 is the first of these, a Hellenistic token that portrays a ship's mast (*stylis*) on wheels being drawn by two horses. The wagon shown was likely used for a Dionysiac festival procession; although Crosby suggested the Anthesteria as a possible occasion, recent work suggests the City Dionysia is a more likely context.[1] A second Hellenistic token type shows Dionysus seated in a cart being drawn by a horse; Crosby also connects this image to a Dionysiac procession.[2] A token dated to the Roman imperial period from Athens showing the bust of Athena on a ship has been connected to the Panathenaic festival by

---

[1] Lang and Crosby, 1964: 95, L88; Gkikaki, 2019: 130 for the connection with the Anthesteria and Gkikaki, 2020 for the Greater Dionysia, citing Csapo, 2012.
[2] Lang and Crosby, 1964: 95, L87.

128 Cult, Euergetism and the Imagery of Festivals

Figure 4.1 Pb token, Athens, 18 mm, 4.72 g, Hellenistic period. A ship's *stylis* on a cart (the 'cart of Dionysus') being drawn by two horses right; prow above. Gkikaki, 2020: cat. no. 21.

Gkikaki; during this festival Athena's *peplos* was suspended on the mast of a ship and brought to the foot of the Acropolis.[3]

Tantalising connections between tokens and festivals can also be found elsewhere in the ancient Mediterranean. Bronze tokens naming Melqart in Tyre from the second and first centuries BC carry dates that almost all correlate to the quinquennial games of Hercules in the city: one imagines they are probably connected with this festival in some way.[4] Hoover has suggested the Hellenistic lead pieces from Nabatea were also likely issued on the occasion of triumphs or religious festivals.[5] Lead tokens from Chersonesus on the Black Sea have been connected to festival distributions of grain, oil and wine, largely on the basis of their imagery.[6] The issuing of tokens by named individuals holding public office in other cities (e.g. in Ephesus and Dobrogea) means these objects have been connected to particular public events: tickets to festivals or distributions.[7]

Previous scholarship on tokens in Italy has also acknowledged the role these pieces may have played in festivals.[8] Indeed, the connection of tokens from Rome and Ostia to various events (e.g. triumph, celebrations of *dies imperii*) has already been noted in the previous chapters. Here we delve deeper into this theme, exploring the full potential of tokens as a source to gain a better understanding of the imagery, emotions and experience of festivals. The chapter begins with a detailed discussion of two particular festival contexts: those connected to Egyptian cults (particularly Isis), and

---

[3] Lang and Crosby, 1964: 111, L256; Gkikaki, 2019: 130, cat. nos. 48–9.
[4] Abou Diwan and Sawaya, 2011.
[5] Hoover, 2006; de Callataÿ, 2010: 228 noting there is no way to definitively support this hypothesis, although it is possible.
[6] Kovalenko, 2002. [7] Kuhn, 2014; Marin and Ionita, 2018.
[8] Garrucci, 1847: 33; Ruggiero, 1878: 149; Rostovtzeff, 1905b: 26, 41, 72; Turcan, 1988: 629.

the Saturnalia held in December. This is followed by a broader discussion of what the imagery of tokens reveals about festival culture in Rome and its port town.

Egyptian Cults in Rome and Ostia

The *Isidis Navigium* was a festival of Isis held on the 5th March each year; the celebrations involved the launching of a votive ship to mark the beginning of the sailing season.[9] One of the most detailed texts connected to the festival is provided by Apuleius in the *Metamorphoses*: this fictional account is set in Corinth, and includes the dedication of the ship, a detailed description of the festival procession and its participants, as well as the vows made for the emperor and various sectors of the Roman population.[10]

It has long been thought that a series of bronze tokens, as well as associated coin fractions, were produced in conjunction with this festival in late antiquity (Figure 4.2).[11] It is not only the late date that separates these particular tokens from those that form the focus of this volume. These late antique pieces were issued officially by the mint (not by private individuals) and are extremely similar to the official small change produced at this time. Some tokens of this category carried obverse imagery of deities, while others possessed obverses that carried portraits and legends naming Roman emperors. In the latter case, the same obverse dies used for official currency were utilised, confirming the hypothesis that these were produced at the mint of

Figure 4.2 Bronze token, 19 mm, 12 h, 2.38 g, AD 317. Laureate bust of Constantine I right, IMP CONSTANTINVS P F AVG / Isis Pharia standing on a ship left, VOTA PVBLICA. Ramskold 2016: no. 33, pl. 1.

---

[9] Ramskold, 2016: 158; Bricault, 2020: 211–27. [10] Apul. *Met.* 11.5–17; Griffiths, 1975: 31–47.
[11] Alföldi, 1937; Ramskold, 2016.

Rome.¹² In spite of the similarities to coinage, however, Ramskold's study of the Constantinian issues noted that none of the specimens were known from hoards, suggesting that users of these objects understood they were not considered official money.¹³ Alföldi initially thought these issues, which carry the legend VOTA PVBLICA, indicated that the *Isidis Navigium* had been moved to coincide with the vows taken for the wellbeing of the emperor on the 3rd January each year. But he later rethought this idea, and further evidence suggests that the festival remained in March.¹⁴

Apuleius does suggest that the festival was connected with vows for the emperor, the senate, the equestrian order and all the Roman people, as well as for the sailors and ships in the empire – this may be the VOTA PVBLICA referred to in the late antique token legends.¹⁵ Ramskold's study of the Constantinian tokens suggest they were issued when the emperor was in Rome, and many issues correlate with major events of Constantine's reign: significant anniversaries (e.g. his *decennalia*) and the introduction of Constantine's heirs.¹⁶ As well as Isis on a ship, the tokens display Isis standing, as well as imagery of Anubis, Sarapis, the Nile and other Egyptian motifs.¹⁷ Alföldi suggested these objects were distributed as small change during the festival (i.e. they were a form of *sparsiones*).¹⁸ Bricault has observed that the messages communicated by these Egyptian deities correlated well with the messages associated with the Roman New Year: health, peace, nourishment, prosperity and birth.¹⁹ The purpose of the objects remains enigmatic for now.

What is rarely realised is that many of the images found on these late antique bronze tokens are also found on the earlier lead tokens of Rome and Ostia. Several lead tokens explicitly connect Isis with ships. One token issue shows Isis (or a worshipper or priestess of Isis) on one side and a ship sailing right on the other.²⁰ Another shows Isis standing on a ship with the legend TI|LA on the other side; the legend suggests an issuer for this series other than the emperor (Figure 4.3).²¹ It is impossible to know whether

---

[12] Ramskold, 2016: 163. For a new study of these pieces see Bricault and Mondello, in press.
[13] Ramskold, 2016: 164.
[14] Alföldi had originally cited the existence of tokens for Jovian, who never ruled in March, as evidence, but the issues may have been created in advance of the festival. The presence of tokens issued by Magnentius, who never ruled in January, is evidence that the festival was never moved; see Ramskold, 2016: 159–61.
[15] Apul. *Met.* 11.17.   [16] Ramskold, 2016: 212–14.   [17] Alföldi, 1937.   [18] Alföldi, 1937: 35.
[19] Bricault, 2008: 32.   [20] *TURS* 3181, Pl. X, 15.
[21] *TURS* 3184, Pl. X, 11. How we might resolve the legend is unknown, but it is not part of the regular abbreviations associated with imperial power. A further token type possibly shows Isis (?) on a ship holding a spear with the letter L on the other side, *TURS* 3183 (no image available).

Figure 4.3 Pb token, 18 mm, 12 h, 3.21 g. TI|LA / Isis standing left on a ship with oars holding sistrum in raised right hand and *situla* in left. *TURS* 3184.

these particular tokens were used during the *Isidis Navigium* or not, but they provide further evidence of Isis' connection to sea faring.[22]

A third token type perhaps refers to the votive ship of the *Isidis Navigium*. On one side stands a figure identified by Rostovtzeff as Anubis holding a caduceus and a long palm branch, while on the other Isis reportedly stands in a small ship woven or entwined with twigs, holding a rudder in her right hand and a sistrum in her left.[23] The token is very small (11 mm) and can no longer be found, so we are reliant on Rostovtzeff's report and the drawing included in his catalogue. The drawing itself shows a ship with vertical lines, which may represent twigs, or may simply be an embellishment or style of the engraver. If we are to interpret these lines as twigs, however, they are suggestive of a votive offering or context.[24] The representation of Anubis is also strikingly close to the description provided by Apuleius of the priest who dressed as Anubis during the *Isidis Navigium*: the priest wore a black and gold Anubis mask and carried a caduceus and a green palm branch.[25] It may be that this token, and others reported by Rostovtzeff showing Anubis, may depict participants in the cult, the *anubophoroi* or *anubiaci* who wore a mask of Anubis on particular cultic occasions.

These mask-wearers are mentioned several times within ancient texts, and would have been present at numerous celebrations within Egyptian cults: in addition to the *Isidis Navigium* there was the *Lychnapsia* (a festival of lamps), the *Pelusia* held in honour of Isis and Harpocrates, the *Serapia* in honour of Sarapis and the *Inventio Osiridis*, which re-enacted Osiris' mythical death and subsequent rebirth.[26] Other evidence also attests to existence of these priests throughout the Roman Empire. A priest wearing the mask of Anubis is shown in a fresco from the *Iseum* in Pompeii.[27] A mask-wearing priest is

---

[22] On this more generally see Bricault, 2020. [23] *TURS* 3191, fig. 214.
[24] On Isis with a rudder see Bricault, 2020: 145. [25] Apul. *Met.* 11. 11. [26] Bricault, 2001: 30.
[27] Museo Archeologico Nazionale, Naples, inv. no. 8920.

also probably shown on the El Djem mosaic in Tunisia as part of the imagery accompanying the month of November – a probable reference to the *Isia* that took place from 28 October to 3 November.[28] A three-handled jug decorated with a terracotta medallion, in all likelihood manufactured in the Rhône valley, shows a procession of Isis with the goddess being pulled by worshippers with a priest wearing the mask of Anubis standing towards the front of the procession (Figure 4.15 below).[29] A clay mask of Anubis, complete with slits for shoulders and eye-holes, has been found in Egypt, dating to between the 26th and 30th dynasties (the sixth–fourth centuries BC).[30] An epitaph for one Lepidus Rufus from Vienna reveals that he was an *anubophorus* or 'Anubis carrier'.[31]

Several lead tokens from Rome and Ostia carry the representation of a male figure with the dog-shaped head of Anubis holding a caduceus and long palm branch (Figure 4.4).[32] An Anubis figure also appears on the *vota publica* tokens of late antiquity; Ramskold argues that when Anubis appears on these pieces in military dress holding a branch, the god himself is represented, while the presence of a palm branch and drapery indicates the depiction of an *anubophorus*.[33] By this reasoning, the Anubis shown on the earlier lead tokens is the depiction of a priest, since the figure always appears with a long palm branch. But there did not seem to be such a distinctive iconographic division between Anubis and the *anubophoroi* in the earlier Roman period: representations of what is believed to be Anubis himself on

Figure 4.4 Pb token, 19 mm, 12 h, 3.05 g. Anubis (or priest of Anubis) draped from the waist down, holding branch in left hand and caduceus in right / Isis (or priestess of Isis) standing right holding sistrum in upraised left hand and *situla* in right, ACICI along on the left. *TURS* 3190, *BMCRLT* 16.

---

[28] Bricault, 2001: 33, 40.
[29] Metropolitan Museum of Art 17.194.870, said to have been found at Arausio (southern France).
[30] Pelizaeus-Museum Hildesheim inv. no. 1585; Bricault, 2001: 37.   [31] *CIL* XII, 1919.
[32] *TURS* 3189–94. The meaning of the legend ACICI is unknown.   [33] Ramskold, 2016: 174–5.

various media show the god holding a long palm branch.³⁴ Thus the representations on the tokens remain ambiguous: the figure may be the god Anubis, or a priest wearing the mask of Anubis during a particular festival.

The users of these pieces may have known what particular representation was intended. But perhaps not: the ambiguity here between the priest and the god would have been similar to the experience of a cultic procession. In Apuleius' procession of the *Isidis Navigium* the *anubophorus* is described as the god himself 'deigning to walk with human feet'.³⁵ Indeed, Apuleius details how participants in the festival dressed up in costume: as a soldier, a gladiator, a woman and even a bear dressed as a Roman matron.³⁶ Of course, there is literary purpose here: this particular occasion, where people could transform into someone or something else via clothing, becomes the perfect backdrop for the physical transformation of Lucius, the main character of Apuleius' tale, from an ass back into a human being and worshipper of Isis. This slippage between worshipper and the divine is also found elsewhere in Isiac cult. Inscriptions within sanctuaries carry first person references to the goddess ('I am Isis'); the reading aloud of such texts by priests (perhaps dressed as Isis) or initiates would have served to blur the boundaries between the cult participant and the deity being worshipped.³⁷ A shared ceremony would have resulted in a shared emotional experience that served to bond the cultic community together; Apuleius' text also captures such emotions.³⁸

The tokens with Egyptian motifs may thus have served to capture and evoke the sense of transformation that occurred during the *Isidis Navigium* and other Egyptian festivals. Indeed, just as the case for the *anubophoroi*, the figure on the other side of these tokens may be the goddess Isis *or* a worshipper of Isis. Both the goddess and her worshippers carried a sistrum and *situla* (sacred bucket).³⁹ The funerary altar of Cantinea Procla found on the via Ostiense in Rome, for example, shows her as a priestess of Isis, veiled and holding what was probably a sistrum in her raised hand and a *situla* at her side, just as on Figure 4.4.⁴⁰ The statue of Isis found at Hadrian's villa shows the goddess with the exact same attributes,

---

³⁴ For example, an intaglio (Metropolitan Museum of Art inv. 41.160.643), funerary altar of Fabia Stratonice (*AE* 1988, 368; Badisches Landesmuseum Karlsruhe inv. 67/134), bronze statuette (BM EA36064), terracotta lamp (BM 1856,1226.397).
³⁵ Apul. *Met.* 11.11.   ³⁶ Apul. *Met.* 11.8.   ³⁷ Martzavou, 2012: 276–86.
³⁸ Chaniotis, 2011: 267–8, discussing Apul. *Met.* 11.7.
³⁹ This particular iconography of Isis first appears on coinage under the Flavians, see Bricault, 2008: 26.
⁴⁰ *CIL* VI, 34776; Friggeri, Granino Cecere and Grigori 2012: 669–70. See *CIL* VI, 13454 for a further representation; there are numerous examples.

held in the same way: the sistrum in a raised hand, the *situla* at her side.[41] Coins of Claudius Gothicus invoking the wellbeing of the emperor (an interesting forerunner of the late antique tokens) also show Isis holding a sistrum and *situla*, accompanied by the legends SALVS AVG or CONSER AVG.[42] Thus the cults of both Anubis and Isis encompassed a slippage between the iconography associated with the god and the iconography associated with the worshipper; a slippage also found in the experience of the cult itself. The imagery selected for the lead tokens may therefore have been intentionally ambiguous, capturing the idea that a worshipper might appear as a deity. Like the tokens from Nemi discussed in the Chapter 3, the imagery perhaps allowed participants in a cult to identify themselves in the image: both male and female participants in this particular instance.

Particular paraphernalia connected to Egyptian cults are also shown on lead tokens. Figure 4.5 appears to show the physical mask of Anubis worn by the *anubophoroi*; the sistrum carried by worshippers of Isis is shown on the other side. Rostovtzeff believed Figure 4.6 was connected to the *Isidis Navigium*, noting that Apuleius reported among the attributes of the gods carried in the procession was a 'deformed left hand with palm extended', which was a symbol of justice.[43] There is not any reason to connect the representation of a left hand with the cult of Isis, however. As with Figure 3.8, the hand may symbolise something else, for example a particular numeral.

Figure 4.5 Pb token, 18 mm. Mask of Anubis right / Sistrum on left, next to patera on right. *TURS* 3206.

---

[41] Capitoline Museums, inv. MC0744.
[42] *RIC* V Claudius Gothicus 202, 217–18. The figure may also be interpreted as a worshipper of Isis.
[43] Apul. *Met.* 11.10.

Figure 4.6 Pb token, 18 mm, 12 h, 2.14 g. Cat (?) crouching right / Left hand, ABR (retrograde) around. *TURS* 3185, Rostovtzeff and Prou, 1900: no. 446b.

The imagery selected from the broader repertoire of Egyptian cults for use on tokens in Rome and Ostia is surely significant: the iconography is predominantly associated with festival processions or worshippers. Several representations of Isis found on Roman imperial coinage are absent on tokens: the goddess holding a sistrum and sceptre seated on a dog leaping right (the image most closely connected with the temple of Isis in Rome), for example, and Isis suckling Horus (connected with the fecundity of the empresses on coinage).[44] This may be because the tokens were utilised within a particular cultic community (or communities); imagery was chosen to reflect the experiences of the members rather than broader ideology. It is also worth mentioning that the imagery chosen for these tokens also differs significantly from the imagery on tokens within the province of Egypt itself: here deities of local and regional significance dominate, with the river god Nilus particularly popular.[45]

Sarapis also appears on tokens in Rome and Ostia, almost always in the form of a bearded head wearing a *modius*.[46] Figure 4.7 shows one such example; the type was catalogued by Rostovtzeff and Prou in their publication of the tokens of the BnF, but it was then overlooked in *TURS*. On this specimen the head of Sarapis is combined with the representation of a river deity reclining on an urn holding a long reed: the representation may be of the Tiber, or perhaps the Nile.

Harpocrates also appears on lead tokens, as do Osiris, Jupiter Ammon and other Egyptian imagery including an ibis, an Egyptian-style headdress,

---

[44] For example, *RIC* II.1² Vespasian 116–17, 204; *RIC* II.3² Hadrian 2919; *RIC* III Antoninus Pius 1197; *RIC* IV.1 Septimius Severus 577, 645, 865. For a discussion of these types see Bricault, 2008: 28, 33. For a discussion of the development of Egyptian motifs on coinage see Bricault, 2015.

[45] Milne, 1971 for a catalogue; Wilding, 2020 for a detailed analysis.

[46] For example, *TURS* 3151–74.

Figure 4.7 Pb token, 17 mm, 12 h, 3.64 g. Head of Sarapis wearing *modius* right / River deity reclining left, leaning on urn from which water flows with left arm and holding long reed in right. *TURS* (Supplement) 3731, Rostovtzeff and Prou, 1900: no. 646.

Figure 4.8 Pb token, 17 mm, 12 h, 3.25 g. Isis or worshipper of Isis standing left holding sistrum in raised right hand and *situla* in left / Two figures on a rectangular object. *TURS* 3179, *BMCRLT* 1286.

a baboon and the eagle form of the god Horus.[47] One of the more peculiar representations is reproduced here as Figure 4.8. This token shows Isis or a worshipper of Isis on one side and on the other side two figures on a rectangular object. What scene the image is meant to capture remains unknown. Egyptian imagery is also paired with other iconography: Mercury, for example, Fortuna, or a dolphin.[48] Each occurrence of Egyptian iconography thus cannot necessarily be connected to a particular Egyptian cult or festival; Sarapis, for instance, might have been used on tokens for other contexts.

The findspots of tokens carrying Egyptian imagery in Rome and Ostia only provide limited information, but this does suggest these objects were used in multiple locations. A token with an image of Isis or worshipper of Isis on one

---

[47] Harpocrates: *TURS* 3196–7. Osiris: *TURS* 3186. Jupiter Ammon: *TURS* 3187–8. Ibis: *TURS* 3178. Egyptian headdress: *TURS* 3196. Baboon: *TURS* 3195. Horus: *TURS* 3200.

[48] *TURS* 3158, 3160, 3167.

side and a semi-nude figure facing right on other was uncovered in the baths of the swimmer (Terme del Nuotatore) in Ostia. The token came from a stratum associated with the levelling of sections E, F and G of the complex during the Antonine period (AD 160–180/90).[49] Several other tokens were found elsewhere in these baths, which evidently manufactured them on site (discussed in Chapter 5). Whether this particular token was manufactured for use in the baths, or was lost by an owner whilst in the complex, cannot be known.[50] A token mould half, designed to produce 11 mm circular tokens showing the head of Sarapis, was uncovered in January 1915 in the area of the via di Diana in Ostia.[51] The area has no known connection with Egyptian cults; the mould, broken in the right hand corner, might have been thrown away as rubbish. The area housed shops and was close to a crossroads shrine (*compitum*). During the third century AD a mithraeum was located for a period of time in room 24 of the House of Diana.[52] Any of these venues, or another, might have produced tokens showing Sarapis, either in connection with a particular festival or simply because he was a popular deity.

Unfortunately the other known find locations of tokens carrying Egyptian imagery are not so precise. A further fragment of a token mould half designed to produce 20 mm tokens showing the head of Sarapis was found in Ostia, but has no further find information.[53] The assemblage of tokens now housed in the Museo Archeologico Nazionale di Palestrina also contains several specimens that carry Egyptian imagery (as well as some Egyptian tokens), but no find information for these are known.[54] Amongst the tokens coming from the Tiber in Rome, two contained Egyptian imagery: one with 'head of Sarapis / Isis or worshipper of Isis' (*TURS* 3151) and the other showing Osiris on one side and a palm branch accompanied by the legend CA N on the other (*TURS* 3186).[55] How tokens, coins and other artefacts ended up in the Tiber is the subject of debate, but one suggestion is that at least some of these artefacts were offered as votives.[56]

---

[49] Pardini, 2014: 46.
[50] Twenty coins were also found during the excavations, including a provincial coin from Alexandria dating from the reign of Domitian, Pardini, 2014: 41.
[51] *GdS* 1915 (vol. 8) 45, inv. 9535.
[52] Bakker suggests that for a period the ground floor of the House of Diana may have been a meeting venue for the *magistri et ministri vici*, see www.ostia-antica.org/regio1/3/3-3.htm.
[53] Ostia Antiquarium inv. 12543; Spagnoli, 2017b: pl. VI, 6.
[54] See Pensabene, 2001-2003: nos. 12, 14, 32, 37 for a selection.
[55] Rostovtzeff and Vaglieri, 1900: 266, nos. 131–2. The meaning of the legend is not known.
[56] Campbell, 2012.

The discussion of the via di Diana in Ostia reveals that it is unhelpful to try and distinguish between 'profane' and 'cultic' space in the Roman world, since shrines and places of cultic significance were located amongst domestic housing, shops and other establishments. But it is worth noting that tokens are also found in dedicated temple and sanctuary spaces. Cultic groups may have created tokens for use in particular events, for example the token series carrying the legend MAG(*istri*)·MINERVALES·M·N·.[57] Tokens may also have acquired a secondary use as cheap and convenient votive offerings that looked like coinage. In Roman Gaul tokens have been uncovered on numerous temple sites, and there are a handful of contexts from Roman Italy as well.[58] The tokens found in the well in the sanctuary of Hercules at Alba Fucens have already been discussed in Chapter 2.[59] A token mould half was found during excavations of the 'Syrian sanctuary' on the Janiculum in Rome: the mould produced tokens showing two nude pankratiasts with raised fists, an amphora between them and leaves blossoming around them.[60] A further mould half, which produced circular tokens possibly showing an altar, was found in the area of the Sabazeum in Ostia.[61] Unfortunately finer contextual detail is lacking from these early finds, but they do suggest some cultic groups may have manufactured tokens.

One can imagine that the lead tokens with imagery pertaining to Egyptian cults and festivals were used within a variety of contexts. Like the imagery connected to the *pompa circensis* discussed in Chapter 2, particular token types bore imagery that evoked particular processions. In the case of the references to Anubis and Isis, the imagery created a slippage between the gods and their worshippers that was also part of the cultic experience. Other tokens with Egyptian imagery may have been used within more quotidian contexts. Regardless of the particular use context, the designs on these tokens would have evoked particular Egyptian cults, shaping experience and memory, and forming part of the religious backdrop to daily life.

The Saturnalia

Several tokens carry a clear connection with the Saturnalia, held each year in late December in honour of Saturn.[62] The festival inverted or suspended many Roman social norms. Masters served their slaves, gifts were given and

---

[57] *TURS* 876. The meaning of M and N is not clear. [58] Discussed in Wilding, 2020.
[59] Ceccaroni and Molinari, 2017; Molinari, 2021. [60] *NSc.* 1909, 410. [61] *NSc.* 1909, 23.
[62] Dolansky, 2011.

households participated in feasting that might last several days. Gambling was allowed, and individuals participated in drinking and games, as well as (according to our surviving literature) learned discussions.[63] Catullus described it as the 'best of days'.[64] Of course, the inversion of social customs in this way would have worked to cement and reinforce those same norms and social hierarchies.[65]

Several lead tokens from Rome and Ostia carry an abbreviated form of the chant *io Saturnalia!*[66] One group carries the legend IO SAT IO accompanied by a palm branch, with a wreath displayed on the other side.[67] Remarkably, the bottom of the palm branch ends in four different designs: a dot, a curve, a cross that Rostovtzeff interpreted as a denarius sign ($\ast$) (*TURS* Pl. IV, 23) and a retrograde F (Figure 4.9), which Rostovtzeff suggested communicated the phrase *feliciter*. The very similar style of these tokens, and the consistent placement of their legend and imagery, suggest that they were probably part of a single series. The engraver of the mould may have playfully embellished the end of each palm branch, or else the slight variations might have acted as a code to represent information (e.g. particular items, gifts or benefactions). If the latter is true, then the users of this series must have had to study the imagery on the pieces extremely closely. The sense of playfulness and fun that permeated the festival is also found on the festival tokens.

In a poem set during the Saturnalia, Martial describes the lavish *nomismata*, the coins or coin-like objects.[68] The same word is used by Martial to describe objects specifically exchanged for goods in the context of

Figure 4.9 Pb token, 17 mm, 12 h, 4.32 g. Palm branch ending in a retrograde F, IO on left, SAT | IO on right / Wreath. *TURS* 507, Rostovtzeff and Prou, 1900: no. 103.

---

[63] Gell. *NA* 18.2, 18.13; Macrob. *Sat.* 1.1.   [64] Catull. 14.15.   [65] Dolansky, 2011: 489.
[66] Mart. *Ep.* 11.2.5; Petron. *Sat.* 58; Dio 60.19.3; Livy 23.1.
[67] *TURS* 504, 506–7; Rostovtzeff, 1905b: 41.
[68] Mart. *Ep.* 12.62.11; Mitchiner, 1984: 99; Harrison, 2001: 304.

a spectacle, discussed in detail in Chapter 2. We possess evidence that coins were exchanged during the Saturnalia, so *nomismata* may not necessarily mean 'tokens' in each instance: Tiberius reportedly gave Claudius *aurei* during one Saturnalia, and among the gifts distributed by Augustus were 'coins (*nummi*) of every device, including old pieces of the kings and foreign money'.[69] Nonetheless, given the existence of tokens carrying specific reference to the Saturnalia, one imagines these may also have formed part of the broader gift giving, perhaps representing a particular gift or gifted experience.

As with the triumphal tokens carrying the chant *io triumphe* discussed in Chapter 2, these tokens were designed to evoke a response from their users. The tokens 'spoke' to their audience, encouraging them to speak in turn. The Saturnalian cry is found on several other token designs. One issue carries the veiled and bearded head of Saturn accompanied by the legend SATVR; the other side of the token is decorated with the image of a palm branch with I on the left and O on the right, all within a wreath.[70] The legend on both sides of the token comes together to read *Satur(nalia) io*! Two specimens of this type are known; the second is very worn on the wreath side and bears a rectangular countermark with the legend I·VE.[71] Rostovtzeff wondered whether the countermark referred to the emperor Vespasian (*I(mperator) Ve(spasianus)*), an idea that can only remain a hypothesis. The token was perhaps countermarked since the wreath side was worn or poorly cast; countermarking on lead tokens from Rome and Ostia is rare when compared to other areas, most notably Athens.[72] The existence of the countermark here does suggest a form of quality control or administrative process, which in turn hints at something more than play objects or joke gifts.

The chant *io Saturnalia* is also referenced on a token now in the British Museum: one side of the piece carries the legend IO | SA, while the other side bears the number IIII.[73] The number I is found on another Saturnalian token, this time accompanied by the legend VAL | SATVR|NALIA on the other side.[74] The VAL here may be understood as *val(eas)* or *val(e)*, a message of good wishes and health given to the user in addition to whatever benefaction the token itself conferred. Other tokens carry simply the legend

---

[69] Suet. *Aug.* 75, *Claud.* 5.   [70] *TURS* 502, Pl. IV, 21.
[71] Scholz, 1894: nos. 99–100, Pl. II no. 100 = Mowat, 1898: no. 21. The VE is ligate.
[72] Mowat, 1898 still remains the best work on countermarked tokens from Rome. For Athens see Lang and Crosby, 1964: 83, 116; Bubelis, 2011: 190; Gkikaki, 2019.
[73] *TURS* 510; *BMCRLT* 2221.   [74] *TURS* 503, Pl. IV, 22.

SAT or IO; Rostovtzeff's connection of the latter with the Saturnalia is hypothetical, since the chant *io* might also be used during other occasions.[75]

A final lead token type connected to the Saturnalia displays Victory on one side and four wreaths on the other (Figure 4.10).[76] The depiction of four wreaths in this manner is also known on a Republican coin issue struck to commemorate Pompey in 56 BC (Figure 4.11): the three smaller wreaths are thought to represent Pompey's three triumphs, while the larger wreath at the top of the coin is the *corona aurea*.[77] One wonders if this earlier coin issue served as inspiration for the design of the token, which most probably dates from the imperial period. Republican coins did circulate well into the principate. In Trajan's reign, for example, Republican coins seem to have been melted down at the Roman mint and also served as models for new issues of restored coins.[78] It is thus possible that this earlier coin served as inspiration for the design of the token, although the layout of the wreaths differs (it is also worth noting in this context that some 'restorations' of Republican coins under Trajan did not slavishly imitate each aspect of the original, but displayed some creativity).[79] Indeed, the rather orderly presentation here also recalls the representation of prize wreaths in reliefs. But the image may have been playfully adapted from the coin type.[80] During a festival that gave licence to satire, the official currency of the Roman government might have been subjected to playful comment.

Figure 4.10 Pb token, 12 mm, 12 h, 1.88 g. Victory standing right with wreath in outstretched hand and palm branch over left shoulder; SAT in field left / Four wreaths. *TURS* 508.

---

[75] *TURS* 509, Pl. IV, 25 with SAT on one side and a helmeted bust of Roma or Minerva on the other side. One specimen of this type (*TURS* 509.4) was reportedly found at Aquileia. See also *TURS* 512 (IO and palm branch / Minerva) and 512 (IO within wreath / Tetrastyle temple accompanied by the legend A T D).
[76] The legend is absent on *BMCRLT* 797.   [77] Crawford, 1974: vol. 1, 450.
[78] Dio 68.15.3; Komnick, 2001: 158; Woytek, 2010: 167–9, nos. 801–73; Woytek, 2022.
[79] Woytek, 2010: nos. 850-77; Woytek, 2022: 256. The relevant coins are *aurei*; as Woytek notes the Trajanic silver restorations are all very faithful to the originals.
[80] Tooker, 2014: 29 on the 'playfulness' with money found in modern token systems.

Figure 4.11 AR denarius, c. 19 mm, 5 h, 3.71 g. Faustus Cornelius Sulla moneyer, 56 BC. Head of Hercules right, wearing lion-skin, S C and monogram behind. Dotted border / Globe surrounded by three small wreaths and one large wreath; below on left, aplustre; below on right, corn-ear. Border of dots. *RRC* 426/4a.

The message communicated by the four wreaths on Figure 4.10 is unknown; surviving material culture that can be connected to the Saturnalian festival is relatively rare and thus there is very little comparative evidence. More generally, however, we might say that wreaths are connected to festivals and sacrifice.[81] Many of the tokens carrying a direct reference to the Saturnalia carry a palm branch and wreath; we might then deduce that this imagery was associated with the festival, as it was with other celebrations in the Roman calendar. The four wreaths might have been meant to indicate the number four, but this is pure speculation.[82] Apart from the token said to be found in Aquileia (n. 75 above), the only other reported findspots for Saturnalia tokens are in Rome. In addition to the possible Saturnalian token carrying the representation of three *Fortunae* (discussed in Chapter 3), the other specimen was acquired by Rostovtzeff in Rome before being donated to the BnF. The token was of the IO SAT IO type with palm branch and wreath.[83] With such tiny find numbers little can be deduced from this data.

The imagery on these tokens would have contributed to the overall experience of a particular festival. Other imagery on tokens communicates a sense of fun and festivity, although the tokens themselves carry no indication of which, if any, festival they might be connected with. It is to these tokens that this work now turns – although these objects cannot be connected to a particular occasion, they nonetheless shed light on the emotions and experiences of Roman festivals, and the transformation of festival imagery into the iconography of the everyday.

---

[81] Macrob. *Sat.* 3.12.1–4 (in connection with the cult of Hercules).
[82] Similarly, the representation of two clubs on tokens might also have a numerical significance, see *TURS* 2548, 2573.
[83] *TURS* 504; Rostovtzeff and Prou, 1900: no. 102.

Festivals, Emotions and Roman Daily Life

Many tokens from Rome and Ostia carry scenes of fun, spectacle and entertainment, themes connected to the celebration of festivals in the Roman world. Many of these images, particularly gladiatorial combat and animal fights, were also popular themes on other small-scale domestic media: terracotta figurines, lamps and glassware, for example.[84] The imagery and emotions captured in these scenes transcended any individual event; they formed an iconographic backdrop to Roman daily life. Imagery placed on tokens, then, might have been representative of a particular festival (whether city-wide or localised within a small community), or it may have been chosen to evoke a particular emotion in the user: a sense of benefaction, of fun, or of joy. Indeed, when studying tokens one cannot escape the conclusion that many of the designs were selected to make users smile. A small figure swinging from a building crane is one example of this, as is the representation of two youths on a swing or the 'monkey-triumph' taking place on the back of a camel (Figure 4.12).[85] The obvious satire of an official Roman ceremony here might also be found on a token (*spintria*) with a sexual scene in which one of the sexual participants carries a rod – this might be an allusion to, and hence satire of, a freedom ceremony.[86]

Figure 4.12 Orichalcum token, 19 mm, 9 h, 4.54 g. A togate figure in a triumphal *quadriga* right holding a sceptre in left hand and with right hand outstretched, being crowned by a monkey who stands behind; all on a camel / XIX within dotted border within wreath. Buttrey, 1973: B25 XIX.

---

[84] Dunbabin, 2016: 4; Popkin, 2022.
[85] Küter, 2019: 88–9. Küter, on the basis of a specimen of the camel token in the Münzkabinett Berlin, suggests that the 'triumph scene' shows one monkey being crowned by another; on the piece from the Hunterian shown here, this is not the case. For the swinging crane scene see Cohen: vol VIII, 267 no. 10 and Küter, 2019: figs. 33–4. For the two youths on a swing see *TURS* 2839, Pl. VII, 26.
[86] Jacobelli, 1997: 10–13; Campana, 2009: 59; Küter, 2019: 88–9.

Satire, of course, was a feature of some Roman festivals, particularly the Saturnalia, as was gambling. Gambling was popular in the Roman world, although it was frequently regulated and confined only to particular festival days.[87] The calendar of AD 354 illustrated December with a figure throwing dice, a reference to the Saturnalia, when such activity was allowed.[88] Several tokens refer to games and/or gambling, which no doubt served to evoke anticipation or remembrance of a particular moment of leisure time. Figure 4.13 is one such example. It shows four knucklebones (*astragali*) used in games of chance on the reverse, accompanied by the legend *qui ludit arram det quod satis sit*, a statement that invites those who would play in the game to place a sufficient *arra* or pledge.[89] The phrase *det, quod satis sit*, is known from legal contexts and testimonies.[90] *Arra* (or *arrha*) is connected to the Greek *arrhabón* (ἀρραβών), which communicated the idea of a pledge or earnest money, deposited by the purchaser and then forfeited if the transaction was not completed. The term is discussed by Gellius in *Attic Nights*: he describes the pledge (*arrabo*) the Romans had given to the Samnites (here referring to 600 hostages), before going on to note that 'nowadays *arrabo* is beginning to be numbered among vulgar words, and *arra* seems even more so, although the early writers often used *arra*, and Laberius has it several times'.[91]

Figure 4.13 was originally published by Cohen in the nineteenth century. The same design was also reported on a lead token said to be found around Autun in France in the nineteenth century, which belonged to the collection of M. Alphonse Renaud.[92] The lead specimen is now lost to time, but the image included in the publication shows that the obverse filled the flan completely, whereas on the specimen shown here the die is much smaller than the flan. There may then truly have been a second example of the type, made of lead rather than bronze alloy. The female depicted on the obverse was interpreted by Mowat as the goddess who presides over games of chance – C(*aput*)

---

[87] Lanciani, 1892; Purcell, 1995: 9. [88] Salzman, 1990: 74–5 and fig. 23. [89] Mowat, 1913: 51.
[90] For example Cic. *Fin.* 2.101, citing another document: 'ut Amynomachus et Timocrates, heredes sui, de Hermarchi sententia dent quod satis sit ad diem agendum natalem suum quotannis mense Gamelione ... ' ('that his heirs, Amynochus and Timocrates, shall after consultation with Hermarchus assign a sufficient sum to celebrate his birthday every year in the month of Gamelion ... '). See also Mowat, 1913: 52.
[91] Gell. *NA* 17.2.21. The term also appears in Gai. *Inst.* 3.139 ('The contract of purchase and sale is complete so soon as the price is agreed upon and before the price or any earnest money is paid. The earnest money is merely evidence of the completion of the contract'). See also Isid. *Etym.* 5.25.20 and Plin. *HN* 33.28 (*arra* used to denote an agreement or contract) and 29.21; a full discussion of the term can be found in the *TLL* (Prinz, 1902).
[92] Castan, 1870: 1870, 261. Image available at https://coins.warwick.ac.uk/token-specimens/id/renaud1.

Figure 4.13 AE token, 25 mm, 7 h, 8.64 g. Female bust right, with hair tied in a bun behind her head. C on left side, S on right. Dotted border / Four knucklebones, two on top of the other. QVI LVDIT above, ARRAM | DET QVOD in the middle between the knucklebones, SATIS SIT below. Cohen vol. VIII, 266 no. 5.

S(ortis) – but this remains speculation.[93] A further lead token may also refer to knucklebones: *TURS* 1381 carries the legend ASTRAGALVS around in a circle on one side and a palm branch and club on the other; Rostovtzeff, however, suggested that this legend be understood as a name.

The action and excitement of gaming (and the gambling that inevitably accompanied it) is also evident on Figure 4.14, a brass token that is die linked to the so-called *spintria* series and associated tokens carrying the portraits of the Julio-Claudian imperial family (see Chapter 1). We might thus conclude it was made at the same workshop around the same period: the first half of the first century AD.[94] On this particular token series (which is issued with a variety of numerals on the reverse, as well as the legend AVG), two men (or boys) are shown playing a board game that appears to be *ludus latrunculorum*. The figure on the right has his right hand raised and is evidently shouting *mora* ('wait!').[95] The scene is reminiscent of the painting from the bar of Salvius in Pompeii where two men are depicted playing dice with their speech written above them – one declares 'I've won' while the other replies 'Its not a three, it's a two'. Further paintings in the bar show the quarrel escalating, with the landlord eventually throwing the two individuals out of the establishment. Clarke notes that these and other paintings in the bar demonstrate a loss of control, a world turned upside down, inviting laughter from the viewer.[96] The

---

[93] Mowat, 1913: 51. [94] Rowan, 2020b.
[95] Mowat, 1913: 52. The word *moraris* is found on rectangular bone gaming pieces (*tesserae lusoriae*); *AE* 1888, no. 116g (with XIIII).
[96] Clarke, 2003: 161–70.

Figure 4.14 Orichalcum token, 21 mm, 5.04 g. Two boys or men seated facing each other, a tablet on their knees, playing a game. The figure on the right has a raised right hand. At the left a cupboard or doorway (?); MORA above / XIII within dotted border within wreath. BnF AF 17088.

representation on Figure 4.14 doesn't seem to carry the same sense of humour, and is perhaps closer in intent to the more straightforward representation of dice playing in the fresco of another bar, that on the Street of Mercury in Pompeii.[97] The frescos and the token possess imagery that invites an emotional response from the viewer, designed to evoke a particular atmosphere of fun, diversion and leisure. Depending on when the token imagery was seen, the viewer might anticipate leisure immediately ahead of them, or be prompted to reminisce about previous gaming experiences.

Remarkably, given its popularity, dice playing does not seem to be represented on tokens. Several decades ago a lead token said to be found at Ostia was sold at auction showing two figures seated facing each other; the catalogue suggested they may have been playing a finger game (*micare digitis* or *morra*), but the token itself is too small (16 mm) to come to any firm conclusions.[98] Overall very few surviving tokens from Roman Italy reference gaming or gambling. The motif was not as popular as others; representations of deities, references to Fortuna and depictions of spectacles seem to have been far more popular choices.

The same sense of festivity might be communicated via more banal imagery, for example the wreaths and palm branches that are to be found on numerous tokens. Both the wreath and palm branch were attributes of Victory, who was connected not only to military victories, but also to victories in the circus, the theatre or other contests. Indeed, the presence

---

[97] Clarke, 2003: 169.
[98] Frank Sternberg, Auktion 17, 9–10 May 1986, Zürich, no. 709, image available at https://coins.warwick.ac.uk/token-specimens/id/antikemuenzen.auction.17.lot.709.

of palms and wreaths on drinking vessels illustrates that the ideology of victory also entered dining and symposium contexts.[99] These images, in fact, were quite widespread – also found on Roman lamps, and even incorporated into a potter's stamp.[100] The imagery of Roman festivals, including associated games and spectacles, was a popular decorative motif for everyday items in the Roman world. Although we may not be able to connect a particular festive token motif to a particular festival, tokens, alongside other everyday objects, served to keep the culture and spirit of festivals fresh in people's minds.

The Rhône valley beakers (terracotta vessels decorated with round medallions, largely produced in the second and third centuries AD) offer a fruitful parallel to the lead tokens of Roman Italy.[101] Like the lead tokens, the exact use context of these objects is debated; Alföldi believed that they formed New Year gifts based on a terracotta medallion showing Isis and Sarapis and resolving a fragmentary inscription as *(annum novu)m lucro accipio*. There is, however, little evidence to link these objects to New Year celebrations, and accepting this idea based on a restored inscription is problematic.[102] Like Roman tokens, these vases show deities, emperors and festival processions: triumphs, for example, and a procession associated with the festival of Isis. The latter shows one participant wearing the mask of Anubis, Isis in a chariot, as well as religious standards that included Horus depicted as an eagle (Figure 4.15).[103] A sense of satire is also found on these artefacts: one terracotta medallion, for example, shows the *Navigium Veneris*, a parody on the *Navigium Isidis*, that shows a nude female figure in a boat (Venus?) being penetrated from behind by a bearded, nude male figure (Mars?).[104] Although the parallels between the erotic representations on tokens and on the Rhône valley beakers has already been noted by Jabobelli, the wider iconographic parallels between the two categories of object – which both show deities, gladiatorial scenes, scenes from the circus, and carry the wish *feliciter* – has had little

---

[99] For example, Metropolitan Museum of Art 81.10.214 and 81.10.210 (glass beakers with two rows of wreaths divided vertically by two palm fronds and a Greek phrase that translates as 'Take the victory'), 59.11.4 (glass beaker with palm branches and the phrase 'Rejoice and be merry!' in Greek).

[100] For example, BM 1904,0204.472.a (FORTIS, with wreath next to palm branch); Metropolitan Museum of Art 74.51.1964 (terracotta lamp decorated with two wreaths and a long palm branch).

[101] Desbat, 2011: 13, 36.   [102] Alföldi, 1965/66: 67; Desbat, 2011: 37.   [103] Desbat, 2011: 35–6.

[104] Jacobelli, 2011: 140, 142.

Figure 4.15 Three-handled jug from the Rhône valley, decorated with a medallion showing an Isiac procession (also shown enlarged in the image). A medallion on the other side (not pictured) shows Atalanta and Hippomenes. Said to be from Arausio (modern Orange, Southern France), Metropolitan Museum of Art, 17.194.1980, public domain.

discussion.[105] Unlike tokens, however, the medallions on the beakers carry specific reference to particular dramatic performances.[106]

One imagines that these beakers, high quality products, would have been used for some period of time. In this way they form a compelling example of the way in which objects in the Roman world created an iconographic backdrop to daily life that frequently referenced festival culture. Importantly, the beakers were artefacts manufactured and used outside of Rome – Popkin observes that some of these items may have acted as 'souvenirs' for events that the owners of the artefact had never experienced (e.g. gladiatorial combat, circus racing in the Circus Maximus); in this case the artefacts enabled users to imagine themselves at various spectacles and hence feel a belonging to the Roman Empire and its culture.[107]

Apart from those tokens that may have been converted into mementoes (by being pierced, for example), tokens likely remained objects of a particular moment. In this sense they differ from the Rhône beakers, but possess parallels with the objects made from the so-called 'cake moulds' found throughout the Roman Empire. The round moulds found along the Danube have been discussed in Chapter 2. Three-dimensional moulds have also been found in number, particularly in Ostia. The largest and best-known find is that of the Caseggiato dei Doli, a building containing some thirty-five *dolia* for wine and oil, as well as c. 400 terracotta moulds.[108] These moulds can be divided into roughly thirty designs, depicting scenes from the theatre, the circus (victorious charioteers), *venationes*, mythological scenes, erotic scenes, and scenes with sea life (e.g. fish). Nothing produced from these moulds has ever been found, suggesting that they were used to create items that were perishable and/or edible: suggestions have ranged from cakes to wax figurines, which perhaps served as a form of *missilia*, objects thrown to a crowd.[109] Whatever these moulds produced, they carried reference to the entertainments that accompanied religious festivals, in the theatre, circus or amphitheatre. It is thought the products of these moulds were distributed during particular festival occasions – like tokens, they would have enhanced the experience of the participant, evoking the spectacles and sights that one might anticipate seeing, or recalling an event already experienced. Like the souvenirs discussed by Popkin, if these objects were given to individuals who did not have the opportunity to

---

[105] For an overview of the subject material shown on the beakers see the collection of essays in Desbat and Savay-Guerraz, 2011.
[106] For example, BM 1904,0204.441, which appears to show a scene from Roman tragedy; Desbat, 2011: 17.
[107] Popkin, 2022: 132, 248.   [108] Pasqui, 1906; Squarciapino, 1954; Salomonson, 1972: 94.
[109] Salomonson, 1972: 112; Simon, 2008: 768.

experience spectacles first hand, they offered the opportunity to vicariously access this particular aspect of Roman culture. In the case of Ostia, which appears to have not had an amphitheatre or circus of its own, the moulds used in the Caseggiato dei Doli likely evoked some experiences that one had to travel to Rome for, or which took place in a temporarily erected structure.[110]

These moulds, like the tokens, at times seem to have taken inspiration from coinage. A mould fragment found in the harbor at Marseille shows a ship with a *spina*; an intact mould with the same design is now on display at the Herakleion Archaeological Museum on Crete, and reveals that the ship has animals bounding beneath it.[111] As Salomonson observed, the design recalls the coinage of Septimius Severus showing a ship surrounded by animals and the legend LAETITIA TEMPORVM, which in turn recalls Dio's description of a boat collapsing to release wild animals in the amphitheatre, a spectacle that likely took place as part of Severus' saecular games.[112] The presence of moulds carrying the same imagery in geographically distant parts of the empire (and this is not the only occurrence), reveals how the celebration of a particular festival might lead to the sharing of similar imagery across the Empire: not only through imperial coinage, which circulated widely, but through the manufacture and distribution of moulds such as these by particular workshops.[113] Further work on these items needs to be performed, but they form a fruitful comparative source from which to better understand tokens and the imagery they carry.

The finds from the Caseggiato dei Doli were likely used within this building, which stored wine or olive oil; the resulting products were thus not given out in the amphitheatre or the theatre, but rather evoked these arenas and their spectacles for recipients. It is likely that a similar phenomenon occurred with lead tokens from Rome and Ostia. Although tokens have been found in the theatre in Ostia (discussed more fully in Chapter 5), one imagines that not all of the tokens carrying reference to particular spectacles were issued in conjunction with a particular event; like lamps and other everyday objects, the imagery of gladiators, animal fights and horse racing might be used in a variety of contexts. The study of this particular imagery on tokens thus remains difficult. Nonetheless, the imagery itself contributes to our understanding of Roman cultural attitudes towards the spectacles and entertainments associated with

---

[110] Bruun, 2007: 129–31. [111] Salomonson, 1972: 109–10.
[112] *RIC* IV.1 Septimius Severus 274, Caracalla 133, 157, Geta 43; Dio 77.1.4–5; Rowan, 2013: 51–2.
[113] As Salomonson observed, the similarities between these moulds are rarely noted (Salomonson, 1972: 101). A further example of the same scene (of comic actors) found in multiple regions is presented by Sifakis, 1966: specimens have been found in Athens, Ostia, Paestum and Egypt, with a further example in the British Museum (1857,1013.5).

festivals, and their almost ubiquitous iconographic presence in Roman society. The images chosen on tokens and other objects shaped the perception of what these spectacles entailed, and contributed to feelings of excitement and belonging, since the use of this imagery on rather modest artefacts offered individuals the opportunity to vicariously participate in particularly Roman cultural events.[114] For token issuers, the designs of tokens offered the opportunity to present themselves to others as individuals with connection to this particular aspect of Roman culture.

The Imagery of Spectacles, Performances and Races

Roman festivals were frequently accompanied by spectacles of different types (gladiatorial or animal fights, for example, or chariot racing). Unsurprisingly given the popularity of these motifs in Roman material culture, we find imagery associated with spectacles on tokens. This includes the representation of spectators. Similar to the images of Isis and Anubis discussed above, and the tokens carrying female worshippers discussed in Chapter 3, the representation of the audience of an event allowed the user to self-identity with the image.

More specifically, the spectators shown on tokens are depicted applauding. The image perhaps evoked the sound of applause in the minds of the users, and subtly acted upon them to contribute applause in turn at a future moment in time. Indeed, if presented in advance of an event, the representation of applause promised a spectacle worthy of such a response. A series of tokens carry the image of two spectators applauding, accompanied by various legends (presumably referring to different individuals, although on one occasion the legend is the number II). The spectators are always two in number, and are consistently shown seated via the use of horizontal lines. The image is not, to the author's knowledge, otherwise known from surviving Roman material culture, and the tokens of this type may all have been cast from moulds coming from the same workshop.

Shown on the other side of these tokens are the imagery of gladiators (Figure 4.16), an eight-horse chariot (*octoiugus*), a ship with a statue of Victory (?), palm branches, as well as representations of Ceres (standing holding a sceptre and corn-ears) and the head of Juno Sospita wearing a goat-skin.[115] One wonders whether the *octoiugus* type is part of the same series as the token carrying a representation of Nero on one side and an

---

[114] Popkin, 2022: 120.   [115] *TURS* 532–49, Supplement 3629.

Figure 4.16 Pb token, 17 mm, 12 h, 1.32 g. Two spectators applauding right / Gladiator standing left with shield in left hand and sword in right. *TURS* 537 variant (no fly).

octoiugus on the other (*TURS* 31), but unfortunately the surviving specimens are not well preserved enough to judge whether they might be the products of the same workshop. The token carrying representations of spectators and a ship (perhaps a reference to a *naumachia*?) survives as a single specimen now preserved in the British Museum; it bears a rectangular countermark beneath the spectators that reads IMP – a reference to the emperor (who would have been one of the few individuals with the resources to stage such a spectacle).[116]

One imagines that the representation of spectators was intended to generate a sense of anticipation, and to serve as a prompt to audiences, much like the tokens carrying acclamations discussed in Chapter 2. The representation of the audience also highlights the importance given to the crowd in situations of this kind: these public gatherings were arenas in which the Roman population might voice its approval or disapproval of particular emperors, and this was a potential source of tension and anxiety; indeed often Roman writers focused more on the actions of spectators than the spectacles themselves.[117] The chanting and involvement of the crowd were a key characteristic of spectacles; acclamations from the audience are even recorded on mosaics that commemorate such events.[118] As Fagan has explored, spectacles formed moments in which people were placed into

---

[116] *TURS* 538; *BMCRLT* 1304. Nero is recorded as hosting the first *naumachia* in an amphitheatre (Suet. *Ner.* 12.1; Dio 61.9.5, see also Dio 62.15.1).

[117] Bartsch, 1994: 1–31; Lim, 1999. Rostovtzeff also included a token with the legend SPEC|TAS on one side and a male figure on the other (*TURS* 565) amongst the tokens referring to spectators, although he admitted that he was not sure how the verb *spectare* was relevant in this context (Rostovtzeff, 1905b: 53). The verb is frequently found, however, on *tesserae nummulariae* (Kay, 2014: 125–6), and the token type thus might be connected to a group that was involved in the inspection or assaying of particular materials.

[118] Most famously perhaps on the mosaic of Magerius, see Adams, 2015. On the activities of the crowd at spectacles see Fagan, 2011.

temporary groups and developed a particular social identity echoed by the collective vocalisations and actions; the depiction of an audience on tokens may also have served to make such temporary identities salient.[119]

Participants in spectacles may also be represented on a series of tokens showing a woman with a cloth held in an arc over her head (Figure 4.17).[120] The representation is similar to *velificatio* (an artistic style where a deity is shown with cloth billowing around their head) but the figure on the token seems to be holding a piece of cloth entirely above their head with no material falling behind her. A variation on this type carries the legend P E C around the female figure.[121] Rostovtzeff wondered if the figure was Diana Lucifera, but the figure lacks the torch that is almost always represented with this particular form of the goddess. Indeed, a closer iconographic parallel can be found in late antiquity. On reliefs from this period (on the column of Porphyrius, the so-called 'Kugelspiel' now in the Bode Museum in Berlin, and the obelisk of Theodosius) we find representations of supporters of circus factions partaking in ceremonial dances; the participants are shown as figures holding a banner over their heads.[122] These dances took place at the conclusion of a race, with individuals waving banners that were the colour of the victorious team. Many (although by no means all) of these dancers, however, are men, and if the token carries a representation of such a dancer here, it is the only one known from the earlier imperial period. It is thus difficult to come to a firm conclusion, and the figure may also represent a Maenad or a different type of female dancer involved in an event. A bronze token type is decorated with three female

Figure 4.17 Pb token, 15 mm, 12 h, 2.19 g. Woman standing left holding cloth over her head in an arch / Lion springing right. *TURS* 2149.

---

[119] Fagan, 2011: 121–46; Carter, in press.
[120] One specimen of this type was found in the Tiber, see *NSc.* 1888, 439 no. 5.
[121] *TURS* 2147 (=2148); *BMCRLT* 1166. The letters may be the initials of a name. Twenty-two specimens of this type were found in the Tiber (*TURS* 2148.1–22).
[122] Cameron, 1973: 32–39; Lim, 1999: 355.

musicians dancing; such performers contributed to the overall experience of an event and are often represented on other media as part of a scene of spectacle or entertainment.[123]

That tokens were used during particular spectacles is evident from the specimens that specifically mention particular games or days. The best example of this is Figure 4.18, which specifically mentions *dies venat(ionis)*, days during which animal fights would take place. Other tokens carry a specific number in connection with a day: DIE I, for example (combined with the legend SPES on the other side), or the legend DIIII, which Rostovtzeff interpreted as a reference to the fourth day (*d(ies) quartus*) (Apollo is shown on the other side).[124] One imagines that tokens like these were used on one particular day during a longer celebration. Another token type carries the image of a female figure standing between two standing male figures who both wear tunics; the other side of the token carries the phrase LVD and a palm branch, a reference to *ludi*.[125] The identification of the three figures standing facing right is uncertain – the type might reference the public procession that took place before the games, which is referenced on other token types (see the discussion in Chapter 2).

The spectacles themselves are also shown on tokens, although the imagery of animal fights, gladiators and chariot racing was so popular in the Roman world we cannot know if these representations refer to specific events. References to *venationes* occurred via the representation of animals, frequently with a single animal shown on one side of a token, at times accompanied by a second animal on the other side, as on Figure 2.13.

Figure 4.18 Pb token, 16 mm, 2.46 g (die axis not provided). DIES VENAT around / palm branch. *TURS* 578.

---

[123] Buttrey, 1973: B 23/VII; Küter, 2019: 86–7. The mosaic in the Villa of Lucius Verus in Rome shows musicians alongside comic actors, and the Zliten mosaic includes musicians amongst its scenes from the amphitheatre, see Dunbabin, 2016: 32, 189.
[124] *TURS* 559–60. [125] *TURS* 561; *BMCRLT* 1322.

A *bestiarius*, an individual who fought animals in the arena, might also appear on one side of a token with an animal on the other; *bestiarii* are also very occasionally shown in the act of attacking an animal.[126] Different types of gladiator are also depicted, either alone or in combat.[127] On one type a gladiator carrying a *clipeus* (oblong shield) and a *gladius* (sword), possibly a Murmillo, stands on one side; on the other side of the token we find a helmeted Thraex (?) wearing greaves and carrying a small shield and curved sword. The legend reads CVR on one side and M on the other, which Rostovtzeff resolved as *cur(ator) m(uneris)*, a reference to an individual responsible for organising gladiatorial games.[128] Animal hunts were traditionally held in the morning, followed by executions at noon, and gladiatorial combats in the afternoon.[129] This programme of events, with different spectacles taking place throughout the day, is suggested by *TURS* 576, which shows two gladiators in combat on one side and an uncertain animal, poorly carved in the mould, on the other.[130] The two images combine to suggest a full day's entertainment.

Rostovtzeff believed this category of tokens constituted tickets to the spectacles shown.[131] But these pieces largely lack any information about dates or seating arrangements, so it is more likely they were used during a festival for distributions, or in another context.[132] Only three tokens featuring gladiators have recorded findspots, and these are all from the Tiber in the nineteenth century.[133] This is also the only recorded findspot to date of tokens carrying imagery of *bestiarii*.[134] The numbers are very small, but the absence of imagery of gladiators or *bestiarii* on tokens found in Ostia may be telling: as mentioned above, those living in Ostia may have had to travel to Rome for more extravagant displays.[135] Tokens showing animals, however, have been found in Ostia, although we cannot know if they were issued in the context of an animal fight. A token showing a lion

---

[126] *TURS* 579–705, although not all tokens listed may be connected to spectacles; some, particularly those showing boars, may also reference hunting activities.

[127] For example, *TURS* 568–77. Reference to gladiators is also made on the lead tokens from Mallorca, see Trilla Pardo and Calero Gelabert, 2008, who suggest the pieces might be entry tickets.

[128] *TURS* 528; Rostovtzeff, 1905b: 51; Lim, 1999: 345. The position of *editor* or 'producer', funnily enough, does not seem to be mentioned on tokens. On this role see Dunbabin, 2016: 172.

[129] Clarke, 2003: 144; Dunbabin, 2016: 173. [130] *TURS* Pl. IV, 57.

[131] Rostovtzeff, 1905b: 43–58, an idea also presented in Toynbee, 1948: 33, amongst others.

[132] Turcan, 1987: 56. Other material that has been viewed as amphitheatre tickets, from Arles, contain information about the *cavea* number, as well as which *cuneus* and tier a person was seated in, see Fagan, 2011: 100–1.

[133] *NSc.* 1888, 40 no. 14 (*TURS* 204); *NSc.* 1900, 261, nos. 61–2.

[134] *NSc.* 1900, 261 nos. 54–55. [135] Bruun, 2007: 131.

walking right was found during excavations of a sewer that ran towards the Tiber (the other side of the token was illegible), and another specimen decorated with the image of a bull on one side and elephant on the other (*TURS* 623) was found near the theatre during cleaning works.[136] A token showing a horse with a rider (with CCC on the other side) was also found in Ostia along the via di Diana; the piece was later moved to the Museo Nazionale in Rome and now cannot be found.[137] Rostovtzeff and Vaglieri also reported a token decorated with a rhinoceros standing right on one side and *modius* on the other as found in Ostia, but no further information is known.[138] In time, specimens showing gladiators or *bestiarii* may eventually come to light in Ostia.

Scenes from the circus also feature on tokens, with many images similar to that found on Roman lamps.[139] The representation of the *pompa circensis*, the procession that took place before spectacles in the circus, has already been discussed in Chapter 2. Tokens also carry imagery of *quadrigae* and *bigae* driven by charioteers or Victory, as well as representations of victorious horses and charioteers (Figure 4.19).[140] One lead token carries the image of a *desultor* on one side and a charioteer in a *biga* on the other.[141] A charioteer in a *biga* also appears on tokens of bronze alloy.[142] Several tokens may name particular horses: a legend reading EYC, for example, has been interpreted as the name *Eustolos* or 'Ready'; a horse is shown standing accompanied by a palm branch on the other side of the token. SACRATVS ('Holy') also appears on a token accompanied by the representation of a horse, as does RUSTIVC(us) ('Peasant').[143]

---

[136] *NSc.* 1908, 471 for the first token. For the second see *NSc.* 1911, 325; *GdS* 1911, 127 no. 4, Ostia Antiquarium inv. no. 4284.

[137] *GdS* 1915, no. 8, 52–3, Ostia Antiquarium inv. no. 9568.2. Another token type showing a horse galloping right with CCC above and a palm branch on the other side (*TURS* 789) is now in Berlin.

[138] Rostovtzeff and Vaglieri, 1900: 268 no. 2, pierced, of the type *TURS* 373.

[139] Rostovtzeff, 1905b: 54, who suggests a date of the first and second centuries AD for many of these tokens based on the similarities with lamp designs.

[140] See *TURS* 706–832, although all the tokens included in this range by Rostovtzeff are not necessarily connected to chariot racing, e.g. *TURS* 832 is likely connected to the *cisiarii* of Ostia, as discussed in Chapter 3.

[141] *TURS* 731; *BMCRLT* 1357. The image of the *desultor* is also known on Roman Republican coinage, see *RRC* 297/1, 346/1, 480/20–22.

[142] Buttrey, 1973: no. B24.

[143] *TURS* 819, 826–7. Rostovtozeff recorded *TURS* 825 as Romulus, thinking that a horse was named after Rome's founder, but close examination of the only surviving specimen of this type, currently in the Münzkabinett in Berlin, suggests that ROMV|TVS is the correct reading. Admittedly an error may have been made by the mould engraver. For a discussion of this category of tokens see Rostovtzeff, 1905b: 54; Toynbee, 1948: 33.

Figure 4.19 Pb token, 16 mm, 3.4 g, 6 h. Charioteer (*auriga*) standing left holding wreath in right hand and long palm branch in his left / Horse galloping right holding palm branch in its mouth. *TURS* 749, *BMCRLT* 1086.

Rostovtzeff suggested that the inclusion of particular names gave the tokens a programme style character, advertising the horses that would make an appearance. But the names of horses are also placed on other objects in the Roman world: late antique contorniates (which have numerous parallels with earlier lead tokens), for example, as well as gems and mosaics.[144] Circus races and charioteers are one of the most popular motifs in Roman art. The scenes on these tokens may have had a programmatic character, perhaps advertising forthcoming events during distributions or in other contexts.[145] But the victorious charioteer was also representative of success in life, as well as the victory of Rome and its rulers.[146] This is embodied in Figure 4.20, previously unpublished, which combines the image of a victorious horse with that of Victory inscribing a shield set upon a column, an image that repeatedly occurs on Roman coinage to communicate imperial military success. We cannot rule out the idea that the imagery of the circus may have been selected by token issuers in order to communicate success, in the same way an issuer might select a phallus, Fortuna or other imagery with positive connotations.

Several of the tokens that carry imagery associated with racing display the bust of Sol on one side. There was a temple to Sol and Luna at the Circus Maximus, and the representation of the deity on tokens no doubt reflects his strong connection to the circus and the events that took place within it.[147] More definitive references to the architecture of the circus are also found; this is unsurprising since, as Dunbabin has observed, most

---

[144] Toynbee, 1948; Henig, 1997: 51; Dunbabin, 2016: 157–67.
[145] Such distributions are, for example, recorded for Hadrian at the circus in Dio 69.8.2, though it is recorded that these distributions were mediated through 'little balls': δῶρα διὰ σφαιρίων καὶ ἐν τῷ θεάτρῳ καὶ ἐν τῷ ἱπποδρόμῳ χωρὶς μὲν τοῖς ἀνδράσι χωρὶς δὲ ταῖς γυναιξὶ διέρριψε.
[146] Henig, 1997: 51; Dunbabin, 2016: 167.
[147] *TURS* 754–7; Humphrey, 1986: 91–4; Hijmans, 2010: 387. The temple is shown on a coin issue of Trajan showing the Circus Maximus, *RIC* III 571 and Woytek, 2010: no. 175.

Figure 4.20 Pb token, 22 mm, 12 h, 7.88 g. Victory standing right inscribing shield that rests on a column / Horse standing right with palm branch in its mouth. *TURS* (Supplement) 3603.

representations of the circus include details of circus architecture.[148] One token type represents the dolphin markers that were used to count the laps of the racers, with a lion standing beneath the structure.[149] The turning posts (*metae*) of the circus also appear, combined with a variety of imagery on the other side of the respective tokens: the head of a victorious charioteer, clasped hands, the legend CAL, the statue of Victory atop a column that stood in the Circus Maximus, and the obelisk that stood in the centre of the track.[150] The Victory atop a column is repeatedly shown in reliefs portraying scenes from the circus. The image is also placed on a previously unpublished quadrangular lead token now in Berlin, where the image is combined with a figure placed within a distyle temple on the other side; unfortunately the token is now too worn to discern whether the structure represents a temple from the area of the circus itself.[151] One type, illustrated only through a line drawing, appears to show the erection of an obelisk via ropes; although Rostovtzeff included this among the tokens showing imagery connected to the Circus Maximus, there is not necessarily any reason that the obelisk shown was that in the hippodrome in Rome.[152]

A fragment of a token mould half that recently appeared on the market carries on it a design to produce circular tokens with the image of a chariot

---

[148] Dunbabin, 2016: 144.
[149] *TURS* 706, Pl. V, 18. On the marker see Humphrey, 1986: 262–4.
[150] *TURS* 707–11. See Humphrey, 1986: 268–9 on the Victory statue and obelisk in the circus.
[151] *TURS* (Supplement) 3636, Tray 12 of the Roman lead tokens in the Berlin Münzkabinett, photograph no. 1010190218050. For the image of Victory on the column see, for example, Musei Vaticani, Museo Gregoriano Profano inv. 9556 (early second century funerary relief), reproduced in Dunbabin, 2016: 145.
[152] *TURS* 712, figure 59.

racer in a *biga*; unfortunately no find information is associated with this piece.[153] A further mould half from Rome (without more precise information) carries the image of a horse; the image may not necessarily be connected to the circus.[154] Two tokens carrying the imagery of a *biga* on one side and Victory on the other (*TURS* 726) have a provenance of Rome, as does one specimen carrying the image of the circus *metae* on one side and a depiction of clasped hands on the other (*TURS* 708).[155] A token with a charioteer in a *quadriga* on one side and three corn-ears on the other was found in Ostia, but is lacking detailed information.[156] The find information associated with this type of imagery is thus scanty; not much can be said beyond the observation that this type of imagery is found on tokens in both Rome and Ostia.

Tokens carrying a reference to the theatre – whether drama, comedy, pantomime or mime – appear to be far less frequent than those referencing spectacles. They do exist though: one issue carries the image of a gladiator on one side and on the other a double-facing mask consisting of the bearded head of Silenus and a satyr; the two images might have been chosen to communicate a particular event that involved both theatre and spectacle.[157] A similar message was communicated by another token, which carried a satyr/Silenus mask on one side accompanied by a legend in Greek (ΑΞΙ), with an animal of some kind (quadruped) on the other.[158] A further possible reference to the theatre might be found on a token now in the British Museum, which shows a crude facing head on one side and a male figure on the other; the facing head may have been intended to represent a mask but we cannot be certain.[159] Rostovtzeff recorded another token showing a theatre mask on one side and clasped hands on the other; the location of the token is now unknown and so the description cannot be verified.[160] Although an enormous achievement for the time, Rostovtzeff's original catalogue does contain some errors and verification of the descriptions provided remains important. Indeed, this is illustrated by another token series recorded by Rostovtzeff as carrying the image of a comic mask

---

[153] Bertolami Fine Arts, Auction 44 (20 April 2018), lot 339.

[154] Cesano, 1904b: 16, fig. 8. Rostovtzeff recorded a further token mould with multiple designs on it, including Victory in a *biga*, as *TURS* 3599 (= *CIL* IX, 6087.1). Rostovtzeff expressed doubts about its authenticity.

[155] Rostovtzeff and Prou, 1900: 154–5, 157. [156] Rostovtzeff and Vaglieri, 1900: 268 no. 1.

[157] *TURS* 571, Pl. IV, 56. [158] *TURS* 2965. The meaning of the legend is not known.

[159] BMCRLT 394. See also Rostovtzeff and Prou, 1900: 150–1, which carry uncertain imagery, thought by Rostovtzeff and Prou to be a theatre mask.

[160] *TURS* 564. Rostovtzeff recorded that he had not seen this token, and reproduced a description given by Garrucci, 1847, 47 no. 10.

on either side (*TURS* 563); in fact the token is decorated on one side with the image of a ring from which a flask (*aryballos*) and two strigils are suspended and the other side of the token displays an uncertain image (a long oval shaped object decorated with five pellets) (Figure 5.10).[161] Representations of dramatic performances in Roman material culture (e.g. on mosaics) often also include musicians and so the bronze token mentioned above carrying representations of female musicians might be relevant to the discussion here, although one imagines that the focus in a dramatic context would likely be on theatrical masks or actors.

In addition to theatrical and musical displays, Greek festivals also frequently involved athletic events.[162] Representations of athletes are difficult to spot on tokens, which often carry crude representations that are little more than 'stick men'. Several tokens carry a male portrait wearing what might be a band or ribbon; Rostovtzeff identified these as the heads of male athletes, but this must remain only a suggestion.[163] Indeed, in some cases it is impossible to identify whether the portrait has a band or wreath, or whether the representation is of an athlete or a male youth more generally.[164] Full figure representations of athletes also remain difficult to identify: without an identifiable pose or attributes it is difficult to know whether the representation of a nude male represents an athlete, a Genius or some other heroic figure. The rounded hands of some figures do suggest boxers, however. Figure 4.21 is one such example: Victory crowns a nude male figure, whose hands seem to indicate that he is a boxer. The other side of the token shows a goddess holding a cornucopia and clasping hands with a smaller figure. The seated goddess may be raising a kneeling figure from the ground, or perhaps giving the figure something; the stark difference in the size of the figures recalls the numismatic representations of imperial *alimenta* given to children.[165] The combination of imagery is certainly unusual. Another token of this type was found during the works along the Tiber in the nineteenth century.[166]

---

[161] Turcan, 1987: no. 764. [162] Dunbabin, 2016: 22.
[163] For example, *TURS* 677, 844 (Pl. VIII, 58); Rostovtzeff and Prou, 1900: no. 533.
[164] For example, *TURS* 754.
[165] For example, *RIC* II Trajan 93 (Trajan standing before two small figures), 243 (Abundantia standing with cornucopia and corn-ears next to much smaller child), 461 (Trajan seated before woman with two children); Woytek, 2010: no. 345 with discussion on pp. 133–4. For the second specimen of this token type see Rostovtzeff and Prou, 1900: no. 169b.
[166] Rostovtzeff and Vaglieri, 1900: 261, no. 63.

Figure 4.21 Pb token, 21.5 mm, 6.29 g, 12 h. Victory, standing right, crowning a nude male figure (boxer?) with a wreath, who stands right before her / Female figure seated left with cornucopia in left arm, clasping hands with a smaller figure standing before her. *TURS* 550, *BMCRLT* 770.

Another possible boxer (a nude male with a clenched fist) appears on *TURS* 917, with an erect phallus shown on the other side.[167] Further victorious athletes may be shown on *TURS* 566–7, which show a nude male figure carrying a wreath and palm branch. *TURS* 579 is described as showing two figures in tunics wrestling, with a *bestiarius* on the other side. A palombino mould half, designed to produce six circular tokens showing two pankratiasts facing each other with raised fists, with an amphora between them and leaves blossoming around them, was found during the 1908 excavations of the 'Syrian Sanctuary' on the Janiculum hill in Rome.[168] Unfortunately no image of the find was provided and its current whereabouts are unknown. No known token matches this description.

There may be one further, as yet unnoticed, reference to Greek festival culture on the tokens of Rome and Ostia. Among the types recorded by Rostovtzeff were three that he described as being decorated with the image of an amphora, from which two or three ears of grain emerged (Figure 4.22).[169] The imagery is better interpreted as an amphora from which palm fronds emerge; this image is found on scenes showing prize tables from the Roman world.[170] Grain ears more normally emerge from a *modius* (see Figure 4.24 below); moreover, as Figure 4.22 demonstrates, the placement of the palm fronds is at each lip of the opening of the amphora, in keeping with the representation of prizes. Although some

---

[167] *BMCRLT* 1084.   [168] *NSc.* 1909, 410.
[169] *TURS* 434–6, Pl. IV, 6 and fig. 34. *TURS* 435 carried the image of a palm branch between two cornucopiae on the other side, and *TURS* 436 the legend AN|E – the meaning of the legend is unknown.
[170] For example, *RPC* VI, no. 6552 (temporary).

Figure 4.22 Pb token, 15 mm, 2.09 g, 12 h. Amphora with two palm branches / Amphora with two palm branches. *TURS* 434, *BMCRLT* 1982.

representations of prize tables referenced specific games, often this imagery was employed more generically to convey prestige, civic pride or acts of euergetism.[171] If these images are to be interpreted as an amphora with palms, the image may have been chosen as a prestige symbol to enhance a particular event or act.

The selection of boxers and pankratiasts for the handful of tokens referencing athletic events, with an apparent omission of other athletic activities, reflects broader iconographic preferences in the west of the Empire.[172] As with the other spectacles discussed in this section, the representation of athletes, or *amphorae* with palm branches, need not reference a particular festival; such images were popular motifs in bath decoration, for example, and in mosaics and paintings.[173] The depiction of a successful athlete on a token may have been intended to evoke a feeling of leisure, success or physical attainment.

While some motifs were more popular than others, the imagery of animal and gladiatorial fights, races within the circus, as well as athletic events, transcended a particular moment in time and appeared on Roman objects, floors, walls and streets. The imagery might serve to immortalise a particular benefactor's actions (and hence status), build anticipation of future experience or connect the viewer to the broader Roman spectacle-going community. These images, however, also acquired numerous other associations connected to leisure, success and victory. The regular occurrence of festivals (it is estimated that at least 135 days of the year were dedicated to games in Rome by the second century AD) and their imagery shaped Roman daily life, providing a framework within which to create and consolidate experiences, identities and communities.[174] Tokens and their imagery contribute a further perspective to this broader picture.

[171] Dunbabin, 2010. [172] Dunbabin, 2016: 50. [173] Dunbabin, 2016: 39.
[174] Dunbabin, 2016: 6.

Festivals, Feasts and Distributions

Large festivals and smaller events also frequently featured banquets or food distributions. As discussed above, the Saturnalia involved banqueting as part of the celebrations, and *collegia* also had particular festival days that involved feasting: an *ordo corporatorum* in Ostia, for example, held an annual banquet on 27 November, likely in connection with the birthday of Antinous.[175] The *collegium* of the *cultores Dianae et Antinoi* in Lanuvium held six banquets a year: on the birthday of the father of L. Caesennius Rufus (a patron of the association) on the 8 March, as well as on the birthdays of Rufus' brother (20 August), his mother (12 September), Rufus' own birthday (14 December), and on the birthday of Antinous (27 November) and of Diana (13 August). Food was provided by the annually elected *magistri*, who were responsible for the provision of sardines, loaves of bread, hot water and good wine. Another official (*quinquennalis*) of the *collegium* was responsible for providing members with oil in the public baths on the festival days of Antinous and Diana, as well as an amphora of good wine for the banquets.[176] Beyond these associations, magistrates or members of the elite might also provide public feasts to enhance their prestige: an inscription found at Portus and now lost recorded that one P. Lucilius Gamala sponsored a feast that was 217 *triclinia* in size; a feast (*epulum*) or a distribution of honeyed cakes and sweet wine (*crustulum et mulsum*) are attested in numerous other inscriptions.[177]

The act of communal dining serves to strengthen social bonds and social hierarchies.[178] Most banquets in the Roman world would have been limited to invited diners, whether members of a particular magisterial or priestly group, a particular *collegium*, or another social grouping. 'Invite only' events contributed to a sense of group cohesion: those holding an invite grouped against those not invited.[179] Who was served when, and what they were served, also reinforced hierarchies: the *collegium* of Asclepius and Hygeia, for example, explicitly details the differing amount of food and money given to individuals of different rank.[180] The sponsor of the feast would also have had their prestige enhanced by the occasion; the public recording of such events, like the feast held by Gamala mentioned above,

---

[175] *CIL* XIV, 246; Bruun, 2016: 361.
[176] *CIL* XIV, 2112; Bollmann, 1998: 38; Bendlin, 2011. On *collegia* and feasting more generally see van Nijf, 1997: 152–88; Perry, 2011: 506–11.
[177] Criniti, 1973; D'Arms, 2000; Donahue, 2003.   [178] van Nijf, 2002; Donahue, 2003: 424.
[179] Donahue, 2003: 432; Raja, 2020: 398.   [180] *CIL* VI, 10234; Donahue, 2003: 433–4.

demonstrate that the sponsoring of acts of commensality were an integral part of a public career.

The connection between tokens, prestige, community and banquets in the Roman world is best illustrated by the tokens of Palmyra (frequently called Palmyrene *tesserae*). Uniquely in the Roman world, Palmyrene tokens overwhelmingly portray and name priests in the city, who are frequently represented on the tokens reclining on a *kline* as during a banquet. Palmyrene tokens are found in large quantity around the banqueting hall of the main temple of Bel, where they were obviously disposed of after use.[181] The legends on these tokens may carry the name of the person or group offering the banquet, the names of the deities involved, the date of the event or even the measures of food or drink to be given to each attendee. The unique focus of Palmyrene token iconography reflects Palmyrene society; as Raja has noted, priestly representations constitute 25 per cent of all male funerary representations from Palmyra – becoming a priest, and all this involved, was clearly an important symbol of status.[182] Religious banquets cemented group cohesion, but also acted as a (unofficial) celebration of the sponsor.[183]

Can we find a similar role for tokens outside Palmyra? In Hellenistic Athens, tokens carrying the legend ΑΓ or ΑΓΟΡ have traditionally been connected with the *agorastikon*, a market tax collected by the *agoranomoi* from merchants; the tokens were seen as a proof of payment. More recently, however, Bubelis has pointed to the use of the word *agorastikon* in connection with the act of animal sacrifice: the word seems to indicate something that had to be purchased, with the resulting money funding the sacrifice; those who purchased the *agorastikon* had access to the sacrifice, or at the very least the feast that followed it.[184] Tokens from Tyre and Dobrogea have also been connected with possible feasts or distributions, but there is no conclusive evidence they were used in this manner.[185]

In Roman Italy, tokens do not overtly refer to banquets as on the issues of Palmyra. Direct references to priesthoods, via legend or imagery, remain relatively rare. But this is unsurprising. The study of tokens across the Roman Empire reveals their extremely local nature; the issues of Roman Italy were created by different types of individuals, who used a different language of prestige, and who operated within a different tradition of token making than those in Palmyra. The evidence from Rome and Ostia in

---

[181] Ingholt, Seyrig et al., 1955; Al-As'ad, Briquel-Chatonnet and Yon, 2005; Raja, 2015; Raja, 2019; Raja, 2020.
[182] Raja, 2019: 249. [183] Raja, 2019: 250; Raja, 2020: 394–5. [184] Bubelis, 2013.
[185] Abou Diwan and Sawaya, 2011: 274; Marin and Ionita, 2018: 589.

particular suggests that tokens were made by a variety of different social classes. As explored in the previous chapters of this volume, many Roman tokens appear to have been issued by those with the position of *curator* or *magister* and many seem to have preferred to have a token carry their portrait without the addition of other symbols. The specific use context of tokens in Roman Italy is rarely, if ever, spelt out in the legend.

Although Roman tokens do not show reclining banquet participants, tokens do portray an array of food and drink, which must have evoked feasting and distributions even if the tokens themselves were not actually used in these contexts. Figure 4.23, reportedly found in Rome, is one such example. Erroneously identified by Rostovtzeff as showing a rose, closer inspection of the image suggests that what is depicted is a loaf of bread seen from above, accompanied on the other side by a vessel with a handle.[186] The combined imagery evokes the idea of the distribution and/or consumption of bread and wine. Overbeck also wondered if many of the 'rosettes' recorded by Rostovtzeff were actually representations of bread; his discussion centred on *TURS* 1023, which shows a 'rosette' or loaf of bread on one side and a fish on the other, a combination that recalls the sardines and bread mentioned above.[187]

The same idea is captured on tokens that carry variations of a cantharus and *modius*, or other vessels that contained grain, wine or oil. An orichalcum issue is known that contains a cantharus on one side and a *modius* on

Figure 4.23 Pb token, 23 mm, 12 h, 6.21 g. Vessel with handle / Loaf of bread seen from above. *TURS* 1021, Rostovtzeff and Prou, 1900: no. 609.

---

[186] Another possible misidentification is *TURS* 382, which similarly probably shows a loaf of bread rather than a rose, with a *modius* shown on the other side. See the specimen *BMCRLT* 2040.
[187] Overbeck, 1995, 38 no. 200, see also nos. 196, 201–3.

Figure 4.24 Pb token, 18 mm, 6 h, 4.53 g. Male head right / *Modius* with three corn-ears. *TURS* 372, Rostovtzeff and Prou, 1900: no. 79.

the other (Figure 5.15), and a lead issue is decorated with a *modius* on one side and a *dolium* on the other.[188] Other issues carry imagery of various *amphorae* or *dolia* or have more creative representations – one issue, for example, carries a *modius* on one side accompanied by the legend FR and a nut or olive tree flanked by corn-ears on the other.[189] A lead token, now in Berlin, displays a bunch of grapes on one side with a measurement, CONGIVS, written on the other – presumably a reference to a specific amount of wine.[190] To reiterate, these tokens need not have been used as invitations for banquets in the same way as the Palmyrene *tesserae*; the imagery may simply have been used to evoke leisure and abundance – the presence of several tokens carrying *dolia* or *amphorae* in the baths of the *Cisiarii* in Ostia demonstrate this (discussed in Chapter 3). *Modii* were also a popular design for Roman coinage, which may have inspired their adoption on other monetiform objects.[191]

The imagery of grain, bread and wine is also associated with particular individuals on tokens in Rome and Ostia, although nowhere near as frequently as in Palmyra. Figure 4.24 is one such example, showing a portrait of an individual on one side and a *modius* on the other; presumably the recipients of the token would have recognised the identity of the individual and the token would have served to further heighten the connection of the benefactor with the benefaction received. Another issue carries an Antonine period portrait on one

---

[188] For the cantharus / *modius* type: Cohen: vol VIII, 272 no. 55 (orichalcum); *TURS* 378 (lead). For the *dolium* / *modius* type: *TURS* 377.

[189] *TURS* 993–1021 for the vessels, *TURS* 346 for the '*modius* / tree'. Rostovtzeff interpreted the FR as *fr(umentum)* or *fr(umentatio)*.

[190] *TURS* 101; Rostovtzeff, 1905b: 56.

[191] For example, *RIC* I^2 Claudius 84, 86–90 (*quadrantes*), *RIC* II.3^2 Hadrian 800, 2316–18 (*denarii*).

side, with two corn-ears and the legend MOD on the other, very probably a reference to a *modius*.[192] One issue combines the image of the *modius* with the legend GPRF on the other side, a reference to the Genius of the Roman people, and another issue combines a *modius* with the image of a rhinoceros.[193]

Moulds bearing this category of imagery have been found in Rome and Ostia. A single mould half that produced both square tokens carrying a cantharus and circular tokens showing a phallus was found on the Aventine hill in Rome; the combination of imagery here – with the erect phallus likely used as a symbol of luck – suggests that *modii* and similar imagery may have at times been chosen to communicate the idea of abundance rather than strictly being connected to a particular occasion.[194] The other two known mould halves with *modii* on them bore no other designs and are said to be found in Rome and Ostia respectively without further find information.[195]

Many of the known meeting houses (*scholae*) of *collegia* in Italy are not large enough to have enabled large groups to meet and banquet at once; as a result it has been suggested that different groups within an association may have feasted at different times.[196] One can imagine the use of tokens to mediate access in such circumstances, particularly for very large associations where members may not have known each other personally. Unfortunately, concrete evidence is once again extremely slim. As discussed earlier in this volume, tokens were issued by particular *collegia*, but their precise use remains uncertain. The only known find of a token in connection with the *schola* of an association in Italy is in Vada Volterrana, and even here the connection is uncertain.[197] The lead token carried the image of a helmeted male bust with a cloak, spear and shield on one side (either Mars or the emperor), and an uncertain image, which looks like a filleted spearhead, on the other. The token, suggested to date to the third or fourth centuries AD (most of the coins from the excavation are from this period), was found in a *horreum* of the port quarter. The surrounding area contained a bath complex and a structure that looks very much like a *schola*; a marble statue of Attis was also found nearby. Sangriso concluded that the workers of the area likely belonged to a *collegium*; given the small evidence available, they may have been *dendrophori*, a college connected to

---

[192] *TURS* 340 = *BMCRLT* 979. Rostovtzeff wondered whether the portrait was of Antoninus Pius, but the piece is too worn to make a definitive identification.
[193] *TURS* 373, 1584.   [194] *TURS* 3589 = Ruggiero, 1878: 218 no. 7.
[195] *TURS* 3585 = Ruggiero, 1878: 317 no. 2 (Rome); *TURS* 3598 (Ostia).
[196] Bollmann, 1998: 50.   [197] Facella, 2004: 52, no. 2153; Sangriso, 2017.

168   *Cult, Euergetism and the Imagery of Festivals*

the worship of Attis. The evidence here is too meagre to come to any firm conclusions; the token may also have been connected to the functioning of the baths or harbour, or may have been a casual loss. Some tokens from *collegia* do reference specific events, suggesting use at a particular moment in time – the adoption of an individual into a *collegium*, for example – but whether these are connected to feasts or not is another matter.[198]

The representation of foodstuffs on mosaics and frescos in the Roman world drew on a Hellenistic tradition that captured the gifts (*xenia*) a host might bestow upon his visitors.[199] These compositions might also include reference to particular festivals or events. Among the painted decoration in the *triclinium* at the House of Spurius Mesor at Pompeii, for example, is a goose and a basket of fruit accompanied by a sistrum; the design also features birds and fruit, athletic equipment and prizes.[200] The combination of foodstuffs and reference to particular festivals is also found in the Casa dei Cervi in Herculaneum: here figs, dates and coins are depicted, the gifts traditionally given on New Year's Day.[201] These representations contributed to the ongoing game of illusionistic art in the classical world (what is more tantalising than a bowl of fruit that looks real?), but they also undoubtedly acted as *omina*, expressing a desire that the inhabitants of the house would have fruitful, successful and sweet existences.[202] The depiction of foodstuffs on tokens may belong to the same tradition: the imagery may have served to act as a promise of the gifts that would be forthcoming from the benefactor (perhaps within a particular festival context), and/or express wishes for a fortunate and happy life. If we adopt such an understanding, these tokens need not have necessarily been used only for the distribution of the items depicted (although some may have been); rather the tokens allowed differing groups to adopt a visual language otherwise found on the walls and floors of elite housing, or on coinage. Viewed this way, the imagery is also an expression of prestige and authority.

The use of festival imagery across a variety of media in the Roman world in contexts not specifically connected with an event makes it difficult to know if a particular token was used as part of a celebration. Festivals,

---

[198] *TURS* 98; Héron de Villefosse, 1893: 350. The token shows three togate figures seated left on curule chairs surrounded by four fasces and accompanied by the legend COLLEGIVM; the other side of the token shows two draped standing figures and carries the legend ADOPTIO.

[199] Vitruv. *De arch.* 6.7.4; Ling, 1991: 154; Dunbabin, 1999: 298.   [200] Ling, 1991: 156.

[201] Thüry, 2012: 65. See also the Villa of Diomedes in Pompeii, which shows moneybags and fruit, another probable reference to the New Year.

[202] Thüry, 2012: 65–6 on *omina*; Squire, 2017 on the contribution of these images to the cultural fascination with illusion.

feasting and those who sponsored them were a key part of Roman culture; reference to and representation of this aspect of Roman life thus appeared on a variety of media throughout Rome and beyond. Tokens belong to this same tradition; while we might guess that some were used to facilitate particular distributions or access particular events, other token issuers may have employed festival imagery in a more abstract capacity. Relatively cheap and easy to produce, tokens underscored the prestige and identity of a particular benefactor while also acting upon the user or participant, shaping their experience of an event. There is still much to understand about the possible roles of tokens in festivals in Roman Italy, but it seems clear that tokens can be used as a source to better understand the imagery associated with such occasions.

5 | Tokens, Finds and Small-Scale Economies

The monetiform nature of lead tokens in Italy has repeatedly led scholars to conclude that these objects operated as a form of alternative currency. Dressel believed that an assemblage from the Tiber he published represented a privately issued emergency coinage, the 'till money' of an innkeeper or grocer.[1] Thornton identified these objects as a form of 'peasants' money'.[2] Rostovtzeff suggested some tokens acted as surrogates for money within small household economies and groups of clients. In this discussion Rostovtzeff cited Figure 5.1, a token that names two individuals, Olympianus and Eucarpus, as well as the sum of 1,000 *sestertii*. The portraiture style of the bust, as well as the dates of the tokens associated with the find (admittedly from the Tiber), suggests a date in the Julio-Claudian period or the first century AD. Rostovtzeff, acknowledging that the relatively large sum of 1,000 *sestertii* was unlikely to be represented by a single lead token, suggested the amount named on the series was the total value of the tokens issued by these two individuals.[3] The hypothesis is an intriguing one, although other interpretations are possible. The sum might represent the amount bequeathed by Olympianus and Eucarpus as capital to fund particular banquets or acts of euergetism (although it would be a modest amount in such a context), or the token issue might be an act of satire, given during the Saturnalia or another festival.[4] Others have seen this issue as evidence that tokens were used as *calculi* or counting pieces.[5]

Lead monetiform objects elsewhere have been interpreted as emergency small change, but for Roman Italy the evidence does not appear sufficient to come to this conclusion.[6] As explored in the previous chapters of this

---

[1] Dressel, 1922: 183.   [2] Thornton, 1980.   [3] Rostovtzeff, 1905b: 109.
[4] Duncan-Jones, 1974: 171–84 lists the capital donations for various foundations in Italy. Twenty-three are for 1,000 *sestertii* or less, the majority from the north of Italy. A sum of this amount for a foundation in Rome is thus not out of the question (especially since more modest foundations may not have been commemorated with a marble inscription and hence are invisible to modern scholarship), although, on the basis of current evidence, it would be unusual.
[5] van Berchem, 1936: 312; Turcan, 1987: 57.
[6] Milne, 1914: 94; Milne, 1971: xvii (Egypt, now questioned by Wilding, 2020); Hoover, 2006 (Nabataea); Amela Valverde, 2011: 124 (Iberia).

Figure 5.1 Pb token, 17 mm, 12 h, 3.95 g. Male bust right, OLYMPIANVS around / EVCARPVS around HS ∞. From the Tiber. *TURS* 1460.

volume, tokens might be utilised in a variety of ways. Some of these roles do overlap with the functions of money. Tokens could represent a particular value (i.e. a product or experience that was worth a certain amount), and, if issued in advance, form a type of credit. The findspots of tokens across Rome, Ostia and elsewhere (discussed in more detail below) do suggest that at least some were issued before a particular occasion or benefaction. An exploration of the use of tokens in the medieval period has demonstrated that they might act as IOUs to defer expenditure, or as a form of payment in kind rather than cash.[7] Some Roman tokens may have functioned in a similar way (with patrons issuing clients or customers tokens to be exchanged for goods rather than money), but there is no surviving evidence to confirm this was the case. This chapter explores the potential economic roles of tokens in Roman Italy, and the extent to which these objects facilitated the functioning of micro economies.

Was there a shortage of small change in Rome and Ostia during the imperial period that led to the creation of tokens similar to that shown in Figure 5.1? The Roman mint produced *quadrantes* and *semisses*, the smallest denominations in the imperial monetary system, throughout the first century AD and into the second, with *semis* production starting again in the later third century.[8] It has traditionally been thought that the *quadrans* denomination was utilised mainly in Italy, particularly in the region

---

[7] Courtenay, 1972: 289; Rennicks, 2019: 174.
[8] See *RIC* III Marcus Aurelius 1213, 1243 – listed by the *Roman Imperial Coinage* as '*semis* or *quadrans*'. Woytek, 2021: 816 observes that Mattingly did not always correctly distinguish between the *quadrans* and the *semis*, consequently some of the *quadrantes* listed in the *RIC* are actually *semisses*. See also Woytek, 2020b: 299, and the coins labelled as *quadrantes* in the *RIC* for Trajan now classified as *semisses* in Woytek, 2010, discussed on pages 158–62. After Marcus Aurelius, we find small bronzes again being produced under Trajan Decius (*RIC* IV.3 Trajan Decius 128). Abdy notes the difficulty in distinguishing between the denominations on the basis of metal alone (*quadrantes* are struck in copper, *semisses* in brass), particularly in connection to specimens which are found on excavation and so adopts a system which may not be strictly

between Rome and Pompeii. However recent work has demonstrated that later *quadrantes*, particularly from the reign of Domitian, travelled beyond Italy to be used elsewhere.[9] Although the find evidence from Italy is patchy, the evidence as it survives suggests Julio-Claudian *quadrantes* were relatively common in the region. Later issues of small change are less frequently found and appear to have been shipped to the provinces in greater quantities.[10] From our current evidence, the production of small change in the first and second centuries largely overlaps with the zenith of lead token production in Rome and Ostia (which begins in the first century and continues into the second).

More research is required to better understand the role of the small bronzes within the Roman monetary system.[11] A *semis* was half an *as*, a *quadrans* a quarter of an *as*. Surviving price lists suggest the *quadrans* was too small to have actually purchased anything on its own, apart from entrance into the Roman baths.[12] Indeed, Reece suggested the denomination served as 'change necessary for equity', that is, solely to be provided as change, much like small one or two cent pieces today.[13] Significant numbers of *quadrantes* in boxes or *dolia* in shops in Pompeii suggest Reece may be correct – the *quadrans* may have existed to 'provide change'.[14] King also pondered the oddity of this denomination, and suggested that perhaps *quadrantes* did not primarily serve as small change, but were instead issued to fulfil some other administrative requirement – imperial *congiaria*, for example, although she admitted there is little evidence to support this idea.[15] Weigel wondered whether some small bronzes (the so-called 'anonymous' issues) were struck for public religious celebrations.[16] This hypothesis provoked a rebuttal by Buttrey, who noted that the small number of issues mean that they cannot have been a regular feature of festivals held each year; he concluded we are unable,

---

accurate for the new *RIC* of Hadrian – only coins smaller than 15 mm in diameter are classified as *quadrantes* (Abdy and Mittag, 2019: 2).

[9] Kemmers, 2003. See also Woytek, 2020b: 299–301, who details finds of *semisses* and *quadrantes* outside of Italy.

[10] For example, to the northern frontier. See King, 1975: 74; Kemmers, 2003: 28.

[11] The most detailed study remains van Heesch, 1979.

[12] Kemmers, 2003: 18, who notes that prices only include *quadrantes* as part of a larger amount, and that the epigraphic evidence from Pompeii suggests that a small family would probably need 6–7 *sestertii* per day for basic foodstuffs, although prices of course might differ over time and in different geographical areas.

[13] Reece, 1982: 129.

[14] Kemmers, 2003: 28. Woytek, 2020b: 298–9 observes that some parts of Pompeii have furnished more *quadrantes* than others, although it is clear the denomination played an important role in the city.

[15] King, 1975: 80–2.   [16] Weigel, 1998.

given the current state of knowledge, to know what the purpose of the *quadrans* denomination was.[17]

Ancient literature, particularly satirists, use the word *quadrans* to highlight a particularly small amount; these same authors also use the phrase 100 *quadrantes* to refer to the dole given by a patron to his client.[18] Martial repeatedly connects this dole with bathing; the entrance to the baths was one *quadrans*.[19] Indeed, Seneca uses the phrase *res quadrantaria* when describing Roman baths.[20] The denomination thus must have been useful in this regard – had there been no *quadrantes*, the purchasing of bath access would have been hampered by lack of appropriate specie. One additional item that might have been purchased for a *quadrans* seems to have been overlooked to date in modern scholarship: Varro tells us that this was the cost charged for ferry transport by raft.[21] That the Roman government issued small change in the form of *quadrantes* and *semisses* reflects that fact that some consideration must have been given to the role of small change in facilitating the economy and everyday transactions.[22]

During the second century AD the Roman mint ceased production of *quadrantes*, perhaps because price rises meant they became even less useful, or perhaps because the cost of their production now outweighed their value. We have little information in this regard. Since token production began in earnest in Rome in the first century AD, we cannot argue that lead tokens were produced to fill a void of small change after production of *quadrantes* ceased. But to what extent did tokens take on some of the roles played by small change, thereby easing any pressure on small change supply that might have occurred?

Quadrantes and *semisses* bear some similarity to lead tokens in that they did not always carry a portrait of the emperor, and at times *quadrantes* also lacked a legend referring to the imperial authority. Many *quadrantes* types, particularly of the Julio-Claudian period (altar, cornucopia, clasped hands and caduceus, *modius*), are also found on tokens. Indeed, one of the most common types amongst the tokens published by Dressel as a merchant's 'till' was Figure 5.2, which carries an altar on one side and a *lituus* on the other. The 'bowl-shaped' altar appears on several *quadrantes* issues under Augustus (Figure 5.3)

---

[17] Buttrey, 2000.
[18] A *quadrans* as a paltry amount: Juv. *Satires* 7.8; Mart. *Ep.* 2.44.9. On 100 *quadrantes* as a dole: Juv. *Satires* 1.120; Mart. *Ep.* 1.59, 3.7, 8.42, 10.70.10 (these texts also mention the use of *quadrantes* in the baths), 6.88. Discussion in Harrison, 2001: 299.
[19] See references in footnote directly above. On the cost of entrance to the baths see also Cic. *Cael.* 62, with discussion in Turcan, 1988: 628; Nielsen, 1990: 131–2.
[20] Sen. *Ep.* 86.9. [21] Varro, *Ling.* 5.44. [22] Woytek, 2020b: 286.

Figure 5.2 Pb token, 14 mm, 2 h, 2.12 g. Garlanded altar / *Lituus*. From the Tiber, *TURS* 1072.

Figure 5.3 Copper *quadrans*, 18.5 mm, 6 h, 3.19 g, 8 BC. Cornucopia flanked by S C, PVLCHER TAVRVS REGVLVS around / Garlanded altar, III·VIR A A F F · around. *RIC* I² Augustus 425.

and the *lituus* also appeared alongside a *simpulum* on *quadrantes* of 9–8 BC.²³ Of the collection of tokens published by Dressel, this type was by far the most numerous: of the 487 tokens, 205 were of this type.²⁴ Dressel suggested that the tokens found in higher numbers were those of the till owners themselves and that the other tokens, present in smaller numbers, represented the issues of others. A significant quantity of this type (139 examples) was also among the Tiber finds published by Rostovtzeff and Vaglieri.²⁵ This token issue, it seems, has survived in much higher quantity than any other. Beyond the two assemblages from the Tiber, however, no further specimens have come to light (in excavation publications or museum collections). This might be a reflection of the very small circulation area of tokens.

---

[23] *RIC* I² 421–2, 424–5, 443–68. The legend III·VIR A A A F F is a reference to the position of moneyer (*tresviri auro argento aere flando feriundo*, the three men for the casting and striking of gold, silver and bronze).

[24] Dressel, 1922: 180 no. 21.   [25] Rostovtzeff and Vaglieri, 1900: 439, no. 1.

But despite these similarities, we should not see Italian lead tokens as emergency or privately issued small change. To begin with, lead tokens simply do not survive in sufficient quantity to have functioned as a currency. The altar and *lituus* token issue discussed above is an anomaly in terms of the quantity that has survived – we otherwise find only a handful of each type preserved, or a single known specimen. The overall picture may have been affected by museum acquisition practice: for Roman coinage, museums historically have focused on obtaining rare pieces, or selected only one or two examples of a type to include in their collections. A similar phenomenon might have occurred with lead tokens. The token assemblage now housed at the Museo Archeologico Nazionale di Palestrina, coming from illicit excavations, contains far more tokens of the same type than other European national collections. It also contains far more examples of tokens that might have been overlooked by antiquarian collectors as not being of great interest – for example, tokens that carry only a single letter on each side. Like Roman coinage, the overall image gained from tokens in museum collections may not necessarily reflect the realities of what was in circulation. But even those tokens which appear in number (e.g. the 344 'altar/*lituus*' tokens from the Tiber) still do not seem to have the characteristics of an alternative currency: their concentrated findspot, for example (the Tiber and nowhere else), suggests they did not 'circulate', even within a relatively small area. Indeed, the 'altar/*lituus*' series may have been used for an event or distribution in a particular moment in time, after which the tokens lost their value and were discarded.

The quantities and findspots of lead tokens in the archaeological record give the impression of accidental survival of artefacts that were otherwise utilised for a moment in time and then melted down for reuse – the tokens we find today are the result of accidental loss, rather than intentionally deposited for their value. Tokens of bronze and orichalcum also do not survive in large quantities, certainly not the numbers known for other issues of emergency small change in antiquity. The pseudo-coinages that acted as unofficial small change in the region around Pompeii and Minturnae, for example, with designs adopted from the coinages of Massalia and Ebusus, survive in significantly higher quantities.[26]

---

[26] Stannard, 2005; Stannard and Frey-Kupper, 2008; Hobbs, 2013: 133–56 records 688 coins of Massalian and Ebusan type from the AAPP excavations of Regio VI, Insula 1 (from a total of 1,512 coins found), although he does not distinguish between imports and products of the pseudo-mints; Stannard, 2019 observes that from a purse of ninety coins from Pompeii, fifty-five are issues of a pseudo-mint.

Moreover, lead tokens do not attempt to imitate official currency; in fact they are consciously different in design, even when coin imagery forms a point of inspiration. Tokens of Roman Italy, in bronze, orichalcum or lead, are also not generally found intentionally hoarded with official Roman coinage, discussed further below. This is an important point of difference from pseudo-coinage or emergency small change, which is found stored together with official coinage – in Pompeii for example.[27] These characteristics suggest tokens served a different purpose to Roman currency, and were recognised as 'different' by users. Some functions of tokens, however, may have overlapped with those of currency.

Tokens and Roman Baths

Some Roman lead tokens specifically name Roman baths, or bath managers (*balneatores*) and scholarship has suggested a connection between these artefacts and the administration of bathhouses. Rostovtzeff suggested these types of tokens were used to gain access to particular bathing establishments.[28] Lead tokens have also been interpreted as a method to carry out euergetism in this context: tokens may have facilitated the sponsoring of free access to the baths by particular individuals.[29] Tokens have also been connected to the internal administration of a bathhouse – used to mediate access to particular services, for example, like massage, oil, food or drink.[30] Scholarship, however, remains rightly tentative – it is extremely difficult to deduce the precise use of tokens in bathing contexts, and studies of bathing in the Roman world more broadly have revealed that we cannot generalise: customs were different from region to region and bathhouse to bathhouse.[31] Nonetheless, several new archaeological finds have come to light since the last published scholarly discussion of this issue, and it is worth revisiting the question in the light of the recent evidence.

Some of the earliest evidence for tokens in Italy is connected with bathing. During excavations in Fregellae, a settlement captured and destroyed by the Romans in 125 BC, tokens of both lead and bone were uncovered. In a stratum associated with the spoliation of a wall (probably of a private house), a bone token was found with the legend L. ATIN | MEM carved on one side and BALN (or BALIN) with ligate lettering on the other.[32] Palaeography and the archaeological context date the piece to

---

[27] For example, the purse hoard analysed by Stannard, mentioned in n. 26 above.
[28] Rostovtzeff, 1905b: 102–3; Turcan, 1988: 629.   [29] Nielsen, 1990: 134; Fagan, 2002: 162.
[30] Pedroni, 1997: 209.   [31] Turcan, 1987: 59; Fagan, 2002.   [32] Sironen, 1990.

c. 150–125 BC. The legend might refer to the position of *balneator*, or a *bal(i)neum*, *bal(i)n(ae)* or *bal(i)ne*; the abbreviated name has been resolved as Lucius Atinius Memmianus. *Balneum*, *balnea*, and *balnae* were words used to refer to baths in the Republic. The term *thermae* appeared only in the first century AD, although *balineum* continued to be used, likely to refer to establishments that were not as lavish as *thermae*.[33]

A structure that has been identified as the baths of Fregellae has been uncovered, thought to have been erected around 190/180 BC. Excavations of this structure uncovered five lead tokens, found close together in a 'gruzzoletto' in the central space of the south entrance of the baths.[34] The context appears to be one of spoliation; the five tokens were all of the same design, and likely made from the same mould. One side of the tokens displayed the bust of Mercury wearing a petasus with three globules before him, while the other side was decorated with a dolphin swimming right. Pedroni noted the water associations of the dolphin, and wondered if the three globules were meant to represent a particular value: a *triens* or *quadrans*, which might have been the cost of entry to the baths.[35] Globules are used to indicate particular values on Republican bronze coinage; *RRC* 97/5c and 98A/5 (c. 211–208 BC) have the head of Mercury on the obverse and a ship's prow accompanied by three globules on the reverse, indicating the coin is a *quadrans*. As in the later imperial period, the tokens of Fregellae appear to have adopted contemporary numismatic imagery while avoiding straight imitation (choosing a dolphin design instead of a prow).[36]

The 'pseudo-coins' and lead tokens in Baetica and Italy in the second and first centuries BC also carry imagery of bathing. As Stannard has established, these lead and bronze pieces were produced in both Baetica and Italy, with issues in both regions carrying similar designs.[37] Amongst the shared imagery is the type of a ring, two strigils and an *aryballos*, at times carried by a dog on Italian pieces.[38] Another series carries an image that was previously identified as a 'miner' but which has now been correctly identified as a *furnacator*, the individual responsible for stoking the fire of a bath's hypocaust.[39] A type in struck lead has also come to light. This

---

[33] Fagan, 2002: 14–18, who observes that this was then a value judgement on behalf of the individual; there does not seem to be a hard and fast rule for the use of either term.

[34] Pedroni, 1997: 206.   [35] Pedroni, 1997: 210.

[36] A dolphin as the main design did occur on earlier Roman bronze, see *RRC* 14/3 (*triens*, 280–276 BC), and 25/6 (*triens*, 241–235 BC).

[37] Stannard, 2007 for a provisional catalogue of these pieces.

[38] Stannard, 1995: 71; Stannard, 2020: 98, where Stannard suggests the dog might be connected to a cult or ritual story associated with the baths.

[39] Stannard et al., 2017: 81; Stannard, Sinner et al., 2019: 127; Stannard, 2020: 98.

shows Apollo seated on an omphalos, offering two strigils and an *aryballos* to a small nude male figure before him; the other side of the token displays a prow and two globules (a design adapted from Roman Republican coinage).[40] In spite of the bathing imagery, the sheer production volume of the Italo-Baetican series, and the fact that bathing imagery is often combined with other types that have no apparent connection to Roman bath culture, meant Stannard concluded that these are more than bathing tokens, although their precise function remains elusive. More recently Stannard has suggested the strigil type might be connected with euergetism – gifts of vinegar and oil to bathers, free entry, or something larger in scale, for example connected to bath building or management.[41]

Although undoubtedly more work needs to be done, there does seem to be a connection between tokens and bathing in the Republic, which continued into the imperial period. The archaeological evidence, particularly from Ostia, suggests the use of lead tokens within bathing houses, although we should remain cautious in our conclusions. Bathhouses, after all, are places where small items like lead tokens are likely to be dropped and lost, and so it is difficult to distinguish between accidental loss and intentional use. What follows is a discussion of the relevant evidence that connects some tokens to bathing; although each individual instance may not be convincing on its own, the combined weight of the data does suggest a connection between bathhouses and lead tokens. The finds from the baths of the *Cisiarii* in Ostia have already been discussed in Chapter 3; all the tokens in that complex came from what is interpreted as the frigidarium (Room C), largely from fill contexts.[42]

Excavations in the Baths of the Swimmer ('Le Terme del Nuotatore') in Ostia uncovered lead tokens, a token mould half, as well as token manufacturing waste. In stratum 1 of area XVI (dated from the middle of the third century to the middle of the fourth century AD), a fragment of a token mould was uncovered, designed to produce circular tokens showing a beetle.[43] In an earlier layer (stratum II, dated to the end of the second century and beginning of the third century AD), lead waste was found, which bears the characteristic 'tree branch' design of the channels carved into token moulds.[44] The logical conclusion is that this is waste from the casting of lead tokens, which in all likelihood took place on site. For the

---

[40] Stannard, 2020: 96.
[41] Stannard et al., 2017: 82; Stannard, 2020: 104. Bathing equipment is also shown on tokens of Hellenistic Athens, see Engel, 1884: no. 218 (with thanks to Mairi Gkikaki for the information).
[42] Spagnoli, 2017b.   [43] Carandini and Panella, 1977: 271; Rowan, 2019: 100–1, no. 52.
[44] Carandini and Panella, 1977: 271, fig. 307.

period in which the casting waste was uncovered, however (Phase 4a, post AD 190–210), the area was likely no longer part of the bathhouse. Area XVI is in the western part of the complex, thought to have been converted into a place of habitation by this time, with XVI identified as a *popina* or wine bar.[45]

In area XXV of the baths, which was an open-air corridor in the northeast of the complex linking several service areas (ovens, a cistern), three lead tokens were uncovered. The first of these carried the imagery of Fortuna and a female figure (probably Juno with patera and sceptre) and was found in stratum VA (dated AD 80–90 and associated with hydraulic installations). The other two tokens were found in stratum III (AD 190/200–225). One was decorated with a *furca* or a stylised caduceus flanked by stars on one side and the legend F C on the other (*TURS* 3065; the meaning of F C is unknown). The second was decorated with a palm branch on one side and what is probably the letters PM on the other (*TURS* 691–2).[46] An additional lead token was later excavated immediately outside the northeast area of the complex, carrying the imagery of Isis or a worshipper of Isis on one side and a semi-nude male figure on the other; the stratum of this piece is dated to AD 160–180/90 and is connected the levelling of the area in the late Hadrianic and Antonine period.[47] The sum total of the token evidence from the Baths of the Swimmer reveals token use throughout the lifetime of the complex (which was built in AD 89–90), although we cannot definitively connect the finds with bathing.

The excavations of the Baths of Neptune ('Terme di Nettuno') in the early twentieth century also uncovered a lead token and a token mould, although as is typical of early excavations, we do not possess detailed stratigraphic data. A hexagonal mould half that created nine quadrangular tokens of 8 × 8 mm, each decorated with three globules, was found during excavations of the southern side of the peristyle of the baths near the via della Fontana.[48] Unfortunately we cannot be certain of the precise context the mould half was found in – whether it was a stratum of use, abandonment or fill.

In the same excavations, conducted by Vaglieri from 1909 to 1910, a lead token was found in a place described as the 'second *taberna*' of the baths, if one counted from the via dei Vigili.[49] The design of the token, as

---

[45] Medri et al., 2013: 64–5.
[46] Carandini and Panella, 1977: 391. The meaning of PM is unknown; it may be the initials of a name.
[47] Pardini, 2014: 4. Twenty coins were also uncovered.   [48] Vaglieri, 1909: 200.
[49] *NSc.* 1910, 553; *GdS* no. 3, 1910, 227, inventory no. 3575.

mentioned in Chapter 3, was the lighthouse of Ostia and the legend TI S on one side, and Fortuna seated left on the other side (*TURS* 61, Figure 3.10; the meaning of the legend remains a mystery). A token of the same type was found in the Terme Bizantine in Room D; Spagnoli suggested this piece likely dates from the earlier period of the baths, in the latter half of the second century AD.[50] Pensabene records a third bath context for this token type, from the Terme di Serapide.[51] Although the discovery of three tokens of the same type in three different bath complexes may suggest the use of this token in a particular citywide benefaction (e.g. gifting of free bath access, granting of particular goods for use in the baths), the finds are solitary and the type is also found elsewhere (stray finds from illegal metal detecting, a token that seems to be of this type was also found in a late antique context from Portus).[52] The finds of the lighthouse token series may thus simply reflect that the piece was carried across the city. Apart from the example of the baths of the *Cisiarii*, tokens are found in very small numbers in bath complexes, and not found collected together as one would expect if they served a particular exchange function within the complex. That said, it may simply be that, since Ostia continued to be inhabited into late antiquity (when tokens appear to have been used differently), no abandoned or preserved 'hoard' exists to be discovered. Spagnoli is currently working on publishing a corpus of eight tokens from the area of the Terme sotto la via dei Vigili, which may serve as a complementary example to the relatively large amount of tokens from the Terme dei *Cisiarii*.[53]

A far more significant number of lead tokens (150 in total) were found during the 1981–3 excavations of a Roman bath complex in Alameda in Spain.[54] The baths were constructed in the latter half of the first century AD. Twenty-seven coins were also found, dating from Augustus to the second half of the second century AD, with one outlier – an *antoninianus* of Galerius. The tokens, also thought to date to the first few centuries AD, were in a poor state of preservation, but carried a variety of designs, including male and female heads (including radiate male heads), animals, vessels, globules, stars and a cross with four globules design. Mora Serrano notes that they seem to fall into two diameter groups: one of 15–16 mm and one of 9–12 mm.[55] The excavation records do not reveal much about the

---

[50] Pensabene, 2001–3: 497; Spagnoli, 2017a: 271; Ostia inv. 33110.
[51] Pensabene, 2001–3: 497; Ostia inv. 4741, Mag. Vet. V, 4.
[52] Pensabene, 2001–3: no. 36; Spagnoli, 2011: 215.   [53] Spagnoli, 2017a: 270.
[54] Mora Serrano, 2002.   [55] Mora Serrano, 2002: 50.

findspots of these tokens within the complex, and Mora Serrano refrains from interpreting their use – the bathhouse may also have had a cultural-religious aspect, indicated by a rectangular edifice at the foot of the adjacent La Camorra mountain and an altar found nearby dedicated to *Isis Bulsae*.[56] Although the quality of the find information is not ideal, the existence of a large number of tokens from this site, in comparison with far fewer coins, does hint at use within the bathing complex, whether or not bathing was undertaken as part of a cultic experience.

No other published bath complexes from the Roman Empire carry such a high number of token finds, but lead tokens are found in these contexts. In Ephesus, four lead tokens were found in a debris layer of the frigidarium of the bath on the western slope of Mount Pion. The tokens are uniface and all carry the same design: the forepart of a boar being speared by Androklos, the mythical founder of the city.[57] A theta is placed above Androklos' spear. The same image (without the theta) is found on Ephesus' third century civic coinage.[58] Baier suggested these tokens might have been used to access the private bath complex, with the theta (Θ) perhaps referring to *therma* (θερμά), warm baths.[59] A second example from outside Italy is the find of a single token with the legend L. II A within a wreath, which was uncovered in the sediments of the frigidarium drain at Caerleon in Britain.[60] This is just as likely to be an accidental loss as an object connected to the functioning of the bathhouse.

Remarkably, the small amount of token finds from baths in Roman Italy contain no examples that make specific reference to particular bathing establishments, bathing activities, or individuals connected to bathing complexes (e.g. those with the position of *balneator*). And yet tokens of this nature exist, offering us further evidence for the connection between at least some tokens and this popular Roman activity. *TURS* 886, for example, carries the legend BALI|NEVM GER|MANI, which has been interpreted as the name of a particular bathing establishment that is otherwise unknown (Figure 5.4).[61]

---

[56] Mora Serrano, 2002: 52–3. [57] Baier, 2017: 125. [58] For example, *RPC* VII.1 369b.
[59] Baier, 2017: 131 n. 39.
[60] Caerleon: *RIB* II.1 2408.3; Boon, 1986; Wilding, 2020. The legend referred to the *legio II Augusta*, which was stationed at Caerleon; similar abbreviations occur on lead seals.
[61] Platner and Ashby, 1929: 69; Richardson, 1992: 49; Fagan, 2002: 365. For another specimen see Harvard Art Museums inv. no. 2008.116.14. *TURS* 1421 also carries the legend GERMANI (but arranged around the edge of the token in a circle), with an image of Mercury on the other side.

Figure 5.4 Pb token, 18 mm, 12 h, 4.09 g. BALI|NEVM / GER|MANI. *TURS* 886. Rostovtzeff and Prou, 1900: no. 415b.

Other tokens types carry the legend BAL, thought to be an abbreviation of *balineum* or *balneator*.[62] *TURS* 888, for example, carries the legend BAL on one side and the legend TIC|ILL on the other. In his catalogue, Rostovtzeff suggested the legend might be understood as *Bal(ineum) Ti. C(laudi) Ill(ustris)* or similar. More recently, Bruun has suggested the type may have referenced the *balneum Tigellini*, an establishment also mentioned by Martial.[63] Quite often the rendering of G on Roman lead tokens looks very close to (or indeed the same as) a C, so the suggested reading is very plausible. Indeed, on the specimen now in the Museo del Castelvecchio of Verona, the letter does appear to be a G.[64] The individual named may be the Tigellinus who acted as praetorian prefect under Nero.[65] A *bal(ineum) nov(u)m* is also mentioned on lead tokens (*TURS* 887). Rostovtzeff believed that a token carrying the legend L·DOMITI·PRIMIG, accompanied by the image of an amphora of oil and a jug, referenced the bathing establishment of one Lucius Domitius Primigenius (the other side of the token issue was decorated with a ring from which strigils and an *ampulla* were suspended).[66] The existence of a name consisting of a *tria nomina* and the absence of the letters BAL on this series leaves open the possibility that these tokens may have been issued as part of a bathing benefaction

---

I was unable to find a specimen of this type for examination, so cannot say whether the token, stylistically speaking, may belong to the same series as *TURS* 886.

[62] *TURS* 887–93. It is worth noting that the entrance fee to the baths could be called a *balneaticum* (Fagan, 2002: 165).

[63] Bruun, 1999: 84; Mart. *Ep.* 3.20, 16. Fagan, 2002: 362 names the baths the *balneum Tigillini*.

[64] Arzone and Marinello, 2019: no. 317. The specimen reproduced in Turcan, 1987: no. 171 is unfortunately worn.

[65] Fagan, 2002: 362.   [66] *TURS* 895; Fagan, 2002: 365.

by Primigenius – free access to a particular bath house, for example, or free oil.

Where a name occurs directly before BAL, it is likely that we have reference to a *balneator*, the manager or contractor of a complex. *TURS* 892 carries the legend IVL | BAL, which likely references a *balneator* named Jul(ius); Mercury seated on a ram is shown on the other side.[67] Another issue carries BAL on one side and IV on the other – one cannot know whether this is a number (IV), a reference to a *balneator* named Julius, or a complex called the *bal(ineum) Iu(lium)*.[68] *TURS* 890 has the same ambiguity, carrying the legend BAL on one side and FEL on the other – this may reference a bath manager, a bathhouse or perhaps communicate a wish for the possessor of the token to have a good bathing experience (*fel(iciter)*). A similar sentiment is expressed on a mosaic from the bathing complex at Thamugadi in North Africa: the image of sandals is accompanied by the text BENE LAVA.[69] *TURS* 893 carries the legend SVB | BAL, which likely refers to someone with the cognomen Sub(erinus) or similar; Victory is portrayed standing on the other side.

Although the full range of responsibilities associated with the position of *balneator* may never be known (and indeed, these may have varied from establishment to establishment), it seems that the word could reference an owner, leaseholder or manager of a private bathhouse.[70] The position was normally found in bathhouses that could not afford numerous employees.[71] Nielson suggests that in the vast majority of cases the leaseholder employed a manager for the bathhouse, normally a freedman, a member of the lower classes, or a slave.[72] Ulpian's *Digest* records *balneatores* and *fornacatores* (fire-stokers) as *instrumenta balnei* ('bath equipment') included as part of the property left in a legacy.[73] Epigraphic evidence does little to clarify the role of these individuals.[74] But textual evidence does provide some insight into at least one of their functions: the *balneator* is mentioned in texts as the person who, among other activities, accepts the fee from a customer and then allows them to enter the bathhouse.[75] This does suggest that those tokens naming

---

[67] Bruun, 1999: 84.   [68] *TURS* 891.   [69] Nielsen, 1990: vol. 1, 141–2, vol. 2, 79.
[70] Bruun, 1993: 223.   [71] Nielsen, 1990: vol. 1, 127.   [72] Nielsen, 1990: vol. 1, 127.
[73] *Dig.* 33.7.13.1, 33.7.17.2, 33.7.14.1, with discussion in Fagan, 2002.
[74] Bruun, 1993: 223 on the small amount of epigraphic evidence for these individuals. In Rome, a *balneator* is mentioned in *CIL* VI, 6243, 7601, 8742, 9102, 9216, 9217 (*balnea(toris)*), 9395 (*balneatoris*), and 9396, but little information is provided other than the name, and occasionally a social status (e.g. *servus*).
[75] Cic. *Cael.* 62; Mart. *Ep.* 3.7.3. For other tasks and characterisations see Plin. *HN* 18.156 (using seeds on coals to drive bathers away), SHA *Comm.* 1.9, *Car.* 17.9 (held responsible for the temperature of the baths), *Alex. Sev.* 42.2 (emperor only employing slaves in the position).

particular *balneatores* may have been used to gain access to particular bathing establishments. The fact that no *thermae* are named on Italian tokens may indicate that these artefacts were mainly used within smaller, private establishments, the type that attracted the term *balineum* and which employed *balneatores*. However, the presence of tokens in larger *thermae* in Ostia suggests otherwise; it may be then that smaller establishments had to take pains to be specific on their tokens, while larger establishments needed no such identifying legend. If the tokens discussed above were issued by particular *balneatores*, they provide a rare piece of material culture associated with these elusive individuals.

If tokens were used within some establishments as access tickets, or to facilitate the distribution of foodstuffs or oil as acts of euergetism, then these objects would have, intentionally or not, lessened the pressure on the Roman supply of small change. Lead tokens may have been supplied as 'change' in the absence of available official specie – customers, for example, may have been given a token for additional future access to the baths in lieu of change. Alternatively, patrons may have given their clients tokens for bathing, although in this case one would imagine the Roman preoccupation with prestige would have meant that the tokens carried direct reference to the benefactor. At any rate, the gifting of a token to use to access a bathhouse would explain why many of the tokens that carry reference to bathing have been found outside of bathing establishments. Tokens may then have, even unintentionally, lessened the pressure on the *quadrantes* in circulation in Rome and Ostia.

Did tokens used in bathing contexts encourage the user to identify themselves in the image? As explored elsewhere in this volume, this practice can be identified for tokens used in other aspects of Roman social life, for example in cults. Rostovtzeff recorded that an unpublished bronze token was in the Bibliothèque nationale de France showing a male standing right dressed in an *exomis*, with his right hand on his breast and carrying a strigil and *ampulla* in his left hand. The other side of the token, Rostovtzeff recorded, carried the image of a ring with strigils and an *ampulla* within a wreath.[76] The token is shown here as Figure 5.5. There appears to be no hard or fast rule about whether bathers went nude or merely scantily clad; both are referenced in surviving evidence.[77] Depictions of bathers in surviving material culture from the Roman world are rare, so there is little evidence to compare against the depiction

---

[76] Rostovtzeff, 1905b: 102, also mentioned in Nielsen, 1990: vol. 1, 134.
[77] Fagan, 2002: 25–6; Yegül, 2010: 34.

Figure 5.5 AE token, 13 mm, 6 h, 1.44 g. Male figure standing right wearing a very short tunic gazing upwards, right hand on his breast, left hand carrying an *ampulla* and strigils (?) / *Ampulla* (?) on left, next to two strigils (?) on right; dotted border. Unpublished, BnF inv. FRBNF45877423.

in Figure 5.5.[78] Unfortunately the items the male figure is holding, and those shown on the other side of the token, are not particularly clear. The figure may indeed be holding the instruments associated with bathing, though one wishes the details of the proposed strigils were clearer. The reverse of the token shows an ovoid vessel which looks very similar to a club, and if the item next to the vessel is to be interpreted as strigils, then the die engraver has run them together so that they form one continuous line. The representation of two strigils facing each other (and ultimately joined) in this way is unusual, if not unique, as is the representation of the individual on the obverse. The rarity of depictions of bathers, however, means the singularity of the representation should not surprise. If this is a bather, we should note that what is represented is not the elite experience of bathing (in which an individual was accompanied by attendants who carried various paraphernalia), but a rather more humble representation.

Cohen connected a further bronze token in the Paris coin cabinet to bathing, reproduced here as Figure 5.6. Cohen reported that the legend, which is located on the lower part of the obverse, reads BAL on the left and LORVS on the right. Cohen suggested that the BAL referred to *balnearius*, and that the two individuals shown may be two bathers. The legend is no longer legible, unfortunately (although 'LORVS' on the right seems plausible with what remains), and the figure on the right hand side of the obverse appears to be leaning on a thyrsus and so is more likely Dionysus. It is not possible, therefore, to confidently place this piece among the tokens connected to bathing. The Paris coin cabinet also possesses a series of orichalcum tokens that show nude figures in a variety of poses, accompanied by numbers on the other

[78] Nielsen, 1990: vol. 1, 111.

Figure 5.6 AE token, 22 mm, 6 h, 3.62 g. Male figure on left standing with right hand on hip, facing Dionysus (?) on right, who leans on thyrsus with left hand and has right leg crossed in front of the left, worn legend around / XV within dotted border within wreath. Cohen: vol. VIII, 266 no. 9.

side.[79] Campana, noting that these pieces appear to be concentrated in one European collection, and that they have a regular die axis of 12, suggested that they were more modern creations, made during the Renaissance or even later.[80] These tokens are certainly of a different style to the orichalcum pieces carrying imperial portraits and other designs that are securely dated to the Roman imperial period.

Lead tokens present similar difficulties in interpretation. A series of tokens showing a nude male crouching with arms outstretched as if he were about to jump were assigned by Rostovtzeff to the section of his catalogue connected to baths, suggesting the figure stood as if he were about to jump into a body of water.[81] On Figure 5.7 the presence of Neptune on the other side of the token does evoke water, but it is uncertain if the nude figure is meant to be a bather. No other surviving material culture from Roman antiquity seems to show bathers acting in such a fashion, although the vibrancy and sense of fun is characteristic of tokens. Indeed, the image recalls Seneca's description of the individual who jumps into the bathing pool with 'unconscionable noise and splashing'.[82] Literary descriptions of such 'characters' with annoying habits at the baths are also found in Martial, and if Rostovtzeff is correct

---

[79] Paris BnF AF 17117–21, and 17123, an ithyphallic herm. A piece from the same series is in the Münzkabinett Berlin inv. 18203168.
[80] Campana, 2009: 91–3.
[81] TURS 901–3. For the type TURS 902 Rostovtzeff reported that the figure seemed to be standing before a bathing tub, but neither of the two specimens in the Berlin Münzkabinett, nor the specimen in Munich (Overbeck, 1995: no. 185) have any hint of such a feature.
[82] Sen. Ep. 56.2.

Figure 5.7 Pb token, 17 mm, no other data recorded. Neptune standing right holding trident in right hand and dolphin in outstretched left / Nude male bending at the knees with both arms outstretched before him. *TURS* 901.

in seeing a connection to bathing here, the design might have been intended to bring a smile to the face of the user as they 'recognised' one such annoying individual.[83]

Tokens showing paraphernalia associated with bathing – strigils and oil flasks – are easier to identify. Several lead tokens amongst the assemblage from Rome and Ostia show strigils and a vessel for oil, at times hanging from a ring or *anulus*.[84] Figure 5.8 shows an oil jug above a strigil; the combination probably references the practice in which oil would be applied to the body, and then dirt and the oil would be scraped off with the strigil after exercise. The same scene (a jug above a strigil) appears on another token series, *TURS* 900. This time the image is combined with a type on the other side that shows an altar inscribed with the letter S, a palm branch and wreath. What the S may signify here is unknown. The use of the same imagery, as well as the common use of S, palm branch and wreath, suggests that these token types may have belonged to a single series or issuer, although no specimen of *TURS* 900 is currently available for first hand examination, meaning we cannot know if they are of the same style as Figure 5.8.

Since Rostovtzeff's catalogue several additional token types referencing bathing have come to light. Amongst the tokens now in the Museo Archeologico Nazionale di Palestrina is a token that carries the image of a dolphin with the legend BAL above; the other side of the token carries an uncertain design (Figure 5.9). A more worn specimen of the same type exists in Milan (also quite heavy at 9.08 g) and was published by Overbeck, who read the legend as 'CAE . . . ' and wondered if the uncertain image was a portrayal

---

[83] For example, Mart. *Ep.* 12.82 (one Menogenes, who pesters others until he receives a dinner invitation).
[84] *TURS* 894–900; Nielsen, 1990: vol. 1, 134.

of gladiatorial weapons.⁸⁵ The reading on the Palestrina piece is quite certain; the representation of a dolphin accompanied by an abbreviation of *balineum* (BALN) is also known on a token found at Puente Melchor, located in Puerto Real in Spain.⁸⁶ The Museo di Castelvecchio in Verona also possesses a lead token issue not known to Rostovtzeff: on this piece two strigils and an *aryballos* hang from a ring on one side, and the legend IVC is found on the other.⁸⁷ TURS 563, which Rostovtzeff reported as bearing a comic mask on either side, may also carry a ring from which two strigils and an *aryballos* are

Figure 5.8 Pb token, 19 mm, 12 h, 5.46 g. Jug above strigil / Wreath on left, next to palm branch and S. *TURS* 899, Rostovtzeff and Prou, 1900: no. 105bis.

Figure 5.9 Pb token, 22 mm, 12 h, 9.43 g. Dolphin swimming right, BAL above / Uncertain image (Column (?) above rectangular object, person holding spear or sceptre on right, horse with head turned back and foreleg raised on left?) cf. Overbeck, 2001: no. 50.

---

⁸⁵ Overbeck, 2001: no. 50. ⁸⁶ Lagóstena Barrios, 1993.
⁸⁷ Arzone and Marinello, 2019: no. 309. The meaning of the legend is unknown; it might be an abbreviation of a *tria nomina*.

suspended (Figure 5.10). The motif on the other side of the token has attracted varying theories without a definitive identification; Scholz entertained the idea it represented an oval-shaped loaf of bread, while Turcan wondered whether it represented the teats of a sow.[88] A decorated oval shield is also a possibility.

Of course, as has already been revealed by the discussion of the tokens in the baths of the *Cisiarii* in Chapter 3, other imagery may equally have been used on tokens within a bathing context. It is hoped that future finds may further elucidate the situation. However, the combination of bathing imagery with legends that may be abbreviations of names (e.g. S, MOF, PVR), the use of festive imagery on Figure 5.8 and, above all, the tiny quantities in which these tokens survive, suggests that euergetism is a likely context for their use. If tokens acted as entry tickets for bathhouses on any regular basis, one would imagine we would find them in much larger quantities. If, however, these items were used to facilitate occasional acts of euergetism (free entry, gifts of oil, or other goods), then their limited occurrence in the archaeological record can be better understood. Indeed, if lead tokens were used in a variety of euergetic acts (e.g. food distributions, banquets, bathing), then they form an important (and recurring) part of the material tradition of this practice within central Italy.

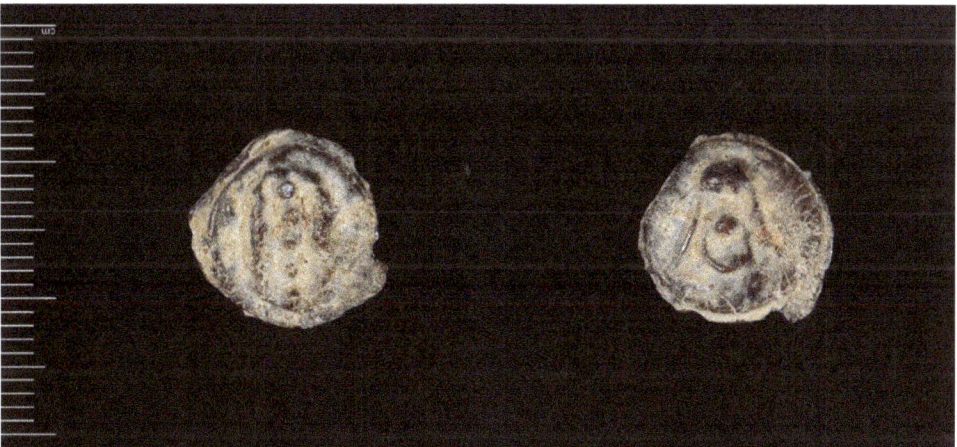

Figure 5.10 Pb token, 14.7 mm, 12 h, 3.51 g. Long oval object decorated with five pellets / Ring with two strigils hanging down on either side of a container of oil (*aryballos*). TURS 563.

---

[88] Scholz, 1894: 45 and pl. III 457–8; Turcan, 1987: 158 no. 764, with accompanying discussion. Another of the same type is in the Münzkabinett Berlin, and three in Paris, Rostovtzeff and Prou, 1900: nos. 146–8.

Tokens and the *Tabernae* in Ostia

The presence of tokens in the *popina* adjacent to the Baths of the Swimmer raises the question: were tokens manufactured and used by small commercial establishments in Ostia? The biggest concentration of tokens in connection to this question comes from the *tabernae* in the theatre. Unfortunately, however, the theatre at Ostia was used in one way or another from late antiquity into the Middle Ages and beyond, which means that the finds may have originally come from a multitude of places – we cannot assume the theatre was the original place of deposition. The wide variety of finds associated with the tokens, detailed below, demonstrates this. Nonetheless, since this evidence has not been gathered together before, it is worth presenting here. Wherever these pieces were originally deposited, they are nonetheless to be connected with Ostia since lead tokens did not frequently travel from their place of issue.

The theatre at Ostia was originally built by Agrippa during the reign of Augustus; it was later renovated under Septimius Severus, before being modified again in the fourth century to allow aquatic displays.[89] Early archaeological investigations were begun in the latter part of the nineteenth century by Lanciani, but of relevance to our discussion here is the later work by Vaglieri, who focused on uncovering the outer structures in the early twentieth century. Vaglieri had an interest in lead tokens, publishing a series from the Tiber with Rostovtzeff in 1900, and making careful mention of any finds of this nature in his reports in the *Notizie degli Scavi* and *Giornali degli Scavi*.[90]

Vaglieri's excavations of the shops running around the outside of the theatre uncovered tokens, moulds and casting waste. Excavations of the back room of one of the *tabernae* beneath the *cavea* uncovered a complete cast from a lead token mould, with the eleven tokens still attached to their casting. On one side the tokens carried the letter S and the other side the letter N; Vaglieri posited that perhaps this particular casting had not been to the maker's satisfaction, and so it was discarded.[91] Small marble figures were also found (including portrayals of a male youth and Venus), as well as part of a marble 'trapezoforo' or table leg. Marble bearing graffiti and

---

[89] Calza, 1927; Cooley, 1999: 173; Sear, 2006: 129 with extensive bibliography and collection of epigraphic evidence.
[90] Rostovtzeff and Vaglieri, 1900.
[91] Vaglieri, 1912: 393; Ostia Antiquarium inv. 6228; *GdS* 1912, 262 no. 5. Vaglieri, in *GdS* describes the location as 'sotto la cavea del teatro, che faceva da dietro botteca alla taberna no. 4 a contrare dall'angolo est del teatro, non compresa la scala'.

part of an inscription (M | ORDIE | IVS) were also found, as well as three bone handles and six coins (one of larger diameter and five smaller in size).

In 1913, Vaglieri turned his attention to the entrance to the theatre and what he labelled 'taberna 2'. He observed that beneath a dump layer was a stratum of fine earth mixed with a dark substance and water, which he suggested might be the remains of marble working.[92] The layer did indeed contain a significant quantity of marble, including a female portrait of the second century AD, the torso of a satyr, the torso of a female maritime (?) divinity, a Hellenistic style head of Venus, two fragmentary inscriptions and a token mould for seven quadrangular tokens of c. 10 mm × 10 mm size. The design of the tokens was only roughly sketched and not fully legible.[93] A mould for circular blank tokens was also found – this mould may not have yet been incised, or else was intended to create a 'blank' design on one side of a token, a phenomenon known on several issues within Rome and Ostia.[94] The moulds were likely present here because of their material, and were assembled alongside other marble objects.

The third *taberna* of the theatre also housed a significant quantity of marble, coming from a fire stratum and the stratum beneath this. The context here, according to Vaglieri, appears to be one of fill and dumped marble, containing numerous sculptures (including the torso of a Nereid and a seated philosopher) and some inscription fragments. Included among these was a further token mould that would have once created tokens carrying the number IV.[95] The fill from around the theatre also uncovered a token mould amongst other marble finds – this mould have would have created circular tokens carrying the letter P.[96]

Although the *tabernae* furnished numerous token moulds, the archaeological contexts of these pieces means it is impossible to extrapolate much. But it is worth noting that tokens have been found associated with theatres elsewhere. As mentioned in Chapter 3, excavations from

---

[92] Vaglieri, 1913: 393. 'Sotto lo strato di scarico si notò uno strato di sabbia triturate, mista a una sostanza nerastra, impastata con l'acqua: forse è il rifiuto di una sega di marmi'.
[93] Vaglieri, 1913: 396; *GdS* 1913, 396, inv. 8367.
[94] Vaglieri, 1913: 133. This may be the same mould that is recorded in *GdS* 1913, p. 30, inv. no. 6976 from this area. The *Giornale* records a mould half for seven round tokens of 9 mm without design, with the mould measuring 142 × 145 mm. In the *NSc.* Vaglieri records a mould for nine tokens and gives the dimensions as 124 × 145 mm. The tokens with one blank side are too numerous to list here but see by way of example *TURS* 1012 (amphora / blank); Pensabene, 2001–3: no. 9.
[95] Vaglieri, 1913: 299; *GdS* no. 6 1913 p. 234, inv. 8156.
[96] Vaglieri, 1910: 185; *GdS* no. 3 1910 p. 73, inv. 2939.

around the theatre at Nemi uncovered three lead tokens.[97] Recent excavations of the theatre in Sardis also uncovered a handful of tokens.[98] A bronze token found in the fill (no. 114.1) was decorated with the bust of Artemis and a stag accompanied by a legend referring to Ephesus (ΕΦΕ-ΣΙΩΝ); DeRose Evans suggested that this piece, and the coins found in the fill, were likely used to buy food and drink in the theatre. As discussed in Chapter 2, Martial also seems to indicate that some sort of token was used to mediate the distribution of food and drink during spectacles.

The state of the evidence in Ostia, however, does not allow us to reach a definitive conclusion about whether particular *tabernae* at the theatre utilised tokens. During cleaning associated with excavations of a *taberna* along a street to the west of the Capitolium and south of the so-called Piccolo Mercato, a token (*TURS* 1478) was uncovered, but the context is not particularly secure.[99] In 1914 two *tabernae* along the *decumanus* were excavated; the *Giornale degli Scavi* records that during this work a mould half was uncovered, which would have created tokens bearing the number IV (the design of the token cavities on the right side of the central casting channel) as well as tokens decorated with a palm branch (token cavities on the left side of the central casting channel).[100] No assemblage of lead tokens in Rome or Ostia has been found inside a *taberna*, which would demonstrate they were used in a manner similar to 'merchant's tokens' of later periods.

Temporal Value? Tokens and Find Contexts in Ostia

An examination of the findspots of tokens in Ostia suggests these objects circulated throughout the city and, as with other small finds of low value, were subject to casual loss.[101] Indeed, this impression confirms the picture

---

[97] Morpugo, 1931: 281, no. 111.

[98] DeRose Evans, 2018: 114.1 (found in the fill), L4 (topsoil). L6 came from a Byzantine context, but was decorated with a theatre mask and thus DeRose Evans suggested it may have been connected with the theatre in some way (perhaps acting as a ticket), before being used as a coin in later periods.

[99] Vaglieri, 1912: 280; *GdS* 1912, no. 5, p. 151 inv. 5781. Four coins, a marble fragment and red slip ware were also uncovered.

[100] The shape of the tokens was not recorded; presumably they were circular. *GdS* 1914 no. 7, 30 inv. 8701.

[101] Rome and other locations in Italy unfortunately do not possess the same quantity of find information and so cannot be the subject of an extended discussion. A map showing the locations discussed in this section can be viewed at https://parcoarcheologicostiantica.it/en/educational-panels/.

presented elsewhere in this volume: tokens were artefacts that were manufactured sporadically and used for brief moments in time. The tokens that survive to the present day appear to be those that were lost or had lost their value, ending up in contexts of fill or abandonment. The findspots of tokens and token moulds from Ostia not already discussed in this volume are presented here. The overview brings this material together for the first time, and in doing so reveals how widespread tokens were in Ostia in antiquity.

Most of the published lead tokens from Ostia come from the early excavations of Vaglieri: his interest in the artefacts meant that he focused on recording them and that he made a particular note of their existence in the *Notizie degli Scavi*. The concentration is thus the result of Vaglieri's interests, which were not shared by later excavators. The recent work of Spagnoli on tokens across the settlement has demonstrated that tokens have also been found elsewhere in Ostia, even if they are not yet published.[102] A preliminary list of moulds from the settlement has been compiled by the present author; more unpublished examples may sit in the stores.[103] Spagnoli's ongoing work will undoubtedly reveal further find contexts from other excavations, but the tokens and moulds published to date already illustrate the widespread nature of token use in Rome's harbour.

Vaglieri's excavations of Ostia's *decumanus* in 1913–14 uncovered several lead tokens. Work in 1913 was carried out along the *decumanus* up to the via della Pistrina: a mould half was uncovered for circular tokens of 13 mm bearing an image of standing Fortuna, as was a token of 23 mm decorated with a rudder on one side and cornucopia on the other (*TURS* 2421).[104] The written records of the excavation (the *Giornale degli Scavi*) record a further four lead tokens associated with the campaign along the *decumanus*; the information given does not provide a precise context.[105]

The tokens of the Baths of Neptune have already been discussed. Across the road from these baths tokens were uncovered around the so-called Caserma dei Vigili, the seat of Ostia's fire brigade (*vigiles*). Excavations uncovered two token mould halves: one in 1911 that created tokens carrying the letter F, and one in 1912 along the via Fullonica which cast tokens showing a cornucopia within a wreath.[106] As Vaglieri observed, the Caserma had already been subject to large

---

[102] Spagnoli, 1992; Spagnoli, 2001; Spagnoli, 2007: 241; Spagnoli, 2017a; Spagnoli, 2017b.
[103] Rowan, 2019.   [104] Vaglieri, 1913: 216; *GdS* 1913, 216 inv. 7572 (mould) and 7587 (token).
[105] *GdS* 1913, no. 6, 88 inv. 7207 (type 'wreath/illegible'); *GdS* 1914, no. 7, 160 inv. 7675 (type 'Apollo / TCE', *TURS* 2035 and also recorded in *NSc.* 1913, 217), 202 inv. 9340 (type 'head right / illegible'), 231 inv. 9445 (type not recorded)
[106] Vaglieri, 1911: 367; *GdS* 1911, no. 4, 151 inv. 4377; Vaglieri, 1912: 434; *GdS* 1912, no. 5, 151 inv. 5776.

amounts of spoliation in antiquity.[107] Excavations of the porticus in front of rooms 1 and 2 on the north side (from which one enters the complex), uncovered two tokens of the same type. Vaglieri recorded that the tokens were worn and so the identification is not definitive, but from his description they appear to be of the type *TURS* 869.[108] Figure 5.11 shows a token of the same type. Rostovtzeff had connected the token with the *iuvenes* of Ulubrae, having interpreted the legend as *Cur(ator) Iu(v)e(nium) Ul(u)b(ris)*. The find of two tokens in the same location suggests that this series is better associated with Ostia. The three birds reference the Capitoline triad (Jupiter, Juno, Minerva). While CVR most likely references a *curator*, IVE and VLB remain difficult to resolve.

Excavations along the via dei Vigili uncovered a lead token showing Fortuna on one side and P within a wreath on the other (*TURS* 2226).[109] The fullonica flanked by the via di Fullonica and via delle Corporazioni furnished a bronze token carrying a palm branch on one side and a figure within a double wreath on the other.[110] The excavations of the Piazzale delle corporazioni to the west also uncovered tokens and token moulds.

Figure 5.11 Pb token, 19 mm, 10 h, 3.72 g. Eagle standing right with head turned back left. CVR above left, IVE on the right / Peacock and owl standing right with closed wings, VLB above left. *TURS* 869, Rostovtzeff and Prou, 1900: no. 247c.

---

[107] Vaglieri, 1911: 366.   [108] Vaglieri, 1912: 26; *GdS* 1911, no. 4, 239 inv. 4891.1–2.
[109] Vaglieri, 1909: 130; *GdS* 1909, no. 2, 110 inv. 1613.
[110] Pietrogrande, 1976: 24, who reports the information was provided by Squarciapino. The type is given as Cohen vol. VII, 272 no. 8, which does not refer to a token, and indeed is an obvious error (page 272 in volume VII of Cohen contains nos. 38–46). The reference may in fact be Cohen vol. VIII, 272 no. 48, which shows Victory with palm and wreath on the obverse and a palm branch on the reverse. This may also be the same piece as that listed in *GdS* 1959 under the date 8.9.59 (no. 3), which is of the same type, said to be found during cleaning in an area to the west of the fullonica. Also recorded were coins of Philip the Arab (Cohen vol. V no. 140) and Salonina (Cohen vol. V no. 60).

The 1912 work along the portico behind the theatre and of the east side of the Piazzale uncovered a token mould half for nine circular tokens of c. 5 mm (the token cavities were blank).[111] A lead token was also uncovered with Salus on one side and Fortuna on the other (*TURS* 1993).[112] During work on the large square in front of the 'Quattro Tempietti', Vaglieri reported that in the ruins from the street a lead token was found, decorated with a wreath on one side and an unidentifiable figure on the other.[113]

Along the via della Fontana, which ran along the western side of the Baths of Neptune and the Caserma dei Vigili, several token mould halves were uncovered. One, intended to create circular tokens of 15 mm bearing the letter E, was found during the clearing of a house.[114] An *antoninianus* of Philip the Arab and a bronze coin of Valerian were also found, along with seals, pieces of lead, lamps, a palombino marble weight, nails, glass vessel fragments and other finds. In the same year a further mould for seven circular tokens of 9 mm was found, as well as a coin of Claudius. The design of the mould cavities on this piece proved too rough to make out.[115] Excavation work in the Casa dei Dipinti, a large apartment block dating to the second century AD, also revealed token activity. A palombino marble mould half was found above the covered corridor at the entrance to the house along the via delle Fontana; the mould was intended to create quadrangular tokens of 13 × 12 mm decorated with five globules.[116] In a room inside the block, which Vaglieri records as being located to the north of that already excavated, three lead tokens were found: one bearing a palm branch on one side and the legend SP on the other (*TURS* 3349), one with the number V on one side and a wreath on the other and the third illegible.[117] The room was decorated with frescoes of fish and goats, and contained a white mosaic pavement. Other finds included a gold ring, three *denarii* (one dated to the reign of Hadrian), bronze objects (e.g. *fibulae*) and an iron key.

In 1914 excavations began to the south west of the via dei Molini and three lead tokens were among the finds. The types were 'AISV(?) | PAN(?) / Centaur', 'SVNV | IVLI / elephant' and 'cuirassed and helmeted bust / figure standing left' (*TURS* 163).[118] Two further tokens were uncovered in October 1916 from excavations on the west side of the large tufa wall that runs along the west side of the street. The designs on the tokens were

---

[111] Vaglieri, 1912: 437; *GdS* 1912, no. 5, 274 inv. 6309 bis.
[112] Vaglieri, 1912: 439; *GdS* 1912, no. 5, 280 inv. 6323.   [113] *NSc.* 1913, 178.
[114] Vaglieri, 1907: 18.   [115] *NSc.* 1907, 121 (with image).   [116] *NSc.* 1913, 78.
[117] *NSc.* 1912, 434; *GdS* 1912, no. 5, 289 inv. 6393.1–3.
[118] *GdS* 1914 no. 7, 52 inv. 8799, 66 inv. 8883, 149 inv. 9169.

unrecorded; the area possessed a large amount of construction materials, which were perhaps accumulated in antiquity.[119] Tokens were also found inside the structures lining the via dei Molini. In Room 14 of the Caseggiato dei Molini, which housed a bakery, a lead token was found – the room originally held an oven but was converted into a shop (not associated with the bakery) in the later third century.[120] The token was decorated with a male figure on one side and a quadruped on the other. On the other side of the via dei Molini stood the Grand *Horrea*, a large warehouse, where in 1956 a token was found, but neither the precise location of the find within the warehouse, or the design of the token is recorded in the *Giornale degli Scavi*.[121]

An alley separates the Caseggiato dei Molini from the Caseggiato di Diana (House of Diana), which sits on the via di Diana and the via dei Balconi. Excavations in 1915 along the via di Diana uncovered three lead tokens, with a fourth uncovered nearby to the west in 1914.[122] To the east of the House of Diana is the so-called Piccolo Mercato, a storage structure. Work around this area in 1911–12 uncovered four lead tokens. In 1911 work began to remove the earth from Petrini's earlier excavations; along the street parallel to the south side of the Piccolo Mercato a lead token decorated with a wreath on one side and an S on the other was uncovered, along with fragments of lamps, a weight, coins and a bone stud.[123] A token of type *TURS* 623 (elephant / bull) was also uncovered in excavation work in the area that year.[124] The continuation of the campaign in 1912 revealed a further token of type *TURS* 2372 (standing Fortuna / PS).[125] In the same year excavations took place on the street parallel to the west side of the Capitolium and the south side of the Piccolo Mercato. Vaglieri records that during cleaning operations another token was found of type *TURS* 1478. Another specimen of the same design is shown as Figure 5.12; the type is found with relative frequency in museum collections. Earlier work on a street parallel to the Capitolium also uncovered a palombino token mould half, designed to create circular tokens carrying the legend CT.[126]

---

[119] *GdS* 1916 no. 9, 181 inv. 10907.1–2.　　[120] Bakker, 1999: 153, inv. 9737.
[121] *GdS* 1956–61, 27-10-1956.1.
[122] *GdS* 1915 no. 8, 52–3 inv. 95681.1 (type 'Head of Mercury right / IVVII'), inv. 9568.2 (type 'Rider on horse galloping right / CCC'), 67 inv. 9635 (*TURS* 2004 'Cupid with wreath / bird right'); *GdS* 1914 no. 7, 203 inv. 9347 (type not recorded).
[123] *NSc.* 1911, 410; *GdS* 1911, no. 4, 198 inv. 4704.
[124] *NSc.* 1911, 325; *GdS* 1911, no. 4, 127 inv. 4284.
[125] *NSc.* 1912, 173; *GdS* 1912, no. 5, 72 inv. 5433.
[126] Vaglieri, 1908: 332; *GdS* 1908, no. 1, 102 inv. 589.

Figure 5.12 Pb token, 22 mm, 7.6 g, die axis not recorded. ROM|VLA / Shield (?) with A above G on left and A above S on right. *TURS* 1478.

Moving further west, a token mould half was uncovered during the excavations of the Insula delle Ierodule in Regio III during 2003–4. The mould half was made of lunense marble, and would have cast quadrangular tokens bearing an anthropomorphic figure holding a sceptre (?) with a container (*modius*?) between its legs. The mould was found in a corridor (Area 10) in a stratum of abandonment. Clay moulds and glass were also found, leading the excavators to wonder if there was not some type of artisanal workshop located within the building. Two coins were also found, both of the third century AD; the building itself was destroyed in the latter part of the third century.[127]

Excavation activity in the sewers of the town, the Tiber and the harbour have also uncovered lead tokens. The 1908 excavations of a sewer that ran towards the Tiber uncovered a token decorated with a lion walking right.[128] In 1910 the excavations of a sewer that ran beneath the pavement of a room that contained two 'vasche' (basins) of the baths along the via del Teatro uncovered two lead tokens; one with the design 'H / CC' and the other 'A / C' (*TURS* 3363). The excavation also uncovered bronze coins, a bronze token (type unrecorded), as well as terracotta and glass fragments.[129] In 1910 excavations of the 'piazzale' between the two streets

---

[127] Falzone and Pellegrino, 2014: 364, Inv. SSBAR-OS no. 62025, 302–7 for a discussion of the stratum in which the mould was found, and p. 365 for the coins (*RIC* IV Philip 168 and *RIC* V Gallienus 587).

[128] *NSc.* 1908, 471.

[129] *GdS* 1910, no. 3, 250 inv. 3631.1–2 (lead tokens), 3634 (bronze token). In 1910 work was associated with the installation of the railroad outside the theatre, as well as the sewer coming from the nearby latrines. Two mould halves were found during this activity. The first would have created tokens bearing the letter C (the shape of the resulting tokens was unfortunately not recorded, they were presumably circular) and the second would have produced tokens bearing the letter L, see *GdS* 1910, 162, inv. 3282–3.

immediately behind the harbour of the town uncovered a 14 mm circular lead token of the type 'palm branch / vessel'.[130]

The dredging of the Tiber riverbed between the Palazzo imperiale and Ponte delle Scafa uncovered thirteen lead tokens. Of those that were legible on both sides three were decorated with a patera on each side, one was of the type 'cornucopiae / CPA' (*TURS* 2432), one was of type *TURS* 2517 (Hercules standing with club and cup, A EV / TFS between two palm branches), one of type *TURS* 2792 (Ram standing right / M), with another token being described as uniface and decorated with a young male (Julio-Claudian?) head next to a *lituus* and *praefericulum*.[131] Twenty-one coins were also recorded, dating from Augustus to late antiquity, as well as other lead, bronze and iron objects.

A token mould half was found during excavation work in the area formerly owned by the Alobrandini family, which would have cast tokens showing an eagle.[132] The ruins to the northwest of the eastern gate of Ostia also furnished two tokens; the first a bronze quadrangular token said to show a horse running and the second a lead piece that was poorly preserved.[133] A token decorated with a wreath on one side and palm branch on the other (*TURS* 3286) was found in the via delle Foce in 1955.[134]

What this brief survey illustrates is that tokens, as well as token moulds, appear to be scattered throughout Ostia. Further finds in the town have been mentioned elsewhere in this volume (e.g. the Sabazeum). Although many of the finds are from fill, disturbed contexts or abandonment strata, the presence of token moulds and tokens across the settlement suggests that these objects were in use amongst a wide segment of the population. If these objects were used to mediate time sensitive acts of euergetism or distribution, then the presence of moulds and tokens in these types of archaeological contexts is understandable – once they had been used for a particular occasion or period of time, the objects became worthless and were thrown away. That only a handful, or even a single, token from a particular series survives suggests an artefact that was used and then

---

[130] *NSc.* 1910, 252.

[131] *GdS* 1961–65, date 5-5-1964, p. 74, inv. 5.5.1964 nos. 22–34. No. 28 is described as having a legend G (?), no. 29 TF(?) / blank, no. 30 is reported as being decorated with a small bird (raven?), nos. 31–3 were illegible.

[132] *NSc.* 1918, 132. The mould described may be that pictured in Spagnoli, 2017b: pl. VI no. 4 (inv. 12544).

[133] *GdS* 1918, no. 11, 39 inv. 12801 (bronze), 12802 (lead). The bronze piece sounds like Type 2 of Stannard's 'Shipping *Tesserae*' series (Stannard, 2015b) but the author was unable to view the artefact in order to provide confirmation. The second, lead, piece is described as having for its type a flying figure (?) on one side and a sword (?) on the other.

[134] Spagnoli, 2001.

destroyed – the majority of tokens, one imagines, were handed in and then melted down for reuse; those that survive escaped this process in some way.

Can we estimate the frequency with which tokens were used in Ostia, and hence whether they served to lessen the pressure on small denominations in the town? The total tokens found in excavations in Ostia, indeed, even the total number of token types recorded by Rostovtzeff (which largely come from Rome and Ostia), seem small when one notes that these are the remnants of an estimated 200 or 250 years. It seems more likely, as this book has suggested, that the tokens were used in occasional acts of euergetism. Sponsoring entry to baths, or distributing particular goods on particular occasions, may have meant that for a small moment in time individuals did not need the specie to purchase these goods themselves, but this would not, one imagines, have had an enormous impact on the demand for small change within daily life.

Travel and the Secondary Lives of Tokens

According to current find evidence, the vast majority of tokens remained close to their place of manufacture. But some did travel, and it is worth exploring the circumstances that resulted in these objects being carried from one region to another. In some instances the materiality of tokens, particularly those made of bronze, which look very much like money, may have meant they acquired a secondary context as a coin to be used in the economy. But if this occurred, it did so as a series of isolated instances: the very small numbers involved suggest tokens were not shipped elsewhere en masse. The study of the shipment of coin blocks by Frey-Kupper and Stannard points out that the low value of bronze coinage (and by extension, tokens) meant that very large numbers of coins would be needed for long distance transfers of this type of specie to be worthwhile. Smaller numbers of finds suggest the movement of people and groups, who carried such pieces on their person.[135] Indeed, the findspots of tokens that travelled, discussed in further detail below, suggest that in many cases they were recognised as something different from official currency or even pseudo-currency. The imagery of tokens, particularly *spintriae*, held evident appeal, which may have resulted in these objects being curated. Finds of lead and bronze tokens far from their place of manufacture, like the lead

---

[135] Frey-Kupper and Stannard, 2018: 285; Frey-Kupper and Stannard, 2019: 156.

Egyptian tokens found in Italy discussed in Chapter 2, may reveal regional networks and commercial relationships.

Bronze and orichalcum tokens have been found across the Empire (for a discussion of these types and images, see Chapter 1). For the issues carrying portraits of Julio-Claudian emperors on the obverse and numbers on the reverse, recorded findspots are rare. Two specimens are recorded as part of the Sottosuolo urbano 2 (SSU2) from Rome ('laureate Augustus / VI', the second illegible); a further findspot is recorded in Pergamum ('radiate Augustus / X').[136] A *tessera* reported to be of the Augustan period was found during a nineteenth century excavation in Nendorp-Wischenborg in Germany, in what has been interpreted as a grave context; the piece is now lost and we cannot know the original design.[137] A token carrying the portrait of Tiberius and the number II appeared on the market with a possible find context of Germany; the piece was reported by Martini alongside a token carrying the radiate head of Augustus on one side and the number XIII on the other, said to have been found in the Garigliano in Italy.[138] The majority of the tokens with Julio-Claudian portraits belong to museum and private collections and possess no find information. Martínez Chico has recently published bronze and orichalcum tokens carrying the portraits of emperors and sexual imagery in Spain; he states that the pieces in the collection of Gonzalo Cores Uría and the archive of Alberto Campana undoubtedly have an Andalucian origin; if the information is correct we have further find information (however vague) for many more specimens.[139] More recently a token showing Drusus the Younger and the number XIIII (a previously unknown combination) came to light near the Giribaile reservoir in Vilches (Jaén, Andalusia), a region that possesses the remains of an Iberian *oppidum*. Martínez Chico suggested these pieces moved to Spain in connection with the movement of troops and elite to Baetica and the increasing Roman municipalisation of the area.[140]

What of other bronze and orichalcum tokens produced from this workshop? Two specimens of tokens released by Gaius Mitreius, both of the basilica type, have known findspots: one was found on the Saalburg in Germany and another on the island of Capri; both specimens are now lost.[141] The findspots of the so-called *spintriae* carrying sexual imagery have seen considerably more scholarly attention; this may explain why there are more recorded findspots

---

[136] Comune di Roma, Musei Capitolini, Inventario Medagliere Nuovo, Med 17980 (online at http://capitolini.net/object.xql?urn=urn:collectio:0001:med:17980), 17692 (Molinari, 2015: 128); Berlin Münzkabinett 18203146.
[137] *FMRD* VII.1-3 no. 2013.1.   [138] Martini, 1997: 7 n. 15 nos. IV and IX.
[139] Martínez Chico, 2019: 112.   [140] Martínez Chico, 2021.
[141] *FMRD* V 1.1. p. 577 no. 1655; Federico and Miranda, 1998: 363, E77, also mentioned in *CIL* X, p. 681; Rowan, 2020b.

for this series than any other. De Callataÿ, who has recently observed that most *spintriae* appear to have been known before 1800, noticed that many of these early finds have a provenance of Capri, but whether this was an invented findspot to enhance the value of these pieces cannot be known.[142] More securely, tokens with sexual imagery have been found in a potter's workshop in Salles, and at Argenton-sur-Cruese, both in France.[143] Two *spintriae* have been recorded as coming from the Thames in London, although it is uncertain if this was an ancient context or a more modern loss.[144] Two further specimens, one pierced, were found in Croatia – one in Narona and the other at Majsan.[145] Another pierced specimen was uncovered as a stray find at Caesarea Maritima.[146] Crisà has recently published a piece found in a Roman villa in Patti Marina near Messina in Sicily.[147] There is no pattern to the distribution of the finds (no one number or scene concentrates in a particular area); the overall picture is one of individual pieces that travelled to particular regions from Italy before being lost or deposited. The pierced specimens at Caesarea Maritima and Majsan suggest that some of the *spintriae* may have been cultivated for their imagery.

It is clear that the fascination with *spintriae* is not confined to the modern world. The same interest can be seen in the various imitations of these artefacts throughout the Roman Empire. Perhaps the most famous example is the imitative *spintria* found in a tomb at Mutina in Italy; the piece was covered in gold leaf and was found alongside four coins.[148] A terracotta imitation is also known from Salone: one side shows a couple engaging in intercourse in a lavishly appointed room complete with drapes and *kline*, while on the other side the number V is depicted within a dotted border and wreath.[149] Buljević posited that the imitation was directly copied from an original *spintria*, and that the terracotta piece was produced for the same reason as the original *spintriae*, whatever this might have been. This need not have been the case: the imagery might have simply appealed to the creator of the terracotta token, who may have used the resulting product in a different way. Martínez Chico's catalogue of *tesserae* from Spain includes what appear to be two imitations in lead, as well as a possible token converted into a pendant; several of the tokens

---

[142] de Callataÿ, 2021: 183–6. [143] Richard Ralite, 2009.
[144] *Numismatic Circular* 1979 no. 10129 (Chelsea); PAS LON-E98F21.
[145] Mirnik, 1985: no. 3 (pierced at 12 h above the number VII); Campana, 2009: 50.
[146] Hamburger, 1986: no. 60. This may be the *spintria* recorded as being found at Caesarea Maritima by Martini, 1997: 7 n. 15 no. iii.
[147] Crisà, 2020. [148] Benassi, Giordani and Poggi, 2003. [149] Buljević, 2008.

in museum collections are also pierced, suggesting later use in jewellery.[150]

A piece once in the Martinetti collection and now in the British Museum also draws inspiration from higher quality bronze and orichalcum tokens: this piece bears the head of Mercury on one side and the number V within a wreath on the other (Figure 5.13). Other pieces that may have functioned as tokens carry sexual imagery that is not so imitative in design. A lead piece measuring 1.8 cm × 1.5 cm found on the Lavanter Kirchbichl in Austria shows two lovers under a roof, with a column on either side.[151] A similar design, in bronze, is found on a quadrangular token now in Paris (Figure 5.14). A further piece in the BnF, shaped like a *tabula ansata*, carries an incuse erotic scene on one side and II on the other.[152] Sexual imagery was a popular motif within Roman visual and material culture, and the *spintriae* appear to have inspired the creation of further paranumismatic objects in different locations.

A specimen of the bronze token series carrying the bust of Dionysus on one side was found north of the baths during the excavation of a large Roman villa on the south-west shore of Lake Nemi.[153] The villa was abandoned in c. AD 150 because of a natural catastrophe, providing a *terminus ante quem* for the type. No die connections between the Dionysus tokens (which appear to be relatively small issue, even for tokens) and the Julio-Claudian types have been found by the author. The numbers on the reverse dies are only

Figure 5.13 AE token, 12 mm, 1.24 g, 3 h. Head of Mercury right wearing petasus, caduceus over shoulder / V within wreath. BM 1940, 0401.60.

---

[150] Martínez Chico, 2019: nos. 24, 41, 46 (converted into a pendant). Nos. 4, 38, and 42 in his catalogue are pierced. Three of the tokens in the Hunterian Museum in Glasgow are also pierced, Bateson, 1991: H6–7 and *tessera* no. 9.

[151] The other side was either worn smooth or blank, Kainrath, 2005.

[152] BnF inv. 17116, pierced on the left hand side.

[153] Poulsen, 2010: no. 7, the type is Cohen: vol. VIII, 262 no. 2 (with number XVII on the other side). Cohen identified the bust as possibly that of Drusilla, sister of Caligula, but the figure wears an ivy-wreath and has tightly curled hair, making Dionysus a more probable identification (although Apollo is also a possibility). See Küter, 2019: 85, who places the type within a broader array of Dionysiac imagery on tokens.

Figure 5.14 AE token, 17 × 15 mm, 4.22 g. Nude female figure reclining left within domed canopy. BnF inv. F 7917.

placed within a dotted border, not a wreath, and the series may be a later issue, or from a different workshop.[154]

A concentration of token finds is present in Lepcis Magna in North Africa: four specimens of the orichalcum issue carrying a cantharus on one side and a *modius* on the other were found in four different tombs in the necropolis.[155] The archaeological context of the finds gives the series a date of c. AD 50–150.[156] In this context it is also worth noting that, like the Dionysus type discussed above, this series has a dotted border and no wreath. The concentration of four tokens of the same type in the same city is remarkable; Munzi suggested they might have come to circulate in Lepcis Magna on the basis of their metal value.[157] Munzi also reported that seven anonymous issues of small bronzes have been found in the *necropoleis* of Lepcis: four specimens of *RIC* II (anonymous) 26 (head of Apollo / tripod with S C) were found in *hypogea* as well as three examples of type *RIC* II (anonymous) 19 (head of Mars / cuirass and S C). A fourth specimen of the Mars type was uncovered as a sporadic find in the funerary region of Uadi er-Rsaf.[158] The concentration of particular designs (two coin types, one token type) amongst the small change found in tombs at Lepcis does suggest that the finds reflect currency that may have been shipped to Lepcis Magna (officially or unofficially) to act as small change – it is hard to explain the repeated recurrence of types if the finds reflected coinage that arrived in Lepcis in the pockets of merchants or other travellers.

---

[154] BM R.4457 (XIIII within dotted border); Gemini, LLC Auction XII (11 January 2015) lot 338 (XIIII within dotted border, this same specimen which has appeared in several previous auctions); Cohen: vol. VIII, 262 no. 1 (III within dotted border); Fritz Rudolf Künker GmbH & Co. KG Auction 124 (16 March 2007) lot 8812 (III within dotted border); Triton III (30 November 1999) lot 995 (II within dotted border); Collection de Feu Monsieur L. Vierordt, J. Schulman, 5–6 June 1930, nos. 680–1 (II with dots above, within dotted border). The specimen found at Nemi (XVII) similarly did not have a wreath on the reverse.

[155] Munzi, 1997; Di Vita-Evrard et al., 1996: 123–6; Rowan, 2020b.   [156] Rowan, 2020b.

[157] Munzi, 1997: 591.   [158] Munzi, 1997: 25–6.

The find contexts of these examples, however, may be significant. Munzi noted the presence of other Trajanic and Hadrianic small bronzes in the *hypogea* at Gasr Gelda, and observed that in general the earlier tombs seem to have contained *asses* and the later burials smaller denominations (e.g. *semisses* or *quadrantes*).[159] As Kemmers demonstrated for the *quadrantes* of Nijmegen, the arrival of small denominations in North Africa may have been later than the use of the denomination in Rome; here it seems to be a phenomenon of the Trajanic and Hadrianic period. Each coin was a single find, not associated with other coins. It seems that these pieces acted as Charon's obol; users selected the lowest value coins for this purpose, which, we might note, included the orichalcum tokens. The value of these orichalcum pieces must have been at the lower or lowest end of the monetary economy. Munzi observes that small bronzes are found elsewhere in Lepcis Magna, but in smaller numbers: of the thirty-eight coins coming from the excavations of the theatre, for example, only four were identified as *quadrantes*.[160] An archaeological survey uncovered a further anonymous *quadrans* (*RIC* II (anonymous) 7) in the region from a mausoleum/villa site and a lead token (illegible) on a villa site.[161] Lepcis Magna should be added to studies exploring the role and circulation of small bronzes in the Roman Empire.

A specimen of the 'cantharus / *modius*' token series has also been found in the river Walbrook in London; although the token came from the silted riverbed, the associated finds suggest deposition sometime after the coins of Antoninus Pius arrived in the region, and before the arrival of coins of Marcus Aurelius.[162] A specimen was also found in Segobriga in Spain, during the excavations of the cryptoporticus south of the theatre.[163] Munzi also recorded possible find locations in Germany and in Siscia.[164] There are at least three obverse dies for this issue: one with the *modius* clearly displaying three legs (with the middle leg quite thick) (Figure 5.15), another displaying the *modius* with two smaller legs at either side (Figure 5.16) and a third on which the *modius* is flanked by the letters Θ E (Figure 5.17). Given that for the token found in Ephesus Θ is thought to refer to *therma*,

---

[159] Di Vita-Evrard et al., 1996: 124. Munzi classified some of the coins as *quadrantes*, but they might also have included some *semisses*. The finds included *RIC* II 977 (= *RIC* II.3² 976, classified as a *semis*), *RIC* II 702 (= Woytek, 2010: no. 602b, a *quadrans*). Munzi also described some of the specimens as '*quadrans* or *semis*'.

[160] Di Vita-Evrard, Musso et al., 1996: 124 n. 7, where he also notes that the coins coming from the excavations of a temple in nearby Sabratha uncovered only four *sestertii* and an *as*.

[161] Munzi, 2017: 198 nos. 15, 22 (the lead token was thought to perhaps date to the second–first centuries BC).

[162] Merrifield, 1962: 45.   [163] Abascal et al., 2010: no. 6; Martínez Chico, 2019: no. 49.

[164] Di Vita-Evrard et al., 1996: 123 n. 2, based on the presence of an example in the Rheinisches Landesmuseum Bonn and in the Arheoloski Musej di Zagabria.

Figure 5.15 Orichalcum token, 19 mm, 6 h, 2.83 g. *Modius* with three corn-ears, dotted border / Cantharus, dotted border. BnF inv. 17070.

Figure 5.16 Orichalcum token, 16 mm, 6 h, 2.57 g. *Modius* with three corn-ears, dotted border / Cantharus, dotted border. The Hunterian Museum Glasgow, *Tessera* no. 25.

Figure 5.17 AE token, 19 mm, die axis not recorded, 3.41 g. *Modius* with three corn-ears, Θ on left, E on right / Cantharus, dotted border. Ex BCD collection.

one wonders whether this is how we are to understand Θ E here, but without a bath find context (as on the Ephesian token) any suggestion can only be speculative. Either these tokens were required in such quantity that multiple dies were needed during a single production, or else production was occasional, with different dies being engraved over time. A full die study may assist in coming to a definitive conclusion. Unfortunately, the specimens with find locations are either very worn or not illustrated, so it is not possible to assess whether the products of different dies travelled to different locations.

It is evident that bronze and brass tokens travelled throughout the Empire. Their small numbers mean that they cannot have seriously impacted the supply of small change, but the monetiform appearance of these pieces meant that they might have occasionally been used in this context. It is worth noting, however, that these tokens are not found hoarded alongside other coins – their unusual appearance, and low value, might have prevented them from being used as stores of wealth. Instead, these pieces seem to have been selected for curation, being employed as pendants, Charon's obol, and as inspirations for new creations. These pieces were intentionally designed to sit apart from official currency, through the choice of design, and the absence of the S C that appears on the anonymous *quadrantes* and other bronze from the Roman mint. It seems that most users recognised their differences from official currency and treated them accordingly.

The finds of the bronze and orichalcum tokens described above are rather dispersed, and largely appear to be the result of individual activity rather than evidence of a particular trade network. Other tokens, however, do seem to reflect on-going connections between particular places. Stannard's exploration of the similarity in imagery between lead pieces in Baetica and Italy in the second and first centuries BC, as well as finds of Spanish lead pieces in Italy and lead pieces from Minturnae in Spain, is material evidence of contact between the two regions; Stannard has suggested this is a trade network.[165] Stannard has also argued that the presence of uniface quadrangular bronze tokens in both Ostia and Minturnae during the imperial period is evidence of movement, perhaps of goods, between the two ports.[166] For lead tokens of Roman imperial Italy, however, the evidence seems consistent with the movement of individuals rather than a sustained connection between two places.

Several examples of lead tokens travelling within Roman Italy, particularly within the region of Latium (Nemi, Minturnae and the Garigliano, Alba Fucens), have already been discussed in this volume. A further example can be found with the type *TURS* 919 (Figure 5.18), decorated with an erect phallus on one side and a pair of scales on the other. The combination of imagery here recalls the famous fresco at the House of the Vetii in Pompeii, in which Priapus is depicted weighting his phallus on a pair of scales; one

[165] Stannard, Sinner and Ferrante, 2019: 129, 163.   [166] Stannard, 2015b.

Figure 5.18 Pb token, 14 mm, 3 h, 3.34 g. Phallus / Pair of scales. *TURS* 919.

imagines the token imagery evoked the same sense of abundance and wishes for wealth. The discovery of two specimens of this type in the Baths of the *Cisiarii* in Ostia dates the series to roughly AD 150–250.[167] Pensabene records a further specimen of this type from Ostia; the archaeological museum at Palestrina has twenty-four specimens of this series from the seized collection acquired from illegal excavation activity.[168] Another example was found in the river Liri at Minturnae during the excavation work undertaken by Ruegg.[169] The presence of only a single specimen at Minturnae, in comparison to the higher number of examples associated with Ostia, suggests that it was the token, and not the token mould, that moved southwards. Of the cast lead tokens coming from the river at Minturnae, a handful seem to have come from Rome or Ostia; many more are not paralleled elsewhere and may have been local designs.[170] Ruegg suggested the lead pieces might have been given as votive offerings in the river; like Charon's obol, the very low value of these pieces may have been what made them attractive as votive offerings.

The scattered finds of tokens from Rome and Ostia reported in Hadrumetum, and occasional Egyptian tokens in Italy, have already been discussed elsewhere in this volume. These also seem indicative of the movement of particular individuals rather than an intentional shipment. Several additional finds of Roman tokens are recorded in southern France. *CIL* XII, 5699.12 reports twenty-one lead tokens found in southern Gaul.

---

[167] Spagnoli, 2017b: nos. 17–18.
[168] Pensabene, 2001–3: no. 25. The specimens at Palestrina are included in the currently unpublished catalogue of the collection, currently being prepared for publication by the author.
[169] Medas et al., 1998: no. 49 = Ruegg 53; Stannard Liri Catalogue 35.083.
[170] Possible lead tokens from Rome and Ostia are Medas et al., 1998: no. 1 (*TURS* 1670), 2 (*TURS* 2740), 6 (possibly *TURS* 2116). Although there are no specific findspots in Rome and Ostia for these pieces, their presence in major museum collections suggest that they likely originate from Rome or Ostia, rather than Minturnae. Many of the other types do not have parallels in Rostovtzeff or in museum collections.

Several of the types reported also have find locations in Rome. For example, one of the specimens from southern Gaul is of the type *TURS* 2817 (rooster / C C on either side of a palm branch). Two further examples of this type are known to have Italian contexts – they were once owned by Rostovtzeff, who said he acquired them in Rome.[171] The specimen found in southern Gaul thus likely travelled from Rome or Ostia. Similarly, two specimens were recorded to be of type *TURS* 692 (bull walking right / PM); the numerous specimens of this type in Italian collections, including that of Ficoroni, suggests this was an issue manufactured in Italy.[172] A similar case might be made for *CIL* XII, 5699.12m, of the type *TURS* 310 (eagle and B / LP|O; the meaning of the legend is unknown). Other tokens in the *CIL* entry may have slight misreadings (e.g. in the aforementioned token the O is reported as Q), which obscure the fact they are known types from Italy. Unfortunately, only two of the tokens found in southern Gaul are now accessible, but both of these have fabric consistent with the tokens of Rome and Ostia.[173] Indeed, the impression given by *CIL* XII, 5699 is that of an assemblage of lead tokens from Rome and Ostia, but without being able to physically examine all the tokens we cannot be certain in this conclusion.

The *CIL* also reports two further lead tokens found at Perpignan, a Roman settlement site on the southern coast of Gaul.[174] The types reported are also the same as known tokens found in Rome and Ostia, and the presence of these types in major museum and antiquarian collections suggest they were used in the imperial capital and/or its harbour. The tokens thus likely travelled from Italy to southern Gaul. The first token displayed Fortuna on one side and the legend TI|CE on the other (a token of the same type is shown as Figure 5.19), while the second carried the representation of an ithyphallic Priapus or Silvanus and the legend C PE|

---

[171] *CIL* XII, 5699 no. 12q; Rostovtzeff and Prou, 1900: 455–6.
[172] *CIL* XII, 5699, nos. 12t, 12u.
[173] *CIL* XII, 5699 no. 12h, reported as 'cornucopia / DFO', may in fact be *TURS* 2435, which is of the type 'cornucopia / DEO'. No. 12n (gate / PNR) may in fact be *TURS* 107 (Figure 2.19 in this volume). No. 12d has the reported legend CP|RF – this may in fact read GP|RF, although the legend on the other side (Θ|P) does not match any known type. No. 12a is likely to be *TURS* 118. No. 12l (bull / QHD) is of the type *TURS* 693 (bull right) or 694 (bull left). The two physically accessible tokens, given by Froehner to the BnF are no.12k = Froehner IV.100 (Venus / QHD), and 12e = Froehner IV.99 (of type *TURS* 1286a, 'CMTE with branch above and TE ligate / retrograde and ligate MAX'). Neither design was recorded by Rostovtzeff, but the fabric is consistent with tokens from Rome and Ostia, and in fact many museum collections contain types not originally included in Rostovtzeff's catalogue. Indeed, the ligate legend CMTE on no. 12e is also found on *TURS* 1809 (a specimen of this type is also housed in the BnF, Rostovtzeff and Prou, 1900: no. 461a).
[174] *CIL* XII, 5699 nos. 10 (*TURS* 1502) and 11 (*TURS* 1299).

Figure 5.19 Pb token, 18 mm, 12 h, 3.09 g. TI|CE / Fortuna standing left holding cornucopia in left hand and rudder in right. *TURS* 1502, Rostovtzeff and Prou, 1900: no. 430a.

Figure 5.20 Pb token, 15 mm, 12 h, 2.87 g. C PE|DANI / Ithyphallic Priapus or Silvanus standing right holding sickle. *TURS* 1299, Rostovtzeff and Prou, 1900: no. 426a.

DANI (*C. Pedani*) (a token of the same type is shown as Figure 5.20). Rostovtzeff wondered whether TI|CE was a reference to *Tyche*, although he also entertained the possibility the letters might be an abbreviated name: *Ti. C(laudius) E(utychus)*. Another token issue showing Fortuna on one side with the legend TIC|EV on the other was resolved by Rostovtzeff as a reference to someone of this name (*TURS* 1171); this token is much smaller than Figure 5.19 (11 mm) and so not directly comparable, but it might be they are tokens of different sizes issued by the same person.[175]

The location of these tokens in Gaul, close to the coast, as well as the finds of Roman or Ostian lead tokens in other ports (Minturnae, Hadrumetum) suggests that the pieces accompanied merchants and sailors on their voyages. Their loss abroad may have been accidental or votive in nature. The small number of finds, and the location of some specimens in rivers, suggest these pieces may have been selected to fulfil particular vows, perhaps because of their low value and monetiform nature. The presence of

---

[175] A specimen of this smaller token is now in Paris, Rostovtzeff and Prou, 1900: no. 416t.

struck lead on the Isla Pedrosa shipwreck, as well as the Egyptian lead tokens found on an imperial period shipwreck off the Carmel Coast, are clear evidence that material of this nature was carried on naval vessels.[176] The presence of imperial period lead tokens from Rome and Ostia in other regions (which largely seem to be ports) provides further evidence to suggest that these pieces were given out in advance of a specific event. That is, rather than being both distributed and used on a particular occasion or within a particular building, tokens appear to have been given to individuals to be redeemed at a later moment in time. This would explain why lead tokens managed to travel, and why some tokens appear never to have been redeemed.

The survey of the evidence, meagre as it is, does not support the idea that tokens acted as a form of supplementary or emergency currency. By mediating exchanges that might otherwise have required small change, tokens may have reduced some of the burden on Rome's official currency, but this was surely not their intended function. As a recent exploration of euergetic acts within *collegia* has suggested, activities of this nature may have served to lower transactions costs for members, but whether euergetic acts were performed with economic aims in mind is less clear.[177]

But can a study of tokens bring anything to our understanding of Roman currency, particularly small change? The stark difference in imagery between Roman *quadrantes* and other denominations of the Roman mint has led to the suggestion that these pieces were distributed during festivals or on special occasions. Buttrey believed that the Domitianic *quadrantes* showing a two-horned rhinoceros, for example, might have been showered on crowds during spectacles.[178] The anonymous *quadrantes* in particular (those without an imperial portrait or legend), have been interpreted as artefacts connected to distributions, religious festivals, or public games.[179] Indeed, small bronzes carrying the imagery of prize tables are thought to have entered circulation as distributions during the events referred to on the coin types.[180] If used for distributions during particular events, one

---

[176] Stannard and Sinner, 2014: 172–3; Meshorer, 2010: 132 nos. 160–1; no. 162, remarkably, seems to be an Athenian bronze token that is much earlier than the rest of the assemblage. The line drawings of the tokens found as surface finds at Caesarea Maritima and published by Hamburger also suggest the movement of Egyptian tokens to the region (Hamburger, 1986: nos. 50–6), photos of the holdings of the Eretz Israel Museum in Tel Aviv suggests this is the case. Mitchiner, 1984: 96 also has evidence of Roman lead tokens found in the Thames, but it is unknown whether these moved in antiquity, or were transported later as part of the ballast of ships.
[177] Kloppenborg, 2019.
[178] Buttrey, 2007: 110. For a detailed study of *quadrantes* see van Heesch, 1979.
[179] Weigel, 1998. [180] van Heesch, 2009: 140; Woytek, 2020b: 293–8.

might see how a *quadrans* or a *semis* gifted by the emperor could be seen as an imperial benefaction, buying the recipient a free bath, for example, while also contributing to the supply of small change (the latter could be seen as an act of euergetism, particularly in Greek cities in the Roman Empire).[181] Buttrey's objection to this idea, that there do not appear to be enough issues of this type to have been regularly used during Roman festivals every year, does not preclude the idea that these coins may have featured occasionally at events, in the same way tokens of differing materials might be used occasionally.[182] Roman religion, and Roman festivals, remained a vibrant ever-changing affair, and we should not assume that an event took place in an identical fashion every time.

Greek cities in all likelihood struck coinage to facilitate transactions during particular festivals; the bronze coins carrying the legend ΕΛΕΥΣΙ produced from the fourth century BC have been interpreted as a festival coinage connected to the Eleusinia, and in the imperial period cities must have produced coinage during festivals even if the imagery of these coins only began to communicate these occasions from the reign of Commodus.[183] The Roman mint may also have struck small change for use during festivals – the *semis* series struck from c. AD 62 under Nero that shows a prize table, accompanied by the legend CERTAMEN QVINQ(ennale) ROM(ae) CO(nstitutum), is plausibly connected to Nero's introduction of the quinquennial games in Rome. These *Neronia* were a Greek style celebration involving musical, gymnastic and equestrian competitions.[184] It is not often commented upon, but the appearance of the prize table on these Roman issues is extraordinary; Greek cities at this stage only rarely included such imagery on their coinage.[185]

There are parallels between *quadrantes*, *semisses* and tokens in terms of their imagery, low value and possible connection with festivals. But there are also clear differences, which throw light on our understanding of both types of artefact. Despite earlier scholarship seeing *quadrantes* as an Italian phenomenon, it is clear this denomination did travel, and in greater volume than tokens. Moreover, *quadrantes* and *semisses* are found stored alongside other coins, a phenomenon that is extremely rare for ancient tokens. Thus *quadrantes* and *semisses* were clearly intended to function as small change,

---

[181] Weiss, 2005: 62–3. [182] Buttrey, 2000: 590.

[183] Thompson, 1942 for the Eleusinia coins, and Gkikaki in press for tokens with similar designs. Klose, 2005: 128 makes the observation that it was only under Commodus that iconography associated with games and festivals flourished on provincial coinage.

[184] *RIC* I² Nero 91–2, 229–48, 427–8, 486–88, 559–63; Suet. *Ner.* 12.3; Tac. *Ann.* 14.20ff and 16.4; Dio 61.21; King, 1975: 64; Woytek, 2020b: 595–6.

[185] One of the rare examples is Corinth under Claudius, *RPC* I 2971. See Klose, 2005: 128.

however they entered circulation. Tokens, by contrast, were unequivocally *not* intended to function in this way. This is underlined by a key difference between tokens and official small change – the legend S C. While this legend appeared on Roman official coinage, tokens, by contrast, overwhelmingly did not carry these letters.[186] Tokens, in the main, appear to be connected with acts of euergetism, and anonymous *quadrantes* and *semisses* functioned as small change. We cannot rule out the idea that some tokens, particularly those made of bronze, came to be used as small change in a secondary capacity. Likewise, we cannot rule out the idea that some coin issues of small change were struck and distributed at particular festivals. But we cannot classify tokens as a substitute small change.

---

[186] For the few exceptions to this rule (e.g. *TURS* 2818, 2873, 3479, 3593) the legend S C likely carried a different meaning.

6 | Conclusion

Tokens and the History of Roman Imperial Italy

This book is intended as a beginning, a demonstration of what the study of tokens might offer the student of antiquity after decades of neglect. There are far more tokens from Roman Italy than have been discussed here, and one imagines far more will be uncovered in the future: in excavations, museum stores and archives. Our knowledge of the potential uses of these objects is thus likely to further develop. The understanding of token use in Roman Italy will also be better contextualised as detailed studies of tokens in other regions are finalised and published.[1] Once the imagery, findspots and possible uses of tokens in other regions are better known, particular aspects of tokens from Rome, Ostia or elsewhere in Italy that are unique to the region will be better identified.

What can tokens contribute to our understanding of Roman history? As the title of this volume suggests, these artefacts provide an abundance of information about Roman social life: relationships between individuals, participation in (and identification with) different communities, euergetism, commensality, festivals and communal occasions (and associated emotions and experiences), as well as an individual's life course, whether this was participation in a youth organisation or the burial of an individual with a token to pay Charon. In the daily social life of Rome and Ostia, tokens served to mediate relationships, distributions and benefits, while prompting users to call forth different identities and actions, whether this be a reminder of one's place in a particular *collegium* or the community-forming action of shouting chants in unison with a larger crowd. As with other objects in the Roman world, tokens acted upon their users to achieve particular desired results.

Although at first glance tokens may look similar to Roman coinage, the information offered by these categories of objects, and their use contexts, are very different. Roman coinage circulated amongst a variety of people for a significant period of time; coin types were thus designed to be intelligible

---

[1] For example, Gkikaki is finalising a new monograph on Athenian tokens, Bricault and Mondello a new volume on the *Vota Publica* tokens of late antiquity, Spagnoli continues her work on tokens found in Ostia, while Stannard continues to work on the Italo-Baetican material. The author intends to move onto a detailed study of the tokens of Roman Asia Minor.

to a range of people and to act upon them over time, while first and foremost serving the needs of the Roman economy. Coinage was issued, in the main, by governmental bodies. By contrast, tokens appear to have been issued for specific occasions or use contexts. The users of a particular token series were smaller in number, and at times, one imagines, also known to the token issuer. As a result, the designs on tokens did not need to be generally intelligible, but rather only had to be able to communicate a particular message to a small group over a defined period. Tokens were issued by a variety of individuals and used in a variety of contexts. Their potential for historians is thus broad, if their seeming unintelligibility can be overcome.

Although tokens may reference the imagery of Roman coinage, their designs also interact with a broad array of other artefacts, including wall paintings, lamps and gems. Tokens also carry imagery that has not survived elsewhere: the possible representation of bathers discussed in Chapter 5 is one such example, as are the various representations of rivers discussed in Chapter 3, or the satirical representation of the Roman triumph discussed in Chapter 4. Representations of the imperial family found on tokens also offer a unique repository for better understanding the creation of the imperial image by multiple sectors of society. Tokens contain formulations not found on other media, for example the combination of Vespasian's portrait with a palm tree on a platform on wheels discussed in Chapter 2. Tokens offer the student of Roman visual culture a rich abundance; the creativity of token issuers in Italy, adapting and remixing the imagery that surrounded them to create new meanings and formulations, underscores the vibrant visual world in which the Romans lived.[2] Incidentally, the various references to particular coin types on tokens provides a solution to the age old question of whether the Romans actually looked at their coinage – evidently they did, and were even inspired to adapt the designs for their own purposes.

Although some tokens may have been issued under imperial authority, or carried portraits of the imperial family, one is led to conclude that a very great many of the lead tokens that survive in Italy were issued by individuals outside of the Roman elite. Many token issuers were members of *collegia*, belonged to lower ranking magistrates, or were individuals not otherwise known in the historical record. Tokens are thus a source base that offers a rare insight into 'history from below'. The organisations,

---

[2] See the studies, for example, of Zanker, 1988; Clarke, 2003; Dunbabin, 2016; Russell and Hellström, 2020b amongst the vast scholarship on this topic.

frameworks and activities that led individuals to issue tokens were, in the main, connected to the value that Roman society placed on social prestige – if one was not born of the elite, then participation in particular associations, the holding of minor offices (e.g. of vicomagistrate), or acts of euergetism offered a method to gain prestige and thus status amongst one's peers.[3] Under the Empire, when the emperor increasingly monopolised traditional Republican expressions of prestige (e.g. the triumph), the Roman elite had to adapt their activities, for example by using circus processions as an occasion to demonstrate their status.[4] The issuing of tokens during particular occasions (whether by elites or non-elites) would have served to highlight the prestige of the issuer as well as the bearer, who possessed a token (and resulting benefit) that was not available to just anyone. In a discussion of modern day tokens and their classical Athenian antecedents, Maurer suggests that even when coins and tokens circulate alongside each other, tokens are associated more with status than with economic value.[5] This volume suggests the same holds true for tokens of Roman imperial Italy; they are objects that communicate and confer status over and above any economic value they might have possessed.

While scholars of the Roman eastern provinces might use provincial coinage issued by local authorities as a source to uncover local myths, civic identities, festivals and cults, no such coins were issued in Rome and Ostia.[6] But here tokens offer the historian an alternative. Issued by multiple individuals and multiple groups, rather than a civic authority, tokens differ significantly from coinage in the ways outlined above. But the tokens of Rome and Ostia nonetheless offer us an insight into particular cults, identities, statues, festivals and other ideologies that existed at a local level; indeed, the wide variety of types available offer a more diverse view than provincial coinage, and reflect a broad spectrum of society.

It is evident that the phenomenon of tokens in Roman Italy is overwhelmingly a phenomenon of Rome and Ostia. Far more tokens have been found here than anywhere else in Italy, and although the picture might further develop in the future, one imagines that this overall trend will not change – it seems logical that the capital of the Roman Empire and its harbour should possess the highest number of specimens in Italy. This might be attributed to the high populations of these areas, but also to the localised nature of token production in the Roman world. The production

---

[3] Lott, 2004: 82. [4] Latham, 2016: 147. [5] Maurer, 2019: 226.
[6] For example, Howgego, Heuchert and Burnett, 2005.

of a series of tokens by one person might encourage another to do the same in the future, with the ensuing mass the result of a local culture in which token production was a recurrent event. Since the who, how and why of token production differed from region to region (as discussed in Chapter 1), the low presence of tokens in other regions in Italy may have been due to the fact that the culture of token use did not take off to the same extent. Work on other regions has also uncovered that tokens are more widely used in some towns than others (e.g. an extraordinary quantity are known from Lugdunum, far more than anywhere else in Roman Gaul), while other regions (e.g. Germany, Britain) had very little token use at all.[7]

As with any study of material that does not form a significant focus in surviving ancient literature, one might hope for a more solid understanding of tokens than what has been possible here. But through a careful collation of the evidence, this volume has moved beyond Virlouvet's conclusion that these objects were not *tesserae frumentariae*, and has demonstrated the variety of possible uses and effects these objects may have possessed in antiquity, as well as their potential as a historical source. The benefits of studying tokens of different metals alongside each other, viewing them as the products of a single tradition, has also been established. We should not be surprised that tokens had a variety of roles; a token, after all, is defined as something that represents something else, multifarious in its very definition.[8] Some of Rostovtzeff's frustrations with tokens remain true today (the bewildering inscriptions, the poor preservation of many specimens), but the body of material is significant, and significantly understudied. The tokens of Roman imperial Italy no doubt continue to hold many future discoveries; it is my hope that this volume convinces readers that the analysis of tokens more than repays the effort.

[7] Wilding, 2020.   [8] Crisà, Gkikaki and Rowan 2019a: 3.

References

Abascal, J. M., Alberola, A., Cebrián, R., and Hortelano, I. 2010. *Segobriga 2009. Resumen de las intervenciones arqueológicas*. Cuenca, Consorcio Parque Arqueológico de Segóbriga.

Abdy, R., and Mittag, P. F. 2019. *The Roman Imperial Coinage Volume II Part 3. From AD 117–38, Hadrian*. London, Spink.

Abou Diwan, G., and Sawaya, Z. 2011. 'Les tessères monétiformes de "Melqart à Tyr"', *Syria* 88: 265–83.

Adams, J. N. 2015. 'The Latin of the Magerius (Smirat) mosaic', *Harvard Studies in Classical Philology* 108: 509–44.

Al-As'ad, K., Briquel-Chatonnet, F., and Yon, J.-P. 2005. 'The sacred banquets at Palmyra and the function of the *tesserae*: reflections on the tokens found in the Arsu temple', in E. Cussini (ed.), *A Journey to Palmyra. Collected Essays to Remember Delbert R. Hillers*. Leiden, Brill, 1–10.

Albertson, F. 2014. 'A distribution scene on a Palmyran funerary relief', *Antike Kunst* 57: 25–37.

Alföldi, A. 1937. *A Festival of Isis in Rome under the Christian Emperors of the IVth Century*. Budapest, Institute of Numismatics and Archaeology of the Pázmány University.

Alföldi, A. 1938–41. 'Tonmodel und Reliefmedaillons aus den Donauländern', in *Laureae aquincenses, memoriae Valentini Kuzsinszky dicatae. Aquincumi baberagak, Kuzsinszky Balint emlekenek szenteli Budapest szekesfovaros kozonsege es a Pazmany-Egyetem rem-s Rgisgtani Intzete. Dissertationes Pannonicae Series 2, 10*. Budapest, Institut fuer muenzkunde und archaeologie der P. Pózmany-Universitaet, 312–41.

Alföldi, A. 1965/66. 'Die Alexandrinischen Götter und die Vota Publica am Jahresbeginn', *Jahrbuch für Antike und Christentum* 8/9: 53–87.

Alföldi-Rosenbaum, E. 1971. 'The finger calculus in Antiquity and the Middle Ages', *Chiron* 5: 1–9.

Alföldi-Rosenbaum, E. 1976. 'Alexandriaca. Studies on Roman game counters III', *Chiron* 6: 205–39.

Alföldi-Rosenbaum, E. 1980. 'Ruler portraits on Roman game counters from Alexandria (Studies on Roman game counters III)', in R. A. Stucky and I. Jucker (eds.), *Eikones. Studien zum griechischen und römischen Bildnis*. Bern, Francke Verlag, 29–39.

Alföldi-Rosenbaum, E. 1984. 'Characters and caricatures on game counters from Alexandria', in N. Bonacasa and A. Di Vita (eds.), *Alessandria e il mondo ellenistico-romano. Studi in onore di Achille Adriani*. Rome, L'Erma di Bretschneider, 378–90.

Amela Valverde, L. 2011. 'Un nuevo plomo monetiforme de Urso (Osuna)', *Habis* 42: 119–25.

Andreau, J. 1999. *Banking and Business in the Roman World*. Cambridge, Cambridge University Press.

Anguissola, A. 2014. 'Remembering with Greek masterpieces: observations on memory and Roman copies', in K. Galinsky (ed.), *Memoria Romana. Memory in Rome and Rome in Memory*. Ann Arbor, University of Michigan Press, 117–34.

Arzone, A., and Marinello, A. 2019. *Museo di Castelvecchio Lead Tokens (Tessere di piombo)*. Modena, Franco Cosimo Panini Editore.

Baier, C. 2017. 'A p(a)lace of remembrance? Reflections on the historical depth of a monumental *domus* in Ephesos', in E. Mortensen and B. Poulsen (eds.), *Cityscapes and Monuments of Western Asia Minor*. Oxford, Oxbow, 122–34.

Bakker, J. T., (ed.) 1999. *The Mills-Bakeries of Ostia. Description and Interpretation*. Amsterdam, J. C. Gieben.

Baldus, H. R. 1971. *Uranius Antoninus Münzprägung und Geschichte*. Bonn, R. Habelt.

Banducci, L. M. 2015. 'A *tessera lusoria* from Gabii and the afterlife of Roman gaming', *Herom* 4: 199–222.

Barenghi, F. 1992. 'Scene leggendarie della storia di Roma su alcuni medaglioni a proposito del medaglione di Enea a Anchise', *Rivista Italiana di Numismatica e Scienze Affini* 94: 113–20.

Bartsch, S. 1994. *Actors in the Audience. Theatricality and Doublespeak from Nero to Hadrian*. Cambridge, MA, Harvard University Press.

Bateson, J. D. 1991. 'Roman *Spintriae* in the Hunter Coin Cabinet', in R. Martini and N. Vismara (eds.), *Ermanno A. Arslan Studia Dicata*. Milan, Edizioni ennerre, 385–415.

Beard, M. 2003. 'The triumph of Flavius Josephus', in A. J. Boyle and W. J. Dominik (eds.), *Flavian Rome*. Leiden, Brill, 543–58.

Beard, M. 2009. *The Roman Triumph*. Cambridge, MA, Belknap Press of Harvard University Press.

Beckmann, M. 2015. 'The function of the attribute of Liberalitas and its use in the congiarium', *AJN* 27: 189–98.

Belting, H. 2011. *An Anthropology of Images. Picture, Medium, Body*. Princeton, Princeton University Press.

Ben Abed, A., (ed.) 2006. *Stories in Stone: Conserving Mosaics of Roman Africa*. Los Angeles, Getty Publications.

Benassi, F., Giordani, N., and Poggi, C. 2003. 'Una tessera numerale con scena erotica da un contesto funerario di *Mutina*', *Numismatica e antichità classiche* 32: 249–73.

Bendlin, A. 2011. 'Associations, funerals, sociality, and Roman law: the *collegium* of Diana and Antinous in Lanuvium (CIL 14.2112) reconsidered', in M. Öhler (ed.), *Aposteldekret und antikes Vereinswesen: Gemeinschaft und ihre Ordnung*. Tübingen, Mohr Siebeck, 207–96.

Benefiel, R. R. 2010. 'Dialogues of ancient graffiti in the House of Maius Castricius in Pompeii', *American Journal of Archaeology* 114: 59–101.

Bianchi, C. 2015. '"Pedine alessandrine": testimoni illustri di un gioco ignoto', in C. Lambrugo, F. Slavazzi and A. M. Fedeli (eds.), *I materiali della collezione archeologica "Giulio Sambon" di Milano. 1: Tra alea e agòn: giochi di abilità e di azzardo*. Milan, Università degli Studi di Milano, 53–65.

Billig, M. 1995. *Banal Nationalism*. London, Sage Publications.

Boatwright, M. 1987. *Hadrian and the City of Rome*. Princeton, Princeton University Press.

Bollmann, B. 1998. *Römische Vereinshäuser*. Mainz, Philipp von Zabern.

Boon, G. C. 1958. 'A Roman pastrycook's mould from Silchester', *The Antiquaries Journal* 38: 237–40.

Boon, G. C. 1986. 'A tessera balnearis', in J. D. Zienkiewicz (ed.), *The Legionary Fortress Baths at Caerleon*. Cardiff, National Museum of Wales, 26–7.

Boulakia, J. D. C. 1972. 'Lead in the Roman world', *American Journal of Archaeology* 76: 139–44.

Boyce, A. A. 1958. 'The harbor of Pompeiopolis', *American Journal of Archaeology* 62: 67–78.

Brandt, E., Krug, A., Gercke, W., and Schmidt, E. 1972. *Antike Gemmen in Deutschen Sammlungen Band I: Staatliche Münzsammlung München*. Munich, Prestel Verlag.

Brenner, P. S., Serpe, R. T., and Stryker, S. 2014. 'The casual ordering of prominence and salience in identity theory: an empirical examination', *Social Psychology Quarterly* 77: 231–52.

Bricault, L. 2001. 'Les Anubophores', *Bulletin de la Société égyptologique de Genève* 24: 29–42.

Bricault, L., (ed.) 2008. *Sylloge Nummorum Religionis Isiacae et Sarapiacae (SNRIS)*. Paris, Diffusion de Boccard.

Bricault, L. 2015. 'The *Gens Isiaca* in the Graeco-Roman coinage', *NC* 175: 83–102.

Bricault, L. 2020. *Isis Pelagia: Images, Names and Cults of a Goddess of the Seas*. Leiden, Brill.

Bricault, L., and Mondello, C. in press. *Isis Moneta. The 'Vota Publica' Tokens from Late Antique Rome. Volume 1: Catalogue*. London, Royal Numismatic Society.

Brubaker, R. 2004. *Ethnicity Without Groups*. Cambridge, MA, Harvard University Press.

Bruun, C. 1993. 'Lotores: Roman bath-attendants', *Zeitschrift für Papyrologie und Epigraphik* 98: 222–8.
Bruun, C. 1999. 'Ownership of baths in Rome and the evidence from lead pipe installations', in J. DeLaine and D. E. Johnston (eds.), *Roman Baths and Bathing*. Portsmouth, Rhode Island, Journal of Roman Archaeology, 75–85.
Bruun, C. 2007. 'Civic rituals in imperial Ostia', in O. Hekster, S. Schmidt-Hofer and C. Witschel (eds.), *Ritual Dynamics and Religious Change in the Roman Empire*. Leiden, Brill, 123–41.
Bruun, C. 2014. 'Civic identity in Roman Ostia: some evidence from dedications (inaugurations)', in A. Kemezis (ed.), *Urban Dreams and Realities in Antiquity*. Leiden, Brill, 347–69.
Bruun, C. 2015. 'La mentalità marinara di Ostia, città portuale, nella documentazione epigrafica e iconografica', in L. Chioffi, M. Kajava and S. Örmä (eds.), *Il Mediterraneo e la storia II: naviganti, popoli e culture ad Ischia e in altri luoghi della costa tirrenica*. Rome, Institutum Romanum Finlandiae, 215–27.
Bruun, C. 2016. 'Remembering anniversaries at Roman Ostia: the *dies natalis* of Antinous, hero and divine being', *Phoenix* 70: 361–80.
Bubelis, W. 2011. 'Tokens and imitation in ancient Athens', *Marburger Beiträge zur antiken Handels-, Wirtschafts- und Sozialgeschichte* 28: 171–95.
Bubelis, W. 2013. 'The agorastikon of Hellenistic Athens: not a market-tax', *Zeitschrift für Papyrologie und Epigraphik* 185: 122–6.
Buck-Morss, S. 2010. 'Obama and the image', in N. Curtis (ed.), *The Pictorial Turn*. London, Routledge, 49–68.
Buljević, Z. 2008. 'Uz spintriju iz Salone u splitskom arheološkom muzeju', *Archaeologica Adriatica* 11: 201–11.
Buora, M. 2008. '*Aquileia Crysopolis*, Geschichte einer Legende', *Anodos. Studies of the Ancient World* 8: 109–14.
Burnett, A. 1999. 'Buildings and monuments on Roman coins', in G. M. Paul and M. Ierardi (eds.), *Roman Coins and Public Life under the Empire*. Ann Arbor, University of Michigan Press, 137–64.
Burnett, A. 2016. 'Zela, acclamations, Caracalla – and Parthia?', *Bulletin of the Institute of Classical Studies* 59: 72–110.
Burnett, A. in press. 'Female signatories to Roman provincial coins', in B. Carroccio, D. Castrizio, K. Mannino, M. Puglisi and G. Salamone, *Scritti in onore di Maria Caltabiano per i suoi 50 anni di studi numismatici*.
Buttrey, T. 1973. 'The *spintriae* as a historical source', *NC* 13: 52–63.
Buttrey, T. 2000. 'Unattributed anonymous quadrantes revisited – RICHARD D. WEIGEL, THE ANONYMOUS QUADRANTES RECONSIDERED (Annotazioni Numismatiche, Supplemento XI, Milan 1998). Pp. 20, figs. 22. ISSN 1121-7464.', *Journal of Roman Archaeology* 13: 589–90.
Buttrey, T. 2007. 'Domitian, the rhinoceros, and the date of Martial's "Liber de Spectaculis"', *Journal of Roman Studies* 97: 101–12.

Buttrey, T., Johnston, A., MacKenzie, K. M. and Bates, M. L. 1981. *Greek, Roman, and Islamic Coins from Sardis*. Cambridge, MA, Harvard University Press.

Calomino, D. 2016. *Defacing the Past. Damnation and Desecration in Imperial Rome*. London, Spink.

Calza, G. 1927. *Il teatro romano di Ostia*. Rome, Societè editrice d'arte illustrata.

Cameron, A. 1973. *Porphyrius The Charioteer*. Oxford, Clarendon Press.

Campana, A. 2009. 'Le spintriae: tessere romane con raffigurazioni erotiche', in *La donna romana. Immagini e vita quotidiana*. Cassino, Diana, 43–96.

Campbell, B. 2012. *Rivers and the Power of Ancient Rome*. Chapel Hill, The University of North Carolina Press.

Carandini, A., and Panella, C., (eds.) 1977. *Ostia IV. Le Terme del Nuotatore. Scavo dell'ambiente XVI e dell'area XXV. (Studi Miscellanei 23)*. Rome, De Luca.

Carradice, I. 1998. 'Towards a new introduction to the Flavian coinage', in M. Austin, J. Harries and C. Smith (eds.), *Modus Operandi. Essays in Honour of Geoffrey Rickman*. London, BICS Supplement, 93–118.

Carter, M. in press. '*Clamor ingens totius populi*. Creating a sonic community in the Roman amphitheatre', in S. Bell and N. Elkins (eds.), *The Spectacle of Everyday Life*. Turnhout: Brepols.

Castan, M. A. 1870. 'Un jeton de jeu de l'époque romaine', *Revue Archéologique* 21: 261–2.

Catalli, F. 2013. 'Le monete', in P. Braconi, F. Coarellli, F. Diosono and G. Ghini (eds.), *Il Santuario di Diana a Nemi. Le Terrazze e il Ninfeo, Scavi 1989–2009*. Rome, Erma di Bretschneider, 529–34.

Ceccaroni, E. and Molinari, M. C. 2017. 'I reperti numismatici provenienti dai recenti scavi del santuario di Ercole di Alba Fucens', in M. Caccamo Caltabiano (ed.), *XV International Numismatic Congress Taormina 2015 Proceedings*. Rome-Messina: International Numismatic Commission, 717–19.

Cesano, L. 1904a. 'Matrici di tessere di piombo nei musei di Roma', *Bullettino della commissione archeologica comunale di Roma* 32: 203–14.

Cesano, L. 1904b. 'Matrici e tessere di piombo nel Museo Nazionale Romano', *NSc.*: 11–17.

Chaniotis, A. 2011. 'Emotional community through ritual. Initiates, citizens, and pilgrims as emotional communities in the Greek world', in A. Chaniotis (ed.), *Ritual Dynamics in the Ancient Mediterranean. Agency, Emotion, Gender, Representation*. Stuttgart, Franz Steiner Verlag, 263–90.

Chantraine, H. 1983. 'Münzbild und Familiengeschichte in der römischen Republik', *Gymnasium* 90: 530–45.

Cheung, A. 1998. 'The political significance of Roman imperial coin types', *Schweizer Münzblätter* 191: 53–61.

Chioffi, L. 2017. *Antium. Collezioni epigrafiche*. Anzio, Edizioni Tipografia Marina.

Cipriani, M. 2018. 'Un ritratto di bambina della collezione Doria Pamphilj: il sorriso di Claudia Augusta', *Rendiconti. Atti della Accademia Nazionale dei Lincei* 29: 163–81.

Clarke, A. J. 2007. *Divine Qualities: Cult and Community in Republican Rome.* Oxford, Oxford University Press.

Clarke, J. R. 2003. *Art in the Lives of Ordinary Romans.* Berkeley, University of California Press.

Coarelli, F. 2007. *Rome and Environs. An Archaeological Guide.* Berkeley, University of California Press.

Coarelli, F. 2010. 'Substructio et tabularium', *Papers of the British School at Rome* 78: 107–32.

Cody, J. M. 2003. 'Conquerors and conquered on Flavian coins', in A. J. Boyle and W. J. Dominik (eds.), *Flavian Rome. Culture, Image, Text.* Leiden, Brill, 103–24.

Cohen, H. 1880–92. *Description historique des monnaies frappées sous l'Empire romain communément appelées, médailles impériales (8 vols).* Paris, M. Rollin.

Coleman, K. M. 2005. 'Martial Book 6: a gift for the Matronalia?', *Acta Classica* 48: 23–35.

Coleman, K. M. 2006. *M. Valerii Martialis Liber spectaculorum.* Oxford, Oxford University Press.

Collins-Clinton, J. 2000. 'The Neronian Odeum at Cosa and its sculptural program: a new Julio-Claudian dynastic group', *Memoirs of the American Academy in Rome* 45: 99–130.

Cooley, A. 1999. 'A new date for Agrippa's theatre at Ostia', *Papers of the British School at Rome* 67: 173–82.

Cooley, A. 2009. *Res Gestae Divi Augusti.* Cambridge, Cambridge University Press.

Courtenay, W. J. 1972. 'Token coinage and the administration of poor relief during the Late Middle Ages', *The Journal of Interdisciplinary History* 3: 275–95.

Crawford, M. H. 1974. *Roman Republican Coinage (2 vols).* Cambridge, Cambridge University Press.

Criniti, N. 1973. 'A proposito di "crustulum" e "mulsum"', *Aevum* 47: 498–500.

Crisà, A. 2020. 'A rare *spintria* from the Roman villa of Patti Marina (Messina-Italy)', *Archeologia Classica* 71: 635–48.

Crisà, N., Gkikaki, M., and Rowan, C. 2019a. 'Introduction', in N. Crisà, M. Gkikaki and C. Rowan (eds.), *Tokens: Culture, Connections, Communities.* London, Royal Numismatic Society, 1–10.

Crisà, N., Gkikaki, M., and Rowan, C., (eds.) 2019b. *Tokens: Culture, Connections, Communities.* London, Royal Numismatic Society.

Csapo, E. 2012. '"Parade abuse", "From the wagons"', in C. W. Marshall and G. Kovacs (eds.), *Festschrift for Ian Storey. No Laughing Matter. Studies in Athenian Comedy.* London, Bristol Classical Press, 19–33.

Cuyler, M. J. 2014. '"Portus Augusti": The Claudian harbour on sestertii of Nero', in N. Elkins and S. Krmnicek (eds.), *Art in the Round: New Approaches to Coin Iconography.* Tübingen: Tübinger Archäologische Forschungen: 121–34.

D'Ambra, E. 2014. 'Beauty and the female Roman portrait', in J. Elsner and M. Meyer (eds.), *Art and Rhetoric in Roman Culture*. Cambridge, Cambridge University Press, 155–80.

D'Arms, J. H. 2000. 'P. Lucilius Gamala's feasts for the Ostians and their Roman models', *Journal of Roman Archaeology* 13: 192–200.

Dalzell, B. 2021. 'Personal, public and mercantile themes on unpublished lead tokens', in A. Crisà (ed.), *Tokens, Value and Identity*. Brussels, European Center for Numismatic Studies, 77–92.

Dancoisne, L. 1891. 'Tessères romaines de plomb', *Revue Belge de Numismatique* 47: 210–18.

Dasen, V., (ed.) 2019. *Ludique: jouer dans l'antiquité*. Lyon, Snoeck Publishers.

Dattari, G. 1901. *Numi Augg. Alexandrini. Catalogo della collezione G. Dattari*. Cairo, Tipografia dell'Instituto Francese d'Archeologia Orientale.

de Belfort, A. 1892. 'Essai de classification des tessères romaines en bronze', *Annuaire de la Société Française de Numismatique* 16: 71–9, 126–33, 237–42.

de Callataÿ, F. 2010. 'Les plombs à types monétaires en Grèce ancienne: monnaies (officielles, votives ou contrefaits), jetons, sceaux, poids, épeuves ou fantaisies?', *Revue Numismatique* 166: 219–55.

de Callataÿ, F. 2021. '*Spintriae*: a rich and forgotten past historiography (16th–18th centuries): why it matters for our present understanding', in A. Crisà (ed.), *Tokens, Value and Identity*. Brussels, European Center for Numismatic Studies, 175–91.

de Certeau, M. 1984. *The Practice of Everyday Life (trans. S.F. Rendall)*. Berkeley, University of California Press.

Del Bufalo, D. 2009. *Catalogo illustrato della glittica nella collezione Santarelli*. Rome, L'Erma di Bretschneider.

Dembski, G. 1973/4. 'Zwei römische Bleitesserae aus Carnuntum', *Mitteilungen der Österreichischen Numismatischen Gesellschaft* 18: 13–14.

DeRose Evans, J. 2018. *Coins from the Excavations at Sardis, Their Archaeological and Economic Contexts. Coins from the 1973 to 2013 Excavations*. Cambridge, MA, Harvard University Press.

Desbat, A. 2011. 'Les vases à médaillons d'applique de la vallée du Rhône', in A. Desbat and H. Savay-Guerraz (eds.), *Images d'Argile*. Gollion, Switzerland, Infolio, 8–43.

Desbat, A., and Savay-Guerraz, H., (eds.) 2011. *Images d'Argile. Les vases gallo-romains à medallions d'applique de la vallée du Rhône*. Gollion, Switzerland, Infolio.

Di Vita-Evrard, G., Musso, L., Mallegni, F., Fontana, S., Munzi, M., and Fontana, S. 1996. 'L'ipogeo dei Flavi a Leptis Magna presso Gasr Gelda', *Libya Antiqua* 2: 85–134.

Dissard, P. 1905. *Collection Récamier*. Paris, Rollin et Feuardent.

Dolansky, F. 2011. 'Celebrating the Saturnalia: religious ritual and Roman domestic life', in B. Rawson (ed.), *A Companion to Families in the Greek and Roman Worlds*. Malden, MA: Blackwell, 487–503.

Donahue, J. F. 2003. 'Towards a typology of Roman public feasting', *The American Journal of Philology* 124: 423–41.

Dressel, H. 1922. 'Römische Bleimarken', *Zeitschrift für Numismatik* 33: 178–83.

Du Mesnil du Buisson, R. 1944. *Tessères et monnaies de Palmyre*. Paris, Bibliothèque nationale (France). Département des médailles et antiques.

Dubuis, B., and de Muylder, M. 2014. 'Une nouvelle série de plombs inscrits antiques: Noyon "La Mare aux Canards" (Oise)', *Instrumentum* 40: 23–5.

Dunbabin, K. M. D. 1999. *Mosaics of the Greek and Roman World*. Cambridge, Cambridge University Press.

Dunbabin, K. M. D. 2010. 'The prize table: crowns, wreaths and moneybags in Roman art', in B. Le Guen (ed.), *L'argent dans les concours du monde grec*. Paris, Presses Universitaires de Vincennes, 301–45.

Dunbabin, K. M. D. 2016. *Theater and Spectacle in the Art of the Roman Empire*. Ithaca, Cornell University Press.

Duncan-Jones, R. 1974. *The Economy of the Roman Empire*. Cambridge, Cambridge University Press.

Elkins, N. 2014. 'The procession and placement of imperial cult images in the Colosseum', *Papers of the British School at Rome* 82: 73–107.

Elkins, N. 2015. *Monuments in Miniature. Architecture on Roman Coinage*. New York, ANS.

Engel, A. 1884. 'Choix de tessères grecques en plomb', *Bulletin de correspondance hellénique* 8: 1–21.

Facella, A. 2004. *Vada Volaterrana. I rinvenimenti monetali dagli horrea*. Pisa, Università di Pisa.

Fagan, G. G. 2002. *Bathing in Public in the Roman World*. Ann Arbor, University of Michigan Press.

Fagan, G. G. 2011. *The Lure of the Arena*. Cambridge, Cambridge University Press.

Falzone, S., and Pellegrino, A., (eds.) 2014. *Scavi di Ostia XV: Insula delle Ierodule (c.d. Casa di Lucceia Primitiva: III, IX, 6)*. Rome, Il Cigno GG Edizioni.

Fears, J. R. 1978. 'Ο ΔΕΜΟΣ Ο ΡΩΜΑΙΩΝ Genius Populi Romani. A note on the origin of the Dea Roma', *Mnemosyne* 31: 274–86.

Federico, E., and Miranda, E., (eds.) 1998. *Capri Antica. Dalla preistoria alla fine dell'età romana*. Capri, Edizioni La Conchiglia.

Ficoroni, F. 1740. *I piombi antichi*. Rome, Girolamo Mainardi.

Floriani Squarciapino, M. 1954. 'Forme ostiensi', *Archeologia Classica* 6: 83–99.

Flower, H. I. 2017. *The Dancing Lares and the Serpent in the Garden: Religion at the Roman Street Corner*. Princeton, Princeton University Press.

Franke, P. R. 1984. 'Q. Caecilius Q.F. Oinogenus F. Curator', *Zeitschrift für Papyrologie und Epigraphik* 54: 125–6.

Frey-Kupper, S., and Stannard, C. 2018. 'Evidence for the importation and monetary use of blocks of foreign and obsolete bronze coins in the ancient world', in B. Woytek (ed.), *Infrastructure and Distribution in Ancient*

Economies: Proceedings of a Conference held at the Austrian Academy of Sciences, 28–31 October 2014. Vienna, Austrian Academy of Sciences Press, 283–354.

Frey-Kupper, S., and Stannard, C. 2019. 'Identifying, documenting and understanding the transfer of blocks of minor foreign and obsolete coins in antiquity, for use as money: a note on methodology', in S. Frey-Kupper, C. Stannard and N. Wolfe-Jacot (eds.), *Contexts and the Contextualisation of Coin Finds*. Lausanne, Éditions du Zèbre, 153–210.

Friggeri, R., Granino Cecere, M. G., and Gregori, G. L., (eds.) 2012. *Terme di diocleziano. La collezione epigrafica*. Rome, Electa.

Frœhner, W. 1881. 'Le comput digital', *Annuaire de la Société de Numismatique*: 3–9.

Gallivan, P. A. 1979. 'The *Fasti* for the reign of Gaius', *Antichthon* 13: 66–9.

Garrucci, R. 1847. *I piombi antichi raccolti dall'eminentissimo principe*. Rome, Clemente Puccinelli.

Giglioli, G. Q. 1913. 'Due matrici di tessere plumblee', *Ausonia. Rivista della società italiana di archeologia e storia dell'arte* 7: 3–6.

Gkikaki, M. 2019. 'Tokens in the Athenian Agora in the third century AD: advertising prestige and civic identity in Roman Athens', in N. Crisà, M. Gkikaki and C. Rowan (eds.), *Tokens: Culture, Connections, Communities*. London, Royal Numismatic Society, 127–44.

Gkikaki, M. 2020. 'Tokens of Hellenistic Athens. Lead tokens in the University Museum Göttingen: Part 1. The Haller von Hallerstein Collection and other Greek tokens with no provenance information', *Revue suisse de numismatique* 98: 91–138.

Gkikaki, M., (ed.) in press. *Tokens in Classical Athens and Beyond: Politics, Communities Contexts*. Liverpool, Liverpool University Press.

Göbl, R. 1978. *Antike Numismatik (2 vols)*. Munich, Battenberg Verlag.

Goodman, P. J. 2020. 'In *omnibus regionibus*? The fourteen regions and the city of Rome', *Papers of the British School at Rome* 88: 1–32.

Green, C. M. C. 2007. *Roman Religion and the Cult of Diana at Aricia*. Cambridge, Cambridge University Press.

Griffiths, J. G. 1975. *The Isis-Book (Metamorphoses, Book XI)*. Leiden, Brill.

Gülbay, O., and Kireç, H. 2008. *Ephesian Lead Tesserae*. Selçuk, Selçuk Belediyesi.

Hamburger, A. 1986. 'Surface-finds from Caesarea Maritima – Tesserae', in L. I. Levine and E. Netzer (eds.), *Excavations at Caesarea Maritima 1975, 1976, 1979 – Final Report*. Jerusalem: The Hebrew University of Jerusalem, 187–206.

Hänninen, M.-J. 2000. 'Traces of women's devotion in the sanctuary of Diana at Nemi', in J. Rasmus Brandt, A.-M. Leander Touati and J. Zahle (eds.), *Nemi – Status Quo*. Rome, L'Erma di Bretschneider, 45–50.

Harris, W. V. 2000. 'A Julio-Claudian business family?', *Zeitschrift für Papyrologie und Epigraphik* 13: 263–4.

Harrison, G. W. 2001. 'Martial on *sportula* and the Saturnalia', *Mouseion: Journal of the Classical Association of Canada* 1: 295–312.

Hekster, O. 2015. *Emperors and Ancestors: Roman Rulers and the Constraints of Tradition*. Oxford, Oxford University Press.

Helbig, W. 1880. 'Über den Pileus der alten Italiker', *Sitzungsberichte der Bayerischen Akademie philosophisch-philologische und historische Klasse* 11: 487–554.

Hemelrijk, E. 2015. *Hidden Lives, Public Personae: Women and Civic Life in the Roman West*. Oxford, Oxford University Press.

Henig, M. 1978. *A Corpus of Roman Engraved Gemstones from British Sites*. Oxford, British Archaeological Reports.

Henig, M. 1984. 'The elephant and the sea-shell', *Oxford Journal of Archaeology* 3: 243–7.

Henig, M. 1997. 'The meaning of animal images on Greek and Roman gems', in M. A. Broustet (ed.), *La glyptique des mondes classiques*. Paris, Bibliothèque nationale de France, 45–53.

Henrich, P. 2009. 'Neue Grabungen im gallo-römischer Theatre von Dalheim', *Empreintes* 2: 68–75.

Héron de Villefosse, A. 1893. 'Rapport sur deux médailles en plomb adressées par M. Wolfgang Helbig', *Comptes rendus des séances de l'Académie des Inscriptions et Belles-Lettres*: 350–5.

Herzog, R. 1919. *Aus der Geschichte des Bankwesens im Altertum: Tesserae nummulariae*. Berlin, De Gruyter.

Highmore, B. 2011. *Ordinary Lives: Studies in the Everyday*. London, Routledge.

Hijmans, S. 2010. 'Temple and priests of Sol in the city of Rome', *Mouseion: Journal of the Classical Association of Canada* 10: 381–427.

Hobbs, R. 2013. *Currency and Exchange in Ancient Pompeii. Coins from the AAPP Excavations at Regio VI, Insula 1*. London, Institute of Classical Studies.

Hoff, M. C. 1992. 'Augustus, Apollo, and Athens', *Museum Helveticum* 49: 223–32.

Holden, A. 2008. 'The abduction of the Sabine women in context: the iconography on late antique contorniate medallions', *American Journal of Archaeology* 112: 121–42.

Hollard, D., Le Brazidec, M.-L. and Gendre, P. 2015. 'Plombs monétiformes gaulois et gallo-romains de Vendeuil-Caply (Oise)', *Cahiers Numismatiques* 203: 27–43.

Hoover, O. D. 2006. 'A reassessment of Nabataean lead coinage in the light of new discoveries', *NC* 166: 105–19.

Howgego, C. 2005. 'Coinage and identity in the Roman provinces', in C. Howgego, V. Heuchert and A. Burnett (eds.), *Coinage and Identity in the Roman Provinces*. Oxford, Oxford University Press, 1–18.

Howgego, C., Heuchert, V., and Burnett, A., (eds.) 2005. *Coinage and Identity in the Roman Provinces*. Oxford, Oxford University Press.

Humphrey, J. H. 1986. *Roman Circuses. Arenas for Chariot Racing*. Berkeley, University of California Press.

Ingholt, H., Seyrig, H., and Starcky, J. 1955. *Recueil des tessères de Palmyre*. Paris, Paul Geuthner.

Jacobelli, L. 1997. 'Tessere numerali bronzee romane nelle civiche raccolte numismatiche del Comune di Milano Parte II', *Annotazione Numismatische Supplemento* 10: 1–28.

Jacobelli, L. 2011. 'Le sujets érotiques', in A. Desbat and H. Savay-Guerraz (eds.), *Images d' Argile. Les vases gallo-romains à medallions d'applique de la vallée du Rhône*. Gollion, Switzerland, Infolio, 116–47.

Joshel, S. R. 1992. *Work, Identity and Legal Status at Rome*. Norman, University of Oklahoma Press.

Kainrath, B. 2005. 'Ars erotica in Osttirol. Eine Bordellmarke aus Levant?', in G. Grabherr, B. Kainrath, A. Larcher and B. Welte (eds.), *Vis Imaginum. Festschrift für Elisabeth Walde zum 65. Geburtstag*. Innsbruck, Institut für Klassische und Provinzialrömische Archäologie der Universität Innsbruck, 154–8.

Kay, P. 2014. *Rome's Economic Revolution*. Oxford, Oxford University Press.

Keay, S. 2018. 'The role played by the Portus Augusti in the flows of commerce between Rome and its Mediterranean ports', in B. Woytek (ed.), *Infrastructure and Distribution in Ancient Economies*. Vienna, Austrian Academy of Sciences Press, 147–92.

Keay, S., Millett, M., Paroli, L., and Strutt, K. 2005. *Portus. An Archaeological Survey of the Port of Imperial Rome*. London, The British School at Rome.

Kemmers, F. 2003. 'Quadrantes from Nijmegen: small change in a frontier province', *Revue suisse de numismatique* 82: 17–35.

King, C. E. 1975. 'Quadrantes from the river Tiber', *NC* 15: 56–90.

Kloft, H. 1970. *Liberalitas Principis. Herkunft und Bedeutung*. Cologne, Böhlau Verlag.

Kloppenborg, J. S. 2019. 'New Institutional Economics, euergetism, and associations', in D. B. Hollander, T. R. Blanton IV and J. T. Fitzgerald (eds.), *The Extramercantile Economies of Greek and Roman Cities*. Abingdon, Routledge, 107–29.

Klose, D. O. A. 2005. 'Festivals and games in the cities of the east during the Roman Empire', in C. Howgego, V. Heuchert and A. Burnett (eds.), *Coinage and Identity in the Roman Provinces*. Oxford: Oxford University Press, 125–33.

Koeppel, G. M. 1980. 'Fragments from a Domitianic monument in Ann Arbor and Rome', *Bulletin of the University of Michigan Museums of Art and Archaeology* 3: 14–29.

Komnick, H. 2001. *Die Restitutionsmünzen der frühen Kaiserzeit*. Berlin, De Gruyter.

Kovalenko, S. 2002. 'Struck lead pieces from Tauric Chersonesos: coins or tesserae?', *NC* 162: 33–58.

Kroll, J. H. 2015. 'Small bronze tokens from the Athenian agora: *symbola* or *kollyboi*?', in U. Wartenberg and M. Amandry (eds.), ΚΑΙΡΟΣ. *Contributions to Numismatics in Honor of Basil Demetriadi*. New York, ANS, 107–16.

Kroll, J. H. unpublished. 'Roman Lead Tokens in Harvard Art Museums'.

Kroll, J. H., and Mitchel, F. W. 1980. 'Clay tokens stamped with the names of Athenian military commanders', *Hesperia* 49: 86–96.

Kuhn, C. T. 2012. 'Emotionality in the political culture of the Graeco-Roman East. The role of acclamations', in A. Chaniotis (ed.), *Unveiling Emotions: Sources and Methods for the Study of Emotions in the Greek World* Stuttgart, Steiner, 295–316.

Kuhn, C. T. 2014. 'Prosopographical notes on four lead tesserae from Roman Ephesos', *Zeitschrift für Papyrologie und Epigraphik* 190: 137–40.

Kulikowski, M. 2017. 'Urban prefects in bronze', *Journal of Late Antiquity* 10: 3–41.

Küter, A. 2016. '*Imitatio Alexandri* – the image of Drusus Minor on brass tokens of the Münzkabinett, Staatliche Museen zu Berlin', *Journal of Ancient Civilizations* 31: 85–122.

Küter, A. 2019. 'Roman *tesserae* with numerals – some thoughts on iconography and purpose', in N. Crisà, M. Gkikaki and C. Rowan (eds.), *Tokens: Culture, Connections Communities*. London, Royal Numismatic Society, 79–94.

Laes, C., and Strubbe, J. 2014. *Youth in the Roman Empire: The Young and Restless Years?* Cambridge, Cambridge University Press.

Lagóstena Barrios, L. 1993. 'Una tésera de plomo hallada en el yacimiento romano de "Puente Melchor" Puerto Real (Cádiz)', *Habis* 24: 307–9.

Lanciani, R. 1892. 'Gambling and cheating in ancient Rome', *The North American Review* 155: 97–105.

Lang, M. 1959. 'Allotment by tokens', *Historia* 8: 80–9.

Lang, M. and Crosby, M. 1964. *The Athenian Agora X: Weights, Measures and Tokens*. Princeton, The American School of Classical Studies at Athens.

Latham, J. A. 2016. *Performance, Memory, and Processions in Ancient Rome: The Pompa Circensis from the Late Republic to Late Antiquity*. Cambridge, Cambridge University Press.

Le Brazidec-Berdeaux, M.-L. 1999. 'A propos de l'iconographie d'une série de tessères gallo-romaines en plomb', *Cahiers Numismatiques* 142: 31–41.

Le Guennec, M.-A. 2017. 'De l'usage de jetons à motifs érotiques: les *spintriae* romaines', *Bulletin de la société française de numismatique* 72: 421–6.

Lim, R. 1999. 'In the "Temple of Laughter": visual and literary representations of spectators at Roman games', *Studies in the History of Art* 56: 342–65.

Linderski, J. 2001. 'Silver and gold of valor: the award of *armillae* and *torques*', *Latomus* 60: 3–15.

Ling, R. 1991. *Roman Painting*. Cambridge, Cambridge University Press.

Lott, J. B. 2004. *The Neighborhoods of Augustan Rome*. Cambridge, Cambridge University Press.

Lott, J. B. 2013. 'Regions and neighbourhoods', in P. Erdkamp (ed.), *The Cambridge Companion to Ancient Rome*. Cambridge, Cambridge University Press, 169–89.

Lovatt 2016. 'Flavian spectacle: paradox and wonder', in A. Zissos (ed.), *A Companion to the Flavian Age of Imperial Rome*. Chichester, John Wiley & Sons, 361–75.

Luschi, L. 2008. 'L'ariete dei "Manlii": note su una "tessera hospitalis" dal Fucino', *Studi Classici e Orientali* 54: 137–86.

MacCartney, E. S. 1919. 'Canting puns on ancient monuments', *American Journal of Archaeology* 23: 59–64.

Maderna-Lauter, C. 1988. 'Glyptik', in W. D. Heilmeyer, E. La Rocca and H. G. Martin (eds.), *Kaiser Augustus und die verlorene Republik*. Berlin, Kulturstadt Europas, 441–73.

Mainardis, F. 2002. 'Ancora sul riordino del lapidari triestini', *Aquileia Nostra* 73: 566–75.

Maionica, E. 1899. 'Chrysopolis Aquileja', *Jahreshefte des Oesterreichischen Archäologischen Institutes in Wien* 2: 105–6.

Malmberg, S. 2011. 'Movement and urban development at two city gates in Rome: the Porta Esquilina and Porta Tiburtina', in R. Laurence and D. Newsome (eds.), *Rome, Ostia and Pompeii: Movement and Space*. Oxford, Oxford University Press, 361–85.

Manning, C. E. 1985. '"Liberalitas" – The decline and rehabilitation of a virtue', *Greece and Rome* 32: 73–83.

Mannino, K. 1993. 'Le monete in terracotta', *Rivista Italiana di Numismatica e Scienze Affini* 95: 207–41.

Marin, S. and Ionita, V. 2018. 'A unique lead *tessera* from Dobrogea', *Pontica* 51: 581–92.

Marshman, I. J. 2017. 'All that glitters: Roman signet rings, the senses and the self', in E. Betts (ed.), *Senses of the Empire: Multisensory Approaches to Roman Culture*. London, Routledge, 137–46.

Martelli, E. 2013. *Sulle spalle dei saccarii. La rappresentazioni di facchini e il trasporto di derrate nel porto di Ostia in epoca imperiale*. Oxford, BAR.

Martínez Chico, D. 2018. 'Sexo y erotismo en las llamadas *spintriae*, las supuestas y problemáticas *tesserae* de lupunar de la Antigua Roma', *Athenaeum* 106: 533–57.

Martínez Chico, D. 2019. '*Tesserae frumentariae, nummariae et 'spintriae' Hispaniae*. Hallazgos y nuevas perspectivas', *Revue Numismatique* 176: 107–38.

Martínez Chico, D. 2021. 'An imperial "*spintria*" found in Vilches, Jaén (Andalusia, Spain)', *NC* 181: 327–30.

Martini, R. 1997. 'Tessere numerali bronzee romane nelle civiche raccolte numismatiche del comune di Milano Parte I', *Annotazione Numismatiche Supplemento* 9: 1–28.

Martini, R. 1999. 'Una tessera numerale bronzea con ritratto di Augustus in collezione privata. "Tessera triumphalium(?)": note per una discussione', *Annotazione Numismatiche Supplemento* 13: 12–15.

Martzavou, P. 2012. 'Isis aretalogies, initiations, and emotions', in A. Chaniotis (ed.), *Unveiling Emotions. Sources and Methods for the Study of Emotions in the Greek World*. Stuttgart, Franz Steiner Verlag, 267–91.

Mattingly, H. 1932. 'A Mithraic tessera from Verulam', *NC* 12: 54–7.

Maurer, B. 2019. 'The politics of token economics, then and now', in A. Crisà, M. Gkikaki and C. Rowan (eds.), *Tokens: Culture, Connections, Communities*. London, Royal Numismatic Society, 215–29.

McIntyre, G. 2013. 'Deification as consolation: the divine children of the Roman imperial family', *Historia* 62: 222–40.

Meadows, A., and Williams, J. 2001. 'Moneta and the monuments: coinage and politics in Republican Rome', *Journal of Roman Studies* 91: 27–49.

Medas, S., Overbeck, M., and Vismara, N. 1998. *Minturnae Antiquarium. Monete dal Garigliano II. Monete greche, provinciali romane e tessere romane (di bronze e di piombo)*. Milan, Edizioni Ennerre.

Medri, M., di Cola, V., Carandini, A. and Panella, C. 2013. *Ostia V. Le terme del nuotatore. Cronologia di un'insula ostiense*. Rome, L'Erma di Bretschneider.

Meiggs, R. 1973. *Roman Ostia*. Oxford, Clarendon Press.

Mercando, L. 1974. 'VI. – Marche. Rinvenimenti di tombe di età romana', *NSc.*: 88–141.

Merrifield, R. 1962. 'Coins from the bed of the Walbrook, and their significance', *The Antiquaries Journal* 42: 38–52.

Meshorer, Y. 2010. 'Coin hoard from a third-century CE shipwreck off the Carmel Coast', *Atiqot* 63: 111–35.

Metcalf, W. E. 1993. 'Whose Liberalitas? Propaganda and audience in the early Roman Empire', *Rivista Italiana di Numismatica e Scienze Affini* 95: 337–46.

Meyers, G. E. 2009. 'The divine river: ancient Roman identity and the image of Tiberinus', in C. Kosso and A. Scott (eds.), *The Nature and Function of Water, Baths, Bathing and Hygiene from Antiquity through the Renaissance*. Leiden, Brill, 233–48.

Millar, F. 2005. 'Last year in Jerusalem: monuments of the Jewish War in Rome', in J. Edmondson, S. Mason and J. Rives (eds.), *Flavius Josephus and Flavian Rome*. Oxford, Oxford University Press, 101–28.

Milne, J. G. 1914. 'Graeco-Roman leaden tesserae from Abydos', *Journal of Egyptian Archaeology* 1: 93–5.

Milne, J. G. 1930. 'Egyptian lead tokens', *NC* 10: 300–15.

Milne, J. G. 1945. 'Leaden currencies in Syria', *NC* 5: 134–6.

Milne, J. G. 1971. *Catalogue of Alexandrian Coins*. Oxford, Oxford University Press.

Mirnik, I. 1985. 'Nalazi novca s Majsana', *VAMZ* 18: 87–96.

Mitchiner, M. 1984. 'Rome: Imperial portrait tesserae from the city of Rome and imperial tax tokens from the province of Egypt', *NC* 144: 95–114.

Mittag, P. F. 1999. *Alte Köpfe in neuen Händen. Urheber und Funktion der Kontorniaten*. Bonn, Dr. Rudolf Habelt GmbH.

Mittag, P. F. 2017. 'Die Triumphatordarstellung auf Münzen und Medaillons in Prinzipat und Spätantike', in F. Goldbeck and J. Wienand (eds.), *Der römische Triumph in Prinzipat und Spätantike*. Berlin, De Gruyter, 419–52.

Mlasowsky, A. 1991. *Die antiken Tesseren im Kestner-Museum Hannover*. Hannover, Kestner-Museum.

Molinari, M. C., (ed.) 2015. *The Julio-Claudian and Flavian Coins from Rome's Municipal Urban Excavations: Observations on Coin Circulation in the Cities of Latium Vetus and Campania in the 1st Century AD*. Trieste, EUT Edizioni Università di Trieste.

Molinari, M. C. 2021. 'Three pewter *tesserae* from the temple of Hercules in *Alba Fucens*: new considerations on the use of official imperial tokens', in A. Crisà (ed.), *Tokens, Value and Identity*. Brussels, European Center for Numismatic Studies, 93–102.

Mondello, C. 2019. 'Using and reusing tokens: some remarks about Christian graffiti on contorniates', in A. Crisà, M. Gkikaki and C. Rowan (eds.), *Tokens: Culture, Connections, Communities*. London, Royal Numismatic Society, 145–61.

Mondello, C. (2020a). 'Casting Roman tokens: Notes on two unpublished token moulds from Florence collections.' *https://blogs.warwick.ac.uk/numismatics/entry/casting_roman_tokens/*.

Mondello, C. 2020b. 'Re-reading the so-called "Asina tokens": religious diversity in late antiquity', *American Journal of Numismatics* 32: 273–312.

Mondello, C. 2021. 'The cult of the saints and Roman communities under the Theodosians. Social and religious memory on the early Christian *tesserae*', *NC* 181: 129–58.

Mora Serrano, B. 2002. 'El depósito de plomos monetiformes de las termas de Alameda (¿Vrgapa?), Màlaga', *Numisma* 246: 39–67.

Mora Serrano, B. 2005. 'Un depósito de plomos monetiformes de procedencia bética conservados en el Museo Arqueológico Nacional', in C. Alfaro Asins, C. Marcos Alonso and P. Otero Morán (eds.), *Actas del XIII Congreso Internacional de Numismática, Madrid, 2003. Vol 1* Madrid, International Numismatic Commission, 517–23.

Morpugo, L. 1931. 'XVI. Nemi – Teatro ed altri edifici romani in contrada "La Valle"', *NSc.*: 237–303.

Mowat, R. 1898. 'Countremarques sur des tesseres romaines de bronze et de plomb', *Rivista Italiana di Numismatica* 11: 21–42.

Mowat, R. 1913. 'Inscriptions exclamatives sur les tessères et monnaies romaine', *Revue Numismatique* 67: 46–60.

Munzi, M. 1997. 'Quadranti anonimi e tessere monetali dalle tombe di Leptis Magna', *Annotazione Numismatiche* 26: 589–93.

Munzi, M. 2017. 'The Tripolitanian countryside: new numismatic data from the survey of the territory of *Leptis Magna* (2013 campaign)', *The Journal of Archaeological Numismatics* 7: 189–200.

Murray, D. R. 2012. 'A Cabinet of Mathematical Curiosities at Teachers College: David Eugene Smith's Collection', PhD, Columbia University.

Nibley, H. 1945. 'Sparsiones', *The Classical Journal* 40: 515–43.

Nicols, J. 2014. *Civic Patronage in the Roman Empire*. Leiden, Brill.

Nielsen, I. 1990. *Thermae et Balnea (2 vols)*. Aarhus, Aarhus University Press.

Nogara, B. 1917. 'Matrici per tessere e coltello di età romana scavati in Como nella Piazza Cavour', *Rivista Archeologica della Provincia e antica Diocesi di Como* 73–75: 3–7.

Noreña, C. 2011. *Imperial Ideals in the Roman West*. Cambridge, Cambridge University Press.

Oestreicher, B. 1962. 'A contemporary picture of Caesarea's harbour', *Israel Numismatic Bulletin* 2: 44–7.

Östenberg, I. 2009. *Staging the World. Spoils, Captives, and Representations in Roman Triumphal Procession*. Oxford, Oxford University Press.

Overbeck, M. 1995. *Römische Bleimarken in der Staatlichen Münzsammlung München. Eine Quelle zur Sozial- und Wirtschaftsgeschichte Roms*. Munich, Staatliche Münzsammlung München.

Overbeck, M. 2001. *Römische Bleimarken im Civiche raccolte numismatiche zu Mailand = Tessere plumbee romane, Civiche raccolte numismatiche*. Milan, Comune di Milano, Settore cultura, musei e mostre, Civiche raccolte numismatiche.

Overbeck, M. 2001/2002. 'Eine römische Beinmarke mit dem Colosseum and weitere, bisher unbekannte Marken aus Bein', *Jahrbuch für Numismatik und Geldgeschichte* 51/52: 49–54.

Overbeck, M., and Overbeck, B. 1996. 'Römische Bleimarken als Zeugnis des ersten Jüdischen Krieges', in W. Leschhorn, A. V. B. Miron and A. Miron (eds.), *Hellas und der griechische Osten*. Saarbrücken, SDV Saarbrücker Druckerei und Verlag GmbH: 211–18.

Palmer, R. E. A. 1975. 'The neighbourhood of the Sullan Bellona at the Colline Gate', *Mélanges de l'Ecole française de Rome* 87: 653–65.

Pardini, G. 2014. 'Le monete', in C. Panella and G. Rizzo (eds.), *Ostia VI: Le Terme del Nuotatore*. Rome: L'Erma di Bretschneider, 41–6.

Pardini, G., Piacentini, M., Felici, A. C., Santarelli, M. L., and Santucci, S. 2016. 'Matrici per tessere plumbee dalle pendici nord-orientali del Palatino. Nota preliminare', in A. F. Ferrandes and G. Pardini (eds.), *Le regole del gioco tracce archeologi racconti. Studi in onore di Clementina Panella*. Rome, Edizioni Quasar, 649–67.

Pasqui, A. 1906. 'Ostia: Nuove scoperte presso il Casone', *NSc.* 3: 357–73.

Patterson, J. R. 1992. 'The *collegia* and the transformation of the towns of Italy in the second century AD', in *L'Italie d'Auguste à Dioclétian. Actes du colloque international de Rome (25–28 mar 1992)*. Rome, École française de Rome, 227–38.

Pedroni, L. 1997. 'Tessere plumbee dalle terme di Fregellae', *Bollettino di Numismatica* 28–29: 203–10.

Pensabene, P. 2001–2003. 'Su alcune tessere plumbee di uso commerciale', *Scienze dell'antichità. Storia archeologia antropologia.* 11: 479–510.

Perry, J. S. 2011. 'Organized societies: *collegia*', in M. Peachin (ed.), *The Oxford Handbook of Social Relations in the Roman World.* Oxford, Oxford University Press, 499–515.

Pietrogrande, A. L., (ed.) 1976. *Scavi di Ostia VIII: Le Fulloniche.* Rome, Istituto Poligrafico dello Stato.

Pilon, F. 2016. *L'atelier monétaire de Châteaubleau. Officines et monnayages d'imitation du IIIe siècle dans le nord-ouest de l'Empire.* Paris, CNRS éditions

Pitts, M. 2007. 'The emperor's new clothes? The utility of identity in Roman archaeology', *American Journal of Archaeology* 111: 693–713.

Platner, S. B., and Ashby, T. 1929. *A Topographical Dictionary of Ancient Rome.* Cambridge, Cambridge University Press.

Platt, V. 2006. 'Making an impression: replication and the ontology of the Graeco-Roman seal stone', *Art History* 29: 233–57.

Popkin, M. L. 2016. *The Architecture of Roman Triumph: Monuments, Memory and Identity.* Cambridge, Cambridge University Press.

Popkin, M. L. 2022. *Souvenirs and the Experience of Empire in Ancient Rome.* Cambridge, Cambridge University Press.

Postolacca, A. 1868. 'Piombi inediti del Nazionale museo numismatico di Atene', *Annali dell'instituto di corrispondenza archeologica* 40: 268–316.

Poulsen, B. 2010. 'Coins, a bronze *tessera* and medallions', in M. Moltesen and B. Poulsen (eds.), *A Roman Villa by Lake Nemi. The Finds.* Rome, Edizioni Quasar, 425–8.

Price, S. 2005. 'Local mythologies in the Greek East', in C. Howgego, V. Heuchert and A. Burnett (eds.), *Coinage and Identity in the Roman Provinces.* Oxford, Oxford University Press, 115–24.

Prinz, O. 1902. '*arra, -ae f.*', in *Thesaurus Linguae Latinae Online (Vol. 2).* Berlin, De Gruyter, 631–3.

Purcell, N. 1995. 'Literate games: Roman urban society and the game of alea', *Past and Present* 147: 3–37.

Raja, R. 2015. 'Staging "private" religion in Roman "public" Palmyra. The role of the religious dining tickets (banqueting *tesserae*)', in C. Ando and J. Rüpke (eds.), *Public and Private in Ancient Mediterranean Law and Religion.* Berlin, De Gruyter, 165–86.

Raja, R. 2016. 'In and out of contexts : explaining religious complexity through the banqueting tesserae from Palmyra', *Religion in the Roman Empire* 2: 340–71.

Raja, R. 2019. 'Dining with the gods and the others. The banqueting tickets from Palmyra as expressions of religious individualization', in M. Fuchs, B.-C. Otto, R. Parson and J. Rüpke (eds.), *Religious Individualization:*

Types and Cases. Historical and Cross-Cultural Explorations. Berlin, De Gruyter, 243–55.

Raja, R. 2020. 'Come and dine with us: invitations to ritual dining as part of social strategies in sacred spaces in Palmyra', in V. Gasparini, M. Patzelt, and R. Raja (eds.), *Lived Religion in the Ancient Mediterranean World: Approaching Religious Transformations from Archaeology, History and Classics.* Berlin, De Gruyter, 385–404.

Ramskold, L. 2016. 'A die link study of Constantine's pagan Festival of Isis tokens and affiliated coin-like "fractions": chronology and relation to major imperial events', *Jahrbuch für Numismatik und Geldgeschichte* 66: 206–29.

Rebillard, E. 2015. 'Material culture and religious identity in Late Antiquity', in R. Raja and J. Rüpke (eds.), *A Companion to the Archaeology of Religion in the Ancient World.* Chichester, John Wiley & Sons, 427–36.

Reece, R. 1982. 'A collection of coins from the centre of Rome', *Papers of the British School at Rome* 50: 116–45.

Rennicks, K. 2019. 'The Holme Cultram Abbey series: English medieval tokens and a Cistercian use case', in N. Crisà, M. Gkikaki and C. Rowan (eds.), *Tokens: Culture, Connections, Communities.* London, Royal Numismatic Society, 163–76.

Richard Ralite, J.-C. 2009. 'Une tessère érotique (spintria) découverte dans les ateliers de potiers de Sálleles (Aude) près de Narbonne (France, Aude)', *NC* 169: 193–7.

Richardson, L. 1992. *A New Topographical Dictionary of Ancient Rome.* Baltimore, Johns Hopkins University Press.

Richter, G. M. A. 1956. *Catalogue of Engraved Gems. Greek, Etruscan and Roman.* Rome, L'Erma di Bretschneider.

Rickman, G. 1971. *Roman Granaries and Store Buildings.* Cambridge, Cambridge University Press.

Rimell, V. E. 2009. *Martial's Rome. Empire and the Ideology of Epigram.* Cambridge, Cambridge University Press.

Robinson, E. W. 2002. 'Lead plates and the case for democracy in fifth century BC Camarina', in V. B. Gorman and E. W. Robinson (eds.), *Oikistes. Studies in Constitutions, Colonies, and Military Power in the Ancient World Offered in Honor of A.J. Graham.* Leiden, Brill, 61–77.

Rodríguez Martín, F. G. 2016. '*Tesserae lusoriae* en Hispania', *Zephyrus* 77: 207–20.

Romano, I. B. 2007. *Classical Sculpture. Catalogue of the Cypriot, Greek, and Roman Stone Sculpture in the University of Pennsylvania Museum of Archaeology and Anthropology.* Philadelphia, University of Pennsylvania Press.

Rostovtzeff, M. 1897. 'Étude sur les plombs antiques', *Revue Numismatique* 1: 462–93.

Rostovtzeff, M. 1900. 'ΔΩΡΕΑ CITOY TAPCΩ', *NC* 20: 96–107.

Rostovtzeff, M. 1902. 'Tessere di piombo inedite e notevoli della collezione Franceso Gnecchi a Milano e la Cura Munerum', *Rivista Italiana di Numismatica e Scienze Affini* 15: 151–64.

Rostovtzeff, M. 1903a. 'Augustus und Athen', in *Festschrift zu Otto Hirschfelds sechzigstem Geburtstage*. Berlin, Weidmannsche Buchhandlung, 303–11.

Rostovtzeff, M. 1903b. *Tesserarum urbis romae et suburbi plumbearum sylloge*. St. Petersburg, Commissionnaires de l'Académie impériale des Sciences.

Rostovtzeff, M. 1903c. Римскія свинцовыя тессеры. St. Petersburg, Commissionnaires de l'Académie impériale des Sciences.

Rostovtzeff, M. 1905a. 'Interprétation des tessères en os avec figures, chiffres et légendes', *Revue Archéologique* 5: 110–24.

Rostovtzeff, M. 1905b. *Römische Bleitesserae. Ein Beitrag zur Sozial- und Wirtschaftsgeschichte der römischen Kaiserzeit*. Leipzig, Dieterich'sche Verlagsbuchhandlung.

Rostovtzeff, M. 1905c. *Tesserarum urbis romae et suburbi plumbearum sylloge. Supplementum I*. St. Petersburg, Commissionnaires de l'Académie impériale des sciences.

Rostovtzeff, M., and Prou, M. 1900. *Catalogue des plombs de l'antiquité*. Paris, Chez C. Rollin et Feuardent.

Rostovtzeff, M., and Vaglieri, D. 1900. 'Alveo del Tevere', *NSc.*: 256–68.

Roueché, C. 1984. 'Acclamations in the later Roman Empire: new evidence from Aphrodisias', *Journal of Roman Studies* 74: 181–99.

Rowan, C. 2013. *Under Divine Auspices. Divine Ideology and the Visualisation of Imperial Power in the Severan Period*. Cambridge, Cambridge University Press.

Rowan, C. 2014. 'Showing Rome in the round: re-interpreting the "Commemorative Medallions" of Antoninus Pius', *Antichthon* 48: 109–25.

Rowan, C. 2019. 'Lead token moulds from Rome and Ostia', in N. Crisà, M. Gkikaki and C. Rowan (eds.), *Tokens: Culture, Connections, Communities*. London, Royal Numismatic Society, 95–110.

Rowan, C. 2020a. 'The imperial image in media of mechanical reproduction. The tokens of Rome', in A. Russell and M. Hellström (eds.), *The Social Dynamics of Roman Imperial Imagery*. Cambridge, Cambridge University Press, 247–74.

Rowan, C. 2020b. 'The Roman tokens in the Ashmolean Museum, Oxford', *NC* 180: 95–125.

Rowan, C. in press a. 'Lead tokens in Julio-Claudian Italy', in C. T. Kuhn (ed.), *The Julio-Claudian Principate: Tradition and Transition*. Stuttgart, Franz Steiner.

Rowan, C. in press b. 'Spectacle and tokens in Rome and Ostia', in S. Bell and N. Elkins (eds.), *The Spectacle of Everyday Life*. Turnhout, Brepols.

Ruciński, S. 2012. 'Arruntius Stella, l'organisateur des jeux de Néron', *Eos* 99: 279–92.

Ruggiero, E. 1878. *Catalogo del Museo Kircheriano*. Rome, Salviucci.

Russell, A. 2020. 'The altars of the *Lares Augusti*: a view from the streets of Augustan iconography', in A. Russell and M. Hellström (eds.), *The Social Dynamics of Roman Imperial Imagery*. Cambridge, Cambridge University Press, 25–51.

Russell, A., and Hellström, M. 2020a. 'Introduction: Imperial imagery and the role of social dynamics', in A. Russell and M. Hellström (eds.), *The Social Dynamics of Roman Imperial Imagery*. Cambridge, Cambridge University Press, 1–24.

Russell, A., and Hellström, M., (eds.) 2020b. *The Social Dynamics of Roman Imperial Imagery*. Cambridge, Cambridge University Press.

Sagiv, I. 2018. 'Victory of good over evil? Amuletic animal images on Roman engraved gems', in A. Parker and S. Mckie (eds.), *Material Approaches to Roman Magic. Occult Objects and Supernatural Substances*. Oxford, Oxbow, 45–56.

Salomonson, J. W. 1972. 'Römische Tonformen mit Inschriften. Ein Beitgrag zum Problem der sogenannten "Kuchenformen" aus Ostia', *BaBesch* 47: 88–113.

Salway, B. 1994. 'What's in a name? A survey of Roman onomastic practice from *c.* 700 B.C. to A.D. 700', *Journal of Roman Studies* 84: 124–45.

Salzman, M. R. 1990. *On Roman Time. The Codex-Calendar of 354 and the Rhythms of Urban Life in Late Antiquity*. Berkeley, University of California Press.

Sánchez-Moreno, E. 2001. 'Cross-cultural links in ancient Iberia: socio-economic anatomy of hospitality', *Oxford Journal of Archaeology* 20: 391–414.

Sangriso, P. 2017. 'Una schola ai Vada Volaterrana', *Fasti Online*: www.fastionline.org/docs/FOLDER-it-2017-385.pdf.

Scheid, J. 1998. 'Déchiffrer des monnaies. Réflexions sur la représentation figurée des Jeux séculaires', in F. Dupont and C. Auvray-Assayas (eds.), *Images romaines: actes de la table ronde organisee a l'Ecole normale superieure, 24–26 Octobre 1996*. Paris, Presses de l'Ecole Normale Supérieure, 13–35.

Schmandt-Besserat, D. 2010. 'The token system of the ancient Near East: its role in counting, writing, the economy and cognition', in I. Morley and C. Renfrew (eds.), *The Archaeology of Measurement*. Cambridge, Cambridge University Press, 27–34.

Schmieder, C. 2008. 'Martial und die *lasciva nomismata*: eine Bestandsaufnahme', *Hermes* 136: 250–4.

Scholz, J. 1894. 'Römische Bleitesserae', *Numismatische Zeitschrift* 25: 5–122.

Sciallano, M. 1987. 'Une collection de plombs romains trouvés à Fos-sur-Mer', *Archaeonautica* 7: 193–201.

Sear, F. 2006. *Roman Theatres: An Architectural Study*. Oxford, Oxford University Press.

Shipley, F. W. 1930. 'C. Sosius: his coins, his triumph, and his temple of Apollo', in *Papers on Classical Subjects in Memory of John Max Wulfung*. St Louis, Washington University, 73–87.

Siciliano, A. 1993. '"Monete" in piombo rinvenute in Messapia', *Rivista Italiana di Numismatica e Scienze Affini* 95: 145–63.

Siciliano, A., Natali, V. and Boffi, P. 1995. 'Monete in piombo rinvenute in Messapia. Nuovi dati', *Studi di antichità. Università di Lecce* 8: 313–28.

Sifakis, G. M. 1966. 'Comedia: an actress of comedy', *Hesperia* 35: 268–73.

Simon, I. 2008. 'Un aspect des largesses impériales: les *sparsiones* de *missilia* à Rome (Ier siècle avant J.-C. – IIIe siècle après J.C.)', *Revue historique* 648: 763–88.

Simonetta, B. and Riva, R. 1981. *Le tessere erotiche romane (spintriae)*. Lugano, Gaggini-Bizzozero SA.

Sironen, T. 1990. 'Una tessera privata del II secolo a.C. da Fregellae', *Zeitschrift für Papyrologie und Epigraphik* 80: 116–20.

Smith, S. D. 2014. *Man and Animal in Severan Rome. The Literary Imagination of Claudius Aelianus*. Cambridge, Cambridge University Press.

Sobocinski, M. G. 2006. 'Visualizing ceremony: the design and audience of the Ludi Saeculares coinage of Domitian', *American Journal of Archaeology* 110: 581–602.

Solin, H. 2015–16. 'Nuove iscrizioni di Antium', *Latium* 32–33: 1–44.

Spagnoli, E. 1992. 'Alcune riflessioni sulla circolazione monetaria in epoca tardoantica a Ostia (Pianabella) e a Porto: i rinvenimenti dagli scavi 1988-1991', in L. Paroli and P. Delogu (eds.), *La Storia economica di Roma nell'alto Medioevo alle luce dei recenti scavi archeologici*. Florence, All'Insegna del Giglio, 247–66.

Spagnoli, E. 2001. 'VII.5-7-10', in J.-P. Descœudres (ed.), *Ostia. Port et porte de la Rome antique*. Geneva, Musée d'art et d'histoire, 408–9.

Spagnoli, E. 2007. 'Evidenze numismatiche dal territorio di Ostia antica (età Repubblicana – età Flavia)', in *Presenza e circolazione della moneta in area vesuviana*. Rome, Istituto italiano di numismatica, 233–388.

Spagnoli, E. 2011. 'Materiali numismatici da contesti portuensi', in S. Keay and L. Paroli (eds.), *Portus and its Hinterland: Recent Archaeological Research*. London, The British School at Rome, 211–30.

Spagnoli, E. 2017a. 'Piombi monetiformi da Ostia e Porto: problematiche interpretative', in M. Caccamo Caltabiano (ed.), *XV International Numismatic Congress Taormina 2015 Proceedings*. Rome and Messina, International Numismatic Commission, 269–72.

Spagnoli, E. 2017b. 'Un nucleo di piombi 'monetiformi' da Ostia, Terme dei *Cisiarii* (II.II.3): problematiche interpretative e quadro di circolazione. Per un contributo di storia economica e di archeologia della produzione tra II e III secolo d.C.', *Annali dell'Instituto Italiano di Numismatica* 63: 179–234.

Squarciapino, M. F. 1954. 'Forme Ostiensi', *Archeologia Classica* 6: 83–99.

Squire, M. 2017. 'Framing the Roman "Still Life"', in V. Platt (ed.), *The Frame in Classical Art. A Cultural History*. Cambridge, Cambridge University Press, 188–254.

Stannard, C. 1995. 'Iconographic parallels between the local coinages of central Italy and Baetica in the first century BC', *Acta Numismàtica* 25: 47–97.

Stannard, C. 2005. 'The monetary stock at Pompeii at the turn of the second and first centuries BC: Pseudo-Ebusus and Pseudo-Massalia', in P. G. Guzzo and M. P. Guidobaldi (eds.), *Nuove richerche archeologiche a Pompei ed Ercolano*. Naples, Electa Napoli, 120–43.

Stannard, C. 2007. The Local Coinages of Central Italy in the Late Roman Republic: Provisional Catalogue. Unpublished.

Stannard, C. 2015a. 'The labours of Hercules on central Italian coins and *tesserae* of the 1st century BC', in P. G. van Alfen, G. Bransbourg and M. Amandry (eds.), *Fides. Contributions to Numismatics in Honor of Richard B. Witschonke*. New York, ANS, 357–78.

Stannard, C. 2015b. 'Shipping tesserae from Ostia and Minturnae?', *NC* 175: 147–54.

Stannard, C. 2019. 'The purse-hoard from the Republican Baths at *Regio* VIII 5.36 in Pompeii', *NC* 179: 109–22.

Stannard, C. 2020. 'Apollo and the little man with the strigils, and the Italo-Baetican iconography', in F. Stroobants and C. Lauwers (eds.), *Detur dignissimo. Studies in Honour of Johan van Heesch*. Brussels, Cercle d'études numismatiques, 95–115.

Stannard, C. and Frey-Kupper, S. 2008. '"Pseudomints" and small change in Italy and Sicily in the Late Republic', *American Journal of Numismatics* 20: 351–404.

Stannard, C. and Sinner, A. G. 2014. 'A Central Italian coin with Dionysus/panther types, and contacts between Central Italy and Spain, in the 2nd and 1st centuries BC', *Saguntum* 46: 159–80.

Stannard, C., Sinner, A. G. and Ferrante, M. 2019. 'Trade between Minturnae and *Hispania* in the Late Republic', *NC* 179: 123–71.

Stannard, C., Sinner, A. G., Moncunill Martí, N. and Ferrer i Jané, J. 2017. 'A plomo monetiforme from the Iberian settlement of Cerro Lucena (Enguera, Valencia) with a north-eastern Iberian legend, and the Italo-baetican series', *Journal of Archaeological Numismatics* 7: 59–106.

Steuernagel, D. 2007. 'Ancient harbour towns – Religious market places? Formation and social functions of voluntary associations in Roman Ostia', in I. Nielsen (ed.), *Zwischen Kult und Gesellschaft: kosmopolitische Zentren des antiken Mittelmeerraumes als Aktionsraum von Kultvereinen und Religionsgemeinschaften: Akten eines Symposiums des Archäologischen Instituts der Universität Hamburg (12.–14. Oktober 2005)*. Augsburg, Camelion-Verlag, 141–51.

Taylor, L. R. 1934. 'New light on the history of the Secular Games', *American Journal of Philology* 55: 101–20.

Tennant, P. and Tennant, P. M. W. 2000. 'Poets and poverty: the case of Martial', *Acta Classica* 43: 139–56.

Thompson, D. L. 1942. 'Coins for the Eleusinia', *Hesperia* 11: 213–29.

Thornton, M. K. 1980. 'The Roman lead *tesserae*: observations on two historical problems', *Historia* 29: 335–55.

Thüry, G. E. 2012. 'Zu Gelddarstellungen auf Wandbildern der Vesuvregion', *Numismatische Zeitschrift* 119: 59–92.

Tomassetti, G. 1887. 'Notizie epigrafiche', *Bullettino della commissione archeologica comunale di Roma* 15: 235–9.

Tooker, L. 2014. 'Conversation with ... Bill Maurer', *Exchanges: The Warwick Research Journal* 2: 20–34.

Totelin, L. 2012. 'Botanizing rulers and their herbal subjects: plants and political power in Greek and Roman literature', *Phoenix* 66: 124–44.

Toynbee, J. M. C. 1948. 'Beasts and their names in the Roman Empire', *Papers of the British School at Rome* 16: 24–37.

Tran, N. 2008. 'Les collèges d'*horrearii* et de *mensores*, à Rome et à Ostie, sous le Haut-Empire', *Mélanges de l'Ecole française de Rome* 120: 295–306.

Tran, N. 2020. '*Imagines et tituli*: Epigraphic evidence of imperial imagery in meeting places of Roman professional *Corpora*', in A. Russell and M. Hellström (eds.), *The Social Dynamics of Roman Imperial Imagery*. Cambridge, Cambridge University Press, 215–46.

Trilla Pardo, E. and Calero Gelabert, A. 2008. 'Los plomos monetiformes de época romana en la isla de Mallorca', *Acta Numismàtica* 38: 55–85.

Tuck, S. K. 2016. 'Imperial image-making', in A. Zissos (ed.), *A Companion to the Flavian Age of Imperial Rome*. Chichester, John Wiley & Sons, 109–28.

Turcan, R. 1987. *Nigra Moneta. Sceaux, jetons, tesseres, amulettes, plombs monétaires ou monétiformes, objects divers en plomb ou en etain d'époque romaine conservés au musée des Beaux-Arts de Lyon*. Lyon, Diffusion de Boccard.

Turcan, R. 1988. 'Jetons romains en plomb: problèmes de datation et d'utilisation', *Latomus* 47: 626–34.

Vaglieri, D. 1907. 'Ostia', *NSc.*: 17–19, 121–3.

Vaglieri, D. 1908. 'XXIII. Ostia', *NSc.*: 329–36.

Vaglieri, D. 1909. 'IV. Ostia – Nuove scoperte presso le Terme e la caserma dei Vigili', *NSc.*: 197–209.

Vaglieri, D. 1910. 'Ostia', *NSc.*: 167–88.

Vaglieri, D. 1911. 'II. Ostia – Scavo nella Caserma dei Vigili e in altri siti dell'antica città', *NSc.*: 363–71.

Vaglieri, D. 1912. 'Ostia', *NSc.*: 273–80.

Vaglieri, D. 1913. 'Ostia', *NSc.*: 120–41.

van Berchem, D. 1936. 'Tessères ou calculi? Essai d'interprétation des jetons romains en plomb', *Revue Numismatique* 39: 297–315.

van Haeperen, F. 2019. 'Portus. Lieu de culte (?) de la speira des Traianenses (localisation incertaine)', in F. van Haeperen, F. Coarelli and J. Scheid (eds.), *Fana, templa, delubra. Corpus dei luoghi di culto dell'Italia antica*

(FTD) 6: *Regio I: Ostie, Porto*. Paris, Collège de France, *http://books.openedition.org/cdf/6850*.

van Heesch, J. 1979. 'Studie over de semis en de quadrans van Domitianus tot en met Antoninus Pius' (MA thesis, Rijksuniversiteit te Gent).

van Heesch, J. 2000. 'La "tessère" mithriaque de Liberchies', *Revue Belge de Numismatique* 146: 9–13.

van Heesch, J. 2009. 'Providing markets with small change in the early Roman Empire: Italy and Gaul', *Revue belge de Numismatique et de Sigillographie* 155: 125–42.

van Nijf, O. 1997. *The Civic World of Professional Associations in the Roman East*. Amsterdam, J.C. Gieben.

van Nijf, O. 2002. '*Collegia* and civic guards. Two chapters in the history of sociability' in W. Jongman and M. Kleijwegt (eds.), *After the Past: Essays in Honour of H.W. Pleket*. Leiden, Brill, 305–40.

Vendries, C. 2016. 'Les romaines et l'image du rhinoceros. Les limites de la ressemblance', *Archeologia Classica* 67: 279–340.

Virlouvet, C. 1995. *Tessera Frumentaria. Les procédures de distribution du blé à Rome à la fin de la République et au débout de l'Empire*. Rome, École française de Rome.

Virlouvet, C. 2015. 'Les métiers du port: les saccarii, dockers du monde romain antique', *Journal of Roman Archaeology* 28: 673–83.

Visonà, P. 1980. 'Ritrovamenti monetali sulla Rocca di Monfalcone (1974–1975)', *Aquileia Nostra* 51: 346–50.

Vitellozzi, P. 2010. *Gemme e cammeo della collezione Guardabassi nel Museo Archeologico Nazionale dell'Umbria a Perugia*. Perugia, Volumnia editrice.

Vollenweider, M.-L. 1963–67. 'Principes iuventutis', *Schweizer Münzblätter* 13–17: 76–81.

Wallace-Hadrill, A. 1986. 'Image and authority in the coinage of Augustus', *Journal of Roman Studies* 76: 66–87.

Walthall, D. A. and Souza, R. 2021. 'Sortition in Hellenistic Sicily: new archaeological evidence from Morgantina', *American Journal of Archaeology* 125: 361–90.

Ward, R. B. 1992. 'Women in Roman baths', *The Harvard Theological Review* 85: 125–47.

Weigel, R. 1984. 'The "Commemorative" coins of Antoninus Pius re-examined', in W. Heckel and R. Sullivan (eds.), *Ancient Coins of the Graeco-Roman World (The Nickle Numismatic Papers)*. Calgary, Wilfrid Laurier University Press, 187–200.

Weigel, R. D. 1998. 'The anonymous quadrantes reconsidered', *Annotazioni Numismatiche Supplemento* 11: 1–24.

Weiller, R. 1994. 'Tessères gallo-romaines en plomb de Dalheim-"Pëtzel" (Site du Vicus "Ricciaco" de la Table de Peutinger)', *Revue Belge de Numismatique* 140: 19–23.

Weiller, R. 2000. 'Tessères gallo-romaines en plomb, précurseurs antiques des jetons modernes', *Hémecht* 2: 175–86.

Weiss, N. A. 2013. 'The visual language of Nero's harbor sestertii', *Memoirs of the American Academy in Rome* 58: 65–81.

Weiss, P. 2005. 'The cities and their money', in C. Howgego, V. Heuchert and A. Burnett (eds.), *Coinage and Identity in the Roman Provinces*. Oxford, Oxford University Press, 57–68.

Wilding, D. 2019. 'Tokens of Antinous from the Roman province of Egypt', in N. Crisà, M. Gkikaki and C. Rowan (eds.), *Tokens: Culture, Connections, Communities*. London, Royal Numismatic Society, 111–26.

Wilding, D. 2020. 'Tokens and Communities in the Roman Provinces: An Exploration of Egypt, Gaul and Britain' (PhD thesis, University of Warwick).

Wistrand, E. 1987. *Felicitas Imperatoria*. Göteborg, Acta Universitatis Gothoburgensis.

Wolters, R. 2002. 'Gaius und Lucius Caesar als designierte Konsuln und principes iuventutis. Die lex Valeria Cornelia und RIC I^2 205ff.', *Chiron* 32: 297–323.

Woolf, G. 2015. 'Ancient illiteracy?', *Bulletin of the Institute of Classical Studies* 58.2: 31–42.

Woytek, B. 2003. *Arma et Nummi*. Vienna, Verlag der Österreichischen Akademie der Wissenschaften.

Woytek, B. 2010. *Die Reichsprägung des Kaisers Traianus (98–117)* (2 vols). Vienna, Verlag der Österreichischen Akademie der Wissenschaften.

Woytek, B. 2013. 'Signatores in der römischen Münzstätte: CIL VI 44 und die numismatische Evidenz', *Chiron* 43: 243–84.

Woytek, B. 2015. 'IO IO TRIVMP und A.P.P.F. Zu zwei Typen römischer Buntmetall-Tesserae', in W. Szaivert, N. Schindel, M. Beckers and K. Vondrovec (eds.), *TOYTO APECH TH XWPA. Festschrift für Wolfgang Hahn zum 70. Geburtstag*. Vienna, Institut für Numismatik und Geldgeschichte, 479–98.

Woytek, B. 2020a. 'Metal and system in Roman imperial mints. Flan production, quality control and the internal organisation of minting establishments during the Principate', in K. Butcher (ed.), *Debasement: Manipulation of Coin Standards in Pre-Modern Monetary Systems*. Oxford, Oxbow, 125–42.

Woytek, B. 2020b. 'A remarkable group of *semisses* of Hadrian', in F. Stroobants and C. Lauwers (eds.), *Detur dignissimo. Studies in Honour of Johan van Heesch*. Brussels, Cercle d'études numismatiques, 285–308.

Woytek, B. 2021. 'Reflections on Nerva's imperial coinage', *Journal of Roman Archaeology* 34: 813–23.

Woytek, B. 2022. 'The imperial afterlife of Roman Republican coins and the phenomenon of the restored denarii', in J. Mairat, A. Wilson and C. Howgego (eds.), *Coin Hoards and Hoarding in the Roman World*. Oxford, Oxford University Press, 237–66.

Woytek, B. and Blet-Lemarquand, M. 2017. 'The C.L. CAESARES denarii *RIC* I^2 Augustus 208. A pseudo-Augustan unsigned restoration issue. Corpus, die study, metallurgical analyses', *Revue Numismatique* 174: 183–248.

Yarrow, L. 2018. 'Markers of identity for non-elite Romans: a prologomenon to the study of glass paste intaglios', *Journal of Ancient History and Archaeology* 5: 35–54.

Yarrow, L. 2021. *The Roman Republic to 49 BCE: Using Coins as Sources*. Cambridge, Cambridge University Press.

Yegül, F. 2010. *Bathing in the Roman World*. Cambridge, Cambridge University Press.

Zanker, P. 1988. *The Power of Images in the Age of Augustus*. Ann Arbor, University of Michigan Press.

Zanker, P. 1997. 'In search of the Roman viewer', in D. Buitron-Oliver (ed.), *The Interpretation of Architectural Sculpture in Greece and Rome*. Washington, National Gallery of Art, Washington, 179–91.

Zarrow, E. M. 2003. 'Sicily and the coinage of Octavian and Sextus Pompey: Aeneas or the Catanean brothers?', *NC* 163: 123–35.

Zwierlein-Diehl, E. 1969. *Antike Gemmen in Deutschen Sammlungen Band II: Staatliche Museen Preußischer Kulturbesitz Antikenabteilung, Berlin*. Munich, Prestel Verlag.

Index

abbreviation, 18, 26, 28, 61, 63, 80–4, 100–1, 107, 113, 182, 188–9
acclamations, 16, 47–9, 62–3, 71, 81, 83, 139, 147, 152, 183, 213
Accoleius Lariscolus, Publius (moneyer), 123
Aelia Septimi (token issuer), 102
Aeneas, 32, 84, 85
Aequitas, 52
Agrippa, Marcus Vipsanius, 45, 190
Alba Fucens (Italy), 138, 206
amphora
    prize table, 161, 210–11
Antinous, 68–9, 163
Antonia the Younger, 40, 44, 75
Antoninus Pius, 66–7, 73, 204
Antonius Glaucus, Marcus (token issuer), 100
Anubis, 53, 130–5, 147, 151
anubophoroi, 131–5
apex, 107
Apollo, 31–2, 99, 113, 154, 178, 203
applause, 66, 151
Aquileia (Italy), 13, 15, 122, 142
Aquillius Florus, Lucius (moneyer), 107
arches, 28, 41
Argenton-sur-Cruese (France), 201
armillae (armbands), 48
Arruntius Stella, Lucius, 57
Asclepius, 112, 163
Asellius Fortunatus, P. (token issuer), 104, 109
Athens (Greece), 1, 9, 11, 27, 29, 31, 33–4, 79, 111, 127, 140, 164
    Dionysiac procession, 127
athletes, 118, 160–2
Atinius Memmianus, L., 30, 176
Attis, 167
Augustus, 16, 31, 38–9, 42, 45, 63–4, 70–1, 74, 90, 105, 109, 125, 140, 173, 180, 190, 198, 200
Autun (France), 144

balneatores, 176–7, 181–4
banquets, 11, 45, 52, 115, 125, 163–8, 189
bathhouse, 29, 97, 120, 125, 163, 167, 172, 176–89, 204
    at Alameda, 180
    at Caerleon, 181
    at Ephesus, 181
    at Fregellae, 30, 177
    at Nemi, 202
    balineum Germani, 181
    balineum novum, 182
    balneum Tigellini, 182
    Baths of Neptune, 96, 179
    Pallacina (?), 92
    Terme bizantine, 96, 118–21, 180, 207
    Terme dei *Cisiarii*, 166
    Terme del Nuotatore, 32, 137, 178
    Terme di Serapide, 96, 180
    Terme sotto la Via dei Vigili, 180
    Terme sulla Semita dei Cippi, 96
bathing, 173, 176–89
belonging, 1, 35, 49, 78, 84, 93, 114, 126, 149, 151
Britannicus, Tiberius Claudius Caesar, 40

Caerleon (UK), 181
Caesar, Julius, 31, 37
Caesarea Maritima (Israel), 34, 201
Caesennius Rufus, L., 163
calculi, 3, 170
Caligula, 45
canting types, 28, 107–9, 122
Capri (Italy), 14, 45, 200
Capricorn, 39, 111
Caracalla, 54, 73, 74
Carinus, 32, 74
Carnuntum (Austria), 31
carriages
    cisium, 118–19
    processional, 64
casting waste, 18, 178, 190
Caucidius (or Caucilius), Marcus (token issuer), 107
Ceres, 100, 151
chariot racing, 10, 39, 149–50, 154, 162
    charioteers (*aurigae*), 149, 156–9
    octoiugus, 151
    supporters, 153

Charon's obol, 204–7, 213
Chersonesus (Ukraine), 128
Circus Maximus, 12, 91, 149, 156–9
  races. See chariot racing
cisiarii, 118–21, 166, 180, 207. *See also* Terme dei *Cisarii*.
Claudia Augusta (daughter of Nero), 42–4
Claudius, 38, 40–1, 44, 66, 74, 95, 121, 140, 195
Claudius Eutychus, Ti. (token issuer), 209
coinage, 10, 21, 28, 42–3, 54, 57, 62, 80, 85, 87, 94, 107, 123, 125, 140, 168, 175, 177, 204
  and civic identity, 79, 215
  and *liberalitas*, 75
  and representation of *congiaria*, 75
  and women, 103
  carrying acclamations, 66
  festival coinage, 129, 211
  found in Alameda (Spain), 180
  found in Lepcis Magna, 203
  found in Mutina (Italy), 201
  found in Ostia, 118, 191, 195–8
  found in Sardis, 192
  found in Vada Volterrana, 167
  of lead, 8
  pseudo-coinage, 8, 175, 177
  quadrantes, 8, 30, 49, 58, 171–5, 177, 184, 204, 210
  reception of numismatic imagery, 36, 39, 40, 51–2, 54, 64, 67, 69, 72, 105, 141, 150, 166, 177–8, 181, 214
  relation to tokens, 7, 16, 30, 32, 40, 49, 77, 81, 85, 105, 109, 129, 134–5, 170–1, 176, 199, 203, 206, 210–11, 213
  representation of monuments on, 70, 88
  semisses, 171–5, 204, 211
  small change, 35, 58, 171–5, 203–4
collegia, 2, 22, 29, 80, 98, 101, 114, 210, 213–15
  and *cisiarii*, 118
  Asclepius and Hygeia, 163
  association of *saccarii*, 115, 117
  cultores Dianae et Antinoi (Lanuvium), 68, 163
  meeting houses (*scholae*), 167
  ordo corporatorum (Ostia), 163
colonia Veneria, 121
Colosseum, 12–13, 47, 56–61, 66, 149, 150
Commodus, 73, 211
Como (Italy), 20
Concordia, 18
congiarium (pl. *congiaria*), 40, 75, 172
Constantine I, Flavius Valerius, 130
contorniates, 10–11, 157

Cornelius Paetus, T. (token issuer), 107
Corneto (Tarquinia, Italy), 20
countermarking, 26–8, 111, 140, 152
Crete, 150
Croatia, 201
Cupids, 18, 121
curatores, 10, 28–9, 42, 64, 90, 106–7, 155, 165, 194
Curtia Flacci (token issuer), 104
curule chair, 39, 105–7

democracy, 30, 36
Diana, 68, 79, 122–4, 153, 163, 192
dies imperii, 37, 65, 128
Diogenes (token issuer), 112
Dionysus, 127, 185, 202
Dobrogea (Balkans), 128, 164
Domitia Flora (token issuer), 102
Domitian, 46, 49, 54–62, 65–6, 86, 92, 125, 172, 210
Domitius Primigenius, Lucius (token issuer), 182
Domna, Julia, 74
Drusus the Younger, 38, 40, 55, 200

Egypt, 68, 71, 97–8, 132, 135, 210. *See also* Memphis, Oxyrhynchus
emotions, 3, 11, 36, 56, 60, 62, 67, 77, 100, 120, 127, 133, 142–3, 146, 151, 162, 213
Ephesus (Turkey), 33–4, 74, 79, 111, 122, 128, 181, 192, 204
Eucarpus (token issuer), 170
euergetism, 2, 31, 34, 67, 74–5, 77, 104, 109, 115, 162, 170, 176, 178, 184, 189, 198–9, 210–13, 215
Eurysaces, 114

Fabius Speratus, Quintus (token issuer), 114
fasces, 105–6
Faustina the Younger, 68
Felicitas, 67, 83, 120
festivals, 64, 71, 77, 81, 83, 107, 168, 170, 213, 215
  and emotion, 143
  and gambling, 144
  and small change, 129–30, 172, 210
  chants, 93, 139
  Compitalia, 91
  in Athens, 127
  Isidis Navigium, 74, 129–35, 147
  new year celebrations. *See* new year celebrations
  participants, 132–4

Saturnalia, 22, 47, 57, 93, 138–42, 144, 163, 170
triumph. *See* triumph
Fides, 52
Flaccus and Gallus (token issuers), 104
Florentia (Florence, Italy), 122
Fortuna, 22–3, 45, 51–2, 61, 66, 69, 82–3, 86, 92, 95–7, 99, 102–3, 107, 109–10, 112, 120, 136, 142, 146, 157, 179–80, 193–6, 208–9
Fos-sur-Mer (France), 31
Fregellae (Italy), 12, 30, 176

Gaius Caesar, 39
Galba, 100
Galerius Antoninus, 73
Galerius Valerius Maximianus, Gaius, 180
games, 4, 6, 11, 14, 39, 61, 139, 144–6
gaming counters. *See* tessera
ludus latrunculorum, 145
Garigliano river, 44, 72, 122, 200, 206
Gaul, 29, 31, 34, 79, 138, 207–8, 216. *See also* Lugdunum
gems, 59, 93, 100, 105, 110–12, 119, 121, 157, 214
Genius, 54, 122, 160
loci, 81, 91
of Pompeii, 83
of the college of the *saccarii*, 117
of the Tiber, 86
of Thysdrus, 79
populi Romani, 80–5, 167
vici, 91
Germanicus Julius Caesar, 38, 40, 67
gladiators, 133, 143, 149–51, 154–6, 159, 162, 188
glass pastes, 105, 110–11, 119
Glitius Gallus, Publius (token issuer), 108
golden age, 66
grain, 31, 44–5, 87, 94, 97, 100, 128, 161, 165–6
Groupness, 78, 80, 121, 126
gryllus, 112

Hadrian, 64–6, 68, 74–5, 118, 133, 195, 204
Hadrumetum (Tunisia), 97, 207, 209
Harpocrates, 92, 131, 135
Hecate, 123–4
Herculaneum (Italy), 33, 168
Hercules, 73, 122, 128, 138, 198
Herennius Rufus (token issuer), 106
Hortensia Sperata (token issuer), 102

identity, 28, 71, 78–80, 102, 108, 110–11, 114–15, 117–19, 122, 153, 215
and language, 112
in Ostia, 94–100
in the city of Rome, 80–94
imitations, 5, 201
Isis, 74, 92, 102, 129–36, 147, 151, 179, 181
Italo-Baetican assemblage, 30, 177, 206
Iulia Iusta (token issuer), 102

Jaén (Spain), 200
Janus, 22
Judaea, 46–54, 59
Juno, 109, 125, 179, 194
Sospita, 151
Jupiter, 51, 194
Ammon, 12, 135

Kerch (Crimea), 5

lares, 91
Lavanter Kirchbichl (Austria), 202
legions, 12, 82
Lepcis Magna (Libya), 33, 203–4
liberalitas, 37–8, 44, 74–7
Liri river, 122, 207
literacy, 113
lituus, 38, 106–7, 173, 198
Livia, 38, 64, 125
Livia Melitine (token issuer), 102
Livilla (wife of Drusus the Younger), 38
Livineus Regulus, L. (moneyer), 105
London (UK), 201, 204
Lucilius Gamala, P., 163
Lucius Caesar, 39
Lugdunum (Lyon, France), 9, 29, 33–4, 74, 114, 216
Luna, 123, 157

Magna Graecia, 30
Marc Antony, 31, 37, 113
Marcus and Manius (token issuers), 42
Marcus Aurelius, 68, 72, 204
Mars, 22, 26, 41, 85, 92, 147, 167, 203
Marseille (France), 150
Martial, 46, 57–60, 139, 173, 182, 186, 192
medallions, 10, 49, 66
Memphis (Egypt), 29, 79
Mercury, 30, 52, 59, 65, 86, 105, 107, 112, 118, 120, 136, 177, 183, 202
Messalina, Valeria, 40–1
Minerva, 26, 62, 194
Minturnae (Italy), 98, 175, 206–7, 209

missilia, 3, 45, 71, 149
Mitreius, Gaius (token issuer), 14, 16, 38, 43, 200
moneyers, 105, 107, 109, 123
mould
  'cake mould', 71, 149
  for token production, 9, 17, 18–25, 32, 34, 88, 102, 107, 137–8, 155, 158, 161, 167, 177–9, 190–9, 207
Mutina (Italy), 6, 201

Nabatea, 128
naumachia, 152
Nemi (Italy), 122–6, 192, 202, 206
Nendorp-Wischenborg (Gemany), 200
Neptune, 94, 99, 186
Nero, 4, 40–5, 47, 66, 75, 88, 151, 182, 211
new year celebrations, 10, 66, 130, 147, 168
Nile river, 87, 97, 130, 135
nomismata, 3, 57–8, 139
number, 4–6, 12–14, 17, 20, 60, 68, 74–5, 82, 140, 142, 151, 154, 183, 185, 191–2, 195, 200–2
  finger calculus, 93, 134

Oinogenus, Q. Caecilius Q.f. (token issuer), 28
Olympianus (token issuer), 170
Osiris, 131, 135, 137
Ostia
  bathhouses. *See* bathhouse
  Casa dei Dipinti, 195
  Caseggiato dei Doli, 149
  Caserma dei Vigili, 193
  decumanus, 192–3
  fullonica, 194
  harbour, 88, 197
  Insula delle Ierodule, 197
  lighthouse, 94–8, 180
  Piazzale delle Corporazioni, 96, 97, 194
  Piccolo Mercato, 196
  Sabazeum, 138
  sewers, 197
  tabernae, 96, 190–2
  the Tiber, 198
  theatre, 150, 190–2
  via dei Molini, 195
  via della Fontana, 195
  via delle Foce, 198
  via di Diana, 137, 156, 196
Oxyrhynchus (Egypt), 29, 34, 79, 87, 97

Palmyra (Syria), 9, 11, 29, 33–4, 125, 164
Patti Marina (Italy), 201
Pedani, C., (token issuer), 209

Pergamum (Turkey), 200
Perinthus (Turkey), 117
Perpignan (France), 208
Petronius Sabinus, P. (token issuer), 15
Pietas, 82, 125
Poetovio (Ptuj, Slovenia), 71
pompa circensis, 63–5, 156, 215
Pompeii (Italy), 8, 33, 63, 83, 91, 101, 107–8, 131, 145–6, 168, 172, 175, 206
Pompeiopolis (Turkey), 89
Pompey the Great, Gnaeus, 141
Pomponeius Musa, Quintus (moneyer), 107
Poppaea Sabina, 43–4
portrait, 36, 198
  imperial, 4–5, 13, 16–17, 28, 31, 35, 37–45, 49, 61–4, 67, 69, 72–7, 121, 173, 200, 214
  non-imperial, 14–15, 31, 100, 102–4, 106, 108, 113, 160, 165–6, 170, 191
Portus, 94–6, 98–9, 114, 126, 163, 180
praeses ludorum, 63–4
prestige, 3, 35, 64, 67, 79, 100, 104–5, 109, 162–4, 168, 184, 215
Priapus, 206, 208
priests, 29, 44, 103, 107, 125, 130–5, 164
Prometheus, 121
Puente Melchor (Spain), 188

Rhegion (Italy), 29
rhinoceros, 52, 58–9, 111, 156, 167, 210
Ricciaco (Dalheim-Pëtzel, Luxembourg), 79
Rocca di Monfalcone (Italy), 122
Roma (goddess), 80, 82, 84, 86
Rome
  ab Isis et Serapis, 91
  ad Martis, 92
  ad nucem, 92
  ad tres Fortunas, 92
  ad tres Silanos, 92
  Aventine Hill, 167
  bathhouses. *See* bathhouse
  Capitoline Hill, 82
  Circus Maximus. *See* Circus Maximus
  Colosseum. *See* Colosseum
  Curiae Veteres (Palatine), 32
  Esquiline Hill, 23, 81, 102
  forum, 82
  Horrea Galbae, 100
  Monte della Giustizia (Termini), 22
  Pallacina, 92
  Porta Maggiore, 114
  porticus Octaviae, 108
  Quirinal Hill, 92
  regions, 91–3

'Syrian Sanctuary', 138, 161
temple of the *gens Flavia*, 53
the Tiber, 84–90, 100, 104, 107, 135, 137, 155, 160, 170, 174–5, 190, *See also* Tiberinus
vici, 90

Saalburg (Germany), 200
Sabina, Vibia, 65
saccarii, 114–18
Salles (France), 201
Sarapis, 92, 130–1, 135, 137, 147
Sardis (Turkey), 31, 34, 192
satire, 141, 143, 147, 170, 214
Saturn, 138, 140
Saturnalia. *See* festivals
Segobriga (Spain), 204
Septimius Severus, 86, 150, 190
Severus and Crispus (token issuers), 104
Sicily, 29, 201
Silvanus, 208
Siscia (Croatia), 204
Smyrna (Turkey), 116
Sol, 54, 157
Sosius, Gaius, 31, 113
souvenir, 52, 149
sparsiones, 45, 130
spectators, 151–3
spintria (pl. spintriae), 5–6, 9, 13, 38, 57, 116, 143, 145, 199–202
symbolon (pl. symbola), 3, 45

Telesia (Italy), 20
tessera (pl. tesserae), 3, 6, 8–9, 20, 45, 57, 164, 166, 200
  frumentariae, 3, 216
  gaming counters, 4–6, 10, 16, 33, 60, 93
  hospitales, 4
  lusoriae, 4, 7
  nummariae, 3
  nummulariae, 4
Tettius Rufus, Publius (token issuer), 105
theatre, 5, 33, 45, 66, 116, 124–5, 146, 149, 150, 156, 159, 190–2, 195, 204
Three Graces, 23, 124
Tiberinus, 85–90
Tiberius, 14, 16, 28, 38, 40, 67, 107, 140, 200
Tiberius Gemellus, 38, 55, 67
Titus, 13, 28, 46–7, 51, 55–6, 59–61, 65
tokens
  date of issue, 6, 32, 49, 70, 73, 128, 167, 176, 203, 207

definition of, 3, 11
manufacture, 15–25, 178, 190
of bone, 12, 30, 60, 176
of stone, 13, 15
of terracotta, 11–12, 29–30, 34, 201
of urban prefects in late antiquity, 66
of wood, 13, 28, 56
pierced, 201–2
previous scholarship, 1, 3, 13
shapes, 22, 202
that travelled, 97, 199–201, 206–10
used for distributions, 29, 31, 40, 44–5, 56, 57, 75, 128, 163–5
volume of production, 8–10, 174–5, 215
vota publica issues, 129–30, 132
with Greek legends in Italy, 31–2, 112, 159
torque, 48
traiectus, 100
Trajan, 41, 64, 74–5, 95, 99–100, 125, 141, 204
triumph, 46–56, 128, 141, 143, 147, 214–15
  io triumphe chant, 47–9, 140
  parade of trees in, 49–51
  triumphal arches. *See* arches
  triumphator, 54, 63
Tunisia, 79, 132, *See also* Hadrumetum, Lepcis Magna
Tyre (Lebanon), 128, 164

Vada Volterrana (Italy), 167
Valerius Etruscus, Marcus (token issuer), 105
value, 30, 36, 170–1, 173, 175, 177, 192, 199–207, 209, 211, 215
venationes, 57–9, 105, 118, 143, 149–51, 154–5, 161–2
Venus, 22, 72, 82–3, 121, 147, 190–1
Verres and Proculus (token issuers), 104
Vespasian, 47, 49–56, 61, 86, 140, 214
Victory, 25–6, 49, 51, 66, 71, 80, 82, 88, 107, 111, 121, 141, 146, 151, 156–60, 183
votives, 123, 125, 129, 131, 137–8, 207, 209
vows, 71, 129–30, 209

wolf and twins, 84, 86
worshippers, 78, 125, 130, 132–3, 135–6, 138, 151, 179

youth, 45, 160, 190
  principes iuventutis, 29, 39
youth organisations, 13, 15, 43, 194, 213

For EU product safety concerns, contact us at Calle de José Abascal, 56–1°,
28003 Madrid, Spain or eugpsr@cambridge.org.

www.ingramcontent.com/pod-product-compliance
Lightning Source LLC
LaVergne TN
LVHW081527060526
838200LV00045B/2028